MW00783738

Crime and Behavior

First Edition

Edited by Sylvia Valenzuela, Paul Kaplan,
and Stuart Henry
San Diego State University

cognella®
academic publishing

Bassim Hamadeh, CEO and Publisher
Michael Simpson, Vice President of Acquisitions
Jamie Giganti, Managing Editor
Jess Busch, Graphic Design Supervisor
Seidy Cruz, Acquisitions Editor
Sarah Wheeler, Senior Project Editor
Stephanie Sandler, Licensing Associate

Copyright © 2014 by Cognella, Inc. All rights reserved. No part of this publication may be reprinted, reproduced, transmitted, or utilized in any form or by any electronic, mechanical, or other means, now known or hereafter invented, including photocopying, microfilming, and recording, or in any information retrieval system without the written permission of Cognella, Inc.

First published in the United States of America in 2014 by Cognella, Inc.

Trademark Notice: Product or corporate names may be trademarks or registered trademarks, and are used only for identification and explanation without intent to infringe.

Printed in the United States of America

ISBN: 978-1-62131-539-1 (pbk)/ 978-1-62131-540-7 (br)

www.cognella.com   800-200-3908

CONTENTS

PART I:
MICRO-LEVEL INDIVIDUAL THEORIES

CHAPTER I: CLASSICAL AND RATIONAL CHOICE THEORIES

CHAPTER II: BIOLOGICAL & BIOSOCIAL THEORIES

CHAPTER III: PSYCHOLOGICAL THEORIES

PART II:
MICRO-LEVEL SOCIAL PROCESS THEORIES

PART III:
MACRO-LEVEL STRUCTURAL THEORIES

PART IV:
MACRO-LEVEL CRITICAL THEORIES

PREFACE

The focus of this text is on crime and behavior. Our purpose is to provide students with an introduction to the causes of crime, also known as the "etiology of crime." We have assembled a set of easily accessible articles that give the reader a clear overview of competing explanations for crime, criminals and criminality, each written by leading criminologists in the field. These articles range from individual-level explanations through group and institutional explanations to explanations highlighting the role of wider social and cultural forces on human behavior. We would like to thank the "Thinking Outside the Book Project" at San Diego State University's School of Public Affairs for making this Reader possible, and particularly to Cognella Academic Publishing for underwriting the project.

INTRODUCTION

This book provides an overview of the scholarly study of criminal behavior. Put another way, it tries to answer the question: "Why do people 'do' crime?" It does so through a collecting works of original research, theoretical essays, and literature reviews addressing the major paradigms (theoretical frameworks) in the field of criminology. These articles address various levels of analysis, from individual-level explanation, to group-level theories, to broader approaches that include the influence of culture, social structure and institutions in explaining criminal behavior.

From the outset it is important to recognize that the behavior called "crime" is a legal category. This means that crimes are definitions of behavior decided on by the political acts of government through its process of making criminal laws and imposing penalties on offenders. A crime is defined as an act that violates a public law forbidding it, or the omission of an act violating a public law commanding it. Crimes are defined by local, state or federal governments, but where no clear law exists, decisions by courts can also define crime.

Crimes typically contains three elements: (1) they harm others, institutions or society in general; (2) there is a degree of consensus among society's members about the immorality of the behavior; and (3) society reacts to the behavior through a series of government authorized processes and imposes and enforces sanctions on the perpetrator(s). The severity of the penalty imposed on perpetrators varies in relation to the perceived seriousness of the crime, with persons committing serious offenses, described as felonies, typically receiving a sanction of at least one year of imprisonment. Those committing less serious offenses, called misdemeanors, receive penalties of less than a year imprisonment; both felonies and misdemeanors can also receive fines or alternative sanctions, including community service, probation, and be forced to pay restitution to the victim(s).

For a person to be found guilty of a crime they have to meet certain standards established by criminal law and determined by a criminal court. Importantly, these include (1) *actus reus* (guilty act), meaning the person has to be proven to have committed the act, and (2) *mens rea* (guilty mind) which means the person has to be proven to have criminal intent or that they acted recklessly.

It is also important to recognize the difference between "crime" which is a violation of criminal law and "social deviance," which is a violation of social norms; while crime is punishable by formal criminal law, deviance is subject to social reaction such as informal social control, shaming, ostracism and public humiliation.

In seeking to understand and explain crime it is important also to distinguish between crime, which is a behavior, and "criminality" which is a characteristic of people committing criminal acts. Some criminologists argue that to understand crime it is necessary to focus on the elements that all criminal behaviors have in common, rather than on specific criminal acts. Others believe that what is important is the motivational intent and personality profile i.e. the "criminality" of the offender.

However, insofar as crime is a legal category it is important to note that as behavior defined by law, there are a variety of different motivations and causes that can result in a single type of crime. Take female rape as an example. Is it caused by male sexual desire, a need to dominate others, disrespect for women based on gender socialization, acting out of masculinity, a lack of penalties or uncertainty of apprehension? Or is it the result of a patriarchal society that treats women as sex objects, which is reinforced by mass media and popular culture? What about the crime of embezzlement? Is it caused by simple greed and opportunity, or by being in a trusted position that provides access to money and having a financial problem (e.g. debt) that needs a solution, by employees' resentment over bad treatment by their boss, or disrespect for their employer? Or is embezzlement the result of a societal system that celebrates monetary success at the expense of other values such as care for others, collaboration and mutual support? Clearly, behavior resulting in particular crimes can have different explanations.

In this book we delineate several competing explanations for crime. The text is divided into four parts, each containing articles on different theories of criminal behavior that point to a certain level of explanation. "Micro-level" theories refers to the range of explanations that focus on the individual or groups. For example, choosing to commit a crime based on a simple cost-benefit analysis suggests *individual rational choice* as an explanation. And even though it is the polar opposite of rational choice, being predisposed to commit a crime because of certain genetic or personality traits that produce an enhanced need for excitement and thrill seeking, points to individual biological or psychological explanations of crime.

Rather than rational choice or inherent predispositions, other micro-level theories look at the role of social interaction and social processes between individuals and other people that may also lead to crime. For example, people learn from, and model, the behavior of others, whether real or fictional; they can also model criminal behavior, as shown by social learning theory. These are also considered micro-level theories, but they focus on the interactive social processes that lead to crime, rather than the qualities of the kinds of people who commit crime.

In contrast to micro-level theory is macro-level theory which refers to large social structures such as the kind of society we live in, whether this is hierarchical or communal, whether it is made up of conflicting groups or broad social classes, whether its structure reflects class, gender or racial divisions. For example, does a society that incorporates the right to bear arms in its Constitution, such as the United States (Second Amendment), facilitate a gun culture that increases the level of violent crime, particularly gun crime, compared with societies that ban guns? Is a society that encourages a free market economy and the pursuit of profit more prone to corporate crime and fraud than one where the founding ethos is social responsibility? Does the mass media and popular culture, particularly violent video games, contribute to excessive violence by providing "scripts" for such behavior, by sensationalizing it, and by desensitizing potential offenders to the harmful outcomes of such behavior. These are all examples of how macro-level forces can affect individual behavior and result in crime.

Theoretical explanations that lie between the micro- and macro-levels are said to be at the meso-level. These explanations focus on social institutions like families, schools, workplaces, or neighborhoods. For example, does the type of school make a difference to how much violence takes place there? Does it matter whether it is large or small, whether it allows students a share in governance, or whether it is run "top-down" by the principal, or whether it has zero-tolerance policies toward threats of violence, or whether it uses restorative justice and peer-problem solving? Is academic "tracking," in which some students are put in lower-competency, lower-expectation classes, and as a result are alienated from the educational system, a precursor to crime or deviance? Do alienated or marginalized students react and form deviant subcultures hostile to the school and society out of a sense of injustice, and is this a cause of school crime and violence, or even a subsequent criminal career? These would be examples of meso-level explanations.

This book contains the following 4 parts. Part 1 focusses on micro-level individual explanation of crime such as rational choice theory or biological theory mentioned above. Part 2 focusses on micro-level social process explanations, such as social learning theory. Part 3 focuses on macro-level explanations such as social ecology theory that looks at space and place as shaping crime. Finally, Part 4 focusses on macro-level critical theories that explain crime as a result of social forces such as class, or gender or culture and that have in common that they are critical of the existing system or structure of society, not least its criminal justice system, and they want to change it.

Each part of the book contains one or more articles by leading criminologists explaining their own theory or reviewing theories related to the category under discussion. Several articles are drawn from specialized encyclopedias as we find that these are written in a comprehensive and accessible style that is easily understandable by anyone without prior criminological knowledge. We also provide an introductory overview that summarizes the ideas and assumptions contained in that part of the book, including the implications of particular theories for criminal justice policy.

PART

I

Micro-Level Individual Theories

PART I INTRODUCTION

Micro-Level Individual Theories

In Part 1 we discuss micro-level theories of crime that locate the cause of crime in the individual. These theories include classical and rational choice theories, biological and biosocial theories, and psychological theories. We will begin our discussion with classical theory which is not precisely a theory of crime, but rather a philosophical perspective about crime and punishment (Garland 1985).

The basic idea underlying classical theory is that human beings choose to act, or not act, based on their calculation of the costs and benefits, where their perception of the potential benefit/pleasure of the act outweighs the potential cost/pain that accompany the consequences of committing the act (Lanier & Henry 2010). Consequently, the underlying assumption of classical theory is that humans are free-thinking, rational, self-interested beings who calculate the costs of committing crime and act accordingly.

These ideas were first introduced during the European classical period[1] by philosophers, such as Cesare Beccaria (1738–1794) and Jeremy Bentham (1748–1832), who were influenced by Enlightenment notions of the "social contract," which was a hypothetical "contract" between individuals and society. This was also tied to notions of rationality, logical deduction, and the emergence of free market economics, in which society was seen as the outcome of a myriad of individual decisions.

From the classical perspective, the general role of law (as well as specific laws) is assumed to be based on a consensus among the general population. The social contract—that assumed we all give up some liberties in exchange for an ordered and secure society—is an integral component of this perspective. It was also assumed that those who break the law do so for hedonistic, selfish reasons and thereby violate the interests and well-being of the wider group, i.e. society as a whole.

If rational cost-benefit calculation is the cause of crime, then criminal justice policies deriving from the classical perspective involve the idea of due process. This assumes that individuals are responsible for the decisions they make, that all individuals are equally able to calculate the costs and benefits of their actions and that each should be treated equally in law and be judged by the same universal standards. These standards include what are now considered basic individual "rights" such as: the presumption of innocence, trial by jury, restraint of the power of government, and fairness in the administration of justice (Williams & McShane 1988; Einstadter & Henry 2006). The 18th century radical argument, that punishment should be swift, certain, and proportional to the crime, is another lasting contribution of classical theory (Beccaria 1764). These rights became crucial since the ideas were developed in response to brutal, unfair, and cruel systems of justice found in the pre-classical period in Europe (Smith 1967).

Following classical ideas, early scientific ideas about the origins of crime led to several criticisms. For example, it became clear that humans are born with different capacities and consequently there needs to be recognition of the special needs of the mentally ill, juveniles, and other populations who enter the criminal justice system (Vold & Bernard 1986). This led to a decreased focus on the idea that all people exercise full rationality, to the argument that offenders sometimes have imperfect rationality and/or reduced capacity. Indeed, in the early implementation of these ideas it was recognized that not everyone had the same ability to reason, and this modification to "pure" classicism was labeled "neo-classicism."

Contemporary classical theories, called neo-classicalist or more recently, rational or situational choice theories, recognize that there are limits to the freedom of individuals to act fully or perfectly rationally (Lanier & Henry 2010). Importantly, these theorists have gone beyond the framework of general laws and penalties to provide a disincentive explanation for crime and have provided concrete policy and practice initiatives designed to reduce crime. These crime-reduction policies are based on analyzing and manipulating the costs, risks, opportunities, incentives and provocations to crime, which is known generally as "target hardening." Rational choice and routine activities theorists, therefore, focus on design, security and surveillance measures that reduce the rewards of crime (Clarke & Cornish 1983). Their approach goes beyond the early focus of classical theorists on the law, legal systems, rights and government. The new focus also places some responsibility on the potential victim, for creating and maintaining crime free environments.

The so-called "classical" ideas about crime and justice, originating in 18th century writings of European philosophers, are important for several reasons. They laid the foundation for many justice systems around the world, including the most expensive and largest system found in the United States. This set of ideas also indirectly led to the development of the scientific study of crime when scientifically grounded theorists (known as "positivists") subsequently criticized classical scholars for "armchair theorizing" and for ignoring the facts of crime. Ironically, the earlier versions that we call "classical theory," were not theories at all but simply philosophies about crime and punishment. Finally, classical thought about crime and justice is still relevant today; many correctional and behavioral strategies employed by justice systems around the world are based on the set of principles that these ideas embodied.

The mirror image of classical theory is biological theory. Whereas classical theory assumed everyone was identical (rational, cost benefit calculators driven by self-interest) biological theories of crime assume that people who break laws are different from those who do not; criminals differ in significant ways from non-criminals and the origin of this difference is biological in nature (Cohen, 1966).

Early biological theory first appeared in the work of criminal anthropologist Cesare Lombroso (1835–1909; see Reading by Gina Lombroso, Cesare's daughter and colleague) who led the "Italian School," and whose research was continued by his students Enrico Ferri and Raffaele Garofalo. These founding fathers of biological criminology were heavily influenced by Charles Darwin's evolutionary theory and as such, they saw the roots of crime in inherited physical characteristics (Schafer 1976). Lombroso and his students sought to measure and identify physical differences between criminals and non-criminals. Thus, some humans were seen as "born criminals," and destined[2] to commit crime, if certain physical characteristics were present, such as bumps on certain parts of the head, protruding eyebrows, sunken cheekbones, and other physical traits. These "born criminals" were characterized as genetic throwbacks (or "atavistic") meaning they were reversions or throwbacks to an earlier stage of human evolution (Gibson & Rafter 2006).

Initially, characteristics such as facial features and the shape of one's skull were used to identify those who are "crime prone," but later a wider variety of factors were identified, including environmental factors. The goal of biological theories of crime, therefore, is to compare offenders and non-offenders by measuring a variety of features in order to identify and catalogue these differences and to develop explanations about how these different "kinds of people" could lead to crime.

By the 1950s the work of Lombrosian criminology had been replaced with ideas about body type and criminal propensity found in the research of anthropologist Ernest Hooton and physician William Sheldon. In this "somatotyping" research certain body types were seen as indicative of a propensity to commit crime, which turned out to be more a reflection of the stereotyping of offenders, and who the criminal justice system arrests, than the inheritability or genetic transmission of criminal tendencies (Sheldon, Hastl, & McDermott 1949). Again, the idea reflected in these beliefs is that criminals can be determined based on their inherited physical features.

Despite the simplistic, and flawed, nature of early biological theory, the contribution of these criminologists is immense. They introduced the use of positivistic[3] methods such as measurement, comparison, diagnosis, prediction, and treatment in studying criminals and crime. Further, this approach would go on to distinguish the differences between different kinds of criminals, the mentally ill, and offenders committing crimes of different severity, and how these patterns may persist, or desist, over time. Such individualized attention to the specific criminal, rather than the crime, on the assumption that criminal offenders are different from the general population, and different from each other, eventually led to variations in how offenders were treated and in how the courts sentenced them. This included indeterminate sentences and much greater discretion on the part of police, judges and correctional officials.

The early biological approach received much criticism for its limited focus and was replaced by more sophisticated and rigorous studies and greater attention to factors that were "more than skin deep" (Fishbein 1998). Contemporary biological and biosocial theories argue that humans inherit a set of biological and genetically determined attributes that differentiate people across a continuum (Ishikawa & Raine 2002). As a result, when situated in certain environmental contexts some will have a greater propensity to break the law than others. Unlike classical theories, biosocial theories suggest that there is something inherently defective in the *individual* who is prone to committing crimes. Such crime-prone people can be identified, and actions and interventions can be taken that will prevent or reduce the probability that they will commit crimes.

It is important to note that most contemporary biosocial criminologists do not give priority to genetic factors over environmental causes of crime; rather they see these as interactive components, such that certain environments may trigger inherited tendencies leading the human brain to make criminogenic behavior choices. Studies of twins separated at birth have provided some confirmation of the role that heredity plays in human behavior, as have studies of adoptees. As scientific techniques advanced so did the range of differences found between criminals and non-criminals, including differences in genes, chromosomes, brain chemistry, brain development, hormones, and diet among many other differences.

The scientific (positivistic) approach to crime via the study of criminals and their offenses, as well as an aid to policing, is increasingly relevant today. Popular television series such as *CSI (Crime Scene Investigation)* show how police agencies rely on physical evidence (particularly DNA), to identify criminals. Modern crime analysis techniques can now examine a person's genetic structure. Unlike the previous deterministic analysis of the founding biological criminologists most theorists today argue that a genetic pattern interacting with the appropriate triggering environment may be responsible for an increased proclivity to anti-social and consequently criminal behavior. Sophisticated analysis of offenders' and potential offenders' brain patterns are explored through magnetic resonance imaging (MRI) and positron emission tomography (PET) scans (though some have criticized this; see Henry and Plemmons 2012). Contemporary biosocial theorists acknowledge that the role of a person's environment in combination with their biological attributes can limit and channel the behavioral choices that individuals make. However, environment here is narrowly conceived, and rarely includes cultural and structural dimensions. The object of biosocial theories of crime is to examine the individual and social factors seeming to make crime more likely led to interventions at the level of both the physiology of the individual and their environment that can be made to prevent future crimes from occurring.

The roots of psychological criminology are found in Sigmund Freud's (1856–1939) psychoanalytical ideas. Psychological theories search for the cause of crime by studying the mind; how people think, how we process and react to inputs (visual, emotional and cognitive information), and how the brain affects our cognitive processes (Lanier & Henry, 2010). A recurrent theme in psychological thinking about crime has been the way that human development, particularly during childhood, results in different personalities, some of which are abnormal or antisocial. These are especially likely to occur when early childhood development is subject to abuse or trauma, which can result in antisocial or in extreme cases sociopathic or psychopathic personality disorders. These personality types are more prone, under triggering environmental contexts, to engage in antisocial behavior, including crime and violence (Abrahamsen 1944).

A significant component of the psychological approach to crime is the examination of how people are socialized into conformity (or nonconformity) during the developmental process (Aichhorn, 1935). Not only are personalities formed but also patterns of behavior are learned in a variety of ways, from being rewarded or punished, to social learning from others, including modeling the behavior of others, and media images. Such personalities are formed through socialization and developmental processes, particularly during the early years of childhood, involving a series of mental, moral, and sexual stages. When this developmental process is abnormal or subject to traumatic events, personality disorders and psychological disturbances may become part of the individual's personality characteristics, or may be constructed as an appropriate behavioral response, under a particular set of emerging circumstances.

From the psychological perspective, although differences between people form the basis of explaining

their antisocial conduct, these differences are seen to have less to do with inherited genetic patterns (as professed by biological theory) and more to do with human development, particularly the development of the mind and thought processes and how these emerge from socialization within families. For example, the failure to control behavior, particularly sensation seeking, became an analysis of the failure of parents' ability to develop children with balanced personalities that could control sensation seeking, impulsivity and the pursuit of immediate gratification (Healy & Bronner 1936). Thus, psychological explanations for crime go beyond personality development to look at social learning processes, from behavioral rewards and punishments to behavioral modeling, which also takes account of the situational and environmental context including images, television and other media. Cognitive psychology contributes the idea that behavior may also result from destructive thinking patterns that respond to frustration and perceived threats with aggression. Indeed, the variety of psychological theories provides an under-acknowledged wealth of explanation to criminological theory (Yochelson & Samenow 1976).

Psychologists have also taken the view that antisocial behavior is not the result of the personality and learning alone, but of an interaction between the person's propensities, learning, and their environmental and situational context (Rappaport 1977). Here criminal or anti-social behavior is an outcome of an interactive process that develops over time, such that social or environmental factors may trigger erratic or criminal behavior in those psychologically predisposed, who may have developed particular learned scripts and thinking patterns that respond to certain situations, such as frustration, or barriers to achievement, that are antisocial, and destructive to others and themselves.

The science of psychology is a way to examine how psychological processes may produce criminal behavior (Lanier & Henry 2010). Psychologists rely heavily on scales, inventories, and questionnaires to identify and classify the differences between individuals who suffer from psychological disturbances and those who do not. In this regard, it is a positivist theory. Measurement is thus a very critical component, since what is "normal" must be differentiated from what is "pathological." Since criminal behaviors are seen to stem from abnormal developmental processes affecting the mind and are influenced by environmental triggers, some form of psychological treatment intervention is necessary to correct or counteract those with criminal predispositions: To change the process whereby these personalities are formed to manipulate the conditions which might trigger antisocial behavior and to correct thinking patterns that lead to antisocial behavior.

As technology has advanced, so too has the study of human behavior and the brain, particularly how it integrates information from various senses and constructs meaning. Psychologists and psychiatrists have shown how humans learn, the role that emotions play in our behavior and, how chemicals, diet, hormones and other substances affect our thought and subsequent behavioral patterns. Each of these factors has been applied to the study of crime, or more specifically, to the behavior of those we classify as criminal.

Moreover, criminal justice agencies often employ some aspect of psychology. For example, all police recruits undergo psychological screening; the FBI has a behavioral unit and develops psychological profiles of offenders and terrorists; police agencies are developing "criminal profiles" but these are often defeated by the evidence, such as in the case of school violence. And the psychological approach has long extended treatment. Some crimes are not "punished" but "treated" due to the psychological state of the defendant and, even while being incarcerated, many inmates are offered therapies such as anger management training and cognitive behavior therapy (CBT).

Considering the general discrediting of early classical theory, policies related to neoclassical revisions highlight the importance of taking into account mitigating and other factors. Moreover, it is important to note the effects that deterministic views of criminals and crime may have on punishment. Psychological and biological theories have, at their core, deterministic assumptions about crime and behavior which can lead to troubling policies that would essentially advocate endless or at least indeterminate treatment in secure institutions until the offender is "cured." This indeterminate treatment brings the injustice of different lengths of "sentence" for the same crime, which was a major reason for the 1970s turn away from biological and psychological theories and toward the neo-classical-type fixed

sentences. However, more recent variations of such theories incorporate the interaction of biological and psychological traits and processes with environmental influences. These theories advocate a more holistic approach to treatment, prevention, and punishment. However, none of these theories deal with the wider culture and social structures that frame and shape these individual acts.

NOTES

1. The classical period is considered "pre-criminological" because it is before the scientific method was established. The emergence of positivism occurred later and will be discussed in the next section.

2. The idea that people are destined, or determined, to become criminals is the central idea behind the concept of "determinism." The inherent problem with determinism is that is does not allow for the possibility for human change.

3. Positivism is defined as the "application of the scientific method to the study of the biological, psychological, and social characteristics of the criminal" (Vold & Bernard 1986, p. 45).

REFERENCES

Abrahamsen, D. (1944). *Crime and the Human Mind.* New York: Columbia University Press.

Aichhorn, A. (1935). *Wayward Youth.* New York: Viking.

Beccaria, C. (1764). *On Crimes and Punishment.* Translated by Henry Paolucci. Indianapolis, IN: Bobbs-Merrill.

Clarke, R. V. & Cornish, D. B. eds (1983). *Crime Control in Britain: A Review of Policy and Research.* Albany: State University of New York Press.

Cohen, A. K. (1966). *Deviance and Control.* Englewood Cliffs, NJ: Prentice-Hall.

Einstadter, W. J., & Henry, S. (1995. 2006). Criminological Theory: An Analysis of Its Underlying Assumptions. New Boulder, CO: Rowman and Littlefield.

Fishbein, D. H. (1998). "Biological Perspectives in Criminology." *Criminology*, 28: 27–72.

Garland, D. (1985). *Punishment and Welfare: A History of Penal Strategies.* Brookfield, VT: Gower.

Gibson, M. & Rafter, N. H. (2006). Introduction to *Criminal Man* by Cesare Lombroso. Durham, NC: Duke University Press.

Healy, W. & Bronner, A. (1936). *New Light on Delinquency and Its Treatment.* New Haven, CT: Yale University Press.

Henry, S. & Plemmons, D. (2012). "Neuroscience, Neuropolitics, and Neuroethics: The Complex Case of Crime, Deception and fMRI." *Science and Engineering Ethics* 18: 573–591.

Ishikawa, S. S. & Raine, A. (2002). "Behavioral Genetics and Crime." In J. Glickson (Ed.), *The Neurobiology of Criminal Behavior* 4: 81–110. Norwell, MA: Kluwer Academic Publishing.

Lanier, M. M. & Henry, S. (2010). *Essential Criminology.* 3rd ed. Boulder, CO: Westview Press.

Rappaport, J. (1977). *Community Psychology: Values, Research, and Action.* New York: Holt, Rinehart, and Winston.

Schafer, S. (1976). *Introduction to Criminology.* Reston, VA: Reston.

Sheldon, W. H., Hastl, E. M., & McDermott, E. (1949). *Varieties of Delinquent Youth.* New York: Harper and Brothers.

Smith, L. B. (1967). *Elizabethan World.* New York: American Heritage.

Vold, G. B. & Bernard, T. J. (1986). *Theoretical Criminology.* 3rd ed. New York: Oxford University Press.

Williams III, F. P. & McShane, M. D. (1988). *Criminological Theory.* Englewood Cliffs, NJ: Prentice-Hall.

Yochelson, S. & Samenow, S. (1976). *The Criminal Personality.* Vol. 1. New York: Jason Aronson.

CHAPTER
I

Classical and Rational
Choice Theories

THE RATIONAL CHOICE PERSPECTIVE[1]

Derek B. Cornish and Ronald V. Clarke

INTRODUCTION

A pressing need for cash, and a lack of other practical alternatives, criminal or noncriminal, can make armed robbery an attractive option for some individuals. And knowing where to find cash-rich victims and how to overcome opposition can make the rewards well worth the risk and effort. For criminals doing their best to "get by" in their everyday lives, choices and decisions such as these play a significant role in determining the crimes they commit. The theoretical importance and practical benefits of investigating such decision-making are two of the main contributions of the rational choice perspective (Clarke and Cornish 1985; Cornish and Clarke 1986; Clarke and Cornish 2001) summarized in this essay. The rational choice perspective begins with the assumption that offenders choose crime because of the benefits it brings them; it treats offenders as decision-makers who calculate where their self-interest lies and then pursue that self-interest. It also explains the conditions needed for specific crimes to occur, not just the reasons people become involved in crime. It draws few distinctions between offenders and non-offenders, and it emphasizes the role of crime opportunities in causation. Finally, it is as much designed to serve policymaking as criminological understanding.

First, we will describe the six basic propositions of the rational choice perspective. We will then outline the main points of difference between the rational choice perspective and other criminological theories. Last, we will discuss its policy relevance and give brief examples of its value in guiding situational crime prevention efforts.

FUNDAMENTALS OF THE PERSPECTIVE

The six basic propositions of the rational choice perspective are summarized in Table 1.1 and explained in greater detail below.

TABLE 1.1   Six Basic Propositions of the Rational Choice Perspective

1. Crimes are purposive acts, committed with the intention of benefiting the offender.
2. Offenders try to make the best decisions they can, given the risks and uncertainty involved.
3. Offender decision-making varies considerably with the nature of the crime.
4. Decisions about becoming involved in particular kinds of crime ("involvement" decisions) are quite different from those relating to the commission of a specific criminal act ("event" decisions).
5. Involvement decisions comprise three stages—initiation, habituation, and desistance. These must be separately studied because they are influenced by quite different sets of variables.
6. Event decisions involve a sequence of choices made at each stage of the criminal act—for example: preparation, target selection, commission of the act, escape, and aftermath.

SOURCE: Adapted from Ronald V. Clarke and Derek. B. Cornish. (2001). "Rational choice." In Raymond Paternoster and R. Bachman eds., *Explaining Criminals and Crime*. CA: Roxbury, p. 24.

The Purposive Nature of Crime

In the rational choice perspective, criminal acts are never "senseless," but are viewed as purposive acts intended to bring some benefit to the offender. The benefits of theft are obvious, but the rewards of crime can also include excitement, fun, prestige, sexual gratification, and the defiance or domination of others. A man might "brutally" beat his wife, not just because he is a violent "thug" but also because this is the easiest way of making her do what he wants. "Senseless" acts of vandalism or gang violence might confer considerable prestige on the perpetrators among their peers. The term "joyriding" accurately conveys the main reason why cars are stolen—juveniles enjoy driving around in powerful machines.

It is tempting to exclude from rational choice analysis crimes that are driven by clinical delusions or pathological compulsions. But even here, rationality is not completely absent. For instance, serial killers who hear voices telling them to kill prostitutes might still take pains to avoid arrest—and might succeed in doing so for a long time. In any case, pathological crimes constitute a tiny proportion of all criminal acts and their exclusion from rational choice theory hardly weakens its claims to generality.

Limited or Bounded Rationality

The rational choice perspective takes the view of Simon (1990) that an individual's decision-making behavior is characterized by "limited" or "bounded" rationality.

To use the technical term, their decision-making is "satisficing" rather than "optimizing"—it gives acceptable outcomes rather than the best that could be achieved. Criminal decision-making is always less than perfect because it reflects the imperfect conditions under which it naturally occurs. These conditions can be summarized as follows:

+ Offenders are rarely in possession of all the necessary facts about the risks, efforts, and rewards of crime.
+ Criminal choices usually have to be made quickly—and revised hastily.
+ Instead of planning their crimes down to the last detail, criminals might rely on a general approach that has worked before, improvising when they meet with unforeseen circumstances.
+ Once embarked on a crime, criminals tend to focus on the rewards of the crime rather than its risks; and, when considering risks, they focus on the immediate possibilities of being caught, rather than on the punishments they might receive.

Much support for the rational choice perspective is found in ethnographic research in which offenders have been interviewed about their lifestyles, their criminal choices, and their motives and methods. Even Don Gibbons, a frequent critic of the perspective, has stated that studies of predatory offenders "provide considerable support for a 'limited rationality' view of offender decision making by lawbreakers" (Gibbons 1994, p. 124).

Like the rest of us, offenders often act rashly and fail to consider the long-term consequences of their actions. They may be encouraged to take risks by their peers, and their decisions may sometimes be made in a fog of alcohol and drugs. As a result, offenders can make foolish choices that result in capture and severe punishment. Mistakes and failures made by offenders contribute to the view that such behavior is irrational. To offenders, however, and to those taking a rational choice perspective on their crimes, they are generally doing the best they can within the limits of time, resources, and information available to them. This is why we characterize their decision-making as rational, albeit imperfect.

The Importance of Crime Specificity

Specific offenses bring particular benefits to offenders and are committed with specific motives in mind. Cash is the motive for bank robbery; whereas for rape it is usually sexual gratification or the desire to dominate women. Similarly, the factors weighed by offenders, and the variables influencing their decision-making, will differ greatly with the nature of the offense. This is especially true of event decisions because these are more heavily influenced by immediate situational factors. For example, the circumstances surrounding the commission of a mugging, and the setting in which it occurs, differ considerably from those of a computer fraud.

For these reasons, criminal choice cannot properly be studied in the abstract. Instead, descriptions of criminal choice in the form of simplified models, such as flowcharts depicting decision processes, must be developed for specific categories of crime. Broad legal categories such as auto theft or burglary are far too general to model because they include so many differently motivated offenses, a wide range of offenders, and a variety of methods and skills. For example, the theft of a car for joyriding is an offense very different from theft for temporary transport. And both are different from the theft of cars for selling to local customers or to overseas customers.

The Distinction Between Involvement and Events

Criminal choices can be divided into two broad groups: "involvement" and "event" decisions. Event decisions relate to the commission of a particular offense. They concern such matters as the choice of a particular target and ways to reduce the risks of apprehension. Involvement decisions are more complex and are made at three separate stages in a delinquent or criminal "career." Offenders must decide (1) whether they are ready to begin committing crime to obtain what they want; (2) whether, having started, they should continue offending; and (3) whether, at some point, they ought-to stop. The technical terms used by criminologists for these three stages of involvement are initiation, habituation, and desistance.

It is easy to see why event decisions need to be understood and modeled separately for different kinds of crime. For example, the task of escaping apprehension is very different for a bank robber than for someone vandalizing a parked car. But crime specificity is just as important at the various stages of involvement. Thus, the issues faced by people deciding whether to become involved in particular crimes, and the background of relevant experience brought to bear, can vary greatly. The factors relevant to the decisions being made by juveniles from the ghetto when thinking about joining the neighborhood drug dealers, and those relevant to the decisions of bank employees when planning to defraud customers, are likely to be so different that they must be separately studied.

The Separate Stages of Involvement

Not only must involvement decisions be separately modeled for specific kinds of crime, so must each stage of criminal involvement—initiation, habituation, and desistance—because decisions at each stage are influenced by different sets of variables. These variables fall into three groups:

1. Background factors, including personality and upbringing
2. Current life circumstances, routines, and lifestyles
3. Situational variables that include current needs and motives, together with immediate opportunities and inducements

These are of differing importance at the various stages of involvement, as follows:

- At *initiation*, background factors have their greatest influence because they shape the nature of the individual's accumulated learning and experience as well as his or her current life circumstances.
- At *habituation*, current life circumstances, which now increasingly reflect the ongoing rewards of crime, may be of principal importance.
- At *desistance*, current life circumstances, together with the accumulating costs of crime, weigh heavily in decisions.
- During all stages, however, it is the immediate influence of situational variables, such as needs, motives, opportunities, and inducements, that trigger the actual decision about whether or not to commit a particular crime.

The Sequence of Event Decisions

"Crime scripts," which are step-by-step accounts of the procedures used by offenders to commit crime, can assist the analysis of event decisions (Cornish 1994). The scripts build on offenders' accounts of their criminal activities and treat crimes as stories involving a cast of characters, props, and locations that unfold in a purposeful sequence of stages, scenes, and actions. Table 1.2 provides one such script for residential burglary in the suburbs. Accounts like these help to identify the decisions that the offender must make at each step and the situational variables that must be taken into account if the rewards of crime are to compensate for the risks and effort involved. The stages also suggest intervention points for preventive efforts.

WHAT MAKES RATIONAL CHOICE THEORY DIFFERENT?

A Theory of Both Crime and Criminality

Most criminological theories are geared to answering just one question: What makes certain people or groups of people more likely to become involved in crime and delinquency? In current criminological language, the answer makes them theories of criminality.

TABLE 1.2 A Simple Crime Script: Residential Burglary in the Suburbs

STAGES	ACTIONS
Preparation	Get van, tools, co-offender (if needed)
	Take drugs/alcohol
	Select general area for crime
	Assume appropriate role for setting
Enter setting	Drive into development
Precondition	Drive around and loiter in development
Target selection	Scan for cues relating to rewards, risks and effort (e.g., potential "take," occupancy, surveillability and accessibility)
Initiation	Approach dwelling and probe for occupancy and accessibility
Continuation	Break into dwelling and enter
Completion	Steal goods
Finish up	Load up goods and drive away from house
Exit setting	Leave development
Further stages (if applicable)	Store, conceal and disguise goods
Further crime scripts (if applicable)	Market and dispose of stolen goods

When it focuses on involvement, the rational choice perspective is also a *theory of criminality*, though one that gives a fuller role to current life circumstances, needs, and opportunities. But when the rational choice perspective focuses on the event and seeks to understand when and where offenders choose to commit particular offenses, or how they undertake them, it also becomes a *theory of crime*. This is one way in which it diverges from ostensibly similar approaches such as social learning theory (Akers 1990). It shares these dual preoccupations with crime and criminality with Gottfredson and Hirschi's (1990) general theory of crime, but, unlike them, we do not think that offending is the result of low self-control. Different offenses require varying degrees of planning, and offenders of different ages, experience, and skills exhibit varying degrees of understanding and concern about the consequences of their actions.

The Dynamic Nature of Criminality

Preoccupied with explaining offending in terms of deep-rooted and relatively unchanging motivations, criminological theories have failed to capture its ever-changing contingent reality. Offenders' readiness to commit particular crimes varies according to their current needs and desires, and they constantly reassess their involvement in criminal activity. This assessment is deeply affected by their experience of committing particular acts and what they learn from the consequences; it can result in desistance from offending or concentrating on some new form of crime. In addition, the commission of a particular crime can bring in its wake the need or the opportunity to commit other crimes. Thus, a burglar might decide to rape a woman he finds sleeping in the house, or a prostitute might decide to rob a drunken client. The notion of the crime script was specially developed to explore extended sequences of criminal decision-making and links between crimes.

The Importance of Situation and Opportunity

With a few exceptions, such as routine activity theory (Cohen and Felson 1979), most criminological theories ignore or downplay the importance of situational factors in determining crime. But even though routine activity theory and the rational choice perspective are both described as opportunity theories, Clarke and Felson (1993) have enumerated important differences between the two approaches. Routine activity is a macro theory dealing with changes at a societal level that expand or- limit crime opportunities. The rational choice perspective, on the other hand, is a micro theory dealing with the ways in which these opportunities are perceived, evaluated, and acted upon by individual offenders. Often, opportunities are sought and created. But they also play a more active role: They may tempt an otherwise law-abiding person into occasional transgressions. And the existence of easy opportunities in society might attract some people into a life of crime. These facts present important implications for prevention, and the rational choice perspective has proved invaluable in thinking about practical ways of blocking opportunities for crime.

The Normality of Crime

Unlike many other theories, the rational choice perspective makes no hard-and-fast distinction between offenders and the law abiding. It recognizes, of course, that for some people crime is more consistently chosen in a variety of circumstances than for other people. However, this is as much the result of their present material circumstances as it is of their backgrounds. Given a change in their circumstances, they might easily begin to choose legal means for meeting their needs and desires. Likewise, people who have generally avoided criminal choices might cease to do so in the face of overwhelming need or temptation. Many respectable bank clerks have resorted to fraud in the face of pressing financial need. On occasion, all of us will commit offenses when we think we can get away with them. Even the most respectable among us, those holding steady, well-paid jobs, will cheat on expense claims and pilfer employers' property. Indeed, the rational choice perspective is a general theory of crime—as much concerned with crime in the suites as in the streets; as much with incivilities and disorder as with organized crime; as much with property crime as with violent crime; and as much with crime committed by women as with crime committed by men. In short, there is no kind of crime in which reason, choice, and purpose play an unimportant part.

Compatibility with Criminal Justice

If crime is a result of social or psychological deprivation, which is the position of most theories, it seems irrelevant or unfair to respond with punishment. This explains why many criminologists are hostile to criminal justice and reluctant to become involved in policy studies. Law enforcement and criminal justice professionals often detect this hostility and, in turn, disparage criminology. This is unfortunate for both sides—and for society.

The rational choice perspective provides a more subtle view of this apparent dilemma. It recognizes that offenders from deprived backgrounds usually have fewer opportunities for meeting everyday needs than more privileged members of society. To this extent, their crime choices are, therefore, more readily understandable. However, only rarely are people forced to commit crime by virtue of background or current circumstances. Nor do all disadvantaged or deprived people turn to a life of crime. On the contrary, every act of crime involves a choice by the offender. If so, then a way is opened to influence such decisions by seeking to make criminal behavior less rewarding, more risky, and more difficult.

Policy Relevance

The rational choice perspective was explicitly developed to assist policy, and its most important policy application to date has been in the field of situational crime prevention—a broad set of techniques designed to reduce opportunities for crime (Clarke 1997). These are classified under the four rational choice objectives: (1) increasing the effort required by crime, (2) increasing the risks, (3) reducing the rewards, and (4) removing excuses for crime. More recently, a further objective—(5) removing provocation— has been added (Cornish and Clarke 2003). Many notable crime prevention successes have been achieved through using these techniques (Clarke 1997), including the virtual elimination of airline hijackings in the 1970s by baggage screening; the elimination of robberies of bus drivers in U.S. cities in the 1970s by

the introduction of exact fare systems; and the virtual elimination in the 1990s of graffiti on New York City subway cars by systematic and prompt graffiti removal.

Situational prevention is vulnerable to the criticism that reducing opportunities merely results in crime's being displaced—for example, to some other target or location. The rational choice perspective has helped to show why displacement does not necessarily occur. Much crime is the result of easy opportunities, and offenders may be unwilling to incur the additional risks and effort involved following the implementation of situational measures. They can make do with less money and fewer drugs, or they can try to obtain these in noncriminal ways. In fact, one review found no evidence of displacement in twenty-two out of fifty-five crime prevention projects studied (Hesseling 1994). Some displacement was reported in the remaining thirty-three projects, but in every one there was still a net gain in preventive benefits. Accumulating evidence has also shown that, far from simply displacing crime with little real benefit, situational measures often reduce crime more widely than expected. Such a "diffusion of benefits" occurs because offenders often believe that situational measures are more far-reaching than they really are.

CONCLUSION

As Herrnstein (1990, p. 356) points out, rational choice theory "comes close to serving as the fundamental principle of the behavioral sciences. No other well-articulated theory of behavior commands so large a following in so wide a range of disciplines." As far as the application of rational choice theory to criminology is concerned, we have yet to set out in detail all the components of this powerful perspective, or to explore its potential fully. But to be of practical utility, the rational choice perspective needs only to be "good enough" for the explanatory or policy purpose in hand. At the same time, it must be flexible enough to accommodate new needs. It is continually being refined, and if we were called upon to make a fresh statement of the theory some years from now, we believe this would incorporate new or more fully developed concepts. Otherwise, we will have failed in our objective of providing a useful tool, one capable of being' honed and improved, to assist criminologists in thinking about the practical business of controlling crime.

NOTE

1. This paper is an abridged version of Clarke and Cornish (2001).

REFERENCES

Akers, Ronald L. 1990. "Rational Choice, Deterrence and Social Learning Theory-in Criminology: The Path Not Taken." *Journal of Criminal Law and Criminology* 81: 653–676.

Clarke, Ronald V., ed. 1997. *Situational Crime Prevention: Successful Case Studies.* 2d ed. Albany, N.Y.: Harrow & Heston.

Clarke, Ronald V., & Derek B. Cornish. 1985. "Modeling Offenders' Decisions: A Framework for Research and Policy." In vol. 6 of *Crime and Justice,* edited by Michael Tonry and Norval Morris. Chicago: University of Chicago Press.

_____. 2001. "Rational Choice." In *Explaining Criminals and Crime* (pp. 23–42), edited by R. Paternoster and R. Bachman. Los Angeles: Roxbury.

Clarke, Ronald V., & Marcus Felson. 1993. "Introduction: Criminology: Routine Activity and Rational Choice." In vol. 5 of *Routine Activity and Rational Choices: Advances in Criminological Theory.* New Brunswick, N.J.: Transaction.

Cohen, Laurence E., & Marcus Felson. 1979. "Social Change and Crime Rate Trends: A Routine Activity Approach." *American* Sociological *Review* 44: 588–608.

Cornish, Derek B. 1994. "The Procedural Analysis of Offending and Its Relevance for Situational Prevention." In vol. 3 of *Crime Prevention Studies,* edited by Ronald V. Clarke. Monsey, N.Y.: Criminal Justice Press.

Cornish, Derek B., & Ronald V. Clarke. 2003. "Opportunities, Precipitators and Criminal Decisions: A Reply to Wortley's Critique of Situational Crime Prevention." In *Theory for Practice in Situational Crime Prevention,* edited by Martha J. Smith and Derek B. Cornish, vol. 16 of *Crime Prevention Studies.* Monsey, N.Y.: Criminal Justice Press.

_____, eds. 1986. *The Reasoning Criminal.* New York: Springer-Verlag.

Gibbons, Don. 1994. *Talking About Crime and Criminals: Problems and Issues in Theory Development in Criminology.* Englewood Cliffs, N.J.: Prentice-Hall.

Gottfredson, Michael. R., & Travis Hirschi. 1990. *A General Theory of Crime.* Stanford: Stanford University Press.

Herrnstein, Richard J. 1990. "Rational Choice Theory: Necessary But Not Sufficient." *American Psychologist* 45: 356–367.

Hesseling, R.B.P. 1994. "Displacement: A Review of the Empirical Literature." In vol. 3 of *Crime Prevention Studies,* edited by Ronald V. Clarke. Monsey, N.Y.: Criminal Justice Press.

ROUTINE ACTIVITIES

Marie Skubak Tillyer and John E. Eck

Routine activities theory is a theory of crime events. This differs from a majority of criminological theories, which focus on explaining why some people commit crimes—that is, the motivation to commit crime—rather than how criminal events are produced. Although at first glance this distinction may appear inconsequential, it has important implications for the research and prevention of crime. Routine activities theory suggests that the organization of routine activities in society create opportunities for crime. In other words, the daily routine activities of people—including where they work, the routes they travel to and from school, the groups with whom the socialize, the shops they frequent, and so forth—strongly influence when, where, and to whom crime occurs. These routines can make crime easy and low risk, or difficult and risky. Because opportunities vary over time, space, and among people, so too does the likelihood of crime. Therefore, research that stems from routine activities theory generally examines various opportunity structures that facilitate crime; prevention strategies that are informed by routine activities theory attempt to alter these opportunity structures to prevent criminal events.

Routine activities theory was initially used to explain changes in crime trends over time. It has been increasingly used much more broadly to understand and prevent crime problems. Researchers have used various methods to test hypotheses derived from the theory. Since its inception, the theory has become closely aligned with a set of theories and perspectives known as *environmental criminology*, which focuses on the importance of opportunity in determining the distribution of crime across time and space. Environmental criminology, and routine activities theory in particular, has very practical implications for prevention; therefore, practitioners have applied routine activities theory to inform police practices and prevention strategies. This chapter contains a review of the evolution of routine activities theory; a summary of research informed by the theory; complementary perspectives and current applications; and future directions for theory, research, and prevention.

THEORY

In 1979, Cohen and Felson questioned why urban crime rates increased during the 1960s, when the factors commonly thought to cause violent crime, such as poor economic conditions, had generally improved during this time. Cohen and Felson (1979) suggested that a *crime* should be thought of as an event that occurs at a specific location and time and involves specific people and/or objects. They argued that crime events required three minimal elements to converge in time and space: (1) an offender who was prepared to commit the offense; (2) a suitable target, such as a human victim to be assaulted or a piece of property to be stolen; and (3) the absence of a guardian capable of preventing the crime. The lack of any of these three elements, they argued, would be sufficient to prevent a crime event from occurring. Drawing from human ecological theories, Cohen and Felson suggested that structural changes in societal routine activity patterns can influence crime rates by affecting the likelihood of the convergence in time and space of these three necessary elements. As the routine activities of people change, the likelihood of targets converging in time and space with motivated offenders without guardians also changes. In other words, opportunities for crime—and, in turn, crime patterns—are a function of the routine activity patterns in society.

Cohen and Felson (1979) argued that crime rates increased after World War II because the routine activities of society had begun to shift away from the home, thus increasing the likelihood that motivated offenders would converge in time and space with suitable targets in the absence of capable guardianship. Routine activities that take place at or near the home tend to be associated with more guardianship—for both the individual and his or her property—and a lower risk of encountering potential offenders. When people perform routine activities away from the home, they are more likely to encounter potential offenders in the absence of guardians. Furthermore, their belongings in their home are left unguarded, thus creating more opportunities for crime to take place.

One of the greatest contributions of routine activities theory is the idea that criminal opportunities are not spread evenly throughout society; neither are they infinite. Instead, there is some limit on the number of available targets viewed as attractive/suitable by the offender. Cohen and Felson (1979) suggested that suitability is a function of at least four qualities of the target: Value, Inertia, Visibility, and Access, or VIVA. All else being equal, those persons or products that are repeatedly targeted will have the following qualities: perceived value by the offender, either material or symbolic; size and weight that makes the illegal treatment possible; physically visible to potential offenders; and accessible to offenders. Cohen and Felson argued that two additional societal trends—the increase in sales of consumer goods and the design of small durable products—were affecting the crime by means of the supply of suitable targets. These trends in society increased the supply of suitable targets available and, in turn, the likelihood of crime. As the supply of small durable goods continued to rise, the level of suitable targets also rose, thus increasing the number of available criminal opportunities.

Since its inception, routine activities theory has been developed to further specify the necessary elements for a criminal event and those that have the potential to prevent it. The people who prevent crime have been subdivided according to whom or what they are supervising—offender, target, or place—and are now collectively referred to as *controllers*. *Handlers* are people who exert informal social control over potential offenders to prevent them from committing crimes (Felson, 1986). Examples of handlers include parents who chaperone their teenager's social gatherings, a probation officer who supervises probationers, and a school resource officer who keeps an eye on school bullies. Handlers have some sort of personal connection with the potential offenders. Their principal interest is in keeping the potential offender out of trouble. *Guardians* protect suitable targets from offenders (Cohen & Felson, 1979). Examples of guardians include the owner of a car who locks his vehicle, a child care provider who keeps close watch over the children in public, and a coworker who walks another to his car in the parking garage. The principal interest of guardians is the protection of their potential targets. Finally, *managers* supervise and monitor specific places (Eck, 1994). Place managers might include the owner of a shop who installs surveillance cameras, an apartment landlord who updates the locks on the doors, and park rangers who enforce

Figure 2.1 The Crime Triangle
SOURCE: Courtesy of John E. Eck. Copyright John E. Eck ©
2003. All rights reserved. Reproduced with permission.

littering codes. The principal interest of managers is the functioning of places. Eck (2003) depicted this more comprehensive version of routine activities theory was as a crime triangle (see Figure 2.1).

The inner triangle represents the necessary elements for a crime to occur: A motivated offender and suitable target must be at the same place at the same time. The outer triangle represents the potential controllers—guardians, handlers, and managers—who must be absent or ineffective for a crime to occur; the presence of one effective controller can prevent the criminal event.

Controllers have been described in greater detail. Felson (1995) indicated who is most likely to successfully control crime as a guardian, handler, or manager. He asserted that individuals' tendency to discourage crime—by supervising targets, offenders, or places—varies with degree of responsibility. He described four varying degrees of responsibility:

1. *Personal*, such as owners, family, and friends
2. *Assigned*, such as employees with a specific assigned responsibility
3. *Diffuse*, such as employees with a general assigned responsibility
4. *General*, such as strangers and other citizens

Controllers who are more closely associated with potential offenders, targets, or places, are more likely to successfully take control and prevent crime.

As responsibility moves from personal to general, the likelihood that crime will be prevented diminishes. For example, a shop owner will be much more likely to take control and prevent shoplifting in her store compared with a stranger who infrequently comes to the store. Residents will be more likely to prevent crime on their own street block, rather than on the blocks they travel to and from work.

The characteristics of a suitable target have been expanded and applied to products that are frequently targeted for theft. Clarke (1999) extended Cohen and Felson's (1979) work on target suitability to explain the phenomenon of "hot products." Clarke suggested that relatively few hot products account for a large proportion of all thefts. He argues there are six key attributes of hot products that increase the likelihood that they will be targeted by thieves. Specifically, crime is concentrated on products that are CRAVED, that is, Concealable, Removable, Available, Valuable, Enjoyable, and Disposable (Clarke, 1999).

To summarize, routine activities theory is a theory of crime events. Routine activities theory differs from other criminological theories in a fundamental way. Before the advent of routine activities theory, nearly all criminological theory had focused solely on factors that motivate offenders to behave criminally, such as biological, sociological, and economic conditions that might drive individuals to commit crimes. Conversely, routine activities theory focuses on a range of factors that intersect in time and space to produce criminal opportunities and, in turn, criminal events. Although standard criminological theories do not explain how crimes happen to occur at some places (but not others), at some times (but not others), and to some targets (but not others), routine activities theory does not explain why some people commit crimes and others do not. It is important to note that routine activities theory suggests that crime can increase and decline without any change in the number of criminals. Instead, there might be an increase in the availability of suitable targets, a decline in the availability or effectiveness of controllers, or a shift in the routine activities of society that increase the likelihood that these elements will converge in time and space. This notion that the offender is but one contributor to the crime event has both theoretical and practical implications. First, it insinuates that theories that focus only on offender factors are not sufficient to explain crime patterns and trends, only the supply of motivated offenders. Second, it suggests a much broader range of prevention possibilities. Whereas other criminological theories suggest changes to the social, economic, and political institutions of society to alter the factors that motivate people to commit crimes, routine activities theory indicates that shifts in the availability of suitable targets; the characteristics of places; and the presence of capable guardians, place managers, or handlers can produce immediate reductions in crime. Furthermore, changes in the routine activity patterns of society that affect the likelihood that these elements will converge in space and time can also prevent crime events without directly affecting the supply of motivated offenders. Given these policy implications, researchers have derived various testable hypotheses from routine activities theory to explore its validity.

METHODS

Routine activities theory has guided research designed to understand a range of phenomena, including crime trends over time, distributions of crime across space, and individual differences in victimization. In addition, researchers have considered how opportunities for crime might exist at multiple levels. For example, the characteristics of one's neighborhood and the features of the home might influence the likelihood of burglary victimization. Researchers have used various research methods to meet these different needs. The selection of research reviewed in the following paragraphs illustrates the different methods researchers have used to test hypotheses developed from routine activities theory.

Using Routine Activity to Predict Crime Trends

Routine activities theory was first used to understand changes in crime trends over time. To do this, researchers examine how crime rates fluctuate over time with changes in macro-level routine activity trends to determine whether changes in routine activities are associated with changes in crime trends. If they are, this indicates support for the theory. In their initial presentation of the theory, Cohen and Felson (1979) pointed to a shift in the structural routine activities of society to explain why urban crime rates increased during the 1960s, when the factors thought to cause violent crime, such as economic conditions, had generally improved during this time period. They argued that the dispersion in activities away from the family and household caused an increase in target suitability and a decrease in guardianship. In other words, people were leaving their households unoccupied and unguarded more frequently, as well as exposing themselves as targets to potential motivated offenders. To test this hypothesis, Cohen and Felson developed a *household activity ratio* to measure the extent to which households were left unattended.[1] They predicted that changes in the dispersion of activities away from the family and household explained crime rates over time, arguing that nonhousehold activities increase the probability that motivated offenders will converge in time and space in the absence of capable guardians. Using a time series analysis, they found that the household activity ratio was significantly related to burglary, forcible rape, aggravated assault, robbery, and homicide rates from 1947 to 1974 (Cohen & Felson, 1979). Consistent with Cohen and Felson's initial study, subsequent macro-level studies have demonstrated that variations in society's structural organization of routine activities are related to variations in crime trends over time (e.g., Felson & Cohen, 1980). In other words, research has generally shown that routine activities that take people away from their home tend to be associated with increases in crime rates.

Using Routine Activities to Predict the Distribution of Crime Across Space

Routine activities theory has also been used to explain distributions of crime across space. Unlike the research just reviewed, which examined how crime rates changed in the same place over time (i.e., the United States from year to year), this type of research examines how crime rates differ across various places at the same time (i.e., different cities in the United States during a given year). Researchers have used routine activities theory to develop testable hypotheses about why some areas have higher crime rates than others. To do this, they examine whether the routine activities of people living in places with higher levels of crime differ from the routine activities of people living in places with lower levels of crime. For example, Messner and Blau (1987) hypothesized that routine leisure activities that take place in the household will result in lower crime rates, whereas those that take people away from their households will result in higher crime rates. To test these hypotheses, they used data from the 124 largest Standard Metropolitan Statistical Areas in the United States during the time period around 1980. Specifically, they hypothesized that higher levels of aggregate television viewing would be associated with lower city crime rates, because routine leisure activities that take place in the household provide potential targets with a greater level of guardianship. Conversely, they hypothesized that a greater supply of sports and entertainment establishments will be associated with higher city crime rates, because leisure activities that remove people from their homes leave suitable targets unguarded. In general, their analyses support these hypotheses. Higher levels of television viewing were associated with lower rates of forcible rape, robbery, aggravated assault, burglary, larceny, and auto theft. Conversely, a greater supply of sports and entertainment establishments was associated with higher rates of murder and non-negligent manslaughter, forcible rape, robbery, aggravated assault, burglary, and larceny.

Using Routine Activities to Predict Differences in Victimization

Routine activities theory has also been used to explain differences in victimization across individuals. Although Cohen and Felson (1979) initially used the theory to explain national-level crime trends, the mechanisms described by the theory are actually micro-level in nature: A victim comes into contact with an offender in the absence of any capable controllers. This has led many researchers to use individual-level victimization data to understand differences in victimization risk given the routine activities of the potential victim. Specifically, researchers compare the routine activities of victims to those of nonvictims to understand the effect of lifestyle and routine activities on the likelihood of victimization.

Victimization survey data have become increasingly available in recent decades, making such methodology more common. Therefore, researchers have examined how the routine activities of individuals affect their likelihood of various forms of victimization, including property crime (e.g., Mustaine & Tewksbury, 1998), violent crime (e.g., Sampson, 1987), and stalking (e.g., Fisher, Cullen, & Turner, 2002)

Miethe, Stafford, and Long (1987) argued that the routine activities of individuals differentially place some people and/or their property in the proximity of motivated offenders, thus leaving them vulnerable to victimization. Using victimization data from the 1975 National Crime Survey, Miethe et al. explored whether individuals' major daily activities and frequency of night-time activities affected their likelihood of property and violent victimization. Their analyses indicated that individuals who performed their major daily activities outside of the home had relatively higher risks of property victimization compared with those whose daily activities kept them at home. The location of major daily activities, however, was not significantly related to the risk of violent victimization. In terms of the frequency of night-time activities, Miethe et al. found that individuals with a high frequency of night-time activities were at an increased risk for property and violent victimization.

Routine Activities and Multilevel Opportunity

At first, researchers examined macro- and micro-level hypotheses derived from routine activities separately. Macro-level routine activities have been used to explain crime rates, and the routine activities of individuals have been used to explain victimization risk. In more recent years, researchers have begun to explore whether opportunity factors operate at both individual and neighborhood levels to impact victimization risk (e.g., Sampson & Wooldredge, 1987; Wilcox Rountree, Land, & Miethe, 1994). In other words, do the routine activities of the neighborhood in which an individual resides independently influence his victimization risk beyond the effect of his own characteristics and routine activities that leave him vulnerable to crime? For example, leaving one's door unlocked might contribute to victimization risk; living in a neighborhood where it is common to leave one's door unlocked might also contribute to victimization risk. In the first case, one's house can be easily entered if a burglar should try to enter. In the second case, a burglar knows to try to enter the home given the neighborhood norm of leaving doors unlocked. These two factors may both contribute to the risk of victimization for this individual.

In addition, researchers have questioned whether the effects of individual routine activities on victimization risk vary by neighborhood. For example, does leaving one's door unlocked increase risk for burglary victimization to a particular level, regardless of whether one lives in the suburbs or in the city, or do the neighborhood characteristics *condition* the effect of individual routine activities on victimization risk? Routine activities theory and these types of research questions have inspired further theoretical developments in the area of multilevel opportunity (Wilcox, Land, & Hunt 2003).

To answer these questions, researchers use data on both the characteristics of the neighborhood that indicate opportunities for crime, as well as the routine activities and other characteristics of the victim that might put him at risk for victimization. To analyze such data, researchers rely on sophisticated multilevel modeling techniques that allow them to determine the effects of individual- and neighborhood-level factors at the same time, as well as the extent to which neighborhood characteristics might condition the effects of individual routine activities on victimization risk.

COMPLEMENTARY THEORIES, PERSPECTIVES, AND APPLICATIONS

Routine activities theory is closely linked to and shares similar assumptions with several other theories and perspectives that are collectively referred to as *environmental criminology*. Unlike traditional criminology, environmental criminology has focused primarily on the proximate environmental and situational factors that facilitate or prevent criminal events. While not discounting individual differences in motivation to commit crime, the primary focus of this area of theory and research has been on understanding the opportunity structures that produce temporal and spatial patterns

of crime. In addition to routine activities theory, environmental criminology encompasses the rational choice perspective (e.g., Clarke & Cornish 1985), situational crime prevention (Cornish & Clarke 2003), and crime pattern theory (P. J. Brantingham & Brantingham 1981, 1993; P. L. Brantingham & Brantingham 1995). Each of these four theories/perspectives provides a unique contribution to the understanding of the criminal event. Their shared assumptions make them complementary, rather than competing, explanations of crime. In addition, a policing approach called *problem-oriented policing* draws heavily from routine activities theory to help understand and interrupt the opportunity structures that produce specific crime problems.

The theories and perspectives reviewed here all point to opportunity blocking for prevention. Environmental criminology and other criminological theories make different predictions about how offenders will respond to blocked opportunities. *Displacement* and *diffusion of benefits*, described later, are two possible offender adaptations to blocked criminal opportunities for crime.

The Rational Choice Perspective

Whereas routine activities theory describes the necessary elements of a criminal event and the controllers who can disrupt that event, the rational choice perspective addresses the processes by which offenders make decisions. Clarke and Cornish (1985) argued that the decision to offend actually comprises two important decision points: (1) an involvement decision and (2) an event decision. The *involvement decision* refers to an individual's recognition of his or her readiness to commit a crime (Clarke & Cornish 1985). The offender has contemplated this form of crime and other potential options for meeting his or her needs and concluded that he or she would commit this type of crime under certain circumstances. This involvement decision process, according to Clarke and Cornish, is influenced by the individual's prior learning and experiences. The second decision point—the *event decision*—is highly influenced by situational factors. Situations, however, are not perceived the same way by all people; instead, the person views them through the lens of previous experience and assesses them using his or her information-processing abilities (Clarke & Cornish, 1985). At times, the information used to make decisions is inaccurate, with judgment being clouded by situational changes, drugs, and/or alcohol. Although this model describes involvement and event decisions as two discrete choices, in reality the two may happen almost simultaneously.

Over time, the involvement decision continues to be shaped by experience. Positive reinforcement from criminal events can lead to increased frequency of offending. The individual's personal circumstances might change to further reflect his or readiness to commit crime. For example, Clarke and Cornish (1985) pointed to increased professionalism in offending, changes in lifestyle, and changes in network of peers and associates as personal conditions that change over time to solidify one's continual involvement decision. Conversely, an offender may choose to desist in response to reevaluating alternatives to crime. This decision could be influenced by an aversive experience during a criminal event, a change to one's personal circumstances, or changes in the larger opportunity context (Clarke & Cornish, 1985). Both the involvement and event decisions can be viewed as rational in that they are shaped by the effort, risks, rewards, and excuses associated with the behavior.

Situational Crime Prevention

Situational crime prevention is grounded in the rational choice perspective in that it manipulates one or more elements to change the opportunities for crime and in turn change the decision making of potential offenders. In terms of routine activities theory, situational crime prevention can be viewed as the mechanisms by which controllers (i.e., guardians, place managers, and handlers) discourage crime. Over the past few decades, researchers and criminal justice practitioners alike have used the techniques of situational crime prevention to understand crime problems, develop interventions, and evaluate the effectiveness of those interventions. Situational crime prevention was designed to address highly specific forms of crime by systematically manipulating or managing the immediate environment in as permanent a way as possible, with the purpose of reducing opportunities for crime as perceived by a wide

range of offenders (Clarke 1997). Situational crime prevention techniques focus on effectively altering opportunity structures of a particular crime by increasing the efforts, increasing the risks, reducing the rewards, reducing provocations, and removing excuses (Cornish & Clarke 2003). On its face, situational crime prevention techniques change the event decision by altering the offender's perceptions of a specific criminal opportunity. However, it should be noted that an offender's experience during a criminal event directly affects his or her continual involvement decision over time. Blocked opportunities not only prevent an impending criminal event but might also nudge the offender in the direction of abandoning crime.

Crime Pattern Theory

Crime pattern theory provides a framework of environmental characteristics, offender perceptions, and offender movements to explain the spatially patterned nature of crime. It is compatible with routine activities theory because it describes the process by which offenders search for or come across suitable targets. P. J. Brantingham and Brantingham (1981) began with the premise that there are individuals who are motivated to commit crime. As these individuals engage in their target selection process, the environment emits cues that indicate the cultural, legal, economic, political, temporal, and spatial characteristics/features of the area. These elements of the environmental backcloth are then perceived by the offender, and he or she interprets the area as being either favorable or unfavorable for crime. Over time, offenders will form templates of these cues on which they will rely to interpret the environment during target selection.

P. J. Brantingham and Brantingham (1993) argued that one common way offenders encounter their targets is through overlapping or shared activity spaces; in other words, offenders come across their targets during the course of their own routine activities, and therefore the locations of these activities, as well as the routes traveled to these locations, will determine the patterning of crime across space. Brantingham and Brantingham referred to the offender's home, work, school, and places of recreation as *nodes*. The routes traveled between these nodes are referred to as the *paths* of the offender. Finally, *edges* are those physical and mental barriers along the locations of where people live, work, or play. The offender is most likely to search for and/or encounter targets at the nodes, along paths, and at the edges, with the exception of a buffer zone around each node that the offender avoids out of fear of being recognized. Brantingham and Brantingham argued that crime events will thus be clustered along major nodes and paths of activity, as well as constrained by edges of landscapes. The spatial patterns of crime will reflect these two features: the environmental back-cloth and the heavily patterned activity paths, nodes, and edges. In addition, Brantingham and Brantingham noted that some places have particularly high levels of crime because of the characteristics of the activity and people associated with it. Specifically, they suggested that some places are *crime generators*, in that people travel to these locations for reasons other than crime, but the routine activities at these places provide criminal opportunities. Conversely, other places are *crime attractors* in that their characteristics draw offenders there for the purpose of committing crimes.

Problem-Oriented Policing and Problem Analysis

Police agencies use routine activities theory as part of problem-oriented policing. In addition, researchers, city planners, nonprofit organizations, and private citizens follow the same problem analysis process used in problem-oriented policing to understand and prevent crime problems. Problem-oriented policing (Goldstein 1979) is a proactive policing approach that focuses on systematically addressing problems that produce numerous crime incidents and calls for service to the police, instead of reacting to and treating each call for service in isolation. The problem, rather than the individual crime incident, becomes the unit of work for the police. Problems are a form of crime pattern. Within problem-oriented policing, police work to define, understand, and prevent problems that generate numerous crime incidents and citizen calls to the police.

Problem-oriented policing is implemented through the use of the SARA process—Scanning, Analysis, Response, and Assessment. The police *scan* crime data and calls for service to identify crime patterns that are produced by a problem. A problem should be narrowly defined; that is, instead of broadly identifying a "theft problem," it is important to be specific and identify the problem as "theft of shoes from unsecured lockers at the roller rink during after-school hours." The police then *analyze* the problem to understand its characteristics and causes. The crime triangle depicted in Figure 2.1 is often used to organize the analysis; police collect information on all sides of the triangle, not just on offenders. On the basis of this analysis, the police develop *responses* to prevent future crimes. These responses go beyond traditional police tools of arrest and citation to include less traditional tools that may help disrupt the causes of the problem. These less traditional approaches involve one or more of the three types of controllers discussed earlier. Finally, police *assess* the overall impact of the response and alter the process accordingly, depending on the results.

It is during the SARA process that routine activities theory can be applied for prevention. Problem-oriented policing complements research that indicates that crime is not randomly distributed (e.g., Eck, Clarke, & Guerette 2007); instead, some people are repeatedly victimized, some places are repeatedly the sites of crime, and some people repeatedly offend. Eck (2001) suggested that not only does routine activities theory describe the six elements of a crime event but also that specific types of repeat crime and disorder problems can be connected to these elements. Using the terms *wolf, duck,* and *den,* problems of repeat victimization, repeat places, and repeat offending can be seen as a function of both the routine activities of potential offenders, victims, and/or places as well as the absence or ineffectiveness of potential handlers, guardians, and/or managers. This in turn sheds light on what steps should be taken to prevent future crimes stemming from the same problem. A "wolf" problem reflects the repeated actions of an offender or group of offenders, with absent or ineffective handlers. A "duck" problem is one in which the same individual or group is repeatedly victimized; this repeat victimization can be attributed to both the routine activities and characteristics of the victims as well as the absence of capable guardians. A "den" problem is one in which a place is both attractive to targets and offenders while also having weak or absent place managers. The repeat-place problem in which an apartment building is consistently the site of police calls for service might indicate that place managers, such as the landlord or building manager, need to be encouraged or coerced to take control of the problem. In other words, using routine activities theory during problem analysis reveals the absent or ineffective controller who needs to be empowered or held responsible. Furthermore, it might also reveal the activity patterns that systematically produce the opportunity for the crime and suggest points of intervention.

Displacement and Diffusion of Benefits

One common concern when implementing opportunity blocking crime prevention strategies is that crime will simply be *displaced*. In other words, a particular crime event that appears to be prevented is inevitably displaced to another time, place, and/or victim. Different theories of crime make different predictions about the likelihood of displacement in response to blocked criminal opportunities (Clarke 1997). Traditional criminological theories of offenders suggest that displacement is inevitable when an opportunity for crime is blocked. This prediction is consistent with the assumptions that (a) only offenders matter because (b) crime opportunities are infinite and evenly spread across time, space, and people. These theories suggest that motivated offenders will adapt and simply move on to another available opportunity. Conversely, opportunity theories such as routine activities theory suggest that displacement is possible, but only to the extent that other available criminal opportunities have similar rewards without an increase in costs to the offender (Clarke 1997). This prediction is consistent with routine activities theory's focus on opportunity. Opportunities are not assumed to be infinite and equally gratifying to the offender. The likelihood of displacement, therefore, is tied to the relative costs and benefits of alternative crime opportunities. If an offender is unaware of alternative crime opportunities or these alternatives are very unattractive (i.e., they are difficult, risky, or less rewarding), then displacement is unlikely.

There is another possible offender adaptation to crime prevention strategies. Not only might displacement not occur, but also it is possible that the gains from a strategy might extend beyond those crimes that

were directly targeted by the strategy. One explanation for this *diffusion of benefits* is that offenders, uncertain of the actual scope of a particular strategy, refrain from offending in situations beyond the scope of the strategy (Clarke & Weisburd 1994). Opportunity theories, such as routine activities theory, predict that there may be a diffusion of benefits in response to opportunity blocking if other crimes share similar opportunity structures with those crimes targeted by the strategy. Conversely, dispositional theories of crime generally cannot account for diffusion of benefits.

Environmental criminologists have dedicated considerable attention to the issue of displacement, producing a body of research on displacement that suggests that displacement is not inevitable, nor is it complete when it does occur. Furthermore, there is evidence to suggest that there is sometimes a diffusion of benefits in response to crime prevention strategies. Hesseling (1994) reviewed 55 published articles and reports suggesting that displacement does not appear to be inevitable. When it does occur, it tends to be limited. Of the 55 studies Hesseling reviewed, 22 found no sign of displacement. Six of these studies reported some diffusion of benefits to crimes beyond those directly targeted. Of the 33 studies that reported displacement, no study found complete displacement. The displacement that did occur generally reflected a shift in time, place, target, or tactic for the offender.

FUTURE DIRECTIONS

Although routine activities theory has informed a wealth of research to date, there are still many avenues of research yet to be exhausted. Several areas of research informed by routine activities theory are in their early stages. Guardianship is one of the earliest concepts within routine activities theory, yet there is relatively little understanding of the various forms of guardianship, when and where these forms are effective, and the means by which guardianship reduces crime. On a superficial level, guardianship appears to deter offending by increasing the likelihood the offender will be detected and sanctioned. As many guardians have limited authority, skills, or means to detect and sanction offenders, one may wonder whether (a) guardianship can be based on some other mechanism other than deterrence or (b) many of the examples of guardianship we assume are effective are really guarding; perhaps other things are preventing crime. More research needs to examine this topic.

Another area for research is the concepts of place manager and management. Recently, the Madensen ORCA model of management unpacks these concepts. It states that place management consists of four activities: (1) the Organization of physical space, (2) the Regulation of conduct, (3) the Control of access, and (4) the Acquisition of resources. The study of management and its influence on crime will have to address all four activities and merge crime science with business and management science.

Handlers have received very little attention by routine activity researchers, relative to guardians and managers, yet recent evidence suggests that they may have powerful influences on crime and crime patterns. Tillyer (2008) showed how the concept of handling can be used to reduce a wide variety of crime, from minor juvenile delinquency to group-related homicide.

Crime concentrations appear when none of the controllers is present or effective and offenders meet targets, but why are these controllers' absent or ineffective? One answer might be that the controllers whom Rana Sampson (1987), a consultant on problem-oriented policing, calls *super controllers* are not exerting sufficient or the right influence on the controllers. Super controllers are people and institutions that control controllers. For example, a bartender and bar owner are managers, and the state liquor regulatory agency is one of their super controllers. Foster parents are handlers of children put in their care. Child welfare agencies act as their super controllers. A security guard is a guardian, and the company that hired the guard is a super controller. There is almost no research in this area, although it holds great promise for understanding crime and developing prevention.

Routine activities theory focuses on offenders malting contact with targets at places. Some crimes, however, involve "crime at a distance." Mail bombers, for example, do not come close to their targets. Internet fraudsters are able to steal from victims from anywhere in the world. Either routine activities theory is limited to place-based crimes or it needs revision. Eck and Clarke (2003) suggested that substituting *system* for *place* solves the problem. Systems connect people, and they are governed by managers. The mail bomber uses the postal system to contact his victim, and the Internet fraudster uses a system of networked computers. Research on routine activities in systems is in its infancy.

Although it is possible to study the contribution of elements of routine activities theory to the study of crime, it is impossible to empirically study all the elements interacting to create crime patterns. That is because even our best sources of information contain data on only one or two of the actors involved: offenders, targets, handlers, guardians, and managers. Also, the best data available are often highly aggregated and rife with errors. Computer simulations of crime patterns, however, provide a method for exploring how these parts interact in a dynamical system. This is a very new area of research that has spawned simulations of a wide variety of crime types: drug dealing, burglary, robbery, welfare fraud, and others (Liu & Eck, 2008).

CONCLUSION

To summarize, routine activities theory is a theory of crime events, which distinguishes it from a majority of criminological theories that focus on explaining why some people commit crimes. Although routine activities theory was initially used to explain changes in crime trends over time, it has been increasingly used much more broadly to understand and prevent crime problems. Routine activities theory has guided research designed to understand a range of phenomena, including crime trends over time, distributions of crime across space, and individual differences in victimization. It also has been used in conjunction with many crime control strategies, including problem-oriented policing and problem analysis. Despite the broad applicability of the theory to date, there are numerous directions for future research. Examples include further research on the controllers of crime as well as the super controllers.

NOTE

1. Cohen and Felson (1979) calculated their household activity ratio by summing the number of married, husband-present female labor force participant households and the number of non-husband-wife households and then dividing by the total number of households in the United States.

REFERENCES AND FURTHER READINGS

Brantingham, P. J., & Brantingham, P. L. (1981). Notes on the geometry of crime. In P. L. Brantingham & P. J. Brantingham (Eds.), *Environmental criminology* (pp. 27–54). Beverly Hills, CA: Sage.

Brantingham, P. J., & Brantingham, P. L. (1993). Nodes, paths, and edges: Consideration on the complexity of crime and the physical environment. *Journal of Environmental Psychology, 13,* 3–28.

Brantingham, P. L., & Brantingham, P. J. (1995). Criminality of place: Crime generators and crime attractors. *European Journal on Criminal Policy and Research, 3,* 5–26.

Clarke, R. V (1997). Introduction. In R. V. Clarke (Ed.), *Situational crime prevention: Successful case studies* (pp. 3–36). Guilderland, NY: Harrow & Heston.

Clarke, R. V. (1999). *Hot products: Understanding, anticipating and reducing demand for stolen goods* (Paper 112, B. Webb Ed.). London: Home Office, Research Development and Statistics Directorate.

Clarke, R. V., & Cornish, D. B. (1985). Modeling offenders' decisions: A framework for research and policy. In M. Tonry & N. Morris (Eds.), *Crime and justice: A review of research* (Vol. 6, pp. 147–185). Chicago: University of Chicago Press.

Clarke, R. V., & Weisburd, D. (1994). Diffusion of crime control benefits: Observations on the reverse of displacement. In R. V. Clarke (Ed.), *Crime prevention studies* (Vol. 2, pp. 165–183). Monsey, NY: Criminal Justice Press.

Cohen, L. E., & Felson, M. (1979). Social change and crime rate trends: A routine activities approach. *American Sociological Review, 44,* 88–100.

Cornish, D. B., & Clarke, R. V. (2003). Opportunities, precipitators and criminal decisions: A reply to Wortley's critique of situation crime prevention. In M. J. Smith & D. B. Cornish (Eds.), *Crime prevention studies: Vol. 16. Theory for practice in situational crime prevention* (pp. 41–96). Monsey, NY: Criminal Justice Press.

Eck, J. E. (1994). *Drug markets and drug places: A case-control study of the spatial structure of illicit drug dealing.* Baltimore: University of Maryland Press.

Eck, J. E. (2001). Policing and crime event concentration. In R. Meier, L. Kennedy, & V. Sacco (Eds.), *The process and structure of crime: Criminal events and crime analysis, theoretical advances in criminology* (pp. 249–276). New Brunswick, NJ: Transaction.

Eck, J. E. (2003). Police problems: The complexity of problem theory, research and evaluation. In J. Knutsson (Ed.), *Crime prevention studies: Vol. 15. Problem-oriented policing: From innovation to mainstream* (pp. 79–113). Monsey, NY: Criminal Justice Press.

Eck, J. E., & Clarke, R. V., (2003). Classifying common police problems: A routine activity approach. In M. J. Smith & D. B. Cornish (Eds.), *Crime prevention studies: Vol 16. Theory for practice in situational crime prevention* (pp. 7–39). Monsey, NY: Criminal Justice Press.

Eck, J. E., Clarke, R. V., & Guerette, R. T. (2007). Risky facilities: Crime concentration in homogeneous sets of establishments and facilities. In G. Farrell, K. Bowers, K. D. Johnson, & M. Townsley (Eds.), *Crime prevention studies: Vol. 21. Imagination for crime prevention* (pp. 225–264). Monsey, NY: Criminal Justice Press.

Felson, M. (1986). Routine activities, social controls, rational decisions, and criminal outcomes. In D. Cornish & R. V. Clarke (Eds.), *The reasoning criminal* (pp. 119–128). New York: Springer-Verlag.

Felson, M. (1995). Those who discourage crime. In J. E. Eck & D. Weisburd (Eds.), *Crime prevention studies: Vol. 4. Crime and place* (pp. 53–66). Monsey, NY: Criminal Justice Press.

Felson, M., & Cohen, L. E. (1980). Human ecology and crime: A routine activity approach. *Human Ecology, 8,* 389–405.

Fisher, B. S., Cullen, F. T., & Turner, M. G. (2002). Being pursued: A national-level study of stalking among college women. *Criminology and Public Policy, 1,* 257–308.

Goldstein, H. (1979). Improving policing: A problem-oriented approach. *Crime & Delinquency, 25,* 236–258.

Hesseling, R. B. P. (1994). Displacement: A review of the empirical literature. In R. Clarke (Ed.), *Crime prevention studies* (Vol. 3, pp. 197–230). Monsey, NY: Criminal Justice Press.

Liu, L., & Eck, J. E. (2008). *Artificial crime analysis systems: Using computer simulations and geographic information systems.* Hershey, PA: IGI Global.

Messner, S. F., & Blau, J. R. (1987). Routine leisure activities and rates of crime: A macro-level analysis. *Social Forces, 65,* 1035–1052.

Miethe, T. D., Stafford, M. C, & Long, J. S. (1987). Social differentiation in criminal victimization: A test of routine activities/lifestyle theories. *American Sociological Review, 52,* 184–194.

Mustaine, E. E., & Tewksbury, R. (1998). Predicting risks of larceny theft victimization: A routine activity analysis using refined lifestyles measures. *Criminology, 36,* 829–858.

Sampson, R. J. (1987). Personal violence by stranger: An extension and test of the opportunity model. *Journal of Criminal Law and Criminology, 78,* 327–356.

Sampson, R. J., & Wooldredge, J. (1987). Linking the micro- and macro-level dimensions of lifestyle-routine activity and opportunity models of predatory victimizations. *Journal of Quantitative Criminology, 3,* 371–393.

Tillyer, M. S. (2008). *Getting a handle on street violence: Using environmental criminology to understand and prevent repeat offender problems.* Unpublished doctoral dissertation, University of Cincinnati.

Wilcox, P., Land, K. C., & Hunt, S. A. (2003). *Criminal circumstance: A dynamic, multi-contextual criminal opportunity theory.* New York: Aldine de Gruyter.

Wilcox Rountree, P., Land, K. C., & Miethe, T. D. (1994). Macro-micro integration in the study of victimization: A hierarchical logistic model analysis across Seattle neighborhoods. *Criminology, 32,* 387–414.

CHAPTER II

Biological & Biosocial Theories

BIOLOGICAL THEORY

Angela D. Crews

B iological theories within the field of criminology attempt to explain behaviors contrary to societal expectations through examination of individual characteristics. These theories are categorized within a paradigm called *positivism* (also known as *determinism*), which asserts that behaviors, including law-violating behaviors, are determined by factors largely beyond individual control. Positivist theories contrast with *classical theories*, which argue that people generally choose their behaviors in rational processes of logical decision making, and with *critical* theories, which critique lawmaking, social stratification, and the unequal distribution of power and wealth.

Positivist theories are further classified on the basis of the types of external influences they identify as potentially determinative of individual behavior. For example, psychological and psychiatric theories look at an individual's mental development and functioning; sociological theories evaluate the impact of social structure on individuals (e.g., social disorganization, anomie, subcultural theories, opportunity, strain) and the impact of social function and processes on individuals (e.g., differential association, social learning, social bonds, labeling). Biological theories can be classified into three types: (1) those that attempt to differentiate among individuals on the basis of certain innate (i.e., those with which you are born) outward physical traits or characteristics; (2) those that attempt to trace the source of differences to genetic or hereditary characteristics; and (3) those that attempt to distinguish among individuals on the basis of structural, functional, or chemical differences in the brain or body.

This chapter is organized in rough chronological order and by historical figures associated with an important development. It is difficult to provide an exact chronology, because several important developments and movements happened simultaneously in various parts of the world. For example, although biological theories are considered positivist, the concept of positivism did not evolve until after the evolution of some early biological perspectives. In addition, biological theories of behavior that involve some aspect of evolution, genetics, or heredity are discussed in terms of those scientific developments, although physical trait theories still continued to be popular.

The following sections discuss some of the more important and relevant considerations in scientific developments that impacted biological theories of behavior. A brief history of positivism also is provided, tracing the development and use of the biological theories from early (largely discredited) beliefs, to the most current theories on the relationship of biology to behavior. This section also provides a conclusion that discusses the role of biological theories in the future of criminological thought.

CLASSICAL AND POSITIVIST VIEWS OF BEHAVIOR

Biological theories are a subtype of positivist theory. Positivism evolved as instrumental in explaining law-violating behaviors during the latter part of the 19th century as a response to the perceived harshness of classical school philosophies. Classical thought, which emerged during the Age of Enlightenment (mid-1600s to late 1700s), asserted that man operated on the basis of free will and rational thought, choosing which courses of action to take. According to classical theorists, individuals would engage in behaviors that were pleasurable and avoid behaviors that were painful. Punishment (of the right type and in the right amounts) would deter an individual from committing an act if that punishment resulted in pain that outweighed the pleasure. Classical theorists, for the most part, denounced torture as a type of punishment because it was more punishment than was necessary to prevent a future occurrence of the act; they believed that punishment should be proportionate to the crime to be effective as a deterrent.

Classical views were not very concerned about the causes of behavior. Behaviors were seen as the result of choice rather than as the result of inherent or external factors largely uncontrollable by the individual. The significant progression of scientific thought and method, however, led to the application of science in the study of human and social behavior. The central focus of these new ideas was that the aim of any social action toward individuals who violated law should be curing them, not punishing them.

Positivist criminology is distinguished by three main elements: (1) the search for the causes of crime, whether biological, psychological, or sociological; (2) the use of

the scientific method to test theories against observations of the world; and (3) the rejection of punishment as a response to law-violating or deviant behavior, replaced with treatment based on the medical (rehabilitation) model. Positivism rejects free will and replaces it with scientific determinism. Finally, it rejects focus on criminal law and replaces it with a study of the individual.

THE SCIENTIFIC METHOD

The scientific method is important to positivism and to biological theories of crime because it provides a systematic way to examine a particular problem or issue, rather than relying on spiritual or mystical explanations or haphazard guesswork. The development of the modern scientific method is credited primarily to Ibn al-Haytham (965–1039), an Iraqi-born scientist who wrote *The Book of Optics* between 1011 and 1021. It consists of the following seven steps:

1. Observation: Visual examination of a problem or issue, noticing characteristics and patterns.
2. Statement of the problem: A verbal description of the problem or issue, noting how it impacts and relates to other events or factors. An explanation of why and how the issue or problem is a problem.
3. Formulation of hypotheses: Development of potential explanations or solutions, educated and informed statements about the expected nature of the problem and relationships among the various components of the problem, specification of variables involved in the problem so that the potential explanation can be tested.
4. Testing of the hypotheses using controlled experimentation: controlled manipulation of the variables to determine whether the hypotheses are supported.
5. Analyses of experimental results; this usually involves examination of statistics.
6. Interpretation of data obtained from the testing and analyses and the formulation of a conclusion: Taking into account all the factors, the researcher makes a conclusion about the nature of the problem or issue.
7. Publication or dissemination of findings to inform interested populations and future research: providing information to the scientific community

about your findings to help future researchers or to inform policy and practice.

Although some variation of the scientific method has been used since ancient times to evaluate and solve many problems, its use to explain social problems, such as crime and criminality, developed more recently. Early types of biological theories of crime were among the first efforts. Given the use of the scientific method in the "hard" or "natural" sciences, early researchers of the causes of crime attempted to explain criminal behaviors by applying the scientific method. The most obvious place to look for differences between criminals and other individuals was on the outside, by studying physical traits.

PHYSICAL TRAIT THEORIES

The belief that one can determine a person's character, moral disposition, or behavior by observing his or her physical characteristics is ancient. Pythagoras, a philosopher, mathematician, and scientist who lived during the period around 500 BCE, may have been one of the first to advocate this practice, known as *physiognomy*.

Physiognomy

The term *physiognomy* comes from the Greek words *physis*, meaning "nature," and *gnomon*, meaning "to judge or to interpret." It refers to the evaluation of a person's personality or character (i.e., his or her nature) through an examination of that person's outward appearance. Early physiognomy concentrated on characteristics of the face through which to judge the person's nature. Aristotle, a Greek philosopher who lived from 384 to 322 BCE, was a proponent of physiognomy, as were many other ancient Greeks. The practice flourished in many areas of the world and was taught in universities throughout England until it was banned by Henry VIII in 1531.

Giambattista della Porta (1535–1615)

The publication of *On Physiognomy* in 1586 by Italian scholar Giambattista della Porta once again brought

renewed focus to this belief and practice of the ancient Greeks. Della Porta, often considered the first criminologist, examined patients during his medical practice and concluded that appearance and character were related. He approached the study of this relationship from a magico-spiritualistic metaphysical perspective instead of a scientific one, classifying humans on the basis of their resemblance to animals. For example, men who look like donkeys are similar to donkeys in their laziness and stupidity; men who resemble pigs behave like pigs.

Johann Kaspar Lavater (1741–1801)

Delia Porta's ideas were extremely influential to Johann Kaspar Lavater, a Swiss pastor who published his painstakingly detailed study of facial fragments in 1783. He concluded that one could determine criminal behavior through an examination of a person's eyes, ears, nose, chin, and facial shape.

Phrenology

Phrenology, from the Greek words *phren*, meaning "mind," and *logos*, meaning "knowledge," is based on the belief that human behavior originated in the brain. This was a major departure from earlier beliefs that focused on the four humors as the source of emotions and behaviors: (1) sanguine (blood), seated in the liver and associated with courage and love; (2) choleric (yellow bile), seated in the gall bladder and associated with anger and bad temper; (3) melancholic (black bile), seated in the spleen and associated with depression, sadness, and irritability; and (4) phlegmatic (phlegm), seated in the brain and lungs and associated with calmness and lack of excitability. Theoretically and practically relocating responsibility for behavior from various organs to the brain represented a major step in the development of the scientific study of behavior and in the development of biological explanations of crime and criminality.

Franz Joseph Gall (1758–1828)

Around 1800, Franz Joseph Gall, a German neuro-anatomist and physiologist who pioneered study of the human brain as the source of mental faculties, developed the practice of *cranioscopy*, a technique by which to infer behaviors and characteristics from external examination of the skull (cranium). According to Gall, a person's strengths, weaknesses, morals, proclivities, character, and personality could be determined by physical characteristics of his or her skull.

Gall mapped out the location of 27 "brain organs" on the human skull. A bump or depression in a particular area of the skull would indicate a strength or weakness in that particular area. For example, several areas of Gall's map of the skull were believed to correspond to that person's tendencies to engage in criminal or deviant acts. One area corresponded to the tendency to commit murder; another area corresponded to the tendency to steal. Although not widely accepted in Europe, the English elite (and others) used Gall's ideas to justify the oppression of individuals whose skulls had bumps or depressions in the wrong areas. The practice also was widely accepted in America between 1820 and 1850. Although crude, and somewhat ridiculous by today's standards, Gall's efforts had significant impact on subsequent research that attempted to identity the brain as the origin of behavior. Although similar to physiognomy in that it tried to make inferences about character and behavior from outward characteristics, cranioscopy attempted to correlate those outward physical characteristics to internal physical characteristics (i.e., brain shape), which was a significant advance.

Johann Spurzheim (1776–1832)

Spurzheim, a German physician and student of Gall's, actually coined the term *phrenology* to replace *cranioscopy*. Spurzheim also expanded the map of the brain organs, developed a hierarchical system of the organs, and created a model "phrenology bust" that depicted the location of the brain organs.

While- the German scientists were focusing attention on the brain as an important determinant of individual behavior, various other scholars were theorizing about the development of man as a biological organism; about the nature of social and political organizations; and about the place of man, as an individual, within those organizations. The synthesis of these ideas would significantly advance the progress of research related to biological perspectives of behavior.

THE ORIGINS OF HUMANITY AND THE MECHANISMS OF INHERITANCE

Since the beginning of time, humans have questioned their origins. Earliest explanations focused on mystical/magical and spiritual forces, often centered on creationism, the theory that life originated from a divine source. The power of the organized religions in shaping man's social, political, economic, and legal systems is testament to their immense influence. For example, religious perspectives dominated philosophical thought until the Scientific Revolution began in the mid-16th century, when advances in theory and practice provided explanations alternative to those promulgated by the church. Galileo Galilei (1564–1642), Johannes Kepler (1571–1630), René Descartes (1596–1650), and Isaac Newton (1643–1727) all made significant contributions that brought scientific reasoning to the forefront of thought as a competitor to spiritual explanations. Although usurping the philosophies of the church were not their main goals, then-revolutionary ideas (that natural events and human behaviors may be explained by the development and application of certain scientific principles) had just that effect. Needless to say, secular science was not very popular with the church and organized religion. However, these changes were vital in advancing understanding of human and societal behavior.

Persistence of Human Traits and Characteristics

In addition to having been the potential source of physiognomy, ancient Greek philosophers also were among the first to recognize and attempt to explain the persistence of traits and characteristics from one generation to the next. Plato and Aristotle used the concept of *association* to explain how current mental processes (especially memories) generate from prior mental processes. These beliefs broadened to include all mental processes in the hands of philosophers such as Hume, Mill, and Locke.

Given that memories and other, possibly undesirable, characteristics and traits could potentially persist through generations, Plato advocated the control of reproduction by the state (government). Infanticide was practiced as a form of population control in ancient

Rome, Athens, and Sparta. Many of the ancient societies also engaged in practices to weed out weak, diseased, malformed, or otherwise unfit members, such as exposing young children to the elements to see which ones had the strength, intelligence, and wit to survive.

Scientists began studying the nature of persistent traits in plants and animals prior to the application of these ideals to humans. Once established, however, it took relatively little time and relatively little effort to explain human patterns with these principles. As readers will note, the mid- to late 18th century was characterized by rapid progress in the natural sciences, which positively impacted biologically oriented research in the social sciences.

Carolus (Carl) Linnaeus (1707–1778)

Linnaeus, a Swedish botanist, zoologist, and physician, was among the first to document traits, patterns, and characteristics among plants and animals, creating hierarchical taxonomies (systems of classification). In *Systema Naturae* (System of Nature), published in 1735, Linnaeus grouped humans with other primates, becoming one of the first to recognize similar characteristics across species, hinting at an evolutionary progression.

Pierre-Louis Moreau de Maupertuis (1698–1759)

In 1745, French philosopher and mathematician Maupertuis published *Venus Physique* (Physical Venus), in which he proposed a theory of reproduction in which organic materials contained mechanisms to naturally organize. He subsequently discussed his views on heredity and examined the contributions of both sexes to reproduction, examining variations through statistics. Whether Maupertuis can be credited with being among the first to attempt to elucidate a theory of evolution is actively debated. He is generally credited with outlining the basic principles of evolutionary thought, along with his contemporary, James Burnett (see *James Burnett, Lord Monboddo [1714–1799]* section).

David Hartley (1705–1757) and the Associationist School

Hartley (borrowing somewhat from philosopher John Locke) published his most influential work—*Observations on Man, His Frame, His Duty, and His Expectations*—in 1749. In it, he attempted to explain memory and thought, in general, through the doctrine of association. This was significant, because he attempted to link the processes of the body to the processes of the brain. He explained that actions and thoughts that do not result immediately from an external stimulus are influenced by the constant activity of the brain because of man's past experiences, mediated by the current circumstances, causing man to act in one way or another. These brain activities that Hartley called *sensations* are often associated together and become associated with other ideas and sensations, forming new ideas. Hartley's work was important in that it brought scientific focus to the process of thought, the origin of emotions, and the impact of feelings on the creation of voluntary action. This is a positivist philosophy in that action is not viewed as being the direct result of strict free will.

George-Louis Leclerc, Comte de Buffon (1707–1788)

From 1749 to 1778, Leclerc published his most famous and influential work in 36 volumes, with an additional 8 volumes published postmortem. It was a study of natural history, from the general to the specific. In this work, he proposed the idea that species, including humans, change (i.e., evolve) throughout generations. Following in the footsteps of Linnaeus, he also proposed the radical idea of a relationship between humans and apes.

In another controversial publication, *The Eras of Nature* (1778), Leclerc questioned the long-standing and sacred belief that the universe was created by a divine power, instead suggesting that our solar system was created by celestial collisions. Finally, he contradicted the notion that seemingly useless body parts on animals were spontaneously generated but instead were vestigial, remnants of evolutionary progress.

Leclerc's influence was widespread and impacted subsequent beliefs about the transmission of traits from one generation to the next (inheritance, heredity) as well as about changes that occur over time with each passing generation (evolution). These ideas significantly impacted biological theories of behavior. Charles Darwin, in fact, credited Leclerc with being the first modern author of the time to treat evolution as a scientific principle.

James Burnett, Lord Monboddo (1714–1799)

Burnett, a Scottish judge, is credited with being another of the first to promote evolutionary ideas, in particular, the idea of natural selection. In *The Origin and Progress of Language* (1773), Burnett analyzed the development of language as an evolutionary process; he clearly was familiar with the ideas of natural selection, although he differed with Leclerc in his support of the notion that humans were related to apes.

Erasmus Darwin (1731–1802)

One individual who took Leclerc's ideas to heart was Erasmus Darwin, grandfather of Charles Darwin and Francis Galton (see subsequent sections on Charles Darwin and Galton). Darwin also integrated ideas from Linnaeus, translating Linnaeus's works from Latin to English and publishing his own book of poetry about plants, *The Botanic Garden* (1791). Between 1794 and 1796, Darwin published *Zöonomia*, which discussed the concept of generation (reproduction) and used Hartley's theory of association (and possibly Linneaus's taxonomies). Many scholars believe Darwin's propositions were the forerunners of a more well-defined theory of inheritance later argued by Jean-Baptiste Lamarck (see *Jean-Baptiste Lamarck [1744–1829]* section).

Thomas Robert Malthus (1766–1834)

In 1798, Malthus, an English demographer and political economist, published *An Essay on the Principle of Population*, in which he proposed that populations struggle for existence in competition over resources. His main premise was that increases in population result in increased competition for scarce resources, primarily food. As a society becomes overpopulated, those at the bottom of the socioeconomic strata suffer the most (and often die). He explained that some natural events and conditions serve to control population growth (e.g., war, disease, famine) and that moral restraint (e.g., abstinence, late marriage) could serve the same function.

Contrary to many economists of the time who believed that increasing fertility rates and populations would provide more workers and would increase the productivity of a society, Malthus argued that the provision of resources could often not keep pace with population growth and would result in more poverty among the lower classes. This depiction of a struggle for existence was applied by subsequent scientists to plants and animals and was instrumental to Charles Darwin (and others) in arguments about "natural selection" and "survival of the fittest" (a phrase coined by Herbert Spencer; see *Herbert Spencer [1820–1903]* section).

Jean-Baptiste Lamarck (1744–1829)

Lamarck was a French naturalist, mentored by Leclerc (see preceding section on Leclerc), who published *Recherches sur l'Organisation des Corps Vivans* (Research on the Organization of Living Things) in 1802. Lemarck was among the first to attempt to classify invertebrates and was among the first to use the term *biology*. He primarily is known for promoting and advocating a theory of *soft inheritance*, or *inheritance of acquired characters*, in which characteristics developed during the lifetime of an organism (e.g., larger or stronger muscles) are passed along to subsequent generations, making them better suited for survival (or better adapted).

Lemarck is considered the first to articulate a coherent theory of evolution, although he believed that organisms came into being through spontaneous generation instead of sharing a common source. His theory was characterized by two main arguments: (1) that organisms progress from simpler to more complex through generations and (2) that organisms develop adaptations because of their environments or because of the necessity (or lack thereof) of particular characteristics (the use-it-or-lose-it aspect).

The Impact of Positivism

In the early 1800s, following the advancement of arguments, proposals, and theories related to the biological sciences, and during the discussions of Malthus's revolutionary "struggle for existence," groundbreaking ideas also were being propagated about the place and function of man within social groups. These developments were instrumental to the application of biological perspectives to human behavior within social groups.

Auguste Comte (1798–1857)

Known as the "Father of Sociology," Comte was a French scholar who published *Plan de Travaux Scientifiques Necessaries Pour Réorganizer la Société* (Plan of Scientific Studies Necessary for the Reorganization of Society) in 1822. In this work, he argued for a universal *law of three phases:* (1) theological, (2) metaphysical, and (3) scientific, through which all societies have, or will, progress.

The theological stage is the most primitive stage, characterized by supernatural, religious, or animistic explanations for events, situations, and behaviors and a lack of interest in the origins of causes. The metaphysical stage is slightly more advanced and identifies abstract forces (fate, accident) as the origin of causes. The most advanced stage, the scientific stage, is what Comte called the *positive* stage. At this point, there is little concern for the origin of actions, but a focus on the outcomes, which man can control.

Positive stages are characterized by observation, experimentation, and logic and attempt to understand the relationships among components. Comte's positivism attempted to apply scientific principles (i.e., the scientific method) to the behavior of societies and to the behavior of groups within societies and emphasized the connectedness of all the elements involved in behavior. Positivism is one of the first theories of social evolution, attempting to explain how societies progress. Comte claimed that the only real knowledge is knowledge gained through actual sense experience (i.e., observation).

Comte's scientific stage also is exemplified by the use of quantitative, statistical procedures to make logical, rational decisions based on evidence. Statistical procedures had been used for some time in the hard sciences (e.g., math, physics), but a positivist perspective required that the use of such measurement techniques be applied to the social sciences, as well.

Statistics and the Social Sciences

Adolphe Quetelet (1796–1894) and Andre-Michel Guerry (1802–1866)

Despite the overwhelming complexity of social phenomena, Quetelet and Guerry were convinced that it was possible to apply statistical techniques to the investigation of social behavior. Both men were primarily interested in unraveling the statistical laws underlying social problems such as crime and suicide. This idea was controversial at the time, because it contradicted prevailing belief in free will. Quetelet's most influential publication was *Sur L 'Homme et le Developpement de ses Facultés, ou Essai de Physique Sociale* (Treatise on Man; 1835), in which he described the "average" man, developed from the calculation of mean values to form a normal distribution. Quetelet called this process *social physics*, a term that Comte had earlier used. Quetelet's appropriation of the phrase *social physics* prompted Comte to adopt the term *sociology* instead.

Guerry is known for developing the idea *of moral statistics* in an 1829 one-page document containing three maps of France, shaded in terms of crimes against property, crimes against persons, and a proxy for education (school instruction). A subsequent publication, *Essay on Moral Statistics of France* (1833), expanded on this technique and developed shaded maps to evaluate crime and suicides by age, sex, region, and season. He found that these rates varied by region but remained remarkably stable across the other factors.

This preliminary work emphasized the possibility that social measurements could provide insight into the regularity of human actions, forming a basis for the development of social laws, similar to the physical laws that govern the behavior of other objects and events in nature. Quetelet and Guerry were instrumental in the development of sociology and criminology, illustrating the possibility of measuring, determining the nature of relationships, and identifying patterns and regularities in social situations.

Heredity and Evolution

As the search for explanations of individual and social behavior improved through the application of statistical methods and the positivist insistence that the only real knowledge was that obtained through systematic observation (i-e., the scientific method), beliefs about the nature and potential of man within society became more sophisticated and grounded. Although Lemarck had earlier discussed the passage of certain acquired traits from generation to generation (soft inheritance), theorists in the mid-1800s benefited from Malthus's propositions about the progress of society and from increasingly sophisticated inquiries into the nature and source of biological and behavioral predispositions.

Herbert Spencer (1820–1903)

An early English social theorist and philosopher, Spencer articulated a theory of evolution in *Progress: Its Law and Cause* (1857), prior to the publication of Charles Darwin's *On the Origin of Species* in 1859. Spencer proposed that everything in the universe developed from a single source and progressed in complexity with the passing of time and generations, becoming differentiated yet being characterized by increasing integration of the differentiated parts. Spencer also coined the phrase *survival of the fittest*, in 1864, after reading Darwin's *On the Origin of Species*, and he applied the idea of natural selection to society.

Charles Darwin (1809–1882)

Although the preceding paragraphs illustrate the development of scientific thought on the concepts of heredity and evolution, most scholars primarily note the impact of Charles Darwin. Darwin described his theories in two main publications: (1) *On the Origin of Species by Means of Natural Selection, or the Preservation of Favored Races in the Struggle for Life* (1859) and (2) *The Descent of Man and Selection in Relation to Sex* (1871).

In *On the Origin of Species*, Darwin detailed the theory that organisms evolve over generations through a process of natural selection. Darwin reached his conclusions and supported his observations through evidence that he collected during a sea voyage on a boat, the *HMS Beagle*, during the 1830s.

The Descent of Man and Selection in Relation to Sex applied Darwin's theory to human evolution and described the theory of sexual selection. Although he had earlier hinted that natural selection and evolution could and should be applied to the development of man, others (Thomas Huxley in 1863, Alfred Wallace in 1864) had actually applied his theories to the human animal first.

Cesare Lombroso (1835–1909)

Among the first to apply Darwin's findings to criminal behavior and criminals, Lombroso was an Italian criminologist and founder of the Italian School of positivist criminology. Lombroso rejected the established Classical School, which held that crime was a characteristic trait of human nature. Instead, using concepts drawn from earlier perspectives, such as physiognomy, Lombroso argued, in essence, that criminality was inherited and that someone "born criminal" (this phrase was coined by his student, Enrico Ferri) could be identified by physical defects, which confirmed a criminal as savage, or atavistic.

Lombroso published *Criminal Man* in 1876, helping to establish the newly forming Positive School of criminology. Inspired by Charles Darwin's evolutionary theory, he believed that criminals were not as evolved as people who did not commit crime and that crime is a result of biological differences between criminals and noncriminals.

A central focus of Lombroso's work is the concept of *atavism*. Atavism describes the reappearance in an organism of characteristics of some remote ancestor after several generations of absence. It often refers to one that exhibits atavism, that is, a throwback. It can also mean a reversion to an earlier behavior, outlook, or approach. Lombroso approached this concept believing that criminals were throwbacks on the evolutionary scale. He believed that modern criminals shared physical characteristics (*stigmata*) with primitive humans. In his later years, he eventually thought that social and environmental factors can contribute to criminality.

Lombroso reached his conclusions by studying the cadavers of executed criminals for physical indicators of atavism, developing a typological system (with four main criminal types) to categorize these individuals. Although his methods were flawed, and most of the traits he listed failed to distinguish criminals from matched samples of noncriminals, he was among the first to apply scientific principles to the collection of data and to use statistical techniques in his data analysis. In addition to examining the physical characteristics of the criminal, he also evaluated the conditions under which crime is committed. He also was among the first to study female criminality, speculating that females were more likely to be criminals "by passion."

Lombroso determined that serious offenders inherited their criminal traits and were "born criminals," atavistic throwbacks to earlier evolutionary ancestors. They had strong jaws, big teeth, bulging foreheads, and long arms. These types of offenders constituted about one third of all criminals. The remaining two thirds were "criminaloids" (minor offenders) who only occasionally commit crime.

Although primarily remembered for his claim that criminal behaviors were inherited, Lombroso also argued that environmental factors can play an important role in crime. He speculated that alcoholism, climate changes, and lack of education may contribute to criminality.

Lombroso's work started other researchers on the path to determine a hereditary source for criminal behavior. His student, Enrico Ferri (1856–1929), disagreed with Lombroso's focus on the physiological, preferring instead to examine the interactive effects of physical factors, individual factors, and social factors and to blame criminality on a lack of moral sensibility.

Another Italian contemporary, Raffaele Garofalo (1851–1934), developed a theory of *natural crime*, focusing on those acts that could be prevented or reduced by punishment. Garofalo also suggested the elimination of individuals who posed a threat to society, to improve the quality of the society and ensure its survival. Like Ferri, he believed crime was more the result of a lack in moral sensibilities rather than a physiological problem.

Lombroso's conclusions were challenged and refuted by Charles Goring (1870–1919), who wrote *The English Convict* in 1913. In a carefully controlled statistical comparison of more than 3,000 criminals and noncriminals, Goring found no significant physical differences between the two populations except height and weight (criminals were slightly smaller). His findings essentially discredited Lombroso's idea of the born criminal, although research into the search for criminal types continued.

The Criminal Physique

Evaluations and categorizations of a person's body build or physique also became popular as researchers attempted to link crime with some outwardly observable differences. In 1925, Ernst Kretschmer (1888–1964), a German psychiatrist, published *Physique and Character*, in which he described three categories of body type (asthenic, athletic, pyknik) associated with three categories of behaviors (cyclothemic, schizothemic, and displastic). *Cyclothemes* were manic-depressive and typified by soft skin, a round shape, and little muscle development, and tended to commit the less serious offenses that were more intellectual in nature. *Schizothemes* were antisocial and apathetic, committing the more serious violent offenses, and were either asthenic (thin and tall) or athletic (wide and strong). *Displastics* could be any body type but were characterized by highly charged emotional states and unable to control their emotions. Kretschmer associated displastics with sexual offenses. Although Kretschmer attempted to develop a typology that associated behaviors with physique, he did not put much consideration into the complex nature of behavior and its interaction with the environment.

Among those who continued this search was a contemporary of Goring, Harvard anthropologist Ernest Hooten (1887–1954). Dissatisfied with Goring's findings, Hooten spent 12 years conducting research into the criminal nature of man to disprove Goring and to support Lombroso. His first influential publication, *Crime and the Man* (1939), documented his study of 14,000 prisoners and 3,000 non-prisoner controls in 10 states. Hooten was more rigorous than Goring in his methods, differentiating his subjects on the basis of types of crime and by geographic, ethnic, and racial backgrounds.

Hooten agreed with Lombroso's idea of a born criminal and argued that most crime was committed by individuals who were "biologically inferior," "organically inadaptable," "mentally and physically stunted and warped," and "sociologically debased." He argued that the only way to solve crime was by eliminating people who were morally, mentally, or physically "unfit," or by segregating them in an environment apart from the rest of society.

As Hooten was conducting his research and developing his conclusions, the sociological world was developing an interest in the contribution of social factors and social environments to the development of criminal behavior. Sociological research out of the University of Chicago (i.e., the Chicago School) stressed the impact of the social environment rather than an individual's biology as crucial to the development of crime. Hooten was widely criticized because of his failure to consider social factors and his myopic focus on biological determinism.

Gregor Mendel (1822–1884)

While scholars debated Darwin's claims and investigated whether criminals were born and were atavistic throwbacks to earlier historical periods, a piece of research on heredity in plants that was largely overlooked at the time it was published in 1866 was being rediscovered. This work provided quantitative evidence that traits were passed on from one generation to the next (or inherited), making it one of the most critical pieces of research related to biological theories of crime.

Mendel, an Austrian scientist, is known as the "father of genetics" (Henig, 2000). Although Mendel's work was largely ignored until after 1900 (in part because of the popularity of Darwin's theories), application of his *laws of inheritance* to individual and social development resulted in significant advances in biological theories of behavior.

Mendel's experiments with plants (in particular, peas) and with annuals (in particular, bees) provided scientific support to some of the propositions suggested by Darwin in 1868, although Mendel's research predates that of Darwin. Darwin theorized that pangenesis explained the persistence of traits from one generation to the next. He discussed transmission and development in his laws of inheritance, arguing that cells within bodies shed "gem-mules" that carried specific traits from the parent organism to the subsequent generation. Darwin insightfully proposed that a parent organism's gemmules could transmit traits to the following generation even though those traits may not have been present in the parent and that those traits could develop at any later point.

Mendel, however, was the one who developed support for the theory of inheritance through his experiments with the cultivation and breeding of pea plants,

and the scientific support for *dominant* and *recessive* characteristics, passed from one generation to the next. His work also led to focus on the study of traits at the cellular level (genotypes) instead of at the observable level (phenotypes).

The Implications of Heredity and Evolution: Eugenics and Social Darwinism

Francis Galton (1822–1911) and Eugenics

It was in the work of Galton, a cousin of Charles Darwin, that statistics, biology, and sociology reached a harmonic state. Reading Darwin's theories about variations in the traits of domestic animals set Galton on a path to study variations in humans. In doing so, he developed measurement techniques and analytic techniques to help him make sense of what he was observing. He first was interested in whether human ability was hereditary, and he collected biographical information about numerous prominent men of the time to chart the families' abilities over several generations. He published his results in a book called *Hereditary Genius* (1869), in which he concluded that human ability was inherited. He followed this work with a survey of English scientists (1883) in which he attempted to determine whether their interest and abilities in science were the result of heredity (nature) or encouragement (nurture). Galton stimulated interest in the question of (and coined the phrase) *nature versus nurture*.

Although Galton's work at that point was useful and had resulted in the development of numerous measurement tools (e.g., the questionnaire; fingerprint analysis) and statistical concepts (standard deviation, correlation, regression), it was his work with twins that provided the impetus for future inquiries into the nature-versus-nurture debate. Galton surveyed sets of twins to determine whether twins who were identical exhibited differences if raised in different environments and whether twins who were fraternal exhibited similarities if raised in similar environments. This work was published as "The History of Twins as a Criterion of the Relative Powers of Nature and Nurture" in 1875.

In 1883, Galton developed the concept of *eugenics*, his most controversial and abused philosophy. Eugenics advocated the encouragement, through the distribution of incentives, of "able" couples to reproduce in an effort to improve human hereditary traits. Part of his proposals included manipulating social morals to encourage the reproduction of the "more fit" and discourage reproduction of the "less fit." Galton's proposals were to change social mores and values rather than forcibly manipulating reproduction or eliminating those who were considered less fit. He believed that, without encouragement, it was the natural state of man (and thus of society) to revert to mediocrity, a phrase that came to be clarified as "regression toward the mean," which he viewed as repressive of social and individual progress.

Prevailing thought at the time was receptive to such ideals, in the belief that these policies would reduce or eliminate poverty, disease, genetic deformities, illnesses, and crime. Eugenics was originally conceived as a concept of social responsibility to improve the lives of everyone in society by encouraging individuals to selectively breed good traits in and bad traits out, but many who followed would use Galton's philosophies toward less than desirable ends.

After Galton's efforts, others attempted to document that crime was a family trait. In 1877, Richard Dugdale (1841–1883) published *The Jukes: A Study in Crime, Pauperism, Disease and Heredity*, in which he traced the descendants of matriarch Ada Jukes and found that most of the Jukes family members (although they were not all biologically related) were criminals, prostitutes, or welfare recipients. Another family study, published in 1912 by Henry H. Goddard (1866–1957), traced 1,000 descendants of a man named Martin Kallikak, comparing his descendants who were conceived within wedlock to a woman of "noble birth" to his descendants who came from the bloodline he conceived out of wedlock with another woman, one of ill repute. Goddard concluded (although he later retracted his conclusions) that the legitimate bloodline was "wholesome," whereas the illegitimate bloodline was characterized by "feeblemindedness."

Social Darwinism

Developments that ensued after Galton's propositions of eugenics, and after the rediscovery and replication of Mendel's work on the heritability of traits, were crucial

to the study of man's behavior, its potential biological roots, and to the study of man's role and obligation in society. Malthus's struggle for existence, Comte's sociology, Quetelet and Guerry's social physics and moral statistics, and the work of scientists (most notably Darwin) on transmutation, natural selection, survival of the fittest, and evolution, resulted in perfect conditions under which scientific principles and statistical analysis could be applied to the human condition and to human behavior. A compilation of these philosophies resulted in the theory of *social Darwinism*, originally applied to the structure and function of social processes and organizations (e.g., government), with the primary belief that competition drives all social progress and only the strongest survive.

Mendel's contribution was critical to the ideas of social Darwinism, explaining how observable characteristics (phenotypes) were inheritable and how a trait may appear in one generation that had not appeared in many prior generations. These atavisms, or throwbacks to an earlier evolutionary period, could be physical (e.g., vestigial tails, useless appendages) or behavioral (e.g., violence). Social Darwinists became interested in the question of whether social development (progress, evolution) could be engineered or controlled through manipulation of these traits. Other scientists studying the more undesirable behaviors of man (e.g., crime) were interested in whether social problems could be controlled through this type of manipulation. Many, however, such as noted political economist William Graham Sumner (1840–1910), advocated a laissez-faire philosophy with respect to the survival and progress of societies, noting that problems like poverty are the natural result of inherent inequalities and that the process of natural selection and survival of the fittest would mean a natural reduction in the problems over time (without social engineering or interference; Hodgson, 2004). Viewing society through the lens of social Darwinism, however, inevitably led to viewing man through the lens of social Darwinism.

During the late 1800s and early 1900s, while Goring, Hooten, and others were debating the role of biology in criminal behavior, others were quietly merging Malthus's ideas on competition and survival among societies, Spencer's insistence that individual evolution leads to social evolution, Mendel's ideas on the heritability of traits, Darwin's ideas on natural selection and evolution, and Galton's ideas on eugenics into warped interpretations and applications of eugenics and social Darwinism.

The Legacy of Eugenics and Social Darwinism

With unprecedented immigration in the late 19th and early 20th centuries, American society struggled with increasing crime, poverty, suicide, and other social problems. Some, such as the theorists of the Chicago School, saw the solution in sociological explanations, whereas others turned to solutions implied in eugenics. Although a complete description of the misapplication of eugenics is beyond the scope of this chapter, it is important for the student of biological theories to understand the impact that eugenics had on the study of biological explanations of behavior.

In theory, eugenics argued for the improvement of human genetic qualities. Positive eugenics aims to increase the reproduction of desirable qualities, and negative eugenics aims to discourage the reproduction of undesirable qualities, to improve humanity and society. The underlying premise is that both positive and negative traits are inherited and passed down through generations. Early eugenicists focused on traits such as intelligence and on hereditary diseases or defects presumed to be genetic (Barrett & Kurzman, 2004). These eugenicists, following Galton's philosophies, focused on societal changes (the provision of incentives) to encourage reproduction among those with positive traits and to discourage reproduction among those with negative traits.

In practice, however, and following a logical progression of thought, some believed eugenics to mean that persons with undesirable traits should be prevented from reproducing, or even be eliminated.

Although social Darwinists and eugenicists are alike in their goal to improve humanity and society through survival of the fittest, social Darwinists were more likely to assert that this improvement would take place in a natural process, with weak, diseased, undesirable, and unfit individuals being eventually weeded out. It is for this reason that social Darwinists opposed government intervention into problems such as poverty and crime, believing that natural forces would result in the reduction of elimination of these undesirable conditions. Eugenicists, on the other hand, encouraged active intervention.

It is this active intervention that became problematic, although it was not initially viewed as such. Activists promoted the use of contraception to prevent unwanted pregnancies, and state laws were written regulating marriages. Individuals who had ailments thought to be genetic were prohibited from marrying and forcibly sterilized. This included individuals deemed to be "feeble-minded" or mentally ill.

The popularity of eugenics spread throughout the United States during the late 1800s and early 1900s. Charles Davenport (1866–1944), an influential American biologist, directed the Cold Spring Harbor Laboratory in 1910 and founded the Eugenics Record Office, hiring Harry H. Laughlin (1880–1943) as superintendent (Kevles, 1985).

Between 1907 and 1914, several states had passed sterilization laws. Laughlin, however, perceived these as ineffective and full of holes, prompting him in 1922 to draft a "model" law that was passed by 18 additional states (Lombardo n.d.). In this model law Laughlin defined the populations that would be targeted by forced sterilization, including criminals, the very poor, epileptics, alcoholics, the blind, the deaf, the insane, and those who had a physical deformity. These practices were upheld as constitutional by the U.S. Supreme Court in 1927 in the case of *Buck v. Bell* and continued until 1981. More than 64,000 individuals in 33 states were forcibly sterilized under these laws.

With increased immigration came increased concerns about the quality and purity of the races. Responding to these concerns, Madison Grant (1865–1937), an American lawyer, wrote one of the first and most influential books about racial integrity, *The Passing of the Great Race* (1916). Grant wrote that the Nordic (i.e., white) racial line was the pinnacle of civilization. He warned against miscegenation (race mixing) and supported legislation against it. He argued for racial hygiene because the Nordic race was superior to any other, and any mixing would taint Nordic bloodlines, making them impure. He also warned that "undesirables" breed in greater numbers and would overrun the superior Nordic population if not controlled. He advocated the eradication of "undesirables" from the human gene pool coupled with the promulgation of more desirable and worthy racial types.

Grant's work was immensely popular and was instrumental in the drafting and passage of the Immigration Act of 1924, which restricted the numbers of immigrants from the less desirable regions, such as southern and eastern Europe. His book also was translated into several languages. In 1925, it was translated into German, in which *Nordic* was replaced by the word *Aryan*. Adolph Hitler, who read the book shortly after its translation into German, would later call Grant's work his "bible."

In 1928, with sterilization laws and immigration restrictions in full swing, E. S. Gosney (1855–1942) founded the Human Betterment Foundation, an entity whose primary purpose was to compile and distribute propaganda about compulsory sterilization. Gosney hired Paul E. Popenoe (1888–1979) to assist him in the study of the impact of these sterilization laws in California. Their collaboration resulted in the publication of *Sterilization for Human Betterment: A Summary of Results of 6,000 Operations in California, 1909–1929* (Gosney & Popenoe 1929), used by Nazi Germany to support its 1934 Law for the Prevention of Hereditarily Diseased Offspring. Furthermore, these arguments were used to justify policies of racial hygiene and racial cleaning that Nazi Germany enacted against Jews and other "undesirable" or "unfit" persons who did not meet the model of the Aryan ideal. The Nuremburg Laws enacted in 1935 consisted of the Law for the Protection of German Blood and German Honor, and the Reich Citizenship Laws, which prohibited the mixing of Germans with Jews (which really meant anyone not deemed to be German) and stripped so-called undesirables of their citizenship.

Although population control policies based on eugenics enjoyed widespread support in many countries prior to World War II, Nazi use of its philosophies to justify the eradication of approximately 6 million Jews and an additional 3 to 5 million others brought an immediate halt to its proliferation. However, sterilizations, marriage restrictions based on fitness, and prohibitions of racial intermarriage continued for decades. Marriage counseling, ironically developed by Paul Popenoe as a eugenic tactic to ensure marriage between fit individuals, also became a viable area of practice.

Despite the fact that the word *eugenics* is usually avoided, modern efforts to improve humanity's gene pool persist. The Human Genome Project is one notable scientific effort to understand the genetic makeup and properties of human beings with an eye toward eradicating or preventing inheritable diseases and defects. Advances in science and the development of ethical guidelines provide hope that struggles to better understand the transmission and development of human traits and characteristics are not yet abandoned. This is especially important to the future of biological theories of criminality.

POST-WORLD WAR II RESEARCH ON BIOLOGY AND BEHAVIOR

Body Physique and Crime

After World War II, research into the biological roots of crime persisted. Following in the footsteps of Lombroso in 1876, Kretschmer in 1925, and Hooten in 1939, William H. Sheldon (1898–1977) attempted to document a direct link between biology (specifically, physique) and personality (specifically, crime) through the development of a classification system of personality patterns and corresponding physical builds (Sheldon 1940).

Running contrary to prevailing sociological emphases on the environmental correlates of crime, Sheldon chose to instead employ beliefs about Darwin's survival of the fittest, Lombroso's criminal man, and Galton's eugenics. Sheldon argued for an "ideal" type, in which perfectly formed physique joined perfectly formed temperament and disposition. Any combination that deviated from this ideal was associated with disorders of both personality and behavior. He claimed a physical basis for all variations in personality and body build.

During the 1940s, Sheldon developed and tested his classification system, known as *somatotyping*. He created three classifications: (1) *ectomorphs*, who were thin, delicate, flat, and linear; (2) *endomorphs*, who were heavy or obese, with a round, soft shape; and (3) *mesomorphs*, who were rectangular, muscular, and sturdy.

In subsequent studies of juvenile delinquency, Sheldon argued that mesomorphic types were more likely to engage in crime, ectomorphs were more likely to commit suicide, and endomorphs were more likely to be mentally ill. Although Sheldon linked physical and psychological characteristics and concluded that both were the result of heredity, he failed to support that conclusion with valid statistical methods.

Also during the late 1940s and early 1950s, Sheldon Glueck and Eleanor Glueck conducted longitudinal research into juvenile delinquency using control groups and added to Sheldon's list of somatotypes. They suggested the addition of a fourth type they called *balanced*. In their research, they found support for Sheldon's proposition that mesomorphs are more likely to commit crime. Among the juveniles they studied, the mesomorphic somatotype was disproportionately represented among delinquents by a ratio of nearly two to one as compared with nondelinquent controls. In addition, whereas only about 14% of delinquents could be classified as ectomorphs, nearly 40% of the nondelinquent controls could be placed in this category. Instead of concluding that body type led to delinquency, the Gluecks (1956) concluded that participation in delinquency (for which individuals are more likely to get arrested) may be facilitated by having a mesomorphic body type rather than an ectomorphic, endomorphic, or balanced body type.

Biological explanations for behavior lost much of their popularity during the 1960s with the belief that their inherent implication of inferiority often was misused to justify prejudice and discrimination. In addition, the 1950s and 1960s brought significant advances in the natural sciences and in the social and behavioral sciences. Once again, criminologists and other scientists turned to evaluating the internal components and processes of the human body.

Genetics in Modern Biological Theories

Efforts to find a genetic explanation for violence and aggression have been met with strong resistance, primarily because of painful memories of how research linking biology and crime were used in the past (eugenics). In 1992, a conference related to the Human Genome Project at the University of Maryland had its federal funding withdrawn for attempting to discuss any particular linkage between genes and violence (Murphy & Lappé 1994). Objections by groups who believed that any such research would be used to oppress poor and minority populations overpowered the quest for knowledge.

Although genetic research began with Mendel's laws of inheritance, our understanding of how genes influence our behaviors is still evolving. Discovery of the genetic code in the mid-1950s took us beyond recognizing that genes were involved in heredity to a greater understanding of the process through which hereditary traits are passed from one generation to another. Part of this discovery process was the clarification of the structure and function of chromosomes, which carry human genetic material.

Chromosomes

Human cells normally have 22 pairs of chromosomes, plus a pair of chromosomes that determines sex, for a total of 46. Sex chromosomes are termed X and Y. Females carry a combination of XX, and males carry a combination of XY. During conception, the male's sperm carries genetic material to the female's egg, if the sperm that fertilizes a female egg is carrying a Y chromosome, the resulting embryo will develop into a male fetus (XY). If the sperm is carrying an X chromosome, the resulting embryo will develop into a female fetus (XX).

During this process, however, things can develop abnormally. For example, during the process, some men are left with an extra Y chromosome (XYY). Erroneously termed *XYY syndrome*, a "supermale" carrying this chromosomal pattern usually has a normal appearance and will probably never know that he carries an extra Y chromosome, unless he is genetically tested for some other reason. Given the Y chromosome's association with the male sex and with increased production in testosterone, many claims have been made in the research literature that XYY males are more aggressive and more violent. This supposition has not been supported with scientifically valid research.

Scientific progress made inquiry into genetic correlates of behavior more precise and less speculative. Although scholars are reluctant to associate criminal behavior with any specific gene, researchers continue to investigate the inheritability of behavioral traits. Some of the most promising work involves the study of twins and adoptees.

Twin Studies

Since Galton's work with twins, twin studies have become more sophisticated and have attempted to respond to methodological criticisms. Distinctions between fraternal (dizygotic [DZ]) and identical (monozygotic [MZ]) twins have contributed to the sophistication of this type of research. DZ twins develop from two eggs and share about half of their genetic material, whereas MZ twins develop from a single egg and share all of their genetic material.

Twin studies attempt to control for the impact of the social environment, hypothesizing that these environments are similar for twins. Twins generally are raised in the same social environment, so the impact of the social environment is considered to be equal and consistent (and thus controlled). Therefore, any greater similarity between identical twins than between fraternal twins would provide evidence for a genetic link.

One of the earlier and simpler twin studies was conducted in the 1920s by Johannes Lange (1929). He studied 30 pairs of twins who were of the same sex. Seventeen of these pairs were DZ twins, and 13 of these pairs were MZ twins. At least one of each twin pair was known to have committed a crime. However, Lange found that both twins in 10 of the 13 MZ twin pairs were known criminals, compared with both twins in only 2 of the 17 DZ pairs.

More sophisticated and extensive studies have followed, In 1974, Karl O. Christiansen evaluated the criminal behavior of 3,586 twin pairs born in Denmark between 1881 and 1910. He found that the chance of one twin engaging in criminal behavior when the other twin was criminal was 50% among the MZ twin pairs but only 20% among the DZ twin pairs. The correlation between the genetic closeness of the biological relationship and crime was especially true for serious violent crime and for more lengthy criminal careers.

These findings were supported by additional work on the self-reported delinquency of twins in the 1980s and 1990s by David C. Rowe and his colleagues. This research found that MZ twins were more likely than DZ twins to both be involved in delinquent activity. Moreover, MZ twins reported more delinquent peers than did DZ twins (Rowe 1983). The work of Rowe and his colleagues supported a genetic component to delinquency but also provided evidence of a social component.

Although twin studies have provided some support for a genetic component to behavior, it is difficult to separate the influence of genetics from the influence of social factors. There also are theoretical problems with the assumption that twins raised in the same home are subject to the same treatment and the same social environment. Even scholars who study the link between criminal behavior and genetics are cautious with their conclusions, arguing that these types of studies reveal only that the similarities between twins have some impact on behavior. Whether these similarities are genetic, social, or some combination of the two is still open for debate. Studies of adopted individuals constitute one attempt to resolve this issue.

Adoption Studies

In adoption studies, the behavior of adoptees is compared with the outcomes of their adopted and biological parents. The aim is to separate out the impact of the environment from the influence of heredity. This research asks whether a child will exhibit traits of the adopted parents or of the biological parents.

Research indicates that an adoptee with a biological parent who is criminal is more likely to engage in property crime than other adoptees and that this effect is stronger for boys. The findings, from a study of 14,427 Danish children adopted between 1924 and 1947, provide evidence that there may be a genetic factor in the predisposition to antisocial behavior (Mednick, Gabrielli, & Hutchins 1984). Studies in both Sweden and in the United States confirm these conclusions.

A meta-analysis of adoption studies, conducted by Walters and White (1989), reinforced the importance of adoption studies as the best way to determine the impact of both environment and genetics on criminal behavior but also emphasized the theoretical and methodological difficulties inherent to this approach. Knowing, for example, whether an adoptive parent has a criminal history provides no information on the social environment provided in the adoptive parents' home. The definitions of crime and criminality also widely vary in these studies and can be challenged. For example, one study may consider as criminal behaviors perhaps best classified as antisocial (e.g., using bad language, adultery). Furthermore, these studies do not account for the quantity or quality of social interactions experienced within the various settings (adoptive vs. biological). Finally, the determination that someone is a criminal simply on the basis of a conviction or incarceration is problematic and does not consider undetected criminal behaviors.

According to researchers who worked on the Human Genome Project, however, twin and adoption studies are the best source for evaluating individual differences in human behavior. Recent studies have consistently demonstrated that genetic variation substantially contributes to behavioral variation across all types of behavior. Two primary conclusions are derived from these studies: (1) Nearly all of the most frequently studied behaviors, characteristics, and conditions (e.g., cognitive abilities, personality, aggressive behavior) are moderately to highly heritable, and (2) nonshared environments play a more important role than shared environments and tend to make people different from, instead of similar to, their relatives.

Most biological scholars now cautiously conclude that there may be a genetic predisposition toward criminal behavior but that the manifestation of these predispositions is dependent on social and environmental factors. However, belief (or not) in a genetic link to criminality does not preclude other potential biological explanations of crime.

Biochemical Explanations: Hormones, Neurotransmitters, Diet

Another biological explanation for criminal behavior involves the body's hormones, released by some of the body's cells or organs to regulate activity in other cells or organs. *Androgens* are hormones associated with masculine traits, and *estrogens* are associated with feminine traits. *Progesterone* is another hormone associated primarily with female reproductive processes, such as pregnancy and menstruation.

Testosterone

Testosterone is considered the male sex hormone. Although persons of both sexes secrete testosterone, males secrete it in higher levels. Researchers have found that higher levels of this hormone are associated with increased levels of violence and aggression, both in males and females. Criminal samples have been found to have higher testosterone levels when compared with noncriminal samples, although these levels were still within normal limits.

Problems with attempting to explain criminal behavior by testosterone levels, however, are problematic. Testosterone levels naturally fluctuate throughout the day and in response to various environmental stimuli. For example, levels among athletes increase prior to competitions, perhaps indicating that testosterone is produced to increase aggression instead of as a response to aggression. This makes correlating levels to behavior and controlling for environmental stimuli extremely difficult.

Recent research conducted by Ellis in 2003, however, has added an evolutionary component. In his *evolutionary neuroandrogenic theory*, Ellis argued that increased levels of testosterone reduce the brain's sensitivity to environmental stimuli, making a person act out, with reduced abilities to control emotions. He also speculated that the development of testosterone's "competitive-victimizing" effects is the result of natural selection, as described by Darwin.

Scholars who study the relationship between testosterone levels and crime cite as support the differences between males and females in terms of levels of crime in general and levels of violence in particular. This work has led to the "treatment" of male sex offenders with chemical derivatives from progesterone to reduce male sexual urges through the introduction of female hormones (e.g., Depo-Provera, a brand of birth control for women). This has been effective in reducing some types of sex offenses (e.g., pedophilia, exhibitionism), but it has had little or no impact on other crimes or violence.

Premenstrual Syndrome and Premenstrual Dysphoric Disorder

Researchers also have investigated the impact of female hormones on behavior in women, beginning with two English cases in 1980 in which two women used *premenstrual syndrome* (PMS) as a mitigating factor in violent offenses. These efforts led to female defendants in the United States being able to argue reduced culpability due to PMS.

More recently, a more severe form of PMS has been identified. *Premenstrual dysphoric disorder* (PMDD) is a severe and debilitating form of PMS, distinguished by the level of interference the menstrual process has on the ability of the woman to engage in the functions of everyday life. Interestingly, researchers have established a genetic link to the development of PMDD. Women with a certain genetic structure have increased (abnormal) sensitivity to their own normal hormones, resulting in increased symptoms of emotional and physical stress.

Another phenomenon associated with female hormones is *postpartum depression syndrome*. Although most new mothers experience symptoms of depression in the weeks or months following birth, which is primarily thought to be due to a decrease in progesterone, approximately 1% to 2% of these mothers exhibit severe symptoms, such as hallucinations, suicidal or homicidal thoughts, mental confusion, and panic attacks. As with PMS and PMDD, postpartum depression syndrome has successfully been used as a mitigating factor in the legal defense of women accused of crimes while suffering from its effects. Both PMS and PMDD, however, are controversial concepts, difficult to diagnose as medical conditions, and argued by some to be social constructions and psychiatric problems instead of medical conditions.

Neurotransmitters

In addition to the possibility that human hormones may directly impact behavior, they also may directly impact chemicals that regulate brain activity. *Neurotransmitters* are chemicals that transmit messages between brain cells, called *neurons*, and have a direct impact on the many functions of the brain, including those that affect emotions, learning, mood, and behavior. Although researchers have extensively studied more than 50 of these chemicals, research on the biological bases of crime has focused on three of these: (1) *norepinephrine*, which is associated with the body's fight-or-flight response; (2) *dopamine*, which plays a role in thinking and learning, motivation, sleep, attention, and feelings of pleasure and reward; and (3) *serotonin*, which impacts many functions, such as sleep, sex drive, anger, aggression, appetite, and metabolism.

High levels of norepinephrine, low levels of dopamine, and low levels of serotonin have been associated with aggression. Results from research that has examined the impact of these neurotransmitters are mixed. With all of these chemicals, fluctuations in their levels may result in certain behaviors, and certain behaviors may contribute to fluctuations in their levels (in a reciprocal interaction effect).

Although there is little doubt that there is a direct relationship between levels of various neurotransmitters and behavior, this relationship is extremely complex and nearly impossible to disaggregate. Chemical changes are part of the body's response to environmental conditions (e.g., threats) and to internal processes (e.g., fear, anxiety), and environmental conditions and internal processes produce chemical changes in the body. This creates a chicken-and-egg question about whether our responses and reactions are the result of changes in our chemistry or changes in our chemistry are the result of our responses and reactions.

Diet, Food Allergies, Sensitivities, Vitamins, and Minerals

What one eats impacts one's body chemistry. High-protein foods, such as fish, eggs, meat, and many dairy products, contain high levels of the amino acid *tryptophan*. Tryptophan produces serotonin (see preceding section). Another amino acid, *tyrosine* (also found in high-protein foods), is related to the production of both dopamine and norepinephrine. These relationships have suggested that many aggressive behaviors may be controlled with a diet higher in protein and lower in refined carbohydrates.

Carbohydrates—specifically, refined carbohydrates, such as white refined flour, white rice, white refined sugar, and any processed foods with high levels of sugar—also are examined as related to problem behavior. Complex carbohydrates are slowly transformed into glucose, which stimulates the production of insulin in the pancreas, which in turn produces energy for the body. Simple or refined carbohydrates are not processed slowly and result in the rapid release of insulin into the bloodstream, causing a sharp decrease in blood sugar, depriving the brain of the glucose necessary for proper functioning. This sharp decline in blood sugar also triggers the release of hormones such as adrenalin and increases in dopamine. This combination has been associated with increased aggression, irritability, and anxiety.

The state of having chronically reduced blood sugar caused by the excessive production of insulin is called *hypoglycemia*. Individuals who are hypoglycemic experience increased levels of irritability, aggression, and difficulty in controlling their emotional expressions. Hypoglycemia has successfully been used to mitigate criminal behavior. The most infamous example occurred during the late 1970s when Dan White killed San Francisco Mayor George Moscone and City Supervisor Harvey Milk after consuming nothing but junk food such as Twinkies and soda for several days. At trial, White's attorney successfully argued that White suffered from "diminished capacity" due to his hypoglycemia. His argument has come to be known as the "Twinkie Defense" (Lilly, Cullen, & Ball 2007).

Experimentation with the diets of criminal populations have indicated that reducing intake of refined carbohydrates and increasing consumption of fruits and vegetables have significantly decreased behavioral problems and disciplinary write-ups. It is difficult, however, to separate the impact of diet from other potential factors that may affect behavior.

Other potential contributors related to food intake involve food allergies and the consumption (or not) of various vitamins and minerals. Once again, refined carbohydrates may be a culprit. These types of foods contain particularly high levels of cadmium and lead, two minerals known to cause damage to brain tissue and impact the production of neurotransmitters.

Several food components have been associated with reactions that may include aggressive, violent, or criminal behavior. Some people may be allergic to or exhibit increased sensitivity to chemicals contained in chocolate (phenylethylamine), aged cheeses and wine (tyramine), artificial sweeteners (aspartame), and caffeine (xanthines). Others may react to food additives, such as monosodium glutamate and food dyes. Criminal populations also have been found to lack vitamins B3 and B6 in comparison to noncriminal populations.

Environmental Toxins

The frontal lobe of the brain, an area that has become the focus of biological investigations into criminal behavior, is particularly sensitive to environmental toxins, such as lead and manganese. Behavioral difficulties, such as hyperactivity, impulsivity, aggression, and lack of self-control, have been associated with increased levels of these heavy metals.

Examination of the impact of environmental toxins on human behavior is very promising because it integrates biological with sociological and criminological theories. Facilities that produce, store, treat, and dispose of hazardous wastes are largely to blame for the production of environmental toxins. Research has shown that proximity to these types of facilities increases the impairment of the brain and of the general central nervous system, producing lower IQs; reductions in learning abilities, frustration tolerance, and self-control; and increases in impulsivity, hyperactivity, antisocial behaviors, violence, and crime.

Researchers who study the relationship of environmental toxins to crime argue that our environment is producing crime by producing neurological damage. Scholars emphasize the fact that minority populations and lower-income groups are the ones most likely to live near these facilities and as a result are more likely than white and higher-income groups to be negatively impacted by these toxins. This, according to the researchers, may help explain why minorities and people from the lower classes seem to catch the attention of the criminal justice system in higher rates than others.

Brain Structure and Function

Whereas earlier biological theories considered the brain to be an organ with various areas of specialized function, modern theories recognize that the brain is a complex organism. Some areas of the brain are associated with specific functions (e.g., speech and vision), but all areas of the brain work together, and a problem or event in one area inevitably affects other areas. Although our understanding of the brain's structure and function has significantly advanced, we still know little about the relationship between the brain and many behaviors, such as those related to crime. In addition, we know little about how the environment affects the brain's structure and function.

The *frontal lobe* and the *temporal lobe* are two parts of the brain examined by researchers interested in criminal behavior. The frontal lobe is responsible for regulating and inhibiting behaviors, and the temporal lobe is responsible for emotionality, subjective consciousness, and responses to environmental stimuli.

Tools to evaluate brain structure, brain function, and behavior rely on sophisticated medical equipment and measurements, such as electroencephalography, computed tomography, magnetic resonance imaging, positron emission tomography, and single photon emission computed tomography. These devices have been used by researchers to compare the brain structures and brain functions between criminal and noncriminal populations. In addition to providing images of structure, many of these technologies can track real-time changes in the brain's neural activity before, during, and after exposure to physical or emotional stimuli.

Preliminary studies indicate that the brains of violent offenders and the brains of other individuals differ in both structure and function, but many of the studies have relied on very small sample sizes, which reduces the generalizability of these findings. Moreover, these studies also are plagued by questions of whether the brain causes the violence or whether violence results in changes to the brain. Evidence of structural or functional abnormalities in the brain has, however, resulted in the mitigation of criminal offenses, such as reducing charges of murder to manslaughter.

Studies of brain development have shown that early and chronic exposure to stress (e.g., abuse, neglect, violence) may cause physiological changes in the brain that impact the way a person responds to stress. Human brains under stress produce the hormone *Cortisol*, which helps to return body functions to normal after a stressful event. However, repeated exposure to Cortisol may result in decreased sensitivity to its effects and either contribute to criminality or contribute to a person's acceptance of being victimized. In addition, this research is supported by studies on the brain development of children raised in high-stress environments (inner city, urban, high-crime areas) that found enhanced fight-or-flight impulses among these children.

A recent study by Diana Fishbein in 2003 concluded that behavioral problems may originate in the *hypothalamic— pituitary-adrenal axis* (HPA) that connects the brain to the adrenal glands, which regulate the production of important hormones. Fishbein claimed that increased levels of Cortisol, produced in response to stressors, cause the HPA to shrink and become ineffective. An ineffective HPA depletes Cortisol and results in the inability to regulate emotions and behavior. A dysfunctional HPA may be caused by stress in childhood that impedes its development, or it may be caused by damage later in life.

Biosocial Perspectives

Some scholars who study criminal behavior began to synthesize sociological perspectives with biological perspectives. One of the most influential publications in this area was *Sociobiology: The New Synthesis*, written by E. O. Wilson in 1975. Wilson was among the first criminologists to express disillusion with current sociological and behavioral theories by emphasizing that an individual was a biological organism operating within social environments. Publications by Dawkins in 1976 (*The Selfish Gene*) and by Ellis in 1977 ("The Decline and Fall of Sociology, 1975–2000") illustrated criminological disillusion with purely sociological explanations and renewed hope for improved biological perspectives that would not operate under the faulty assumptions of earlier biological research. Major scientific developments from the 1950s to the mid-1970s (e.g., in the study of genetics) also contributed to the resurgence of interest in explanations of behavior with biological bases. Other advances in the mid-1980s led scholars to examine the brain more closely as a potential factor in criminal behavior.

Modern biosocial theories attempt to integrate beliefs about the sociological development of behavior (i.e., social learning, conditioning) with the biological development of the individual who engages in behavior. In contrast to earlier biological theories that imply the heritability of behaviors, biosocial theories suggest there may be a genetic predisposition for certain behaviors.

These predispositions are expressed in terms of biological risk factors associated with increased probabilities of delinquency and crime when paired with certain environmental (social) conditions. Various risk factors that have been evaluated include IQ levels and performance, attention deficit hyperactivity disorder, and conduct disorder. Although low IQ is not directly associated with crime or delinquency, individuals with lower IQs may experience frustration and stress in traditional learning environments, resulting in antisocial, delinquent, or criminal behaviors. A diagnosis of attention deficit hyperactivity disorder also has been associated with increased levels of delinquent and criminal behavior. However, some scholar's point out that this is true only for individuals who also are diagnosed with conduct disorder. Both disorders can be traced to abnormalities in the frontal lobe, so it is difficult to disentangle the relationship of each to undesirable behaviors.

In contrast to risk factors that may enhance the probabilities of an individual engaging in delinquency and crime, biological protective factors, such as empathy, may inhibit this development. *Empathy* is the ability of one person to identify with another person and to appreciate another person's feelings and perspectives. Research has indicated that empathy is largely (68%) inherited. This biological tendency may counter the impact of biological risk factors. Research on these inhibiting protective factors is still quite sparse but may help explain why some people who have genetic predispositions toward delinquency and crime refrain from those behaviors.

CONCLUSION

Biological theories have evolved significantly with advances in our theoretical understanding of human behavior and in our technological capabilities of measuring human biological characteristics and processes. Whereas earliest attempts to understand the relationships between biology and behavior focused on the outwardly observable, modern efforts are looking inward, to the chemical and structural foundations of our bodies. Contemporary biological theories also recognize the interactive relationship between internal biological events and external sociological events. Moreover, increasing awareness of the complex interrelationships among our environment, our biology, and our behavior is contributing to the development of a rich and promising epistemology of criminal behavior.

Our scientific advancements, however, still have not reached the level where we can definitively determine that antisocial, deviant, or criminal acts have biological roots or correlations. Increasing awareness of how our genes pass along (or do not pass along) our behavioral characteristics, of how our brain structures and functions are interrelated, of how our body chemistry affects and is affected by our behavior and reacts to environmental stimuli, and of how our development in a social environment impacts all of these biological processes will bring us closer to being able to predict behavior and therefore being able to better control it.

Care must be taken to separate the act from the actor and to avoid the atrocities of the past. As our ability to determine biological correlates of behavior expands, so too does the danger of using such information in unethical and inhumane ways that would stigmatize or punish people on the basis of what prohibited behaviors their biological profiles suggest they might do. It is hoped that progress in these areas of inquiry will parallel corresponding advances in our capabilities to prevent initial undesirable behaviors and to treat individuals who do behave undesirably because of biological or biosocial influences.

REFERENCES AND FURTHER READINGS

Adler, F., Mueller, G. O. W., & Laufer, W. (2004). *Criminology and the criminal justice system* (5th ed.). New York: McGraw-Hill.

Barrett, D., & Kurzman, C. (2004). Globalizing social movement theory: The case of eugenics. *Theory and Society, 33,* 505.

Burnett, J. (1773). *The origin and progress of language.* Edinburgh, Scotland: A Kincaid.

Christiansen, K. O. (1974) Seriousness of criminality and concordance among Danish twins. In R. Hood (Ed.), *Crime, criminology, and public policy* (pp. 63–77). New York: Free Press.

Comte, A. (1822). Plan des travaux scientifiques nécessaires pour réorganiser la société [Plan of scientific studies necessary for the reorganization of society]. In *Suite des travaux ayant pour objet de fonder le système industriel, Du Contrat Social.* Paris: Par Saint-Simon.

Curran, D. J., & Renzetti, C. M. (2001). *Theories of crime* (2nd ed.). Needham Heights, MA: Allyn & Bacon.

Darwin, C. (1859). *On the origin of species by means of natural selection, or the preservation of favored races in the struggle for life.* Cambridge. MA: Harvard University Press.

Darwin, C. (1871). *The descent of man and selection in relation to sex.* London: John Murray.

Darwin, E. (1791). *The botanic garden.* New York: T & J Swords.

Darwin, E. (1794–1796). *Zöonomia or the laws of organic life.* London: J. Johnson.

Dawkins, R. (1976). *The selfish gene.* New York: Oxford University Press.

della Porta, G. (1586). *De humana physiognomonia* [On physiognomy]. Vico Equense, Italy: Apud Iosephum Cacchium.

de Maupertuis, P. M. (1745). *Venus physique.* Paris: NP.

Dugdale, R. L. (1877). *The Jukes: A study in crime, pauperism, disease and heredity.* New York: Putnam.

Ellis, L. (1977). The decline and fall of sociology, 1975–2000. *American Sociologist, 12,* 56–66.

Ellis, L. (2003). Genes, criminality, and the evolutionary neuroandrogenic theory. In A. Walsh & L. Ellis (Eds.), *Biosocial criminology: Challenging environmentalism's supremacy* (pp. 13–36). Hauppauge, NY: NovaScienee.

Ferri, E. (1896). *Sociologia criminate* [Criminal sociology] (5th ed., 2 vols.). Turin, Italy: UTET.

Fishbein, D. (2003). *Biobehavioral perspectives in criminology.* Belmont, CA: Wadsworth.

Galton, F. (1869). *Hereditary genius: An inquiry into its laws and consequences.* London: Macmillan.

Galton, F. (1875). The history of twins as a criterion of the relative powers of nature and nurture. *Fraser's Magazine, 12,* 566–576.

Galton, F. (1883). *Inquiries into human faculty and its development.* London: Macmillan.

Garafalo, R. (1885). *Criminologia* [Criminology]. Naples, Italy: NP.

Glueck, S., & Glueck, E. (1956). *Physique and delinquency.* New York: Harper.

Goddard, H. H. (1912). *The Kallikak family.* New York: Macmillan.

Goring, C. (1913). *The English convict: A statistical study.* London: His Majesty's Stationery Office.

Gosney, E. S., & Popenoe, P. E. (1929). *Sterilization for human betterment: A summary of results of 6,000 operations in California, 1909–1929.* New York: Macmillan.

Grant, M. (1916). *The passing of the great race.* New York: Scribner's.

Guerry, A. M. (1833). *Essay on moral statistics of France.* Paris: Crochard.

Hartley, D. (1749). *Observations on man, his frame, his duty, and his expectations* (2 vols.). London: Samuel Richardson.

Henig, R. M. (2000). *Monk in the garden: The lost and found genius of Gregor Mendel, the Father of Genetics.* New York: Houghton Mifflin.

Hodgson, G. M. (2004). Social Darwinism in Anglophone academic journals: A contribution to the history of the term. *Journal of Historical Sociology, 17,* 428–463.

Hooten, E. (1939). *Crime and the man.* Cambridge, MA: Harvard University Press.

Kevles, D. (1985). *In the name of eugenics: Genetics and the uses of human heredity.* New York: Knopf.

Kretschmer, E. (1925). *Physique and character* (W. J. Sprott, Trans.). New York: Harcourt Brace.

Lamarck, J.-B. (1802). *Research on the organization of living things.* Paris: Maillard.

Lange, J. (1929). The importance of twin pathology for psychiatry. *Allgemeine Zeitschrift fur Psychiatric und Psychisch-Gerichtliche, 90,* 122–142.

Lavater, J. C. (1783). *Essays on physiognomy; for the promotion of the knowledge and love of mankind.* London: T. Holcroft.

Leclerc, G. (1778). *The eras of nature.* Paris: NP.

Lilly, J. R., Cullen, F., & Ball, R. A. (2007). *Criminological theory: Context and consequences* (4th ed.). Thousand Oaks, CA: Sage.

Linnaeus, C. (1735). *Systema naturae* [System of nature]. Holmiae: Laurentii Salvii.

Lombardo, P. (n.d.). *Eugenic sterilization laws.* Retrieved from http://www.eugenicsarchive.org/html/eugenics/essay8text.html.

Lombroso, C. (1876). *L'uomo delinquent* [Criminal man]. Milan, Italy: Hoepli.

Malthus, T. R. (1798). *An essay on the principle of population.* London: J. Johnson.

Mednick, S., Gabrielli, W. F., & Hutchins, B. (1984, May 25). Genetic influences in criminal convictions:

Evidence from an adoption cohort. *Science, 224,* 891–894.

Murphy, T., & Lappé, M. (1994). *Justice and the Human Genome Project.* Berkeley: University of California Press.

Quetelet, A. (1835). *Treatise on man.* Paris: Bachelier.

Rowe, D. C. (1983). Biometrical models of self-reported delinquent behavior: A twin study. *Behavior Genetics, 13,* 473–489.

Sabra, A. (1989). *The optics of Ibn al-Haytham.* London: Warburg Institute.

Sheldon, W. H. (1940). *The varieties of human physique: An introduction to constitutional psychology.* New York: Harper and Brothers.

Spencer, H. (1857, April). Progress: Its law and causes. *The Westminster Review, 67,* 445–447, 451, 454–456, 464–65.

Walters, G. D., & White, T. W. (1989). Heredity and crime: Bad genes or bad research? *Criminology, 27,* 455–485.

Wilson, E. O. (1975). *Sociobiology: The new synthesis.* Cambridge, MA: Belknap Press.

CESARE LOMBROSO'S
THE BORN CRIMINAL

Gina Lombroso-Ferrero

A criminal is a man who violates the laws decreed by the State to regulate the relations between its citizens, but the voluminous codes which in past times set forth these laws treat only of crime, never of the criminal. That ignoble multitude whom Dante relegated to the Infernal Regions were consigned by magistrates and judges to the care of jailers and executioners, who alone deigned to deal with them. The judge, immovable in his doctrine, unshaken by doubts, solemn in all his inviolability and convinced of his wisdom, which no one dared to question, passed sentence without remission according to his whim, and both judge and culprit were equally ignorant of the ultimate effect of the penalties inflicted.

In 1764, the great Italian jurist and economist, Cesare Beccaria first called public attention to those wretched beings, whose confessions (if statements extorted by torture can thus be called) formed the sole foundation for the trial, the sole guide in the application of the punishment, which was bestowed blindly, without formality, without hearing the defense, exactly as though sentence were being passed on abstract symbols, not on human souls and bodies.

The Classical School of Penal Jurisprudence, of which Beccaria was the founder and Francesco Carrara the greatest and most glorious disciple, aimed only at establishing sound judgments and fixed laws to guide capricious and often undiscerning judges in the application of penalties. In writing his great work, the founder of this School was inspired by the highest of all human sentiments—pity; but although the criminal incidentally receives notice, the writings of this School treat only of the application of the law, not of offenders themselves.

This is the difference between the Classical and the Modern School of Penal Jurisprudence. The Classical School based its doctrines on the assumption that all criminals, except in a few extreme cases, are endowed with intelligence and feelings like normal individuals, and that they commit misdeeds consciously, being prompted thereto by their unrestrained desire for evil. The offence alone was considered, and on it the whole existing penal system has been founded, the severity of the sentence meted out to the offender being regulated by the gravity of his misdeed.

The Modern, or Positive, School of Penal Jurisprudence, on the contrary, maintains that the anti-social tendencies of criminals are the result of their physical and psychic organization, which differs essentially from that of normal individuals; and it aims at studying the morphology and various functional phenomena of the criminal with the object of curing, instead of punishing him. The Modern School is therefore founded on a new science, Criminal Anthropology, which may be defined as the Natural History of the Criminal, because it embraces his organic and psychic constitution and social life, just as anthropology does in the case of normal human beings and the different races.

If we examine a number of criminals, we shall find that they exhibit numerous anomalies in the face, skeleton, and various psychic and sensitive functions, so that they strongly resemble primitive races. It was these anomalies that first drew my father's attention to the close relationship between the criminal and the savage and made him suspect that criminal tendencies are of atavistic origin.

When a young doctor at the Asylum in Pavia, he was requested to make a post-mortem examination on a criminal named Vilella, an Italian Jack the Ripper, who by atrocious crimes had spread terror in the Province of Lombardy. Scarcely had he laid open the skull, when he perceived at the base, on the spot where the internal occipital crest or ridge is found in normal individuals, a small hollow, which he called median occipital fossa. ... This abnormal character was correlated to a still greater anomaly in the cerebellum, the hypertrophy of the vermis, i.e., the spinal cord which separates the cerebellar lobes lying underneath the cerebral hemispheres. This vermis was so enlarged in the case of Vilella, that it almost formed a small, intermediate cerebellum like that found in the lower types of apes, rodents, and birds. This anomaly is very rare among inferior races, with the exception of the South American Indian tribe of the Aymaras of Bolivia and Peru, in whom it is not infrequently found (40%). It is seldom met with in the insane or other degenerates, but later investigations have shown it to be prevalent in criminals.

This discovery was like a flash of light. "At the sight of that skull," says my father, "I seemed to see all at once, standing out clearly illumined as in a vast plain under a flaming sky, the problem of the nature of the criminal, who reproduces in civilized times characteristics, not only of primitive savages, but of still lower types as far back as the carnivora." ...

Thus was explained the origin of the enormous jaws, strong canines, prominent zygomæ, and strongly developed orbital arches which he had so frequently remarked in criminals, for these peculiarities are common to carnivores and savages, who tear and devour raw flesh. Thus also it was easy to understand why the span of the arms in criminals so often exceeds the height, for this is a characteristic of apes, whose fore-limbs are used in walking and climbing. The other anomalies exhibited by criminals—the scanty beard as opposed to the general hairiness of the body, prehensile foot, diminished number of lines in the palm of the hand, cheek-pouches, enormous development of the middle incisors and frequent absence of the lateral ones, flattened nose and angular or sugar-loaf form of the skull, common to criminals and apes; the excessive size of the orbits, which, combined with the hooked nose, so often imparts to criminals the aspect of birds of prey, the projection of the lower part of the face and jaws (prognathism) found in negroes and animals, and supernumerary teeth (amounting in some cases to a double row as in snakes) and cranial bones (epactal bone as in the Peruvian Indians): all these characteristics pointed to one conclusion, the atavistic origin of the criminal, who reproduces physical, psychic, and functional qualities of remote ancestors.

Subsequent research on the part of my father and his disciples showed that other factors besides atavism come into play in determining the criminal type. These are: disease and environment. Later on, the study of innumerable offenders led them to the conclusion that all law-breakers cannot be classed in a single species, for their ranks include very diversified types, who differ not only in their bent towards a particular form of crime, but also in the degree of tenacity and intensity displayed by them in their perverse propensities, so that, in reality, they form a graduated scale leading from the born criminal to the normal individual.

Born criminals form about one third of the mass of offenders, but, though inferior in numbers, they constitute the most important part of the whole criminal army, partly because they are constantly appearing before the public and also because the crimes committed by them are of a peculiarly monstrous character; the other two thirds are composed of criminaloids (minor offenders), occasional and habitual criminals, etc., who do not show such a marked degree of diversity from normal persons.

Let us commence with the born criminal, who as principal nucleus of the wretched army of law-breakers, naturally manifests the most numerous and salient anomalies.

The median occipital fossa and other abnormal features just enumerated are not the only peculiarities exhibited by this aggravated type of offender. By careful research, my father and others of his School have brought to light many anomalies in bodily organs, and functions both physical and mental, all of which serve to indicate the atavistic and pathological origin of the instinctive criminal.

It would be incompatible with the scope of this summary, were I to give a minute description of the innumerable anomalies discovered in criminals by the Modern School, to attempt to trace such abnormal traits back to their source, or to demonstrate their effect on the organism. This has been done in a very minute fashion in the three volumes of my father's work Criminal Man and his subsequent writings on the same subject, Modern Forms of Crime, Recent Research in Criminal Anthropology, Prison Palimpsests, etc., etc., to which readers desirous of obtaining a more thorough knowledge of the subject should refer.

The present volume will only touch briefly on the principal characteristics of criminals, with the object of presenting a general outline of the studies of criminologists.

PHYSICAL ANOMALIES OF THE BORN CRIMINAL

The Head. As the seat of all the greatest disturbances, this part naturally manifests the greatest number of anomalies, which extend from the external conformation of the brain-case to the composition of its contents.

The criminal skull does not exhibit any marked characteristics of size and shape. Generally speaking, it tends to be larger or smaller than the average skull common to the region or country from which the criminal hails. …

The Face. In striking contrast to the narrow forehead and low vault of the skull, the face of the criminal, like those of most animals, is of disproportionate size, a phenomenon intimately connected with the greater development of the senses as compared with that of the nervous centers. …

The excessive dimensions of the jaws and cheekbones admit of other explanations besides the atavistic one of a greater development of the masticatory system. They may have been influenced by the habit of certain gestures, the setting of the teeth or tension of the muscles of the mouth, which accompany violent muscular efforts and are natural to men who form energetic or violent resolves and meditate plans of revenge.

Asymmetry is a common characteristic of the criminal physiognomy. The eyes and ears are frequently situated at different levels and are of unequal size, the nose slants towards one side, etc. This asymmetry, as we shall see later, is connected with marked irregularities in the senses and functions.

The Eye. This window, through which the mind opens to the outer world, is naturally the centre of many anomalies of a psychic character, hard expression, shifty glance, which are difficult to describe but are, nevertheless, apparent to all observers. Side by side with peculiarities of expression, we find many physical anomalies—ptosis, a drooping of the upper eyelid, which gives the eye a half-closed appearance and is frequently unilateral; … Other anomalies are asymmetry of the iris, which frequently differs in color from its fellow; oblique eyelids, a Mongolian characteristic, with the edge of the upper eyelid folding inward or a prolongation of the internal fold of the eyelid, which Metchnikoff regards as a persistence of embryonic characters.

The Ear. The external ear is often of large size; occasionally also it is smaller than the ears of normal individuals. Twenty-eight per cent. of criminals have handle-shaped ears standing out from the face as in the chimpanzee: in other cases they are placed at different levels. … Anomalies are also found in the lobe, which in some cases adheres too closely to the face, or is of huge size as in the ancient Egyptians; in other cases, the lobe is entirely absent, or is atrophied till the ear assumes a form like that common to apes.

The Nose. This is frequently twisted, up-turned or of a flattened, negroid character in thieves; in murderers, on the contrary, it is often aquiline like the beak of a bird of prey. ...

The Mouth. This part shows perhaps a greater number of anomalies than any other facial organ. We have already alluded to the excessive development of the jaws in criminals. ...

The lips of violators of women and murderers are fleshy, swollen and protruding, as in negroes. Swindlers have thin, straight lips. Hare-lip is more common in criminals than in normal persons.

The Cheek-pouches. Folds in the flesh of the cheek which recall the pouches of certain species of mammals, are not uncommon in criminals.

The Palate. ... Another frequent abnormality is cleft palate, a fissure in the palate, due to defective development.

The Teeth. These are specially important, for criminals rarely have normal dentition. The incisors show the greatest number of anomalies. Sometimes both the lateral incisors are absent and the middle ones are of excessive size, a peculiarity which recalls the incisors of rodents. ...

Very often the teeth show a strange uniformity, which recalls the homodontism of the lower vertebrates. In some cases, however, this uniformity is limited to the premolars, which are furnished with tubercles like the molars, a peculiarity of gorillas and orang-outangs. ... Premature caries is common.

The Chin. Generally speaking, this part of the face projects moderately in Europeans. In criminals it is often small and receding, as in children, or else excessively long, short or flat, as in apes.

Wrinkles. Although common to normal individuals, the abundance, variety, and precocity of wrinkles almost invariably manifested by criminals, cannot fail to strike the observer. ...

The Hair. The hair of the scalp, cheeks and chin, eyebrows, and other parts of the body, shows a number of anomalies. In general it may be said that in the distribution of hair, criminals of both sexes tend to exhibit characteristics of the opposite sex. Dark hair prevails especially in murderers, and curly and woolly hair in swindlers. ...

The blemishes peculiar to the delinquent are not only confined to the face and head, but are found in the trunk and limbs.

The Thorax. An increase or decrease in the number of ribs is found in 12% of criminals. This is an atavistic character common to animals and lower or prehistoric human races and contrasts with the numerical uniformity characteristic of civilised mankind. Polymastia, or the presence of supernumerary nipples (which are generally placed symmetrically below the normal ones as in many mammals) is not an uncommon anomaly. ... In female criminals, on the contrary, we often find imperfect development or absence of the nipples, a characteristic of monotremata or lowest order of the mammals; or the breasts are flabby and pendent like those of Hottentot women.

The chest is often covered with hair which gives the subject the appearance of an animal.

The Pelvis and Abdomen. The abdomen, pelvis, and reproductive organs sometimes show an inversion of sex-characters. ...

The Upper Limbs. One of the most striking and frequent anomalies exhibited by criminals is the excessive length of the arms as compared with the lower limbs, owing to which the span of the arms exceeds the total height, an ape-like character. Six per cent exhibit an anomaly which is extremely rare among normal individuals—the olecranon foramen, a perforation in the head of the humerus where it articulates with the ulna. This is normal in the ape and dog and is frequently found in the bones of prehistoric man and in some of the existing inferior races of mankind.

Several abnormal characters, which point to an atavistic origin, are found in the palm and fingers. Supernumerary fingers (polydactylism) or a reduction in the usual number are not uncommon. ... The length of the fingers varies according to the type of crime to which the individual is addicted. Those guilty of crimes against the person have short, clumsy fingers and especially short thumbs. Long fingers are common to swindlers, thieves, sexual offenders, and pickpockets. The lines on the palmar surfaces of the finger-tips are often of a simple nature as in the anthropoids. The principal lines on the palm are of special significance.

Normal persons possess three, two horizontal and one vertical, but in criminals these lines are often reduced to one or two of horizontal or transverse direction, as in apes.

The Lower Limbs. Of a number of criminals examined, 16% showed an unusual development of the third trochanter, a protuberance on the head of the femur where it articulates with the pelvis. This distinctly atavistic character is connected with the position of the hind-limb in quadrupeds.

The Feet. Spaces between the toes like the inter-digital spaces of the hand are very common, and in conjunction with the greater mobility of the toes and greater length of the big-toe, produce the prehensile foot, of the quadrumana, which is used for grasping. The foot is often flat, as in negroes. ...

The Cerebrum and the Cerebellum. The chief and most common anomaly is the prevalence of macroscopic anomalies in the left hemisphere, which are correlated to the sensory and functional left-handedness common to criminals and acquired through illness. The most notable anomaly of the cerebellum is the hypertrophy of the vermis, which represents the middle lobe found in the lower mammals. ...

In born criminals and epileptics there is a prevalence of large, pyramidal, and polymorphous cells, whereas in normal individuals small, triangular, and star-shaped cells predominate. ... Whereas, moreover, in the normally constituted brain, nervous cells are very scarce or entirely absent in the white substance, in the case of born criminals and epileptics they abound in this part of the brain. ...

These anomalies in the limbs, trunk, skull and, above all, in the face, when numerous and marked, constitute what is known to criminal anthropologists as the criminal type, in exactly the same way as the sum of the characters peculiar to cretins form what is called the cretinous type. In neither case have the anomalies an intrinsic importance, since they are neither the cause of the anti-social tendencies of the criminal nor of the mental deficiencies of the cretin. They are the outward and visible signs of a mysterious and complicated process of degeneration, which in the case of the criminal evokes evil impulses that are largely of atavistic origin. ...

The above-mentioned physiognomical and skeletal anomalies are further supplemented by functional peculiarities, and all these abnormal characteristics converge, as mountain streams to the hollow in the plain, towards a central idea—the atavistic nature of the born criminal.

CHAPTER
III

Psychological Theories

Psychological
Theories of Crime

John W. Clark

W hy do individuals commit crimes? At the same time, why is crime present in our society? The criminal justice system is very concerned with these questions, and criminologists are attempting to answer them. In actuality, the question of why crime is committed is very difficult to answer. However, for centuries, people have been searching for answers (Jacoby 2004). It is important to recognize that there are many different explanations as to why individuals commit crime (Conklin 2007). One of the main explanations is based on psychological theories, which focus on the association among intelligence, personality, learning, and criminal behavior. Thus, in any discussion concerning crime causation, one must contemplate psychological theories.

When examining psychological theories of crime, one must be cognizant of the three major theories. The first is *psychodynamic theory*, which is centered on the notion that an individual's early, childhood experience influences his or her likelihood for committing future crimes. The second is *behavioral theory*. Behavioral theorists have expanded the work of Gabriel Tarde through behavior modeling and social learning. The third is *cognitive theory*, the major premise of which suggests that an individual's perception and how it is manifested (Jacoby, 2004) affect his or her potential to commit crime. In other words, behavioral theory focuses on how an individual's perception of the world influences his or her behavior.

Also germane to psychological theories are personality and intelligence. Combined, these five theories or characteristics (i.e., psychodynamic, cognitive, behavioral, personality, and intelligence) offer appealing insights into why an individual may commit a crime (Schmalleger 2008). However, one should not assume this there is only one reason why a person commits crime. Researchers looking for a single explanation should be cautious, because there is no panacea for the problem of crime.

EARLY RESEARCH

Charles Goring (1870–1919) discovered a relationship between crime and flawed intelligence. Goring examined more than 3,000 convicts in England. It is important to note that Goring found no physical differences between noncriminals and criminals; however, he did find that criminals are more likely to be insane, to be unintelligent, and to exhibit poor social behavior. A second pioneer is Gabriel Tarde (1843–1904), who maintained that individuals learn from each other and ultimately imitate one another. Interestingly, Tarde thought that out of 100 individuals, only 1 was creative or inventive and the remainder were prone to imitation (Jacoby 2004).

PSYCHODYNAMIC THEORY

Proponents of psychodynamic theory suggest that an individual's personality is controlled by unconscious mental processes that are grounded in early childhood. This theory was originated by Sigmund Freud (1856–1939), the founder of psychoanalysis. Imperative to this theory are the three elements or structures that make up the human personality: (1) the *id*, (2), the *ego*, and (3) the *superego*. One can think of the id is as the primitive part of a person's mental makeup that is present at birth. Freud (1933) believed the id represents the unconscious biological drives for food, sex, and other necessities over the life span. Most important is the idea that the id is concerned with instant pleasure or gratification while disregarding concern for others. This is known as the *pleasure principle*, and it is often paramount when discussing criminal behavior. All too often, one sees news stories and studies about criminal offenders who have no concern for anyone but themselves. Is it possible that these male and female offenders are driven by instant gratification? The second element of the human personality is the *ego*, which is thought to develop early in a person's life. For example, when children learn that their wishes cannot be gratified instantaneously, they often throw a tantrum. Freud (1933) suggested that the ego compensates for the demands of the id by guiding an individual's actions or behaviors to keep him or her within the boundaries of society. The ego is guided by the *reality principle*. The third element of personality, the *superego*, develops as a person incorporates the moral standards and values of the community; parents; and significant others, such as friends and clergy members. The focus of the superego

is morality. The superego serves to pass judgment on the behavior and actions of individuals (Freud 1933). The ego mediates between the id's desire for instant gratification and the strict morality of the superego. One can assume that young adults as well as adults understand right from wrong. However, when a crime is committed, advocates of psychodynamic theory would suggest that an individual committed a crime because he or she has an underdeveloped superego.

In sum, psychodynamic theory suggests that criminal offenders are frustrated and aggravated. They are constantly drawn to past events that occurred in their early childhood. Because of a negligent, unhappy, or miserable childhood, which is most often characterized by a lack of love and/or nurturing, a criminal offender has a weak (or absent) ego. Most important, research suggests that having a weak ego is linked with poor or absence of social etiquette, immaturity, and dependence on others. Research further suggests that individuals with weak egos may be more likely to engage in drug abuse.

MENTAL DISORDERS AND CRIME

Within the psychodynamic theory of crime are *mood disorders*. Criminal offenders may have a number of mood disorders that are ultimately manifested as depression, rage, narcissism, and social isolation. One example of a disorder found in children is *conduct disorder*. Children with conduct disorder have difficulty following rules and behaving in socially acceptable ways (Boccaccini, Murrie, Clark, & Cornell 2008). Conduct disorders are ultimately manifested as a group of behavioral and emotional problems in young adults. It is important to note that children diagnosed with conduct disorder are viewed by adults, other children, and agencies of the state as "trouble," "bad," "delinquent," or even "mentally ill." It is important to inquire as to why some children develop conduct disorder and others do not. There are many possible explanations; some of the most prominent include child abuse, brain damage, genetics, poor school performance, and a traumatic event.

Children with conduct disorder are more likely to exhibit aggressive behaviors toward others (Boccaccini et al. 2008), and they may be cruel to animals.

Other manifestations include bullying; intimidation; fear; initiating fights; and using a weapon, such as a gun, a knife, a box cutter, rocks, a broken bottle, a golf club, or a baseball bat. Adolescents with conduct disorder could also force someone into unwanted sexual activity. Property damage may also be a concern; one may observe these children starting fires with the ultimate intent to destruct property or even kill someone. Other unacceptable behaviors associated with conduct disorder include lying and stealing, breaking into an individual's house or an unoccupied building or car, lying to obtain desirable goods, avoiding obligations, and taking possessions from individuals or stores. Last, children with conduct disorder are more likely to violate curfews despite their parents' desires. These children also are more likely to run away from home and to be late for or truant from school. There is no question that children who exhibit the above-mentioned behaviors must receive a medical and psychological examination. It is important to note that many children with conduct disorder could very well have another existing condition, such as anxiety, posttraumatic stress disorder, drug or alcohol abuse, or attention deficit disorder (Siegal 2008). It is important to recognize that children with conduct disorder are likely to have continuing, long-lasting problems if they do not receive treatment at the earliest onset. Without treatment, these children will not be able to become accustomed to the demands of adulthood and will continue to have problems and issues with a variety of relationships and even with finding and maintaining a job or occupation. Treatment of children with conduct disorder is often considered complex and exigent. It is rarely brief, because establishing new attitudes and behavior patterns takes time. As mentioned previously, early treatment offers a child a greater probability for improvement and for ultimately living a productive and successful life. An important component for the medical doctor or psychological clinician to consider is convincing the child to develop a good attitude, learn to cooperate, trust others, and eliminate fear in their lives. Behavior therapy and psychotherapy may be necessary to help the child learn how to control and express anger. Moreover, special education classes may be required for children with learning disabilities. In some cases, treatment may include prescribed medication,

although medicine would ideally be reserved for children experiencing problems with depression, attention, or spontaneity/impulsivity.

A second example of a disorder found in children is *oppositional defiant disorder* (Siegal 2008). This is most often diagnosed in childhood. Manifestations or characterizations of oppositional defiant disorder include defiance; uncooperativeness; irritability; a very negative attitude; a tendency to lose one's temper; and exhibiting deliberately annoying behaviors toward peers, parents, teachers, and other authority figures, such as police officers (Siegal 2008). There is no known cause of oppositional defiant disorder; however, there are two primary theories that attempt to explain its development. One theory suggests that problems begin in children as early as the toddler years. It is important to note that adolescents and small children who develop oppositional defiant disorder may have experienced a difficult time developing independent or autonomous skills and learning to separate from their primary caretaker or attachment figure. In essence, the bad attitudes that are characteristic of oppositional defiant disorder are viewed as a continuation of developmental issues that were not resolved during the early toddler years.

The second theory to explain oppositional defiant disorder focuses on learning. This theory suggests the negative characteristics of oppositional defiant disorder are learned attitudes that demonstrate the effects of negative reinforcement used by parents or persons in authority (Siegal 2009). It is important to recognize that the majority of symptoms observed in adolescents and children with oppositional defiant disorder also occur, at times, in children without this disorder. Relevant examples include a child who is hungry, tired, troubled, or disobeys/argues with his or her parent. It is important to note that adolescents and children with oppositional defiant disorder often exhibit symptoms that hinder the learning process, lead to poor adjustment in school, and most likely hurt the child's relationships with others. Some of the symptoms of oppositional defiant disorder include frequent temper tantrums, excessive arguments with adults, refusal to comply with adult requests, questioning rules, refusing to follow rules, engaging in behavior intended to annoy or upset others, blaming others for one's misbehaviors or mistakes, being easily annoyed by others, frequently having an angry attitude, speaking harshly or unkindly, and deliberately behaving in ways that seek revenge.

In regard to diagnosis, it is often teachers and parents who identify the child or adolescent with oppositional defiant disorder. However, children must be taken to a qualified medical doctor and/or mental health professional who will make an official diagnosis. Doctors will inquire into the history of the child's behavior, which includes the perspective of all interested parties (i.e., parents and teachers) and will verify the results of any previous clinical observations of the child's behavior. Psychological testing also may assist in assigning a diagnosis. As always, early detection and treatment are desirable. Actually, early treatment can often prevent future problems.

Oppositional defiant disorder may exist alongside other mental health problems, including mood and anxiety disorders, conduct disorder, and attention deficit hyperactivity disorder. Treatment for children and adolescents with oppositional defiant disorder will be determined by a physician who considers the child's age, overall health, and medical history. The physician also considers the extent or totality of a child's symptoms, the child's tolerance for certain medications or therapies, expectations for the course of the condition, and the opinion or preference of the caretaker or parent. Most important, treatment could include psychotherapy that teaches problem-solving skills, communication skills, impulse control, and anger management skills. Treatment may also be in the form of family therapy. Here, the approach is focused on making changes within the family system with the desired goal of improved family interaction and communication skills. Peer group therapy, which is focused on developing social skills and interpersonal skills, also is an option. The last and least desirable treatment option is medication.

MENTAL ILLNESS AND CRIME

The most serious forms of personality disturbance will result in mental disorders. The most serious mental disturbances are referred to as *psychoses* (Siegal 2008). Examples of mental health disorders include bipolar disorder and schizophrenia. Bipolar disorder is marked by extreme highs and lows; the person alternates between excited, assertive, and loud behavior and lethargic, listless, and melancholic behavior. A second mental health disturbance is schizophrenia. Schizophrenic individuals often exhibit illogical and incoherent thought processes, and they often lack insight into their behavior and do not understand reality. A person with paranoid schizophrenia also experiences complex behavior delusions that involve wrongdoing or persecution (Jacoby 2004). Individuals with paranoid schizophrenia often believe everyone is out to get them. It is important to note that research shows that female offenders appear to have a higher probability of serious mental health symptoms than male offenders. These include symptoms of schizophrenia, paranoia, and obsessive behaviors. At the same time, studies of males accused of murder have found that three quarters could be classified as having some form of mental illness. Another interesting fact is that individuals who have been diagnosed with a mental illness are more likely to be arrested, and they appear in court at a disproportionate rate. Last, research suggests mat delinquent children have a higher rate of clinical mental disorders compared with adolescents in the general population (Siegal 2008).

BEHAVIORAL THEORY

The second major psychological theory is *behaviorism*. This theory maintains that human behavior is developed through learning experiences. The hallmark of behavioral theory is the notion that people alter or change their behavior according to the reactions this behavior elicits in other people (Bandura 1978). In an ideal situation, behavior is supported by rewards and extinguished by negative reactions or punishments. Behaviorists view crimes as learned responses to life's situations. *Social learning theory*, which is a branch of behavior theory, is the most relevant to criminology. The most prominent social learning theorist is Albert Bandura (1978). Bandura maintains that individuals are not born with an innate ability to act violently. He suggested that, in contrast, violence and aggression are learned through a process of behavior modeling (Bandura 1977). In other words, children learn violence through the observation of others. Aggressive acts are modeled after three primary sources: (1) family interaction, (2) environmental experiences, and (3) the mass media. Research on family interaction demonstrates that children who are aggressive are more likely to have been brought up by parents or caretakers who are aggressive (Jacoby 2004).

The second source of behavioral problems, environmental experiences, suggests that individuals who reside in areas that are crime prone are more likely to display aggressive behavior than those who reside in low-crime areas (Shelden 2006). One could argue that high-crime areas are without norms, rules, and customs (Bohm 2001). Furthermore, there is an absence of conventional behavior. Manifestations of unconventional behavior include the inability to gain employment; drug or alcohol abuse; and failure to obey the local, state, and federal laws. Most important, individuals who adhere to conventional behavior are invested in society and committed to a goal or belief system. They are involved in schools or extracurricular activities, such as football, baseball, or Girl Scouts, and often they have an attachment to family (Kraska 2004).

The third source of behavioral problems is the mass media. It is difficult to discern the ultimate role of the media in regard to crime. Scholars have suggested that films, video games, and television shows that depict violence are harmful to children. Ultimately, social learning theories beckon us to accept the fact that the mass media are responsible for a great deal of the violence in our society. They hypothesize that children who play violent video games and later inflict physical or psychological damage to someone at school did so because of the influence of the video game. Important to note that in the above-mentioned media outlets (e.g., video games), violence is often acceptable and even celebrated. Moreover, there are no consequences for the actions of the major players. Professional athletes provide an interesting example of misbehavior without significant consequences. Over the last 50 years, there have been many documented cases of professional athletes who engaged in inappropriate behavior on and off the field. These cases have important implications for the children who observe this behavior. Thus, when a 10-year-old amateur athlete imitates behavior that he has learned by observing professional sports figures,

whom does society blame or punish? Substantiating the relationship between the media and violence is the fact that many studies suggest that media violence enables or allows aggressive children or adolescents to justify or rationalize their behavior. Furthermore, consistent media violence desensitizes children and adolescents. A person could argue that viewing 10,000 homicides on television over a 10-year period prevents (i.e., desensitizes) an individual from adjusting to the appropriate psychological response. Thus, when the local news reports about a homicide, does the child or adolescent respond with sorrow or indifference (Jacoby 2004)? When searching for stimuli that foster violent acts, social learning theorists suggest that an individual is likely to inflict harm when he or she is subject to a violent assault, verbal heckling or insults, disparagement, and the inability to achieve his or her goals and aspirations (Siegal 2009).

COGNITIVE THEORY

A third major psychological theory is *cognitive theory*. In recent years, significant gains have been made in explaining criminal behavior within the cognitive theory framework. Here, psychologists focus on the mental processes of individuals. More important, cognitive theorists attempt to understand how criminal offenders perceive and mentally represent the world around them (Knepper 2001). Germane to cognitive theory is how individuals solve problems. Two prominent pioneering 19th-century psychologists are Wilhelm Wundt and William James. Two subdisciplines of cognitive theory are worthy of discussion. The first subdiscipline is the *moral development* branch, the focus of which is understanding how people morally represent and reason about the world. The second subdiscipline is *information processing*. Here, researchers focus on the way people acquire, retain, and retrieve information (Siegal, 2009). Ultimately, scholars are concerned with the process of those three stages (i.e., acquisition, retention, and retrieval). One theory within the cognitive framework focuses on moral and intellectual development. Jean Piaget (1896–1980) hypothesized that the individual reasoning process is developed in an orderly fashion. Thus, from birth onward an individual will continue to develop. Another pioneer of cognitive theory is Lawrence Kohlberg (1927–1987), who applied the concept of moral development to criminological theory. Kohlberg (1984) believed that individuals pass through stages of moral development. Most important to his theory is the notion that there are levels, stages, and social orientation. The three levels are Level I, preconventional; Level II, conventional; and Level III, postconventional. With respect to the different stages, Stages 1 and 2 fall under Level I. Stages 3 and 4 fall under Level II, and Stages 5 and 6 fall under Level III.

Stage 1 is concerned with obedience and punishment. This level is most often found at the grade levels of kindergarten through fifth grade. During this stage, individuals conduct themselves in a manner that is consistent with socially acceptable norms (Kohlberg 1984). This conforming behavior is attributed to authority figures such as parents, teachers, or the school principal. Ultimately, this obedience is compelled by the threat or application of punishment. Stage 2 is characterized by individualism, instrumentalism, and exchange. Ultimately, the characterization suggests that individuals seek to fulfill their own interests and recognize that others should do the same. This stage maintains that the right behavior means acting in one's own best interests (Kohlberg 1984).

The conventional level of moral reasoning is often found in young adults or adults. It is believed that individuals who reason in a conventional way are more likely to judge the morality of actions by comparing those actions to societal viewpoints and expectations (Kohlberg 1984). The third and fourth stages fall under this level of development. In Stage 3, the individual recognizes that he or she is now a member of society. Coinciding with this is the understanding of the roles that one plays. An important concept within this stage is the idea that individuals are interested in whether or not other people approve or disapprove of them (Kohlberg 1984). For example, if you are an attorney, what role does society expect you to play? Tangentially, what role does the clergy hold in society? It is important to note that perception is germane to this stage as well. Ultimately, the literature suggests this is where a "good" boy or girl attempts to ascertain his or her standing or role within society. With respect

to stage four, the premise is based on law and order. In this stage, individuals recognize the importance of laws, rules, and customs. This is important because in order to properly function in society, one must obey and recognize the social pillars of society. Ultimately, individuals must recognize the significance of right and wrong. Obviously, a society without laws and punishments leads to chaos. In contrast, if an individual who breaks the law is punished, others would recognize that and exhibit obedience. Kohlberg (1984) suggested that the majority of individuals in our society remain at this stage, in which morality is driven by outside forces.

Stages 5 and 6 exist at the postconventional level. Stage 5 is referred to as the *social contract*. Here, individuals are concerned with the moral worth of societal rules and values, but only insofar as they are related to or consistent with the basic values of liberty, the welfare of humanity, and human rights. Fundamental terms associated with this stage are *majority decision* and *compromise*. Stage 6 is often termed *principled conscience*. This stage is characterized by universal principles of justice and respect for human autonomy. Most important to criminal justice and criminology is the notion that laws are valid only if they are based on or grounded in justice. It is important to recognize that justice is subjective. Thus, Kohlberg argued that the quest for justice would ultimately call for disobeying unjust laws. He suggested that individuals could progress through the six stages in a chronological fashion. Important for criminology is that Kohlberg suggested that criminals are significantly lower in their moral judgment development.

The next subdiscipline is the *information-processing* branch. This area is predicated on the notion that people use information to understand their environment. When an individual makes a decision, he or she engages in a sequence of cognitive thought processes. To illustrate, individuals experience an event and encode or store the relevant information so it can be retrieved and interpreted at a later date (Conklin 2007). Second, these individuals search for the appropriate response, and then they determine the appropriate action. Last, they must act on their decision. There are some vital findings regarding this process. First, individuals who use information properly are more likely to avoid delinquent or criminal behavior (Shelden 2006).

Second, those who are conditioned to make reasoned judgments when faced with emotional events are more likely to avoid antisocial behavioral decisions (Siegal 2008). Interestingly, an explanation for flawed reasoning is that the individual may be relying on a faulty cognitive process; specifically, he or she may be following a mental script that was learned in childhood (Jacoby 2004). A second reason that may account for flawed reasoning is prolonged exposure to violence. A third possibility of faulty reasoning is oversensitivity or rejection by parents or peers. Contemplating the consequences of long-lasting rejection or dismissal is likely to produce damage to an individual's self-esteem. Research has demonstrated that individuals who use violence as a coping mechanism are substantially more likely to exhibit other problems, such as alcohol and drug dependency (Piquero & Mazarolle 2001).

PERSONALITY AND CRIME

Personality can be defined as something that makes us what we are and also that which makes us different from others (Clark, Boccaccini, Caillouet, & Chaplin 2007). Ideally, personality is stable over time. Examinations of the relationship between personality and crime have often yielded inconsistent results. One of the most well-known theories of personality used to examine this relationship is the Big Five model of personality. This model provides a vigorous structure into which most personality characteristics can be categorized. This model suggests that five domains account for individual differences in personality: (1) Neuroticism, (2) Extraversion, (3) Openness, (4) Agreeableness, and (5) Conscientiousness (Clark et al. 2007). Neuroticism involves emotional stability. Individuals who score high on this domain often demonstrate anger and sadness and have irrational ideas, uncontrollable impulses, and anxiety. In contrast, persons who score low on Neuroticism are often described by others as even tempered, calm, and relaxed.

The second domain, Extraversion, is characterized by sociability, excitement, and stimulation. Individuals who score high on Extraversion (extraverts) are often very active, talkative, and assertive. They also are more optimistic toward the future. In contrast, introverts are

often characterized by being reserved, independent, and shy (Clark et al. 2007).

The third domain is Openness, referring to individuals who have an active imagination, find pleasure in beauty, are attentive to their inner feelings, have a preference for variety, and are intellectually curious. Individuals who score high on Openness are willing to entertain unique or novel ideas, maintain unconventional values, and experience positive and negative emotions more so than individuals who are closed-minded. In contrast, persons who score low in Openness often prefer the familiar, behave in conventional manners, and have a conservative viewpoint (Clark et al. 2007).

The fourth domain is Agreeableness. This domain is related to interpersonal tendencies. Individuals who score high on this domain are considered warm, altruistic, softhearted, forgiving, sympathetic, and trusting. In contrast, those who are not agreeable are described as hard-hearted, intolerant, impatient, and argumentative.

Conscientiousness, the fifth domain, focuses on a person's ability to control impulses and exercise self-control. Individuals who score high on Conscientiousness are described as organized, thorough, efficient, determined, and strong willed. In addition, those who are conscientious are more likely to achieve high academic and occupational desires. In contrast, people who score low on this domain are thought to be careless, lazy, and more likely assign fault to others than to accept blame themselves (Clark et al. 2007).

One personality study discovered that the personality traits of hostility, impulsivity, and narcissism are correlated with delinquent and criminal behavior. Furthermore, research conducted by Sheldon and Eleanor Glueck during the 1930s and 1940s identified a number of personality traits that were characteristic of antisocial youth (Schmalleger 2008). Another important figure who examined the criminal personality is Hans Eysenck (1916–1997). Eysenck identified two antisocial personality traits: (1) extraversion and (2) neuroticism. Eysenck suggested that individuals who score at the ends of either domain of extra-version and neuroticism are more likely to be self-destructive and criminal (Eysenck & Eysenck 1985). Moreover, neuroticism is associated with self-destructive behavior (e.g., abusing drugs and alcohol and committing crimes).

PSYCHOPATHIC PERSONALITY

Antisocial personality, psychopathy, or *sociopath* are terms used interchangeably (Siegal 2009). Sociopaths are often a product of a destructive home environment. Psychopaths are a product of a defect or aberration within themselves. The antisocial personality is characterized by low levels of guilt, superficial charm, above-average intelligence, persistent violations of the rights of others, an incapacity to form enduring relationships, impulsivity, risk taking, egocentricity, manipulativeness, forcefulness and cold-heartedness, and shallow emotions (Jacoby 2004). The origin may include traumatic socialization, neurological disorder, and brain abnormality (Siegal 2008). Interestingly, if an individual suffers from low levels of arousal as measured by a neurological examination, he or she may engage in thrill seeking or high-risk behaviors such as crime to offset their low arousal level. Other dynamics that may contribute to the psychopathic personality is a parent with pathologic tendencies, childhood traumatic events; or inconsistent discipline. It is important to note that many chronic offenders are sociopaths. Thus, if personality traits can predict crime and violence, then one could assume that the root cause of crime is found in the forces that influence human development at an early stage of life (Siegal 2008).

INTELLIGENCE AND CRIME

Criminologists have suggested for centuries that there exists a link between intelligence and crime (Dabney, 2004). Some common beliefs are that criminals and delinquents possess low intelligence and that this low intelligence causes criminality. As criminological research has advanced, scholars have continued to suggest that the Holy Grail is causality. The ability to predict criminals from noncriminals is the ultimate goal. The ideology or concept of IQ and crime has crystallized into the nature-versus-nurture debate (Jacoby 2004).

The nature-versus-nurture debate is a psychological argument that is related to whether the environment or heredity impacts the psychological development of individuals (Messner & Rosenfield 2007). Science recognizes that we share our parents' DNA. To illustrate, some people have short fingers like their mother and brown eyes like their father. However, the question remains: Where do individuals get their love of sports, literature, and humor? The nature-versus-nurture debate addresses this issue. With respect to the nature side, research on the prison population has consistently shown that inmates typically score low on IQ tests (Schmalleger 2008). In the early decades of the 20th century, researchers administered IQ tests to delinquent male children. The results indicated that close to 40% had below-average intelligence (Siegal 2008). On the basis of these data and other studies, some scholars argue that the role of nature is prevalent. However, can researchers assume *a priori* that heredity determines IQ, which in turn influences an individual's criminal behavior? One criticism of this perspective is the failure to account for free will. Many individuals in our society believe in the ability to make choices. Last, there are many individuals who have a low IQ but refrain from committing crime.

With respect to nurture theory, advocates ground themselves on the premise that intelligence is not inherited. There is some recognition of the role of heredity; however, emphasis is placed on the role of society (i.e., environment).

To demonstrate, parents are a major influence on their children's behavior. At an early age, parents read books; play music; and engage their children in art, museum, and sporting events. Some parents spend no quality time with their children, and these children are believed to perform poorly on intelligence test. Other groups important in a child's nurturing are friends, relatives, and teachers. Ultimately, the child who has no friends or relatives and drops out of school is destined for difficult times. Research has demonstrated that the more education a person has, the higher his or her IQ.

The nature-versus-nurture debate will continue. The debate has peaks and valleys. For years, the debate subsides, and this is followed by years of scrutiny and a great deal of attention. One of two major studies that highlighted this debate was conducted by Travis Hirschi and Michael Hindelang (1977). These scholars suggested that low IQ increases the likelihood of criminal behavior through its effect on school performance. This argument seems somewhat elementary. Their argument is that a child with a low

IQ will perform poorly in school. In turn, this school failure is followed by dropping out. Given the poor school performance, a child is left with very few options (Hirschi & Hindelang 1977). This ultimately leads to delinquency and adult criminality. Support of this position has been widespread. Furthermore, it is important to note that U.S. prisons and jails are highly populated with inmates who only have an average of eighth-grade education. At the same time, these same inmates at the time of their offense were unemployed.

The second nature-versus-nature study that warrants attention was conducted by Richard Herrnstein and Charles Murray (1994). In their book *The Bell Curve*, these scholars suggested individuals with a lower IQ are more likely to commit crime, get caught, and be sent to prison. Importantly, these authors transport the IQ and crime link to another level. Specifically, they suggested that prisons and jails are highly populated with inmates with low IQs; however, what about those criminals whose actions go undetected? Through self-reported data, the researchers discovered that these individuals have a lower IQ than the general public. Thus, research concludes those criminal offenders who have been caught and those who have not have an IQ lower than the general population (Herrnstein & Murray 1994).

CONCLUSION

The relationship between psychology and criminal behavior is significant. For centuries, scholars have been attempting to explain why someone commits a crime. This chapter examined the role of psychodynamic theory as developed by Sigmund Freud. Included here are the roles of the id, ego, and superego in criminal behavior. This was followed by a discussion of mental disorders and crime. Under examination here were conduct disorder and oppositional defiant disorder. Through both disorders, we learned that children possess many characteristics associated with delinquency and adult criminality, ultimately concluding that treatment is a necessity and early intervention is paramount.

Discussed next was the role of mental illness and crime. Bipolar disorder and schizophrenia are two of the most serious disorders. Research suggests that there is a correlation between individuals with bipolar disorder and schizophrenia and delinquency and/or criminal behavior. The second major psychological theory is behaviorism. As previously mentioned, behavioral theory suggests human behavior is fostered through learning experiences. At the forefront of this theory is the premise that individuals change their behavior according to reactions from others. In the real world, there exists the assumption that behavior is reinforced via rewards and eliminated by a negative reaction or punishment. Social learning theory, which is a branch of behavior theory, is the most relevant to criminology. Moreover, the most prominent social learning theorist is Albert Bandura,

The third psychological theory examined is cognition. Here, the importance of mental processes of individuals is examined. A discussion followed on how individuals perceive and mentally represent the world. Furthermore, how do individuals solve problems? Two important subdisciplines examined were Kohlberg's moral development theory and information-processing theory. Ultimately, we can conclude that criminal offenders are poor at processing information and evaluating the world around them. The next major topics discussed were personality and intelligence. Concerning personality, we learned that personality can be measured via the domains of Neuroticism, Extraversion, Openness, Agreeableness, and Conscientiousness. We learned that Extraversion and Neuroticism are related to criminal behavior. Last, the intelligence debate has existed for centuries, and data demonstrate that individuals with a low IQ are more likely to engage in criminal behavior. Important to the discussion of intelligence and IQ is school performance. Research studies that have examined future delinquency and adult criminality have consistently demonstrated the link between the two. In reality, it is not difficult to understand why a person who fails or drops out of school is limited in his or her career or future options. Occupations that have desirable salaries often require a high school degree as well as a bachelor's or master's degree. In sum, when citizens and scholars attempt to understand why people commit a crime, recognition must be given to psychological theories. Not doing so would be a serious error in judgment.

REFERENCES AND FURTHER READINGS

Bandura, A, (1977). *Social learning theory*. Englewood Cliffs, NJ: Prentice Hall.

Bandura, A. (1978). Social learning theory of aggression. *Journal of Communication, 28*, 12–29.

Bandura, A. (1986). *Social foundations of thought and action*. Englewood Cliffs, NJ: Prentice Hall.

Boccaccini, M., Murrie, D., Clark, J., & Cornell, D. (2008). Describing, diagnosing, and naming psychopathy: How do youth psychopathy labels influence jurors? *Behavioral Sciences & the Law, 26*, 487–510.

Bohm, R. (2001). *Primer on crime and delinquency theory* (2nd ed.). Belmont, CA: Wadsworth.

Clark, J., Boccaccini, M., Caillouet, B., & Chaplin, W. (2007). Five factor model or personality traits, jury selection, and case outcomes in criminal and civil cases. *Criminal Justice and Behavior, 34*, 641–660.

Conklin, J. (2007). *Criminology* (9th ed.). Boston: Allyn & Bacon.

Dabney, D. (2004). *Crime types: A text/reader*. Belmont, CA: Cengage Learning.

Eysenck, H., & Eysenck, M. (1985). *Personality and individual differences*. New York: Plenum Press.

Freud, S. (1933). *New introductory lectures on psychoanalysis*. New York: Norton.

Herrnstein, R., & Murray, C. (1994). *The bell curve: Intelligence and class structure in American life*. New York: Free Press.

Hirschi, T., & Hindelang, M. (1977). Intelligence and delinquency: A revisionist review. *American Sociological Review, 42*, 471–741.

Jacoby, J. (2004). *Classics of criminology* (3rd ed.). Long Grove, IL: Waveland Press.

Knepper, P. (2001). *Theories and symptoms in criminology*. Durham, NC: Carolina Academic Press.

Kohlberg, L. (1984). *The psychology of moral development: Essays on moral development*. New York: Harper & Row.

Kraska, P. (2004). *Theorizing criminal justice*. Long Grove, IL: Waveland Press.

Messner, S., & Rosenfield, R. (2007). *Crime and the American dream* (4th ed.). Belmont, CA: Wadsworth.

Piquero, A., & Mazarolle, P. (2001). *Life course criminology: Contemporary and classic readings*. Belmont, CA: Wadsworth.

Schmalleger, F. (2008). *Criminal justice: A brief introduction* (7th ed.). Englewood Cliffs, NJ: Prentice Hall.

Shelden, R. (2006). *Delinquency and juvenile justice in American society*. Long Grove, IL: Waveland Press.

Siegal, L. (2008). *Criminology: The core* (3rd ed.). Belmont, CA: Cengage Learning.

Siegal, L. (2009). *Criminology* (10th ed,). Belmont, CA: Cengage Learning.

Silver, E. (2002). Extending social disorganization theory: A multilevel approach to the study of violence among persons with mental illness. *Criminology, 40*, 191–212.

Tarde, G. (1903). *The laws of imitation*. New York: Holt.

PART
II

Micro-Level Social
Process Theories

PART II INTRODUCTION

Micro-Level Social Process Theories

I n Part 2 we examine micro-level social process theories, focusing specifically on social learning and social control theories. The theories covered in Part 2 mark a shift away from the individually oriented theories (rational choice, biological, and psychological theories) discussed in Part 1 toward micro-level social process theories that incorporate social, cultural, structural, and interactive factors. This is in stark contrast to psychological and biological theories which argue that the locus of criminal behavior lies within the individual. Contrary to early biological and psychological arguments that criminals were atavistic throwbacks or inferior to normal human beings, or that they had traits that made them criminal, social process theories argue that criminal behavior is developed through individual socialization, learning, supervision, monitoring, and interaction with others. A key assumption made by social process theorists is that delinquents or criminals are essentially no different from non-criminals.

The authors of the Readings in Part 2 discuss two different social process theories, social learning theory and social control theory (a third theory, social interactionism and a related theory of social constructionism are not covered here). What leads to criminal behavior for social learning theorists is what people learn through the socialization process that occurs primarily during early child developmental periods. In other words, normal human beings can learn criminal techniques, behaviors, norms, attitudes, and rationalizations that provide them with the skills and excuse the morality of offenses that make it possible for them to harm others. For social control theorists what leads to criminal behavior is the failure of childhood socialization to develop effective inner controls or the lack of self-control. Social control theories then shift attention away from the causes of crime to focus on what keeps most people from committing crime.

Social learning theory focuses on how normal people learn 'wrong' behavior and values that both teach them how, and allows them, to justify engaging in criminal or delinquent behavior. Consequently, social learning theory is considered sociological, insofar as it goes beyond the stimulus-response learning associated with theories of behavioral psychology[1] and beyond the trait-based and genetic components of biological theories. And, social learning theory continues the positivist push for the study of crime and behavior using scientific principles.

The founding social learning theorists Sutherland and Cressey (1966) argued that criminals were no different from non-criminals. Instead, they saw the fundamental difference between offenders and non-offenders as rooted in the learning process. Whereas non-criminals learn values and norms conducive to conventional life, criminals learn norms and values, as well as justifications, for law offending behavior. The primary learning mechanism occurs in close association with "significant others." This is because social learning is conveyed in close association with others, usually in small intimate groups. Those most influential in the learning process are those we have a close relationship with such as parents, family, friends, and peers. However, learning not only occurs in close association with others but can also occur vicariously, or through social modeling from role models, celebrities, or others who may be available via social media and television (Bandura 1973; 1977; 2001). Celebrities, cultural heroes, and other personas on television, the Internet, or other social media and gaming can also transmit knowledge and thus, may play a part in the transmission of knowledge, values, and/or norms. People are influenced, taught, and ultimately act on what others around them expose them to, whether these are parents, peers, gang members or cultural heroes.

Social learning theory developed as a reformulation of Edwin Sutherland's (1947) differential association theory. Drawing from the symbolic-interactionist perspective, differential association theory proposes that criminal behavior is learned within contexts of social interaction. Social interaction provides exposure to varying configurations of definitions of behavior; when definitions favorable to crime exceed those unfavorable to crime, criminal behavior results. Social learning was founded in behavioral components of psychological theory but its adaptation to explaining criminal behavior moved the concept from its early behaviorist roots toward recognizing the importance of the social context of learning through symbolic interaction with others. Unlike the passive stimulus-response mechanism posited in behavioral models, social learning theorists propose that learning is active and occurs through association with others in small groups. While Sutherland did not specify how the transmission of social learning occurs, Akers (1968) went on to do so

and moved the theory closer to the cognitive learning theory of psychologist Albert Bandura.

Social learning theory posits that the learning process is the same for all forms of learning, criminal or noncriminal. The key difference is the *content* of what is learned. Non-offenders learn the values, norms, skills, and motives that conform to convention, whereas offenders learn values, norms, skills, and motives that are contrary to the convention and which equip them with the knowledge, and values, to commit crime. Crime is most likely to happen when 'criminal' values outweigh "conventional" values.

Along with learning the specific knowledge, skills, motives and techniques about how to commit a criminal act, individuals also learn rationalizations, or neutralizations, that excuse or justify their criminal or delinquent behavior. Neutralization theory (Sykes & Matza 1957) which is another social process theory, challenges the idea that there is a stark contrast between conventional mainstream society and delinquent or criminal subcultures. Rather, individuals learn both conventional and non-conventional norms and values through their involvement in mainstream society, and its subterranean underbelly. Neutralization theory thus explains how offenders are able to neutralize feelings of guilt while still maintaining a connection to conventional society. In other words, no one engages in criminal behavior all the time; rather people drift in and out of crime and conventional behavior and neutralizations allow them to be morally free to do so (Matza 1964).

Unlike the previous theories discussed, social control theorists do not see the cause of crime as rooted in biological, psychological, or even social learning mechanisms. Instead, social control theorists turn the question of what causes crime around and instead they ask what keeps most people from offending? Similar to classical theory, social control theorists believe that without restraint there would be a universal motivation to crime. In essence, they explore what controls, or restrains people from committing crimes. However, they go beyond classical theory's limited view of control because of 'costs' to examine a variety of control mechanisms: internal and external controls, parental controls, disciplinary controls, societal controls, etc. Controls may also include the failure to form attachments and commitments to conventional others, especially parents and teachers (Hirschi 1969). Social control theories are considered sociologically rooted since they look at the social processes and social organizational arrangements to help explain crime and deviance.

More recently, Hirschi and Gottfredson (2001) have developed a theory of the failure of self-control. This suggests that a lack of adequate parental controls and inadequate child rearing, lead some to seek immediate gratification through engaging in sensation and thrill-seeking behavior.

There are two main types of social control theory, broken bond theory and failure to bond theory (Lanier and Henry 2010). Broken bond theory argues that human beings are socialized into conventional behavior from an early age, but something breaks or weakens the bonds to convention, freeing a person to deviate (Akers 1994). As we have seen this "broken bond" can occur through the neutralization of the moral bind of law or as we shall see in Part 3 of this book, social disorganization—isolation and breakdown of communities—can undermine a person's commitment to conform to the dominant or mainstream culture.

Failure to bond theory assumes that the very creation of a commitment to convention, and to socially approved norms and values is difficult to achieve (Box 1971). This requires much investment of time and energy and considerable maintenance and can easily go wrong. Without this attachment, commitment or "stake in conformity" forming in the first place, humans are more likely to deviate and to break the law. This failure to bond has been attributed to a variety of factors, including parents' failure to provide a "secure attachment" which requires a responsible, lovingly responsive and sensitive mother-figure who is empathetic and able to satisfy childhood needs for emotional and physical security (Bowlby 1946).

Others suggest the cause of a failure to bond is the inability to internalize personal self-control and the absence of direct external social controls such as the threat of punishment, the failure of indirect controls from parental monitoring and supervision and a failure of internal or self-control, which for some depends on an internalized sense of guilt (Hirschi & Gottfredson 2001). This too is seen as the result of a failure by parents to adequately train their children to resist the lure of sensation-seeking behavior for immediate gratification. The main idea behind control theory is that the ties, or bonds, to conventional parents, school, friends, employers, and so on make crime too much of a risk for most people.

Because social process theories focus on the learning processes that involve interaction, group dynamics, behavior and exchange of knowledge, then crime reduction policies should be social psychological in nature. Policymakers are urged to implement programs that would identify potential offenders and provide group therapy, counseling or other interventions such that they learn to substitute legal behaviors for illegal ones. Furthermore, prevention involves exposing the reasons, rationalizations or neutralizations for crime as incorrect, inaccurate or misguided. Control theories advocate creating or strengthening ties to conventional society by strengthening involvement in conventional institutions, activities, and improving the quality of parenting, and both direct and indirect controls and supervision.

NOTE

1. Although leading social learning theorist Ronald Akers (1973), incorporates many of these principles into his "sociological" learning theory. Social learning theorists generally reject the personality-type psychological analysis that criminals are different from non-criminal. Psychology has several versions of learning, beyond behaviorism, and its social learning theory involves not just learning from others, but also from images presented via the mass media (Bandura, 1977; 2001).

REFERENCES

Akers, R. (1968). "Problems in the Sociology of Deviance: Social Definitions and Behavior." *Social Forces*, 46: 455–465.

Akers, R. (1973). *Deviant Behavior: A Social Learning Approach*. Belmont, CA: Wadsworth.

Akers, R. (1994). *Criminological Theories: Introduction and Evaluation*. Los Angeles: Roxbury Press.

Bandura, A. (1973). *Aggression: A Social Learning Analysis*. Englewood Cliffs, NJ: Prentice Hall.

Bandura, A. (1977). *Social Learning Theory*. Englewood Cliffs, NJ: Prentice Hall.

Bandura, A. (2001). "Social Cognitive Theory of Personality." In *Handbook of Personality: Theory and Research*, 2nd ed. edited by L. A. Pervin and P. J. Oliver, 154–196. New York: Guilford Press.

Bowlby, J. (1946). *Forty-four Juvenile Theives: Their Characters and Home Life*. London: Bailliere, Tindall, and Cox.

Box, S. (1971). *Deviance, Reality, and Society*. New York: Holt, Reinhart, and Winston.

Hirschi, T. (1969). *The Causes of Delinquency*. Berkeley: University of California Press.

Hirschi, T. & Gottfredson, M. (2001). "Self-Control Theory." In *Explaining Criminals and Crime*, Edited by R. Paternoster and R. Bachman, pp. 81–96. Los Angeles: Roxbury Press.

Lanier, M.M. & Henry, S. (2010). *Essential Criminology*. 3rd Edition. Boulder, CO: Westview Press.

Matza, D. (1964). *Delinquency and Drift*. New York: John Wiley.

Sutherland, E. H. (1947). *Principles of Criminology*. Philadelphia: J. B. Lippencott.

Sutherland, E. H. & Cressey, D. R. (1966). *Principles of Criminology*. Philadelphia: J. B. Lippencott.

Sykes, G. & Matza, D. (1957). "Techniques of Neutralization: A Theory of Delinquency." *American Sociological Review*; 22: 664–670.

CHAPTER
IV

Social Learning Theories

A THEORY OF DIFFERENTIAL ASSOCIATION

Edwin H.
Sutherland and
Donald R. Cressey

*S*utherland's theory is stated in the form of nine propositions. He argues that criminal behavior is learned by interacting with others, especially intimate others. Criminals learn both the techniques of committing crime and the definitions favorable to crime from these others. The sixth proposition, which forms the heart of the theory, states that "a person becomes delinquent because of an excess of definitions favorable to law violation over definitions unfavorable to violation of law." According to Sutherland, factors such as social class, race, and broken homes influence crime because they affect the likelihood that individuals will associate with others who present definitions favorable to crime.

The following statement refers to the process by which a particular person comes to engage in criminal behavior:

1. *Criminal behavior is learned.* Negatively, this means that criminal behavior is not inherited, as such; also, the person who is not already trained in crime does not invent criminal behavior, just as a person does not make mechanical inventions unless he has had training in mechanics.
2. *Criminal behavior is learned in interaction with other persons in a process of communication.* This communication is verbal in many respects but includes also "the communication of gestures."
3. *The principal part of the learning of criminal behavior occurs within intimate personal groups.* Negatively, this means that the impersonal agencies of communication, such as movies and newspapers, play a relatively unimportant part in the genesis of criminal behavior.
4. *When criminal behavior is learned, the learning includes (a) techniques of committing the crime, which are sometimes very complicated, sometimes very simple; (b) the specific direction of motives, drives, rationalizations, and attitudes.*
5. *The specific direction of motives and drives is learned from definitions of the legal codes as favorable or unfavorable.* In some societies an individual is surrounded by persons who invariably define the legal codes as rules to be observed, while in others he is surrounded by persons whose definitions are favorable to the violation of the legal codes. In our American society these definitions are almost

always mixed, with the consequence that we have culture conflict in relation to the legal codes.

6. *A person becomes delinquent because of an excess of definitions favorable to violation of law over definitions unfavorable to violation of law.* This is the principle of differential association. It refers to both criminal and anti-criminal associations and has to do with counteracting forces. When persons become criminal, they do so because of contacts with criminal patterns and also because of isolation from anti-criminal patterns. Any person inevitably assimilates the surrounding culture unless other patterns are in conflict; a Southerner does not pronounce "r" because other Southerners do not pronounce "r." Negatively, this proposition of differential association means that associations which are neutral so far as crime is concerned have little or no effect on the genesis of criminal behavior. Much of the experience of a person is neutral in this sense, e.g., learning to brush one's teeth. This behavior has no negative or positive effect on criminal behavior except as it may be related to associations which are concerned with the legal codes. This neutral behavior is important especially as an occupier of the time of a child so that he is not in contact with criminal behavior during the time he is so engaged in the neutral behavior.

7. *Differential associations may vary in frequency, duration, priority, and intensity.* This means that associations with criminal behavior and also associations with anti-criminal behavior vary in those respects. "Frequency" and "duration" as modalities of associations are obvious and need no explanation. "Priority" is assumed to be important in the sense that lawful behavior developed in early childhood may persist throughout life, and also that delinquent behavior developed in early childhood may persist throughout life. This tendency, however, has not been adequately demonstrated, and priority seems to be important principally through its selective influence. "Intensity" is not precisely defined but it has to do with such things as the prestige of the source of a criminal or anti-criminal pattern and with emotional reactions related to the associations. In a precise description of the criminal behavior of a person these modalities

would be stated in quantitative form and a mathematical ratio be reached. A formula in this sense has not been developed, and the development of such a formula would be extremely difficult.

8. *The process of learning criminal behavior by association with criminal and anti-criminal patterns involves all of the mechanisms that are involved in any other learning.* Negatively, this means that the learning of criminal behavior is not restricted to the process of imitation. A person who is seduced, for instance, learns criminal behavior by association, but this process would not ordinarily be described as imitation.

9. *While criminal behavior is an expression of general needs and values, it is not explained by those general needs and values since non-criminal behavior is an expression of the same needs and values.* Thieves generally steal in order to secure money, but likewise honest laborers work in order to secure money. The attempts by many scholars to explain criminal behavior by general drives and values, such as the happiness principle, striving for social status, the money motive, or frustration, have been and must continue to be futile since they explain lawful behavior as completely as they explain criminal behavior. They are similar to respiration, which is necessary for any behavior but which does not differentiate criminal from non-criminal behavior.

It is not necessary, at this level of explanation, to explain why a person has the associations which he has; this certainly involves a complex of many things. In an area where the delinquency rate is high, a boy who is sociable, gregarious, active, and athletic is very likely to come in contact with the other boys in the neighborhood, learn delinquent behavior from them, and become a gangster; in the same neighborhood the psychopathic boy who is isolated, introverted, and inert may remain at home, not become acquainted with the other boys in the neighborhood, and not become delinquent. In another situation, the sociable, athletic, aggressive boy may become a member of a scout troop and not become involved in delinquent behavior. The person's associations are determined in a general context of social organization. A child is ordinarily reared in a family; the place of residence of the family is determined largely by family income; and the delinquency rate is in many respects related to the rental value of the houses. Many other aspects of social organization affect the kinds of associations a person has.

The preceding explanation of criminal behavior purports to explain the criminal and non-criminal behavior of individual persons. As indicated earlier, it is possible to state sociological theories of criminal behavior which explain the criminality of a community, nation, or other group. The problem, when thus stated, is to account for variations in crime rates and involves a comparison of the crime rates of various groups or the crime rates of a particular group at different times. The explanation of a crime rate must be consistent with the explanation of the criminal behavior of the person, since the crime rate is a summary statement of the number of persons in the group who commit crimes and the frequency with which they commit crimes. One of the best explanations of crime rates from this point of view is that a high crime rate is due to social disorganization. The term "social disorganization" is not entirely satisfactory and it seems preferable to substitute for it the term "differential social organization." The postulate on which this theory is based, regardless of the name, is that crime is rooted in the social organization and is an expression of that social organization. A group may be organized for criminal behavior or organized against criminal behavior. Most communities are organized both for criminal and anti-criminal behavior and in that sense the crime rate is an expression of the differential group organization. Differential group organization as an explanation of variations in crime rates is consistent with the differential association theory of the processes by which persons become criminals.

SOCIAL LEARNING THEORY

Ronald L. Akers and Wesley G. Jennings

The purpose of this chapter is to provide an overview of Akers' social learning theory with attention to its theoretical roots in Sutherland's differential association theory and the behavioral psychology of Skinner and Bandura. Empirical research testing the utility of social learning theory for explaining variation in crime or deviance is then reviewed; this is followed by a discussion of recent macro-level applications of the theory (i.e., social structure and social learning). The chapter concludes with a brief offering of suggestions for future research and a summary of the importance of social learning theory as a general theory in the criminological literature.

ORIGIN AND OVERVIEW OF SOCIAL LEARNING THEORY

Burgess and Akers' (1966) differential association-reinforcement theory was an effort to meld Sutherland's (1947) sociological approach in his differential association theory and principles of behavioral psychology. This was the foundation for Akers' (1968, 1973; Alters, Krohn, Lanza-Kaduce, & Radosevich 1979) further development of the theory, which he came more often to refer to as *social learning theory*). Sutherland's differential association theory is contained in nine propositions:

1. Criminal behavior is learned.
2. Criminal behavior is learned in interaction with other persons in a process of communication.
3. The principal part of the learning of criminal behavior occurs within intimate personal groups.
4. When criminal behavior is learned, the learning includes
   (a) techniques of committing the crime, which are sometimes very complicated, sometimes very simple, and
   (b) the specific direction of motives, drives, rationalizations, and attitudes.
5. The specific direction of motives and drives is learned from definitions of the legal codes as favorable or unfavorable.

6. A person becomes delinquent because of an excess of definitions favorable to violation of law over definitions unfavorable to violation of the law.
7. The process of learning criminal behavior by association with criminal and anti-criminal patterns involves all of the mechanisms that are involved in any other learning.
8. Although criminal behavior is an expression of general needs and values, it is not explained by those general needs and values, because noncriminal behavior is an expression of the same needs and values.
9. Differential association varies in frequency, duration, priority, and intensity. The most frequent, longest-running, earliest and closest influences will be most efficacious or determinant of learned behavior. (pp. 6–7)

Sutherland (1947) referred to the sixth statement as the *principle of differential association*. According to Sutherland, an individual learns two types of definitions toward committing a particular behavior. He can either learn favorable definitions from others that would likely increase the probability that he will commit the behavior, or he can learn unfavorable definitions that would likely decrease the probability that he would engage in a particular behavior. Stated in terms of criminal involvement, when an individual learns favorable definitions toward violations of the law in excess of the definitions unfavorable to violations of the law, that individual is more likely to commit the criminal act(s).

Learning favorable versus unfavorable definitions can also be described as a process whereby individuals attempt to balance pro-criminal definitions against prosocial or conforming definitions. It is logical to assume that individuals learn favorable or pro-criminal definitions for committing crime from those involved in crime themselves (i.e., the criminals) and, in contrast, learn unfavorable definitions for committing crime from those individuals who are not involved in crime, and this assumption is supported empirically. It should be remembered, however, that it is possible for law-abiding persons to expose individuals to pro-criminal attitudes and definitions, just as it is possible for an individual to learn conforming definitions from

criminals (see Cressey 1960, p. 49). According to Sutherland's (1947) seventh principle, the theory does not merely state that being associated with criminals leads to crime or that being associated with law-abiding persons leads to conforming behavior. It is the nature, characteristics, and balance of the *differential* association that affect an individual's likelihood of violating the law. More specifically, if a person is exposed to pro-criminal definitions first (priority), and these definitions increase in frequency and strength (intensity) and persist for some time (duration), the individual is more likely to demonstrate involvement in criminal and deviant acts.

Although Sutherland's (1947) differential association theory began to accumulate a rather large amount of attention throughout the sociological and criminological literature in the years after its emergence, Burgess and Akers (1966) noted that the theory had still failed to receive considerable empirical support and had yet to be adequately modified in response to some of its shortcomings and criticisms. Some of these issues included the inconsistency both within and between studies regarding the support for differential association and a common criticism among scholars on the difficulty of operationalizing the theory's concepts. In response to these criticisms and the prior failure of differential association theorists in specifying the learning process of the theory, Burgess and Akers presented their reformulated version of the theory, that is, *differential association-reinforcement theory*.

To describe their revised version in terms of its modifications and derivations from the original theory (as exemplified in Sutherland's [1947] nine principles), Burgess and Akers (1966) offered the following seven principles that illustrate the process wherein learning takes place:

1. Criminal behavior is learned according to the principles of operant conditioning (reformulation of Sutherland's Principles 1 and 8).
2. Criminal behavior is learned both in nonsocial situations that are reinforcing or discriminative and through that social interaction in which the behavior of other persons is reinforcing or discriminative for criminal behavior (reformulation of Sutherland's Principle 2).

3. The principal part of the learning of criminal behavior occurs in those groups which comprise the individual's major source of reinforcements (reformulation of Sutherland's Principle 3).

4. The learning of criminal behavior, including specific techniques, attitudes, and avoidance procedures, is a function of the effective and available reinforcers, and the existing reinforcement contingencies (reformulation of Sutherland's Principle 4).

5. The specific class of behaviors which are learned and their frequency of occurrence are a function of the reinforcers which are effective and available, and the rules or norms by which these reinforcers are applied (reformulation of Sutherland's Principle 5).

6. Criminal behavior is a function of norms which are discriminative for criminal behavior, the learning of which takes place when such behavior is more highly reinforced than noncriminal behavior (reformulation of Sutherland's Principle 6).

7. The strength of criminal behavior is a direct function of the amount, frequency, and probability of its reinforcement (reformulation of Sutherland's Principle 7). (pp. 132–145)[1]

Akers (1973, 1977, 1985, 1998) has since discussed modifications to this original serial list and has further revised the theory in response to criticisms, theoretical and empirical developments in the literature, and to ease the interpretation and explanations of the key assumptions of social learning theory, but the central tenets remain the same. It is important to note here that, contrary to how social learning is often described in the literature, social learning is not a rival or competitor of Sutherland's (1947) theory and his original propositions. Instead, it is offered as a broader theory that modifies and builds on Sutherland's theory and integrates this theoretical perspective with aspects of other scholars' principles explicated in behavioral learning theory, in particular behavioral acquisition, continuation, and cessation (see Akers 1985, p. 41). Taken together, social learning theory is presented as a more comprehensive explanation for involvement in crime and deviance compared with Sutherland's original theory; thus, any such support that it offered for differential association theory provides support for social learning theory, and findings that support social learning theory do not negate/discredit differential association theory.

The behavioral learning aspect of Akers' social learning theory (as first proposed by Burgess and Akers, 1966) draws from the classical work of B. F. Skinner, yet, more recently, Akers (1998) commented on how his theory is more closely aligned with cognitive learning theories such as those associated with Albert Bandura (1977), among others. According to Burgess and Akers (1996) and, later, Akers (1973, 1977, 1985, 1998), the specific mechanisms by which the learning process takes place are primarily through operant conditioning or differential reinforcement. Stated more clearly, operant behavior, or voluntary actions taken by an individual, are affected by a system of rewards and punishments. These reinforcers and punishers (described later) ultimately influence an individual's decision of whether to participate in conforming and/or nonconforming behavior.

Burgess and Akers (1966) originally considered the imitation element of the behavioral learning process (or modeling) to be subsumed under the broad umbrella of operant conditioning; that is, imitation was itself seen as simply one kind of behavior that could be shaped through successive approximations and not a separate behavioral mechanism. However, Akers later began to accept the uniqueness of the learning mechanism of imitation from operant or instrumental learning and to discuss it in terms of *observational learning* or *vicarious reinforcement*. Burgess and Akers also recognized the importance of additional behavioral components and principles of learning theory, such as classical conditioning, discriminative stimuli, schedules of reinforcement, and other mechanisms.

Considering the brief overview of social learning theory as described earlier, the central assumption and proposition of social learning theory can be best summarized in the two following statements:

> The basic assumption in social learning theory is that the same learning process in a context of social structure, interaction, and situation, produces both conforming and deviant behavior. The difference lies in the direction … [of] the balance of influences on behavior.

The probability that persons will engage in criminal and deviant behavior is increased and the probability of their conforming to the norm is decreased when they differentially associate with others who commit criminal behavior and espouse definitions favorable to it, are relatively more exposed in-person or symbolically to salient criminal/deviant models, define it as desirable or justified in a situation discriminative for the behavior, and have received in the past and anticipate in the current or future situation relatively greater reward than punishment for the behavior. (Akers 1995, p. 50)

It is worth emphasizing that social learning theory is a general theory in that it offers an explanation for why individuals first participate in crime and deviance, why they continue to offend, why they escalate/deescalate, why they specialize/generalize, and why they choose to desist from criminal/deviant involvement. Social learning theory also explains why individuals do not become involved in crime/deviance, instead opting to participate only in conforming behaviors. Thus, considering the generality of the theory as an explanation for an individual's participation in (or lack thereof) prosocial and pro-criminal behaviors, more attention is devoted in the following paragraphs to fleshing out the four central concepts of Akers' social learning theory that have received considerable (yet varying) amounts of attention and empirical support in the criminological literature: differential association, definitions, differential reinforcement, and imitation (Akers 1985, 1998; Akers et al. 1979).

DIFFERENTIAL ASSOCIATION

The *differential association* component in Akers' social learning theory is one of primary importance, Although its significance cannot simply be reduced to having "bad" friends, the individuals with whom a person decides to differentially associate and interact (either directly or indirectly) play an integral role in providing the social context wherein social learning occurs. An individual's direct interaction with others

who engage in certain kinds of behavior (criminal/deviant or conforming) and expose the individual to the norms, values, and attitudes supportive of these behaviors affects the decision of whether the individual opts to participate in a particular behavior.

Akers has indicated that family and friends (following Sutherland's [1947] emphasis on "intimate face-to-face" groups) are typically the primary groups that are the most salient for exposing an individual to favorable/unfavorable definitions and exhibiting conforming and/or nonconforming behaviors. For the most part, learning through differential association occurs within the family in the early childhood years and by means of the associations formed in school, leisure, recreational, and peer groups during adolescence. In contrast, during young adulthood and later in life, the spouses, work groups, and friendship groups typically assume the status of the primary group that provides the social context for learning. Secondary or reference groups can also indirectly provide the context for learning if an individual differentially associates him-or herself with the behaviors, norms, values, attitudes, and beliefs with groups of individuals, including neighbors, church leaders, schoolteachers, or even what Warr (2002) called *virtual groups*, such as the mass media, the Internet, and so on.

According to the theory, the associations that occur early (priority); last longer or occupy a disproportionate amount of one's time (duration); happen the most frequently; and involve the intimate, closest, or most important partners/peer groups (intensity) will likely exert the greatest effect on an individual's decision to participate in either conforming or nonconforming behavior. Taking these elements into consideration, the theory proposes that individuals are exposed to pro-criminal and prosocial norms, values, and definitions as well as patterns of reinforcement supportive of criminal or prosocial behavior. The more an individual is differentially associated and exposed to deviant behavior and attitudes transmitted by means of his or her primary and secondary peer groups, the greater his or her probability is for engaging in deviant or criminal behavior:

The groups with which one is in differential association provide the major social contexts in which all of the mechanisms of social learning operate. They not only expose one to definitions, but they also present one with models to imitate and differential reinforcement (source, schedule, value, and amount) for criminal or conforming behavior. (Akers & Sellers 2004, pp. 85–86)

DEFINITIONS

Definitions are one's own orientations and attitudes toward a given behavior. These personal as opposed to peer and other group definitions (i.e., differential association) are influenced by an individual's justifications, excuses, and attitudes that consider the commission of a particular act as being more right or wrong, good or bad, desirable or undesirable, justified or unjustified, appropriate or inappropriate. Akers considered these definitions to be expressed in two types: (1) general and (2) specific. *General beliefs* are one's personal definitions that are based on religious, moral, and other conventional values. In comparison, *specific beliefs* are personal definitions that orient an individual either toward committing or away from participating in certain criminal or deviant acts. For example, an individual may believe that it is morally wrong to assault someone and choose not to partake in or condone this sort of violence. Yet, despite his belief toward violence, this same individual may not see any moral or legal wrong in smoking a little bit of marijuana here and there.

Akers also has discussed personal definitions as comprising either conventional beliefs or positive or neutralizing beliefs. *Conventional beliefs* are definitions that are negative or unfavorable toward committing criminal and deviant acts or favorable toward committing conforming behaviors. In contrast, positive or neutralizing beliefs are those that are supportive or favorable toward crime and deviance. A *positive belief* is a definition an individual holds that committing a criminal or deviant act is morally desirable or wholly permissible. For instance, if an individual believes that it is "cool" and wholly acceptable to get high on marijuana, then this is a positive belief favorable toward smoking marijuana. Not all who hold this attitude will

necessarily indulge, but those who adhere to these definitions have a much higher probability of using marijuana than those who hold to conventional or negative definitions. A *neutralizing belief* also favors the commission of a criminal or deviant act, but this type of belief is influenced by an individual's justifications or excuses for why a particular behavior is permissible. For instance, one may have an initially negative attitude toward smoking marijuana but through observation of using models and through associating with users come to accept it as not really bad, or not as harmful as using alcohol, or otherwise come to justify or excuse its use.

Akers' conceptualization of *neutralizing definitions* incorporates notions of verbalizations, techniques of neutralization, and moral disengagement that are apparent in other behavioral and criminological literatures (see Bandura 1990; Cressey 1953; Sykes & Matza 1957). Examples of these neutralizing definitions (i.e., justifications, rationalizations, etc.) include statements such as "I do not get paid enough, so I am going to take these office supplies"; "The restaurant makes enough money, so they can afford it if I want to give my friends some free drinks"; "I was under the influence of alcohol, so it is not my fault"; and "This individual deserves to get beat up because he is annoying." These types of beliefs have both a cognitive and behavioral effect on an individual's decision to engage in criminal or deviant behavior. Cognitively, these beliefs provide a readily accessible system of justifications that make an individual more likely to commit a criminal or deviant act. Behaviorally, they provide an internal discriminative stimulus that presents an individual with cues as to what kind of behavior is appropriate/justified in a particular situation. For example, if a minimum-wage employee who has been washing dishes full-time at the same restaurant for 5 years suddenly gets his or her hours reduced to part-time because the manager chose to hire another part-time dishwasher, then the long-time employee might decide to steal money from the register or steal food because she believes that she has been treated unjustly and "deserves" it.

Akers and Silverman (2004) went on to argue that some personal definitions are so intense and ingrained into an individual's learned belief system, such as the radical ideologies of militant and/or terrorists groups, that these definitions alone exert a strong effect on an individual's probability of committing a deviant or criminal act. Similarly, Anderson's (1999) "code of the street" can serve as another example of a personal definition that is likely to have a significant role in motivating an individual to participate in crime or deviance. For example, if an urban inner-city youth is walking down the street and observes another youth (who resides in the same area) flaunting nice jewelry, then the urban juvenile might feel justified in "jumping" the kid and taking his jewelry because of the code of the street or the personal belief that "might makes right." Despite these examples, Akers suggested that the majority of criminal and deviant acts are not motivated in this way; they are either weak conventional beliefs that offer little to no restraint for engaging in crime/deviance or they are positive or neutralizing beliefs that motivate an individual to commit the criminal/deviant act when faced with an opportunity or the right set of circumstances.

DIFFERENTIAL REINFORCEMENT

Similar to the mechanism of differential association, whereby an imbalance of norms, values, and attitudes favorable toward committing a deviant or criminal act increases the probability that an individual will engage in such behavior, an imbalance in *differential reinforcement* also increases the likelihood that an individual will commit a given behavior. Furthermore, the past, present, and future anticipated and/or experienced rewards and punishments affect the probability that an individual will participate in a behavior in the first place and whether he or she continues or refrains from the behavior in the future. The differential reinforcement process operates in four key modes: positive reinforcement, negative reinforcement, positive punishment, and negative punishment.

Consider the following scenario. John is a quiet and shy boy who has difficulty making friends. Two of his classmates approach him on the playground and tell him that they will be his friend if he hits another boy because they do not like this particular child. John may know that hitting others is not right, but he decides to go along with their suggestion in order to gain their friendship. Immediately after he punches the boy, his classmates smile with approval and invite John to come over to their house after school to play with them. This peer approval serves as *positive reinforcement* for the assault. Positive reinforcement can also be provided when a behavior yields an increase in status, money, awards, or pleasant feelings.

Negative reinforcement can increase the likelihood that a behavior will be repeated if the act allows the individual to escape or avoid adverse or unpleasant stimuli. For example, Chris hates driving to and home from work because every day he has to drive through the same speed trap on the interstate. One day, Chris decides to come into work 1 hour early so he can in turn leave 1 hour early. Chris realizes that by coming in early and subsequently leaving early, he is able to avoid the speed trap because the officers are not posted on the interstate during his new travel times. He repeats this new travel schedule the following day, and once again he avoids the speed trap. His behavior (coming in an hour early and leaving an hour early) has now been negatively reinforced because he avoids the speed trap (i.e., the negative stimulus).

In contrast to reinforcers (positive and negative), there are positive and negative punishers that serve to increase or decrease the probability of a particular behavior being repeated. For example, Rachel has always had a designated driver when she decides to go out to the bar on Friday nights, but on one particular night she decides to drive herself to and from the local bar. On her way home, she gets pulled over for crossing the yellow line and is arrested for driving under the influence. Her decision and subsequent behavior to drink and drive resulted in a painful and unpleasant consequence: an arrest (a *positive punishment*).

This last scenario is an example of *negative punishment*. Mark's mom decides to buy him a new car but tells him not to smoke cigarettes in the car. Despite his mom's warning, Mark and his friends still decide to smoke cigarettes in the vehicle. His mom smells the odor when she chooses to drive his car to the grocery store one day and decides to take away Mark's driving privileges for 2 months for not following her rules. Mark's behavior (smoking cigarettes in the car) has now been negatively punished (removal of driving privileges).

Similar to differential association, there are modalities for differential reinforcement; more specifically, rewards that are higher in value and/or are greater in number are more likely to increase the chances that a behavior will occur and be repeated. Akers clarified that the reinforcement process does not necessarily occur in an either/or fashion but instead operates according to a *quantitative law of effect* wherein the behaviors that occur most frequently and are highly reinforced are chosen in favor of alternative behaviors.

IMITATION

Imitation is perhaps the least complex of the four dimensions of Akers's social learning theory. Imitation occurs when an individual engages in a behavior that is modeled on or follows his or her observation of another individual's behavior. An individual can observe the behavior of potential models either directly or indirectly (e.g., through the media). Furthermore, the characteristics of the models themselves, the behavior itself, and the observed consequences of the behavior all affect the probability that an individual will imitate the behavior. The process of imitation is often referred to as *vicarious reinforcement* (Bandura 1977). Baldwin and Baldwin (1981) provided a concise summary of this process:

> Observers tend to imitate modeled behavior if they like or respect the model, see the model receive reinforcement, see the model give off signs of pleasure, or are in an environment where imitating the model's performance is reinforced.... Inverse imitation is common when an observer does not like the model, sees the model get punished, or is in an environment where conformity is being punished. (p. 187)

Although social learning theory maintains that the process of imitation occurs throughout an individual's life, Akers has argued that imitation is most salient in the initial acquisition and performance of a novel or new behavior. Thus, an individual's decision to engage in crime or deviance after watching a violent television show for the first time or observing his friends attack another peer for the first time provides the key social

context in which imitation can occur. Nevertheless, the process of imitation is still assumed to exert an effect in maintaining or desisting from a given behavior.

TESTING SOCIAL LEARNING THEORY

Although full empirical tests of all of the dimensions of Akers' social learning theory did not emerge in the literature until the late 1970s, early research, such as Sutherland's (1937) qualitative study of professional theft and Cressey's (1953) well-known research on apprehended embezzlers, provided preliminary support for differential association (e.g., also offering support for social learning). Following these seminal studies, research now spanning more than five decades has continued to demonstrate varying levels of support for the various components of social learning theory, and the evidence is rather robust (see Akers & Jensen 2006).

There are far too many studies to make an attempt to list or discuss each individually; therefore, the following discussion is limited to noting the findings of some of the most recognizable and comprehensive tests of Akers' social learning theory performed by Akers and his associates.

Akers has tested his own theory with a number of scholars over the years across a variety of samples and on a range of behaviors from minor deviance to serious criminal behavior, and this research can best be summarized in terms of four projects: (1) the Boys Town study, (2) the Iowa study, (3) the elderly drinking study, and (4) the rape and sexual coercion study. The first of these projects, and by far the most well-known and cited, is the Boys Town study (for a review, see Akers & Jensen, 2006). This research project involved primary collection of survey data from approximately 3,000 students in Grades 7 through 12 in eight communities in the Midwest. The majority of the survey questions focused on adolescent substance use and abuse, but it was also the first survey that included questions that permitted Akers and his associates (Akers et al. 1979) to fully test the four components of social learning theory.

The results of the studies relying on the Boys Town data provided overwhelming support for Akers' social learning theory, including each of its four main sets of variables of differential association, definitions, differential reinforcement, and imitation. The multivariate results indicated that greater than half of the total variance in the frequency of drinking alcohol (R^2 = .54) and more than two thirds of the variance in marijuana use (R^2 = .68) were explained by the social learning variables. The social learning variables also affected the probability that the adolescent who began to use substances would move on to more serious involvement in drugs and alcohol. Not only did the social learning variables yield a large cumulative effect on explaining substance use, but also each of the four elements exerted a substantial independent effect on the dependent variable (with the exception of imitation). The more modest results found for the effect of imitation on substance use was not surprising considering the hypothesized interrelationships among the social learning variables. Also, imitation is expected to play a more important role in initiating use (first use) versus having a strong effect on the frequency or maintenance of use. Lanza-Kaduce, Akers, Krohn, and Radosevich (1984) also demonstrated that the social learning variables were significantly correlated with the termination of alcohol, marijuana, and hard drug use, with cessation being related to a preponderance of nonusing associations, aversive drug experiences, negative social sanctions, exposure to abstinence models, and definitions unfavorable to continued use of each of these substances.

The second research project, the Iowa study, was a 5-year longitudinal examination of smoking among junior and senior high school students in Muscatine, Iowa (for a review, see Akers & Jensen 2006). Spear and Akers (1988) provided the initial test of social learning theory on the first wave (year) of the Iowa data in an attempt to replicate the findings of the Boys Town study. The results of the cross-sectional analysis revealed nearly identical results among the youth in the Iowa study as was previously found in the Boys Town study. Once again, the social learning variables explained over half of the variance in self-reported smoking, and each of the social learning variables had a rather strong independent effect on the outcome (with the exception of imitation). Additional evidence provided by Akers (1998) illustrated the substantial influence of the adolescents' parents and peers on their behavior. When neither of the parents or friends smoked, there was a

very high probability that the adolescent abstained from smoking, and virtually none of these youth reported being regular smokers. In contrast, when the adolescent's parents and peers smoked, more than 3 out of every 4 of these youth reported having smoked, and nearly half reported being regular smokers.

The longitudinal analysis of the Iowa data also provided support for social learning theory. Path models constructed using the first 3 years of data indicated that the direct and indirect effects of the social learning variables explained approximately 3% of the variance in predicting who would be a smoker in Year 3 if that individual had not reported being a smoker in either of the 2 prior years. Although this evidence was relatively weak, stronger results were found for the ability of the social learning variables to predict the continuation and the cessation of smoking by the third year (approximately 41% explained variance; Krohn, Skinner, Massey, & Akers 1985). Akers and Lee (1996) also provided longitudinal support for the social learning variables' capacity to predict the frequency of smoking using the complete 5 years of data from the Iowa study and revealed some reciprocal effects for smoking behavior on the social learning variables.

The third project was a 4-year longitudinal study of the frequency of alcohol use and problem drinking among a large sample of elderly respondents in four communities in Florida and New Jersey (for a review, see Akers & Jensen, 2006). Similar to the results of the Boys Town and Iowa studies, which examined substance use among adolescents, the multivariate results in this study of elderly individuals also demonstrated significant effects for the social learning variables as predictors of the frequency of alcohol use and problem drinking. The social learning process accounted for more than 50% of the explained variance in self-reported elderly alcohol use/abuse.

The last project by Akers and his associates reviewed here is a study of rape and sexual coercion among two samples of college men (Boeringer, Shehan, & Akers 1991). The findings in these studies also mirrored the results of the previous studies by Akers and his associates, with the social learning variables exerting moderate to strong effects on self-reported use of nonphysical coercion in sex in addition to predicting rape and rape proclivity (i.e., the readiness to rape). Although Akers and his associates have continued to test social learning theory to various degrees using dependent variables such as adolescent alcohol and drug use (Hwang & Akers 2003), cross-national homicide rates (Akers & Jensen 2006), and even terrorism (Akers & Silverman 2004), the findings from the classic studies just reviewed clearly identify the strength of the empirical status of social learning theory.

SOCIAL STRUCTURE AND SOCIAL LEARNING: THEORETICAL ASSUMPTIONS AND PRELIMINARY EVIDENCE

Akers' social learning theory has explained a considerable amount of the variation in criminal and deviant behavior at the individual level (see Akers & Jensen 2006), and Akers (1998) recently extended it to posit an explanation for the variation in crime at the macro-level. Akers' *social structure and social learning* (SSSL) theory hypothesizes that there are social structural factors that have an indirect effect on individuals' behavior. The *indirect effect hypothesis* is guided by the assumption that the effect of these social structural factors is operating through the social learning variables (i.e., differential association, definitions, differential reinforcement, and imitation) that have a direct effect on individuals' decisions to engage in crime or deviance. Akers (1998; see also Akers & Sellers, 2004, p. 91) identified four specific domains of social structure wherein the social learning process can operate:

1. *Differential social organization* refers to the structural correlates of crime in the community or society that affect the rates of crime and delinquency, including age composition, population density, and other attributes that lean societies, communities, and other social systems "toward relatively high or relatively low crime rates" (Akers 1998, p. 332).
2. *Differential location in the social structure* refers to sociodemographic characteristics of individuals and social groups that indicate their niches within the larger social structure. Class, gender, race and ethnicity, marital status, and age locate the positions and standing of persons and their roles, groups, or social categories in the overall social structure.
3. *Theoretically defined structural variables* refer to anomie, class oppression, social disorganization, group conflict, patriarchy, and other concepts that have been used in one or more theories to identify criminogenic conditions of societies, communities, or groups.
4. *Differential social location* refers to individuals' membership in and relationship to primary, secondary, and reference groups such as the family, friendship/peer groups, leisure groups, colleagues, and work groups.

With attention to these social structural domains, Akers contended that the differential social organization of society and community and the differential locations of individuals within the social structure (i.e., individuals' gender, race, class, religious affiliation, etc.) provide the context in which learning occurs (Akers & Sellers 2004, p. 91). Individuals' decisions to engage in crime/deviance are thus a function of the environment wherein the learning takes place and the individuals' exposure to deviant peers and attitudes, possession of definitions favorable to the commission of criminal or deviant acts, and interactions with deviant models. Stated in terms of a causal process, if the social learning variables mediate social structural effects on crime as hypothesized, then (a) the social structural variables should exhibit direct effects on the social learning variables; (b) the social structural variables should exert direct effects on the dependent variable; and (c) once the social learning variables are included in the model, these variables should demonstrate strong independent effects on the dependent variable, and the social structural variables should no longer exhibit direct effects on the dependent variable, or at least their direct effects should be substantially reduced.

Considering the relative novelty of Akers' proposed social structure and social learning theory, only a handful of studies thus far have attempted to examine its theoretical assumptions and/or its mediation hypothesis. However, the few preliminary studies to date have demonstrated positive findings in support of social structure and social learning for delinquency and substance use, elderly alcohol abuse, rape, violence, binge drinking by college students, and variation in cross-national homicide rates (for a review, see Akers & Jensen 2006). Yet, despite the consistency of positive preliminary findings in support of Akers' social structure and social learning theory, there are some nonsupportive findings, and it is still too soon to make a definitive statement that social learning is the primary mediating force in the association between social structure and crime/deviance. Nevertheless, these few studies provide a suitable benchmark against which future studies testing the theory can build upon and improve.

FUTURE DIRECTIONS

The future of social learning theory lies along three paths. First, there will continue to be further and more accurate tests of social learning at the micro- or process level (i.e., at the level of differences across individuals), including measures of variables from other criminological theories, and these studies will use better measures of all of the central concepts of the theory. Having said this, it is not likely that the empirical findings will be much different from the research so far, but these future studies should continue to include more research on social leaning explanations of the most serious and violent criminal behavior as well as white-collar and corporate crime.

Second, there is need for continued development and testing of the SSSL model, again using better measures. A very promising direction that this could take would follow the lead of Jensen and Akers (2003, 2006) to extend the basic social learning principles and the SSSL model "globally" to the most macro-level. Structural theories at that level are more apt to be valid the more they reference or incorporate the most valid principles found at the individual level, and those are social learning principles.

Third, social learning principles will continue to be applied in cognitive-behavioral (Cullen, Wright, Gendreau, & Andrews 2003) prevention, treatment, rehabilitation, and correctional programs and otherwise provide some theoretical underpinning for social policy. Research on the application and evaluations of such programs have thus far found them to be at least moderately effective (and usually more effective

than alternative programs), but there are still many unanswered questions about the feasibility and effectiveness of programs designed around social learning theory.

Future research along all of these lines is also more likely to be in the form of longitudinal studies over the life course and to be cross-cultural studies of the empirical validity of the theory in different societies. If social learning is truly a general theory, then it should have applicability to the explanation and control of crime and deviance not only in American and Western societies but also societies around the world. There have already been some cross-cultural studies supporting the social learning theory (see, e.g., Hwang & Akers 2003; Miller, Jennings, Alvarez-Rivera, & Miller 2008), but much more research needs to examine both how well the theory holds up in different societies and on how much variation there is in the effects of the social learning variables in different cultures.

CONCLUSION

The purpose of this chapter was to provide a historical overview of the theoretical development of Akers' social learning theory, review the seminal research testing the general theory, and discuss the recently proposed macro-level version of social learning theory (i.e., social structure and social learning), as well as offer suggestions of where future research may wish to proceed in order to further advance the status of the theory. What is clear from the research evidence presented in this chapter, along with a number of studies that have not been specifically mentioned or discussed in this chapter (for a review, see Akers & Jensen 2006), is that social learning has rightfully earned its place as a general theory of crime and deviance. One theorist has referred to it (along with control and strain theories) as constituting the "core" of contemporary criminological theory (Cullen, Wright, & Blevins 2006). The theory has been rigorously tested a number of times, not only by the theorist himself but also by other influential criminologists and sociologists; it has been widely cited in the scholarly literature and in textbooks; it is a common topic covered in a variety of undergraduate and graduate courses; and it provides a basis for sound policy and practice.

Ultimately, the task levied at any general theory of crime and deviance is that it should be able to explain crime/deviance across crime/deviance type, time, place, culture, and context. Therefore, if past behavior is the best predictor of future behavior, then the expectation is that social learning theory will continue to demonstrate its generalizability across these various dimensions and that future tests of Akers's SSSL theory will also garner support as a macro-level explanation of crime. Yet these outcomes are indeed open to debate. No theory can account for all variations in criminal behavior, Only through the process of continuing to subject the theory and its macro-level version to rigorous and sound empirical tests in sociology and criminology can it be determined how much the theory can account for on its own and in comparison to other theories.

NOTE

1. In their reformulation of the theory, Burgess and Akers chose to omit Sutherland's ninth principle.

REFERENCES AND FURTHER READINGS

Akers, R. L. (1968). Problems in the sociology of deviance: Social definitions and behavior. *Social Forces, 46,* 455–465.

Akers, R. L. (1973). *Deviant behavior: A social learning approach.* Belmont, CA: Wadsworth.

Akers, R. L. (1977). *Deviant behavior: A social learning approach* (2nd ed.). Belmont, CA: Wadsworth.

Akers, R. L. (1985). *Deviant behavior: A social learning approach* (3rd ed.). Belmont, CA: Wadsworth.

Akers, R. L. (1998). *Social learning and social structure: A general theory of crime and deviance.* Boston: Northeastern University Press.

Akers, R. L., & Jensen, G. F. (2006). The empirical status of social learning theory of crime and deviance: The past, present, and future. In. F. T. Cullen, J. P. Wright, & K. R. Blevins (Eds.), *Taking stock: The status of criminological theory* (pp. 37–76). New Brunswick, NJ: Transaction.

Akers, R. L., Krohn, M. D., Lanza-Kaduce, L., & Radosevich, M. (1979). Social learning and deviant behavior: A specific test of a general theory. *American Sociological Review, 44,* 636–655.

Akers, R. L., & Lee, G. (1996). A longitudinal test of social learning theory: Adolescent smoking. *Journal of Drug Issues, 26,* 317–343.

Akers, R. L., & Sellers, C. S. (2004). *Criminological theories: Introduction, evaluation, and application* (4th ed.) Los Angeles: Roxbury.

Akers, R. L., & Silverman, A. (2004). Toward a social learning model of violence and terrorism. In M. A. Zahn, H. H. Brownstein, & S. L. Jackson (Eds.), *Violence: From theory to research* (pp. 19–35). Cincinnati, OH: LexisNexis–Anderson.

Anderson, E. (1999). *Code of the street: Decency, violence, and the moral life of the inner city.* New York: W. W. Norton.

Baldwin, J. D., & Baldwin, J. I. (1981). *Beyond sociobiology.* New York: Elsevier.

Bandura, A. (1977). *Social learning theory.* New York: General Learning Press.

Bandura, A. (1990). Mechanisms of moral disengagement. In W. Reich (Ed.), *Origins of terrorism: Psychologies, ideologies, theologies, and states of mind* (pp. 161–191). Cambridge, UK: Cambridge University Press.

Boeringer, S., Shehan, C. L., & Akers, R. L. (1991). Social contexts and social learning in sexual coercion and aggression: Assessing the contribution of fraternity membership. *Family Relations, 40,* 558–564.

Burgess, R. L., & Akers, R. L. (1966). A differential association-reinforcement theory of criminal behavior. *Social Problems, 14,* 128–147.

Cressey, D. R. (1953). *Other people's money.* Glencoe, IL: Free Press.

Cressey, D. R. (1960). Epidemiology and individual conduct: A case from criminology. *Pacific Sociological Review, 3,* 47–58.

Cullen, F. T., Wright, J. P., &Blevins, K. R. (Eds.). (2006). *Taking stock: The status of criminological theory.* New Brunswick, NJ: Transaction.

Cullen, F. T., Wright, J. P., Gendreau, P., & Andrews, D. A. (2003). What correctional treatment can tell us about criminological theory: Implications for social learning theory. In R. L. Akers & G. F. Jensen (Eds.), *Advances in criminological theory: Vol. II. Social learning theory and the explanation of crime: A guide for the new century* (pp. 339–362). New Brunswick, NJ: Transaction.

Hwang, S., & Akers, R. L. (2003). Substance use by Korean adolescents: A cross-cultural test of social learning, social bonding, and self-control theories. In R. L. Akers & G. F. Jensen (Eds.), *Advances in criminological theory: Vol. 11. Social learning theory and the explanation of crime: A guide for the new century* (pp. 39–64). New Brunswick, NJ: Transaction.

Jensen, G. F. (2003). Gender variation in delinquency: Self-images, beliefs, and peers as mediating mechanisms. In R. L. Akers & G. F. Jensen (Eds.), *Advances in criminological theory: Vol. 11. Social learning theory and the explanation of crime* (pp. 151–178). New Brunswick, N J: Transaction.

Krohn, M. D., Skinner, W. F., Massey, J. L., & Akers, R. L. (1985). Social learning theory and adolescent cigarette smoking. *Social Problems, 32*, 455–473.

Lanza-Kaduce, L., Akers, R. L., Krohn, M. D., & Radosevich, M. (1984). Cessation of alcohol and drug use among adolescents: A social learning model. *Deviant Behavior, 5*, 79–96.

Miller, H. V., Jennings, W. G., Alvarez-Rivera, L. L., & Miller, J. M. (2008). Explaining substance use among Puerto Rican adolescents: A partial test of social learning theory. *Journal of Drug Issues, 38*, 261–284.

Spear, S., & Akers, R. L. (1988). Social learning variables and the risk of habitual smoking among adolescents: The Muscatine study. *American Journal of Preventive Medicine, 4*, 336–348.

Sutherland, E. H. (1937). *The professional thief* Chicago: University of Chicago Press.

Sutherland, E. H. (1947). *Principles of criminology* (4th ed.). Philadelphia: Lippincott.

Sykes, G., & Matza, D. (1957). Techniques of neutralization: A theory of delinquency. *American Journal of Sociology, 22*, 664–670.

Warr, M. (2002). *Companions in crime: The social aspects of criminal conduct.* Cambridge, UK: Cambridge University Press.

CHAPTER V

Social Control Theories

SELF-CONTROL THEORY

Travis Hirschi and Michael R. Gottfredson

In the summer of 1998, three white men in east Texas chained a black man to the rear of a pickup truck and dragged him for several miles along the backroads near his hometown. The victim's remains were found strewn along the road the next morning. When arrested that same day, the three men had in their possession a large quantity of meat they had stolen during a burglary of a packing plant. According to media reports, all had served time in prison and all had been drinking heavily at the time the crimes were committed. In federal law, murder involving race hatred is punishable by death. In Texas law, murder involving kidnapping (forcing the movement of the victim) is also subject to the death penalty. Many calls for speedy execution of the offenders were heard in the days that followed. These calls were not limited to one area of the country or to one ethnic group. In fact, a good guess would be that about 95 percent of the U.S. population favored the death penalty in this case. Through his lawyer, one of the arrested men quickly denied participation in the act.

A theory of crime should be able to make sense of these facts, however rare and horrible they may be. A general theory should also make sense of the far more common crimes and delinquencies at the other end of the seriousness scale: truancy, shoplifting, underage smoking, bicycle theft, cheating on tests.

What are "the facts" in this case? You may have heard that theories favor some facts and ignore others. If so, what you have heard is true. Facts accepted by one theory may be rejected or ignored by other theories. Self-control theory focuses on the typical features of criminal acts and on the criminal record of the offender. In the case in question, self-control theory would emphasize the following: (1). The offenders had long records of involvement in criminal and deviant acts. (2). They did not limit themselves to one kind of crime, but engaged in a wide variety of criminal and deviant acts, even in a short period of time (burglary, murder, kidnapping, drinking excessively, driving under the influence). (3). Everyone believes that these acts are criminal or deviant and that some of them deserve severe punishment. (4). The potential costs to the offenders of the crimes described are considerable and long term; the benefits are minimal and of short duration. (5). Despite the enormity of the crimes described, no special skill or knowledge is required to commit them. (6). Although three offenders were involved in these crimes, they did not act as an organized group. Indeed, one offender took the first opportunity to claim that he did not participate in the most serious offense.

Self-control theory would largely ignore the two features of the homicide that made it so newsworthy: its unusual brutality and its element of race hatred. Self-control theory pays little attention to the seriousness of crimes and is not interested in the motives of offenders. It is also relatively uninterested in the social or economic backgrounds of the perpetrators. The theory would lead us to guess that the offenders in this case were uneducated and unskilled, but it would do so because it assumes that people committing such crimes are unlikely to have exerted the effort required to obtain an education or a high level of occupational skill, not because poverty forced them into the acts in question. In short, self-control theory takes the social and economic conditions of offenders as a reflection of their tendency to offend, not as a cause of their offending. By the same token, the theory would pay little attention to the time and place of the crime. In its view, there is nothing special with respect to crime about east Texas or the end of the twentieth century.

Which of the facts listed is most important? We begin to answer this question by asking another: What fact best predicts crime? The answer is previous crime. If you want to know the likelihood that a person will commit criminal or deviant acts in the future, you can do no better than count the different kinds of criminal and deviant acts he or she has committed in the past. This is the central fact on which self-control theory is based. It says to the self-control theorist that all criminal and deviant acts, at whatever age they are committed, whatever their level of seriousness, have something in common. It says also that people differ in the degree to which they are attracted to or repelled by whatever it is crime and deviance have to offer.

We know that criminal and deviant acts have something in common because participation in any one of them predicts participation in all of the others. People who smoke and drink are more likely than people who do not smoke or drink to use illegal drugs, to cut classes, to cheat on tests, to break into houses, to rob and steal. People who rob and steal are more likely than people who do not rob and steal to smoke and drink, use illegal drugs, break into houses, and cheat on tests.

What do robbery, theft, burglary, cheating, truancy, and drug use (and the many forms of criminal and deviant behavior not listed) have in common? They are all quick and easy ways of getting what one wants. They are all also, in the long run, dangerous to one's health, safety, reputation, and economic well-being.

The features common to various crimes and deviant acts would not cause them to predict one another unless these features were reflected in some relatively enduring tendency of individuals. People must differ in the likelihood that they will take the quick and easy way regardless of long-term consequences. This enduring difference between people the theory calls *self-control*. Those who have a high degree of self-control avoid acts potentially damaging to their future prospects, whatever the current benefits these acts seem to promise. Those with a low degree of self-control are easily swayed by current benefits and tend to forget future costs. Most people are between these extremes, sometimes doing things they know they should not do, other times being careful not to take unnecessary risks for short-term advantage.

So, a *fact* at the heart of the theory is the ability of previous criminal and deviant acts to predict future criminal and deviant acts. The *concept* at the heart of the theory is self-control, defined as the tendency to avoid acts whose long-term costs exceed their immediate or short-term benefits. This concept, in our view, accounts for the important facts about crime. In our view, it also questions the meaning of the facts claimed by competing theories. Where did our version of self-control theory come from?

BACKGROUND AND HISTORY

For a hundred years or so, criminologists, social workers, and ordinary citizens have tried to draw a clear line between the delinquencies of children and the crimes of adults. As a result, juveniles and adults have separate justice systems, universities offer separate courses in juvenile delinquency and criminology, and theories continue to focus on the activities of one group and to ignore the other. Beginning in the 1960s, academics became interested in the connection between juvenile delinquency and adult crime, often called the *issue of maturational reform*. It was then widely believed that most delinquents quit delinquency as they enter adulthood, with only a small number going on to criminal careers. Although reform was thought to be common, explanations of it tended to be vague and unsatisfactory. In most accounts, the justice system was given little credit. Indeed, before Robert Martinson (1974a) popularized the view that "nothing works" in the justice system, two famous delinquency researchers, Sheldon and Eleanor Glueck (1940), had concluded that reform was simply the work of Mother Nature and Father Time.

Because reform was thought to be common, it was seen as a serious problem for the delinquency theories popular at the time. The most popular was what is now called *strain theory*, the theory behind the Great Society and War on Poverty programs of the 1960s and 1970s. This theory said that people turn to crime because they cannot realize the American Dream through conventional means. So, according to the theory, poverty, discrimination, and lack of opportunity are major causes of crime. This sounded plausible to many Americans and to most academics. But the theory had an obvious flaw. It could perhaps explain why some kids become delinquent, but it could not explain why they stop being delinquent. It predicted too much delinquency. Poverty, discrimination, and lack of opportunity do not go away in the middle teens. They are still there when delinquency begins to decline.

Social control theory was developed in part to remedy this defect. This theory says that delinquent acts result when an individual's bond to society is weak or broken. In one version (Hirschi 1969), the bond to society, the individual's ties to institutions and other people, is made up of four elements: (1). *Attachment*, the bond of respect, love, or affection. The more the adolescent cares for the opinion of others, the less likely he or she is to commit delinquent acts. (2). *Commitment*, the bond of aspiration, investment, or ambition. The greater the individual's stake in conformity (Toby 1957), the greater the individual's social and personal capital (Coleman 1990), the more he or she has to lose by the commission of delinquent acts. (3). *Involvement*, the restriction of opportunity to commit delinquent acts by engaging in conventional activities. (4). *Belief*, the bond to conformity created by the view that criminal and delinquent acts are morally wrong. Hirschi assumed that these causes could change over the life course, and could thus account for corresponding changes in delinquency.

Social control theory was testable in ways not true of earlier theories. When tested, it worked reasonably well. Kids attached to their parents, kids attached to school, ambitious and diligent kids were less likely to Commit delinquent acts whether delinquency was measured by self-reports or police records. Initial research on the theory did not, however, test its ability to account for change in delinquency over time.

Hirschi's exposition and test of social control theory was published in 1969 as *Causes of Delinquency*. In 1974, Robert Martinson published his famous article just mentioned, "What Works—Questions and Answers about Prison Reform," concluding that indeed nothing works. In the same year, he delivered at a conference a paper titled "The Myth of Treatment and the Reality of Life Process." The second paper attempted to deal with issues raised by his first paper and by social control theories of delinquency.

Martinson saw that the failure of treatment said something important about the theories of crime then dominant in the social and behavioral sciences. Put bluntly, the failure of treatment said there was something wrong with the theories of crime on which the treatment enterprise was based. To illustrate this inadequacy, Martinson turned to the relation between age and crime: 140 years earlier, the French statistician Quetelet (1833) had said: ". . . among all the causes that influence the growth and abatement of the penchant for crime, age is without question the most energetic."

Martinson admitted that we did not know the shape of the entire age-crime curve, but he thought we knew enough to use it to judge theories. We knew when crime tends to begin and we knew something about the peak age. We also knew that what he called *drop out* after the peak age is quite common, and that complete remission usually takes place sometime before the end of life. Another thing we knew, he said, was that there are chronic or persistent offenders. This "knowledge" allowed Martinson to sketch a hypothetical age-crime curve for two societies (see Figure 8.1).

Martinson then applied the major theories of delinquency to these facts, quickly concluding that none of them was adequate to the task. He then introduced a

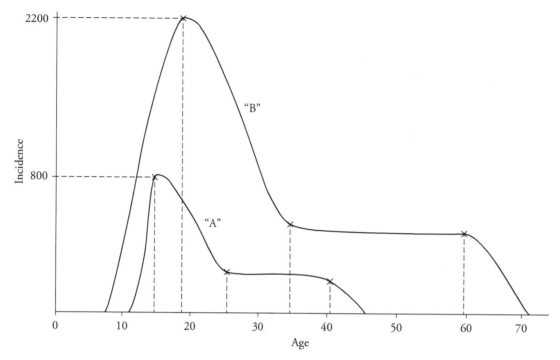

Figure 8.1 *Hypothetical Curves of the Age Distributions of Acts Definable as Deliquency or Crime in Birth Cohorts in Two Societies*

theory he thought might be useful in this effort, which he called "A New Beginning" and "commend[ed] to the attention" of his audience. This was social control theory. The question was whether the concepts of attachment, commitment, involvement, and belief could actually account for the hypothetical age curves Martinson had before him.

After much effort, he concluded that they could not. Martinson's (1974b) conclusions deserve repeating here.

1. The idea that criminal offenders may be induced to desist from offending through correctional treatment is a myth.
2. The failure of correctional treatment is a failure of the idea that crime is analogous to a disease which may be cured by appropriate treatment of the individual.
3. An adequate theory of ... crime must be able to account for the complex relationship between crime and age, and should therefore include variables reflecting variations in the life course of both offenders and nonoffenders.

4. No existing sociological theory is able to account for such age distributions, although control theory has the potential to do so.
5. Control theory must be expanded to include: a) the deterrent effect of the threat of legal punishment; and b) a notion of social damage which is adequate to account for the persistence of offenders in crime. (16–17)

Martinson himself later expanded on the idea of social damage, arguing in a book-length unpublished work that prison may in fact delay maturation by shielding offenders from ordinary social processes. Attempts at treatment, therefore, extend the criminal career beyond its normal age limits.

We did not agree with Martinson's idea of delayed maturation, arguing that such an effect of treatment was contrary to his position that treatment does not work, one way or the other. (If treatment does not make offenders better, it also does not make them worse [Hirschi 1975].) We did agree, however, that no evidence had shown that change in the strength of social bonds actually accounts for the reformation of

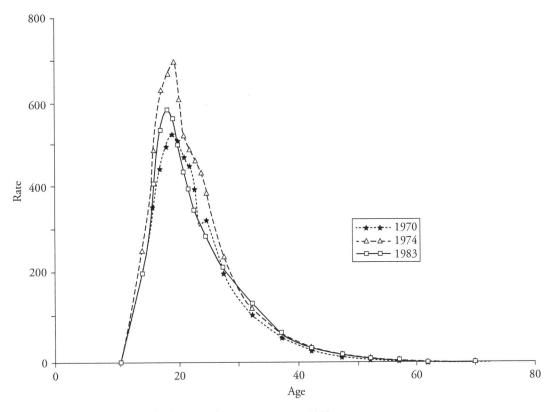

Figure 8.2 *Arrests for Burglary by Age, United States, 1970, 1974, 1983*

juvenile delinquents. It seemed necessary to look more closely at the connection between age and crime. Does crime follow the path described by Martinson?

In 1983, we published our answer to this question in a paper titled "Age and the Explanation of Crime." This paper rediscovers what Quetelet 150 years earlier had called the most "energetic" cause of crime, and what the English physician Charles Goring 70 years earlier (1913) had called "a law of nature."

This law of nature is illustrated in Figure 8.2, which shows that the facts are more dramatic but less complex than Martinson guessed them to be. Crime rates vary from group to group and from one society to another, and they often change over time. But wherever the place and whatever the time, they are highest in adolescence and early adulthood, decline rapidly from peak levels, and continue to decline throughout life. This appears to be true for all, or almost all, crimes. It appears to be true as well for behavior similar to crime:

accidents, legal drug use, promiscuous sexual activity. It appears to be true for all groups and societies, at all times and places, even in prisons. It is true whether crime is measured by police records or by asking people to report their own delinquent acts.

At the time we published our article, we were restricted largely to measures of crime based on police, court, or prison records—so-called official data. Although self-report measures of crime and delinquency had been in use for some time, they had not yet been applied in a convincing way to the age question. This allowed doubters to argue that the decline in crime with age shown in official data was evidence only that the ability of offenders to avoid detection improves as they get older. We believed facts already available undermined such skepticism. Criminal, deviant, and reckless acts differ greatly in the likelihood that they will be observed or recorded, yet almost all decline with age. Automobile accidents, for example, are in important ways analogous to crimes. They may result from short-term advantage (speeding, drinking, inattention) and may produce long-term ill effects. Precisely because they are considered accidents, those involved feel no need to conceal them—and could not even if they wished to do so. The decline in automobile accidents with age, which is much like the decline in crime with age, could not be accounted for by a quirk of measurement. We therefore predicted that self-report measures would confirm the age-crime relation described by official data. Our prediction turned out to be true, something all too rare in social science (see Table 8.1).

Once recognized, these facts changed everything. It was no longer meaningful to ask, why do delinquents quit? because they do not. Active, high-rate offenders slow down with age, but so does everyone else. Differences between people in their criminal and deviant behavior seen early in life are still present long after the peak ages of crime are behind them. It was no longer meaningful to ask how the criminal justice system changes, for good or for ill, the tendency to offend—because it does not. It was no longer meaningful to require sociological theories to explain the decline in crime with age. The decline is found everywhere. It, therefore, cannot be explained by factors that differ from one society to another.

So, we began with the idea that a theory of crime must explain the tendency of offenders to reform with age. We ended up with facts suggesting that reform is not the issue. Criminal activity declines with age, but it declines for everyone. True reform is too rare to show itself in statistics on crime. What was needed was a theory capable of explaining persistent differences in the tendency to offend over the life course.

Table 8.1 Self-reported Illegal Behavior by Age and Sex: Percent Reporting One or More Offenses

Offense	17	18	19	20	21	22	23	Chi²	Gamma
Males									
Hit Supervisor	3.8	1.8	.1	1.1	.7	2.5	1.3	18.2*	−.38
Fight at Work/School	16.2	14.1	7.9	10.2	5.3	8.7	6.2	32.7*	−.27
Gang Fight	20.3	15.9	11.6	12.0	7.5	8.7	3.1	47.7*	−.32
Hurt Someone Badly	15.6	14.8	9.7	6.4	4.5	4.1	1.6	53.6*	−.38
Robbery	4.2	3.0	1.5	1.2	.0	1.1	.3	21.7*	−.52
Steal < $50	41.2	39.9	37.3	32.1	31.3	24.3	21.7	31.8*	−.18
Steal > $50	8.9	7.3	4.2	7.5	5.7	6.2	2.1	12.1	−.17
Shoplift	39.0	28.8	22.8	16.4	19.4	10.4	11.5	102.8*	−.36
Joyride	5.2	4.2	3.2	2.8	1.2	.5	.0	18.2*	−.39
Steal Car Parts	11.5	10.2	6.0	6.3	3.7	3.3	2.3	31.0*	−.33
Trespass	34.0	25.8	16.4	19.3	9.2	10.4	5.7	111.3*	−.40
Arson	3.2	2.2	.5	.7	.1	.5	.0	20.3*	−.59
Damage School Property	19.5	14.5	4.9	4.3	3.1	2.7	.8	113.0*	−.56
Damage Work Property	10.4	10.7	5.5	6.7	3.1	4.4	3.1	25.4*	−.29
Any Aggressive Offense	34.9	28.0	21.8	20.6	13.8	17.0	8.7	77.2*	−.32
Any Property Offense	68.5	59.6	47.8	46.4	42.1	31.0	27.7	140.2*	−.36
Any Offense	74.3	65.4	54.6	53.1	45.7	40.7	29.7	149.8*	−.38
Sample Size (Weighted)	593	289	246	269	241	122	127		

Table (continued)

Offense	17	18	19	20	21	22	23	Chi²	Gamma
	Age								
Females									
Hit Supervisor	1.6	.1	.2	.0	.2	.0	.0	18.8*	−.80
Fight at Work/School	9.9	7.2	7.1	6.3	6.1	3.2	7.4	11.4	−.16
Gang Fight	10.9	9.1	8.6	3.0	3.2	2.7	1.6	45.3*	−.38
Hurt Someone Badly	2.8	1.9	1.0	1.1	.5	.6	.7	12.3	−.41
Robbery	.7	1.0	1.0	.2	.1	.2	.0	5.6	−.34
Steal < $50	23.2	23.0	19.3	19.2	13.3	16.4	11.2	23.5*	−.17
Steal > $50	1.6	1.0	1.1	.6	2.3	1.1	1.6	4.0	−.01
Shoplift	26.6	18.2	15.4	12.7	8.0	11.8	7.0	80.4*	−.35
Joyride	2.3	1.9	2.0	.8	.4	.0	.9	9.8	−.36
Steal Car Parts	1.9	1.0	1.3	.1	.6	.0	1.3	9.5	−.35
Trespass	18.8	9.6	10.5	8.2	6.1	4.4	2.9	69.6*	−.38
Arson	.3	.0	.4	.1	.0	.0	.2	3.2	−.30
Damage School Property	6.4	3.3	2.5	1.5	1.4	1.1	.2	34.7*	−.50
Damage Work Property	1.9	1.7	1.1	2.0	1.1	1.7	1.1	2.0	−.09
Any Aggressive Offense	19.5	15.0	14.6	9.3	8.5	5.4	9.3	44.7*	−.28
Any Property Offense	45.0	34.7	29.3	28.3	18.9	22.7	16.8	104.1*	−.31
Any Offense	50.8	40.1	35.9	32.1	25.3	25.2	24.3	98.3*	−.29
Sample Size (Weighted)	676	318	304	314	306	157	147		

* p < .05

Source: Osgood et al. (1989, 398)

THE THEORY

To construct such a theory, it was first necessary to distinguish between crime and criminality, a distinction forced upon us by the age distribution of crimes. Crimes rise and fall during the life course, but *differences* in the tendency to commit criminal acts do not follow this pattern. Children in trouble with teachers in the 2nd and 3rd grades are more likely to be in trouble with juvenile authorities at 15 and 16; they are more likely to serve prison terms in their 20s; they are more likely to have trouble with their families and jobs at all ages.

So, to discuss the facts sensibly, we need something that may change with age and something that may not.

The changeable element is crime. Crimes are acts or events that take place at specific points in space and time. We began this chapter describing an event in east Texas in the summer of 1998. Three men tied another man to a battered pickup truck and dragged him to his death.

That is a crime: murder. A witness in a criminal trial lies under oath. That is a crime: perjury. A man drives after drinking ten cans of beer. That is a crime: driving under the influence. Crimes are very common. Each year in the United States, the police report about 15 million arrests to the Federal Bureau of Investigation (FBI).

The unchangeable element is criminality, the tendency of people to engage in or refrain from criminal acts.

Because criminality is a propensity or tendency, it cannot be counted, but it can be observed or measured. From such observation, we know that few people would allow themselves to be involved in the murder of a stranger. (In context, the oft-repeated statement that "everybody does it" is obviously foolish. It is usually foolish elsewhere as well.) We know that more people might, under the right circumstances, commit perjury. And we know that many would and do drive after drinking more than the law allows. In fact, experience shows that everyone is capable of criminal or deviant acts. More meaningfully, however, it shows that some are more likely than others actually to commit them. Criminality is a matter of degree.

With this distinction, the task of theory is clear: It is to identify and explain criminality and to relate it to the commission of criminal acts.

We begin by looking more closely at crimes and deviant acts. What do murder, perjury, and driving under the influence (and theft, assault, cheating on tests, burglary, robbery, forgery, and fraud) have in common? The Chinese have a saying: "Crime is as easy as falling down a mountain." Indeed, most crimes require no special learning or knowledge. Children invent them without help. Young people are their major practitioners. A fiendish and relatively complex murder may be committed by (1). wrapping a chain around an outnumbered man; (2). hooking it to a pickup bumper; (3). driving away. Most people know or could learn on the spot how to wrap and hook a chain, and most adults know how to drive. Perjury may be accomplished by saying "No" when what actually happened would require "Yes." The capacity for perjury is thus present the moment the child is able to affirm or deny the occurrence of an event. Driving drunk requires only the ability to drink and the ability to drive. The highest rates of drunk driving are found among those still learning these skills.

Most crimes take little time or effort. They are rarely the product of lengthy and elaborate preparation. Among our examples, drunk driving appears to be the most time-consuming but would not normally be considered hard work. In the United States, homicide is most often committed with a gun. In the typical case, the decision to aim and fire is made instantaneously, on the spot. Compared to this, our east Texas homicide

was unusually difficult, possibly requiring several minutes to accomplish. Perjury too may take only a split second. The consequences of perjury may be complicated, but the difficulties following the commission of a criminal or deviant act should not be confused with the act itself.

Indeed, another characteristic of criminal and deviant acts is that they entail just such long-term complications, difficulties, or costs. These costs or penalties are called *sanctions*. Following the British philosopher Jeremy Bentham ([1789] 1970), we identify four kinds of sanctions. *Physical* sanctions are those that follow naturally from the act, without the active intervention of others. Examples include hangovers and diminished health from the consumption of drugs, disease from promiscuous sexual activity, injuries from the actions of victims attempting to defend their persons or property, and diminished earning capacity from repeated truancy. *Moral* or *social* sanctions are those imposed by family, friends, neighbors, employers, clients, and constituents in the court of public opinion. They include divorce, shaming, shunning, and reduced responsibility and trust. *Political* or *legal* sanctions are those imposed by governments and organizations for violations of law. They include lines, imprisonment, and even execution. They also include expulsion and impeachment. *Religious* sanctions are those imposed by supernatural authorities, now and in the hereafter. Their form varies from one religion to another, but they are usually pictured as long-term and serious.

We often refer to the *risk* of legal and moral sanctions because they cannot be imposed unless the offender is convicted or caught in the act. This suggests the possibility of cost-free crime and deviance, depending on the luck of offenders or their ability to avoid detection. Indeed, religious sanctions are sometimes explained as an effort to solve this problem, as devices that punish deviant behavior whether or not it is seen by others. Self-control theory does not require supernatural or religious sanctions for several reasons: (1). It emphasizes often serious physical or natural sanctions whose application does not require third-party knowledge or intervention; (2), It emphasizes the generality of deviance, the tendency of people to repeat offenses and to be involved in a wide variety of them. As the level and variety of deviant activity increase, detection and automatic penalties become more and more certain; (3). It emphasizes the spontaneous and unplanned nature of criminal and deviant acts, a characteristic inconsistent with successful long-term concealment.

We now see another reason that reckless, deviant, criminal, and sinful acts tend to go together, to be committed by the same people: They all produce potentially painful consequences. Distinctions among deviant acts on the basis of the sanction system most concerned with them are to some extent arbitrary and misleading. Murder is a crime punished by the legal system, but it is also reckless, deviant, and sinful. In fact, one reason it is judged a crime is to control the natural tendency of the victim's family and friends to seek their own revenge. Perjury (lying under oath) is sometimes said to be the quintessential criminal act, but lying in other contexts is also subject to natural, social, and religious penalties. Driving under the influence of alcohol has only recently become a major concern of the criminal justice system. Not long ago, it was widely practiced and considered only mildly deviant. This should not be taken to mean that it was not punished. Whatever its legal or moral status, few acts are more reckless than drunk driving. Since the invention of the automobile, in the United States alone, drunk driving has killed hundreds of thousands of its practitioners (as well as countless others).

The idea that murder, perjury, drunk driving, and marijuana smoking (and all other criminal and delinquent acts) have something in common is sometimes met by such statements as: "Marijuana smoking is not murder!" "Sex is not shoplifting!" "Perjury is not driving under the influence!" Self-control theory does not say these acts are the same thing. It says they have something in common. This common element may be identified more clearly by focusing on the logical structure of criminal and deviant acts.

The logical structure of an act is the set of conditions necessary for it to occur. Each distinct criminal or deviant act has a unique set of necessary conditions. For example, smoking marijuana requires attractive (for reasons of cost, quality, and reputation) and available marijuana. It also requires an offender unrestrained by the consequences of marijuana use. Homicide is more complex. It requires interaction between an offender and a victim, an offender with the means of taking the

life of another, an offender insufficiently restrained to prevent the crime, a victim unable to remove himself from the scene, and absence of life-saving third-party intervention. (Life-saving intervention would make the crime attempted murder or aggravated assault.) Perjury is ultimately simple. It requires only a question asked of a person who has sworn to tell the truth, where that person is insufficiently restrained to prevent the crime. Driving under the influence combines the logical structure of two distinct acts. It requires a drug (usually alcohol) that is available and attractive to the offender, a vehicle that is accessible to the offender, an offender capable of operating the vehicle while intoxicated, and an offender insufficiently restrained to prevent the crime.

The element common to these acts (and all other criminal and deviant acts) is an unrestrained offender, a person willing to risk long-term costs for immediate personal benefits. Self-control theory says there is nothing extraordinarily attractive about the benefits of crime, that they may be found in noncriminal activities as well, and that in practice crime is not an efficient method of producing them. It says further that awareness and appreciation of the benefits of crime are not restricted to offenders. Everyone enjoys money, sex, power, excitement, ease, euphoria, and revenge. Everyone can see that crime provides a direct and easy way of obtaining them. So, according to the theory, the difference between offenders and nonoffenders is in their awareness of and concern for the long-term costs of crime—such things as arrest, prison, disgrace, disease, and even eternal damnation.

The idea that crime satisfies special needs and that offenders are strongly motivated to accomplish their purposes is accepted in many theories of crime and discussions of crime control policy. The source of this idea may be the obvious imbalance between the short-term and uncertain rewards of crime and its long-term and more certain penalties. Offenders often appear to trade a cow for a bag of beans, to risk powerful positions for brief sexual pleasures or small monetary gains. To strike such bargains, the logic goes, offenders must be driven by emotions (seductions and compulsions) of considerable strength. Self-control theory solves this "problem" by reducing the offender's awareness of or concern for the long term. What distinguishes offenders from others is not the strength of their appetites but their freedom to enjoy the quick and easy and ordinary pleasures of crime without undue concern for the pains that may follow them.

From the nature of crime, and acts analogous to crime, we thus infer the nature of criminality. People who engage in crime are people who tend to neglect long-term consequences. They are, or tend to be, children of the moment. They have what we call low self-control.

Where does low self-control come from? All of us, it appears, are born with the ability to use force and fraud in pursuit of our private goals. Small children can and do lie, bite, whine, hit, and steal. They also sometimes consider horrendous crimes they are too small to carry off. By the age of 8 or 10, most of us learn to control such tendencies to the degree necessary to get along at home and school. Others, however, continue to employ the devices of children, to engage in behavior inappropriate to their age. The differences observed at ages 8 to 10 tend to persist from then on. Good children remain good. Not so good children remain a source of concern to their parents, teachers, and eventually to the criminal justice system. These facts lead to the conclusion that low self-control is natural and that *self-control is acquired* in the early years of life.

Children presumably learn from many sources to consider the long-range consequences of their acts. One important source we previously called natural sanctions, penalties that follow more or less automatically from certain forms of behavior. The list is long. It include burns from hot stoves, bruises from falling down stairs or out of trees, and injuries from efforts to take things thought by others to belong to them. Obviously, natural sanctions can be dangerous and painful. In fact, the natural system is so unforgiving that parents and other adults spend a lot of their time protecting children from it.

But the major sources of self-control, in our view, are the actions of parents or other responsible adults. Parents who care for their children watch them as best they can. When they *see* their children doing something they should not do, they correct, admonish, or punish them. The logical structure of successful socialization thus has four necessary conditions: care, monitor, recognize (deviant behavior), and correct.

When all of these conditions are present, the child presumably learns to avoid acts with long-term negative consequences, whatever their legal or moral status. When any one of them is missing, continued low self-control may be the result. Delinquency research provides strong support for these conclusions. It shows that the greater the attachment of the parent to the child, the lower the likelihood of delinquency. It shows that careful supervision and adequate discipline are among the most important predictors of nondelinquency. By extension, this child-rearing model goes a long way toward explaining all of the major family factors in crime; neglect, abuse, single parents, large number of children, parental criminality. All of these are measures of the extent of parental concern for the child or are conditions that affect the ability of the parent to monitor and correct the child's behavior. As would be expected, they are also major predictors of behaviors we call analogous to crime: truancy, quitting school, smoking, excessive drinking, and job instability.

We are now ready to use the theory to explain criminal, deviant, and reckless acts. Persons deficient in self-control are attracted to acts that provide immediate and apparently certain pleasure with minimal effort, whatever their collateral consequences. Criminal, deviant, and reckless acts fit this definition. In many, force and fraud speed up the process and reduce the effort required to produce the desired result. In others, mind-altering chemicals provide shortcuts to happiness. In still others, the pleasure inheres in the act itself or in the risks it entails.

Persons sufficient in self-control avoid such acts because they find that their collateral consequences outweigh their benefits. Force and fraud in the service of self-interest are opposed by the law and by most people (including those lacking self-control). Drugs entail risks to self and others inconsistent with long-term goals. And reckless behavior gains its charm from the very possibility that it may put an end to future prospects, whatever they may be.

Theories explain facts by stating general propositions from which specific facts may be derived. For example, in Newton's theory, apples fall to earth *because* every particle of matter in the universe is attracted by every other particle. The larger the particle, the stronger the attraction. We often condense this explanation into one word, *gravity*, but the truth and value of the explanation are not reduced by this practice. By the same logic, in self-control theory, people commit criminal acts because they fail to consider their long-term consequences. This explanation, too, may be condensed into a single concept, (low) self-control, but its truth and value are not reduced by this practice.

Other theories of course also explain crime by stating general principles from which specific acts can be derived. For example, traditional strain theory would say that people commit criminal acts because they have been blocked from attaining success by noncriminal or conventional means. And social learning theory might explain crime by saying that people commit criminal acts because they have learned such behavior from their peers. Choosing among theories is not, then, so much a matter of their logic as of their relative ability to predict the facts about crime and criminals.

TESTS OF SELF-CONTROL THEORY

Our version of self-control theory was published in 1990, which makes it a new or contemporary theory. Given the traditions of the field, new theories are by definition untested. They are hypotheses or conjectures whose fate depends on the results of research not yet conducted. This suggests that new theories are more problematic than theories that have withstood efforts to test or falsify them. Actually, the reverse should be true. If theories are logical systems based on current understandings of the facts, new theories should be especially consistent with the results of current research. And the use of old theories to explain facts they once ignored or denied should be viewed with considerable suspicion.

Self-control theory is based on and, therefore, "predicts" the following facts:

- Differences between high- and low-rate offenders persist over the life course. Children ranked on the frequency of their delinquent acts will be ranked similarly later in life. This is not to say "once a criminal always a criminal." It is to say that differences in tendencies to commit crime, like differences in height, maintain themselves over long

periods of time. This is among the best-established facts in criminology (Nagin and Paternoster 1991; Gendreau, Little, and Goggin 1996).

- Efforts to treat or rehabilitate offenders do not produce the desired results. The search for effective treatment programs of course continues. But research continues to show that once tendencies to engage in crime and delinquency have been established, successful treatment is, at a minimum, extraordinarily difficult; (Martinson 1974a; Sechrest et al. 1979. For a strongly contrary view, see Andrews et al. 1990).
- Intervention efforts in childhood offer the greatest promise of success in crime reduction (Tremblay et al. 1992).
- The law enforcement or criminal justice system has little effect on the volume of criminal behavior. Offenders do not attend to increases in the number of police or in the severity of penalties for violations of law (Andrews et al. 1990).
- Crimes may be prevented by increasing the effort required to commit them (Murray 1995).
- Crime declines with age among all groups of offenders and in almost all types of offending (Cohen and Land 1987; Gottfredson and Hirschi 1990).
- Offenders do not specialize in particular forms of crime. Career criminals are extremely rare (Wolfgang et al. 1972; Britt 1994).
- Offenders have higher accident, illness, and death rates than nonoffenders (Farrington and Junger 1995).
- Offenders are more likely than nonoffenders to use legal and illegal drugs (Boyum and Kleiman 1995).
- Offenders are more frequently involved in noncriminal forms of deviance (Evans et al. 1997).
- Offenders are more weakly attached than nonoffenders to restrictive institutions and long-term careers—families, schools, jobs (Glueck and Glueck 1968).
- Compared to nonoffenders, offenders are disadvantaged with respect to intellectual or cognitive skills (Hirschi and Hindelang 1977).
- Family structure, family relations, and childrearing practices are important predictors of deviant

behavior (Glueck and Glueck 1950; Loeber and Stout Hamer-Loeber 1986).

In our view, these facts have been repeatedly confirmed by research. In our view, self-control theory is consistent with all of them, something that cannot be said for any of its competitors.

POLICY IMPLICATIONS OF THE THEORY

The control theory approach to policy is to analyze the features of the criminal act and the characteristics of offenders and to pattern prevention efforts accordingly. The major relevant characteristics of offenders are youthfulness, limited cognitive skills, and low self-control. Because the rates of such important crimes as burglary, robbery, theft, shoplifting, and vandalism all peak in mid- to late adolescence and fall to half their peak levels as early as the mid-twenties, effective crime control policies will naturally focus on the interests and activities of teenagers. Because the cognitive skills of offenders are relatively limited, their criminal acts are typically simple and easily traced. As a result, policies targeting sophisticated offenders or career criminals are unnecessarily complex and inefficient. Because offenders have low self-control, they are easily deterred by increasing the immediate difficulties and risks of criminal acts and are generally unaffected by changes in the long-term costs of criminal behavior. Consequently, steering wheel locks are more effective than increased penalties in reducing auto theft, and moving in groups is more effective than increased police presence in preventing robbery.

The characteristics of criminal acts relevant to their prevention have been listed earlier. Crimes provide immediate, obvious benefit, are easily accomplished, and require little skill, planning, or persistence. They involve no driving force beyond the satisfaction of everyday human desires. Because people do not suffer when criminal opportunities are unavailable to them, crimes can be prevented by making them more complex or difficult. For example, increasing the cost of alcohol or banning its use in particular settings will often produce the desired result with little effort. Guarding parking lots or apartment complexes can also be effective in preventing theft and vandalism.

Although it focuses on an element common to all forms of crime and deviance, low self-control, self-control theory actually supports an offense-specific approach to crime prevention. Procedures for preventing one type of crime may be inapplicable to others. Effective efforts to control hijacking have no impact on vandalism or burglary. Offense-specific approaches begin by analyzing the conditions necessary for a particular act to occur. Graffiti, for example, requires spray paint and large, accessible, paintable, generally observable surfaces that are unguarded for a predictable period of time. It also requires an unrestrained offender. Graffiti may be controlled by removing any one of its necessary physical conditions or by altering the behavior of unrestrained offenders. Clearly, efforts directed at offenders—treatment, deterrence, incapacitation—will be highly inefficient compared to programs that restrict access to paint and to paintable surfaces.

Self-control theory is based on the idea that behavior is governed by its consequences. As we have seen, this idea is also central to the criminal justice system, according to which crime may be reduced by increasing the likelihood and severity of such legal sanctions as fines and imprisonment. Nevertheless, self-control theory leads to the conclusion that the formal criminal justice system can play only a minor role in the prevention and control of crime. Because potential offenders do not consider the long-term legal consequences of their acts, modification of these consequences will have little effect on their behavior. Because criminal acts are so quickly and easily accomplished, they are only rarely directly observed by agents of the criminal justice system. As a result, even large increases in the number of such agents would have minimal effect on the rates of most crimes.

These and other considerations led us to advance the following recommendations for crime control policy (from Gottfredson and Hirschi 1995):

1. Do not attempt to control crime by incapacitating adults. A major factor in the decision to incarcerate offenders is the number of prior offenses they have committed. The result is that adults are much more likely to be imprisoned than adolescents. Most people would agree that prior records

should be considered, but the age distribution of crime (see Figure 2) shows us that putting adults in prison is ineffective because by then it is too late. They are too old. The average age of persons sentenced to prison is the late twenties, more than ten years after the peak age of crime.

2. Do not attempt to control the crime rate by rehabilitating adults. As has been shown above, there are two very good arguments against treatment programs for adult offenders. The first is the age effect, which makes treatment unnecessary. The second is that no treatment program for adults has been shown to be effective. If nothing but time works, it seems ill-advised to pretend otherwise.

3. Do not attempt to control crime by altering the penalties available to the criminal justice system. Legal penalties do not have the desired effect because offenders do not consider them. Increasing their certainty and severity may make citizens and policymakers feel better about the justice system, but it will have a highly limited effect on the decisions of offenders.

4. Restrict the unsupervised activities of teenagers. Crime requires opportunity and unrestrained individuals. Much can be gained from limiting access of teenagers to guns, cars, alcohol, unwatched walls, unattended houses, and to each other. One of the great success stories of the last quarter of the century was the reduction in fatal auto accidents that followed increases in the drinking age. Curfews, truancy prevention programs, school uniforms, and license restrictions—all of these have potential value for the same reason.

5. Limit proactive policing including police sweeps, police stings, intensive arrest programs, and aggressive drug policies. Control theory sees crime as a product of human weakness. It sees no point in creating opportunities for crime in order to identify those suffering from such weakness. It sees no point in exploiting such weakness merely for the benefit of the law enforcement establishment.

6. Question the characterization of crime offered by agents of the criminal justice system and uncritically repeated by the media. The evidence suggests that offenders are not the dedicated, inventive, and clever professionals law enforcement and the media often make them out to be. In fact, control theory questions the very existence of huge juvenile gangs and highly organized criminal syndicates. Where, the theory asks, do people unable to resist the pleasures of drugs and theft and truancy and violence find the discipline to construct organizations that force them to resist such pleasures?

7. Support programs designed to provide early education and effective child care. Programs that target dysfunctional families and seek to remedy lack of supervision have been shown to have promise. This does not contradict the control theory notion that self-control is acquired early in life. The finding that nothing works in the treatment area may be limited to programs focusing on adolescents and adults.

8. Support policies that promote and facilitate two-parent families and that increase the number of caregivers relative to the number of children. Large families and single-parent families are handicapped with respect to monitoring and discipline. As a consequence, their children are more likely to commit criminal acts and are especially more likely to become involved with the criminal justice system. A major source of weak families is unmarried pregnancy among adolescent girls, which is itself important evidence of low self-control. Programs to prevent such pregnancies should therefore be given high priority.

CRITICISMS OF THE THEORY

Self-control theory is among the most frequently tested theories in the field of crime and delinquency. It is also frequently criticized. These criticisms are concentrated around three more or less traditional issues: (1) the definition of the dependent variable—crime and deviant behavior; (2) the logical structure of the theory; and (3) the ability of the theory to deal with particular offenses.

THE DEPENDENT VARIABLE

Self-control theory attempts to explain short-term self-interested behavior that entails the risk of long-term sanctions. Because it is framed without regard to the law, this definition includes acts that may not be defined as criminal and may exclude acts defined as criminal by the jurisdiction in question. Examples of the first are behaviors we have labeled "analogous to crime" (e.g., premarital pregnancy, divorce, job-quitting, accidents). Examples of the second are terrorism and espionage, acts committed on behalf of political organizations. The definition also excludes the use of force or fraud in the public interest or as required by the legal system (e.g., killings by soldiers, undercover activities by police, forced removals of property owners by university officials).

This definition of crime is very different from the traditional definition, according to which crime is restricted to and includes all behavior "in violation of law." How can we exclude behavior that is clearly criminal by the laws or norms of all societies (terrorism) and include behavior that is rarely if ever punished by the state (accidents)? The answer is that we have no choice in this matter. Theories define the behavior they explain and their definition cannot be changed without changing them. Terrorist acts are excluded from self-control theory because they are assumed to reflect commitment to a political cause or organization. Terrorists do not act without regard for the broad or long-term consequences of their acts. On the contrary, their purpose is to alter the status quo. However heinous the consequences of their acts, and however severely they are punished by the state, they do not meet the requirement common to acts explained by control theory—that they be committed by an unrestrained offender.

The seriousness of this criticism of self-control theory will depend on the range and frequency of acts it fails to cover As far as we can see, this number is small, especially when compared to the theory's coverage of the very large number of acts ignored by traditional definitions of crime.

LOGICAL STRUCTURE

Self-control theory says that crime is the best predictor of crime and that self-control is the element common to the crimes of interest. These statements are often described as tautological, a serious criticism of the theory in the eyes of many social scientists. One meaning of *tautology* is "repetition; saying or, by extension, doing the same thing again." The *Oxford Universal Dictionary* lists an example from 1687: "Our whole Life is but a nauseous Tautology." This statement introduces another meaning of the term: The repetition described is trivial, pointless, or worse.

That crimes repeat themselves may be tautological, and some criminologists have indeed labeled this fact "trivial and theoretically pointless" (Akers 1998, 168–169). But such repetition is neither logically nor empirically necessary. It cannot therefore possibly be a valid criticism of control theory. Theories are not responsible for the nauseousness of the behavior they attempt to explain.

Another meaning of *tautology* is that the logical relations among concepts may be derived from their definitions. Thus, if low self-control is defined by willingness to engage in behavior with long-term negative consequences, and *crime* is defined as behavior with long-term negative consequences, a relation between low self-control and crime is logically necessary or tautological. The theory repeats the definition and vice versa. We do not deny the tautological or circular nature of self-control theory. On the contrary, we believe that pure theory is always tautological in this sense of the term (Hirschi and Selvin [1967] 1994). Definitions entail theories. Theories entail definitions, It cannot be otherwise. The source of confusion appears to be the belief among social scientists that tautological theories cannot be falsified. This belief, in our view, is demonstrably false.

Applicability of the Theory to Particular Crimes.

In constructing self-control theory, we tried to concentrate on the characteristics of ordinary crimes. This led us to emphasize their triviality and predictability, the ease and speed with which they are committed, the small losses and smaller gains they typically involve. The purpose was to avoid the distractions that come from looking first or mainly at large, serious, or apparently bizarre crimes, crimes that attract the attention of the media and criminal justice system. This strategy has led some critics of the theory to the conclusion that it applies only to the ordinary, mundane crimes from which it was constructed. We believe this conclusion ignores the success of our strategy in revealing features shared by rare and common, serious and trivial offenses. Indeed, we began this essay with a rare and most serious offense to show that it fell easily within the scope of the theory.

Other crimes said at one time or another to fall outside the scope of the theory include income tax evasion, white-collar crime, corporate crime, organized crime, and gambling. Tests of these alleged exceptions seem to us straightforward. Those involved in crimes where self-control is not a factor should be otherwise indistinguishable from the law-abiding population. As of now, it seems to us, the evidence on these matters points in directions favorable to the theory. Those involved in such apparently exceptional crimes tend to have been involved in other forms of crime and deviance as well (Le Blanc and Kaspy 1998).

REFERENCES

Akers, Ronald. (1998). *Social Learning and Social Structure: A General Theory of Crime and Deviance.* Boston: Northeastern University Press.

Andrews, D.A., Ivan Zinger, Robert D. Hoge, James Bonta, Paul Gendreau, & Francis T. Cullen. (1990). "Does correctional treatment work? A clinically relevant and psychologically informed meta-analysis." *Criminology,* 28:369–404.

Bentham, Jeremy. [1789] (1970). *An Introduction to the Principles of Morals and Legislation.* Reprint. London: The Althone.

Boyum. David & Mark A. R. Kleiman. (1995). "Alcohol and other drugs." Pp. 295–326 in J.Q. Wilson and J. Petersilia (eds.). *Crime.* San Francisco: ICS.

Britt, Chester L. (1994). "Versatility." Pp. 173–192 in T. Hirschi and M.R. Gottfredson (eds.), *The Generality of Deviance.* New Brunswick, NJ: Transaction.

Cohen, Lawrence C. & Kenneth C. Land. (1987). "Age structure and crime: Symmetry versus asymmetry and the projection of crime rates through the 1990s." *American Sociological Review,* 52:170–183.

Coleman, James. (1990). *Foundations of Social Theory.* Cambridge, MA: Belknap.

Evans, T., F. Cullen, V. Burton, R. Dunaway, & M. Benson. (1997). "The social consequences of self-control: Testing the general theory of crime." *Criminology,* 35:475–504.

Farrington, David P. & Marianne Junger (eds.). (1995). *Criminal Behavior and Mental Health,* 5(4): Special Issue.

Gendreau, Paul, Tracy Little, & Claire Goggin. (1996). "A meta-analysis of the predictors of adult offender recidivism: What works!" *Criminology,* 34:575–607.

Glueck, Sheldon & Eleanor Glueck. (1940). *Juvenile Delinquents Grown Up.* New York: Commonwealth Fund.

_____. (1950). *Unraveling Juvenile Delinquency.* Cambridge, MA: Harvard University Press.

_____. (1968). *Delinquents and Nondeliquents in Perspective.* Cambridge, MA: Harvard University Press.

Goring, Charles. (1913). *The English Convict.* Montelair. NJ: Patterson Smith.

Gottfredson, Michael R. & Travis Hirschi. (1990). *A General Theory of Crime.* Stanford, CA: Stanford University Press.

_____. (1995). "National crime control policies." *Society,* 32:30–37.

Hirschi, Travis. (1969), *Causes of Delinquency.* Berkeley: University of California Press.

_____. (1975). "Labeling theory and juvenile delinquency: An assessment of the evidence." Pp. 181–203 in Walter Gove (ed.), *The Labeling of Deviance.* Halsted.

Hirschi. Travis & Michael Gottfredson. (1983). "Age and the explanation of crime." *American Journal of Sociology,* 89:552–584.

Hirschi, Travis & Michael J. Hindelang. (1977). "Intelligence and delinquency: A revisionist review." *American Sociological Review.* 42:571–187.

Hirschi. Travis & Hunan C. Selvin. [1967] (1994). *Delinquency Research: An Appraisal of Analytic Methods.* New Brunswick. NJ: Transaction.

Le Blanc, Marc & Nathalie Kaspy. (1998). "Trajectories of delinquency and problem behavior: Comparison of social and personal control characteristics of adjudicated boys on synchronous and nonsynchronous paths." *Journal of Quantitative Criminology,* 14:181–214.

Loeber, Rolf & Magda Stouthamer-Loeber. (1986). "Family factors as correlates and predictors of juvenile conduct problems and delinquency." Pp. 29–149 in M.H. Tonry & N. Morris (eds.), *Crime and Justice: A Review of Research*. Chicago: University of Chicago Press.

Martinson, Robert. (1974a). "What works? Questions and answers about prison reform." *The Public Interest*, Spring, 35:22–54.

_____.(1974b). The myth of treatment and the reality of life process. April. Paper delivered at the Eastern Psychological Association, "Philadelphia."

Murray, Charles. (1995). "The physical environment." Pp. 349–361 in J.Q. Wilson and J. Petersilia (eds.), *Crime*. San Francisco: ICS.

Nagin, Daniel S. & Raymond Paternoster. (1991). "On the relationship of past to future participation in delinquency." *Criminology*, 29:163–189.

Osgood, D. Wayne, Patrick M. O'Malley, Jerald G. Bachman, & Lloyd D. Johnston. (1989). "Time trends and age trends in arrests and self-reported illegal behavior." *Criminology*, 27:389–417.

Quetelet, Lambert A.J. [1833] (1969). *A Treatise on Man*. Gainesville, FL: Scholars' Facsimiles and Reprints.

Sechrest, Lee, Susan O. White, & Elizabeth Brown (eds.): (1979). The *Rehabilitation of Criminal Offenders: Problems and Prospects*. Washington, DC: National Academy of Sciences.

Toby, Jackson. (1957). "Social disorganization" and stake in conformity: Complementary factors in the predatory behavior of hoodlums." *Journal of Criminal Law, Criminology, and Police Science*, 48:12–17.

Tremblay, Richard E., Frank Vitaro, Lucie Bertrand, Marc LeBlanc, Helene Beauchesne, Helene Boileau, & Lucille David. (1992). "Parent and child training to prevent early onset of delinquency: A Montreal Longitudinal-Experimental Study." Pp. 117–138 in J. McCord and R. Tremblay (eds.), *Preventing Antisocial Behavior*. New York: Guilford.

Wolfgang. Marvin, Robert Figlio, & Thorsten Sellin. (1972). *Delinquency in a Birth Cohort*-Chicago: University of Chicago Press.

PART
III

Macro-Level Structural Theories

PART III INTRODUCTION

Macro-Level Structural Theories

So far we have only looked at micro-level theories that either focus on individual free choice (classical and rational choice, routine activities) or on the more deterministic biological differences and psychological and personality propensities that predispose people to the potential for committing crime. We have also seen social process theories that explain crime by humans' exposure to different kinds of interaction with their peers and parents that socialize them into the norms and values of deviant subcultures, or that fail to sufficiently bond them into the norms, values and behavior of convention. In Part 3 of this book we change up the analytical level of theory from the individual/group to social institutions, social structure, and culture of the wider society.

These kinds of analysis are described as "macro-level," which refers to social and cultural forces that shape the institutions, families and groups as well as the individual social actor embedded within them. Social forces include class, race and gender each of which, or their intersections, can significantly impact a person's life choices by limiting them from what they might have been and channeling them toward a certain set of choices. A simple example will illustrate the point. Consider the different life chances of a white female teen from an established well-to-do family in Wellfleet, Massachusetts who goes to Wellesley College, compared with a black female from New Orleans' 9th Ward who stops attending high school to look after her younger siblings because her single parent mother is working. The "life chances" for each of these teenagers is likely to be very different as each has a different cultural, structural, and class location which transcends their individual characteristics, personality and abilities. If we add gender to the demographic profile the teenager from Wellfleet is likely to experience an even greater experiential divide than an African American male from New Orleans. But these forces are not inevitable or consistent in determining outcomes as New Orleans native and jazz impresario Branford Marsalis or Serena and Venus Williams from Compton California, demonstrate; however, as far as the general trend is concerned Branford, Serena and Venus are exceptions. From a criminological perspective, even though we might think of these wider systems and structures as having distant (distal rather than proximate) effects, those effects acutely reach into family, education, and career possibilities and they also channel children and teenagers subject to them into different kinds of encounters with the law. These encounters have different consequences and are shaped by the structural and cultural contexts in which people are located.

There are a number of macro-level forces and in this part of the book (Part 3) we are going to consider just two kinds: (1) Social Ecology Theory and (2) Anomie/Strain Theory. In the next part of the book (Part 4) we will consider a range of critical macro-theories that take a different interpretation of the way structural and cultural forces shape crime and behavior.

SOCIAL ECOLOGY AND SUBCULTURAL THEORIES

Influenced by geography and the importance of a person's spatial location, social ecology theories (Amos 1950), founded by the Chicago School of Sociology in 1920s and 30s (Park et al. 1925; Shaw & McKay 1942; Shaw, Burgess & McKenzie 1929; Thrasher 1927) share a view "that the characteristics of specific places and/or cultural groups may make a person who inhabits those spaces, or who is engaged in the social networks formed in them, more or less prone to engage in crime" (Henry & Lanier 2006, p. 129). Research over the years tends to support the common-sense view that some neighborhoods are "bad" or more crime-prone than others, e.g. "crack city," the "red light district," "the barrio," etc. As Robert Sampson (1997, p. 38) has argued "the empirical data suggest that the structural elements of social disorganization have relevance for explaining macro-level variations in violence." This means that these locations contain a higher than average rate of street crime. Whether this crime is indigenous to the area or imported into the area because of its reputation is not always clear. What is clear is that rates of arrest for "street crime" in these areas are higher than in other areas, and that people who do not want to participate in crime, as a perpetrator or a victim, avoid the area. Social ecologists ask questions about whether there is something about the area and about those drawn to an area that makes it more crime prone than other areas.

One answer to this provided by social ecologists is social disorganization. Areas with dilapidated housing stock, that have become run down or "blighted," encourage a diverse range of immigrants and others at the bottom end of the socio-economic spectrum to the area because of low rents. However, these areas typically lack community integrity and experience fragmentation that reduces the effectiveness of informal social control among neighbors and community members over each other and each other's children. This absence of control allows conflict between groups to gain traction and for crime and law violation to go uncontrolled. In short, communities in transition lead to low levels of social organization that reduce informal social control which allows crime to run rampant.

As mentioned earlier, crime as an outcome is not inevitable. Where neighborhoods within crime-prone areas seem insulated from, or experience less crime, this is believed to result from supportive community or church-based networks with close ties in organized communities. Where neighborhoods are more prone to crime these communities are seen as fractured or broken: "Crime occurs not because residents are forced into offending, but because they make choices that are environmentally structured toward predatory actions—choices limited by the meaning of life in impoverished and disorganized settings" (Henry & Lanier 2006, p. 129).

Areas of cities that are constantly in population transition with people moving in and out, coming as immigrants, tend to become areas with higher rates of crime (at least street crime), relative to those found in more stable suburban environments. Chicago sociologists were one of the first to point his out, although 19th Century English historians and demographers such as Charles Booth, documented such neighborhoods in the heart of London. These "rookeries" were rife with gin houses and houses of debauchery, as well as infamous gambling parlors and shops for receiving stolen property: "Generally, the geographic area in question is a particular neighborhood and the crime-promoting tendency is often related to the economic and social factors that shape and sustain these neighborhoods, such as poverty, high density population, social disorganization, and conflicting cultures or subcultures. The economic factors are themselves tied to the politics of urban development, urban land use, and the alienation and abandonment experienced by those who inhabit these areas. Inhabitants of blighted neighborhoods feel excluded from the mainstream of society and, as a result, become hostile to all but those in, or closest to, their particular ethnic group" (Henry & Lanier 2006, pp. 129–130).

Perhaps not surprisingly, residents strive to leave these blighted unstable neighborhoods to live in better areas, and this movement out (whether white or black flight) has an intensifying or amplifying effect on a deteriorating neighborhood. This is because when the most successful residents are able to move out to the suburbs, those with the greatest amount of problems remain and become concentrated. This results in a loss of adequate role models for children in those neighborhoods, children who didn't choose to be born there, which further demoralizes the remaining residents who often live in isolation. This in turn makes those left behind even more vulnerable to victimization as vital networks of informal social control are further undermined.

There are pockets of resistance to the circumstances ordained by such crime-prone locations and these areas typically become the catalyst for gangs to form which provide protection to their members from the anonymity and lack of community in the neighborhoods. Gangs, criminal or deviant, form because of the migration and transience of the areas, rather than anything particular about the individuals who live in the neighborhoods.

One pattern of gang formation deriving from socially disorganized neighborhoods occurs because of migration to a neighborhood that is affordable, which is typically low income and already rife with problems. Sub-groups within a larger culture may have long-standing differences with the mainstream culture from which they disaffect, and they also may have differences with other subcultures in a neighborhood. Feelings of isolation and alienation from the mainstream and other cultural groups can lead to formation of self-protective groups, including gangs, that are in conflict with each other struggling over territory, identity and reputation. Some gangs have become permanent features of certain urban areas with organizational features that span generations. As a means to sustain their autonomy and enhance their reputation these gangs may be involved in both violent crime and property crime, as well as drug trafficking and human sex trafficking.

Such crime creating or "socially toxic" environments provide a policy challenge since it is not effective to deal with crime at an individual or group level. Even if treatment, training, skill development and the inculcation of coping strategies are able to insulate some individuals from the impact of the toxic social environment, the major challenge is at a different structural level. Consider the analogy of the bad apple verses the bad barrel. Even putting good apples in a bad barrel will turn many of them bad; the problem, in other words, is more systemic than individual. Indeed, the level of community or neighborhood is seen as a sociological problem requiring change to communities, geographic regions, and particularly to the economic and political forces that shape these areas.

One such local-level but national policy that can make a difference to the structure of a neighborhood or community is problem-solving community policing where police work in partnership with community members to develop solutions to area problems to prevent crime, rather than simply engaging in arrest and incarceration. This is combined with the idea of "broken windows" in which dilapidations, vandalism and graffiti are removed and cleaned up immediately, to demonstrate that people care and are in control.

At a broader level beyond policing practices are policies that lie outside the criminal justice system that affect land use and urban design that change the face of neighborhood blight. The permanence, rather than transience, of criminal areas has led to social disorganization theorists, and social ecologists more generally, to explore the importance of "collective efficacy" and neighborhood empowerment, not least through the concept of "'social capital,' the dense social ties that produce supportive, nurturing, resource-sponsoring, self-monitoring, and safe and social environments" (Henry & Lanier 2006, p. 131).

ANOMIE AND STRAIN THEORIES

The second kind of macro-level theory stems from the work of one of the "Founding Fathers" of sociology, Emile Durkheim (1892), who wrote about the challenges to society in the 19th century as it underwent major structural change: from one dominated by agriculture and small-scale, face-to-face communities to one dominated by industrial production, specialization and high levels of division of labor. Like social disorganization theory, anomie contrasts tight-knit communities that have high levels of informal social control, with fragmented communities having fewer obligations among their members and lower levels of social control. However, unlike social disorganization theory, which talks about community breakdown in urban contexts, specifically cities, anomie theory talks about a system-wide societal change that moves society from a social structure characterized by similarity and common or shared values among its members, to one characterized by differences, including differences in values.

Anomie states that at times of rapid change the divisions created to maximize the production of goods and services through manufacturing, and eventually services, can undermine the moral regulation of behavior. Where this structural change is accompanied by a culture that celebrates individual achievement and success (egotistical), and de-emphasizes social responsibility, altruism and mutual interdependence, then the outcome is unlimited aspirations, some of which are pursued through criminal behavior. Durkheim argued that this didn't have to be the outcome if people recognized their interdependence on each other and if those with the best abilities rose to the positions in society to which they were best suited (meritocracy). He also said that new forms of moral regulation would emerge around occupational specializations. However, he did not anticipate that this would more likely lead to a competition of special interest groups, than to mutual collaboration and interdependent community.

Anomie theory then explicitly links macro-level variables (the type of society, free market capitalism, for example) with micro-level behavior (such as frustration, anger, depression, suicide, or crime). It explores how the total organization of a society impacts the behavior of its members, and asserts that some *forms* of societal organization produce more crime than others. As Durkheim revealed, from the point of view of these theories, "crime is a normal reaction to abnormal circumstances. Thus, the 'health' of a society can be determined by the amount of crime present or by the ineffectiveness of the society's social institutions

to ameliorate these problems. Surprisingly, too little crime is just as pathological as too much crime. Too little crime would represent a rigid, over-controlling social system. Too much crime would be found in societies undergoing rapid transformation" (Henry & Lanier 2006, p. 154).

In this tradition a recent theoretical development is "institutional anomie theory" (Messner & Rosenfeld 1994), in which the materiality of industrial society is based on success, measured by monetary achievements, is manifest in the American Dream, and is seen to drive the character of its social institutions, such as education, health care, etc. This over-emphasis on materiality undermines these institutions' ability to provide adequate moral control, resulting in higher rates of crime since all means to achieve material goals are believed to be acceptable, including illegal ones.

Institutional anomie theory not only builds on Durkheim's original insights but also that of Robert Merton (1934; 1957) who in the 1930s after the Great Depression wrote about the differential access to the American Dream. What has become known as "strain theory," sees a clash between the inequality of the social structure and its culturally uniform goals that drive society's members to pursue the American Dream. "Pursuing the American Dream is a driving force for much behavior; if the Dream is blocked, the result can be frustration, depression and anger, emotions that can convert to illegal behavior, either as an illicit means to achieve the desired goals, or as a reaction to what is perceived as unjust treatment by the system" (Henry & Lanier 2006, p. 154). This mismatch between goals and the institutionally provided means to achieve them leads to structural strain and relative deprivation; those without the means are denied reaching these commonly shared cultural goals, such as material success: owning a house, a car etc. In contrast, those who have the means succeed in achieving these goals, forcing the under-achievers into a state of relative deprivation. Adaptations to the strain of perceived relative deprivation included deviance, some of which can involve crime, committed individually or collectively through subcultures and gangs who use illegitimate means to achieve these same material goals of success.

However, some such as Nicos Passas (1990), point out that strain does not just affect lower class members of society who cannot achieve the culturally prescribed goals of materialism, but it also impacts corporations and white collar offenders who cheat (use illegitimate means) to maximize their achievement of goals.

Robert Agnew (1992) developed what he calls a "General Strain Theory" that took this theory in a different direction, giving less importance to structural strain and more importance to social and psychological and emotional strain that results from situations in which people find their lives and opportunities blocked or are unachievable and they are forced to suffer pain and frustration as a result. His version of strain is more micro- than macro- in its level of analysis but shows how people can become alienated and frustrated from their inability to escape their present situation and that this results in anger that can turn violent.

As Henry and Lanier (2006) point out, the policy implications of these various macro-level theories involve a variety of ways to change the society, including lowering aspirations, reducing inequalities, and enabling those suffering strain to better cope with it. By far the majority of policy suggestions and implementations from traditional strain theories have attempted to increase access to legitimate opportunities. Others, such as Agnew, have suggested intervening at the micro-level by stopping people treating others badly, increasing their social supports and coping mechanisms. Few have been brave enough to challenge the deep-seated forces that create these structural strains in the first place.

REFERENCES

Agnew, R. (1992). "Foundation for a General Strain Theory." *Criminology* 30(1), 47–87.

Durkheim, E. (1893; 1933). *Division of Labor in Society.* New York: Free Press.

Durkheim, E. (1897/1997). *Suicide.* NY: Free Press.

Hawley, A. H. (1950). *Human Ecology: A Theory of Community Structure.* New York: Ronald Press.

Henry, S. & Lanier, M. M. (Eds.) (2006). *The Essential Criminology Reader.* Boulder, CO: Westview Press.

Merton, R.K. (1957). *Social Theory and Social Structure.* New York: Free Press.

Messner, S. & Rosenfeld, R. (1994). *Crime and the American Dream.* Belmont: Wadsworth.

Park, R. E., Burgess, E., & McKenzie, R. (1925). *The City.* University of Chicago Press.

Passas, N. (1990). "Anomie and Corporate Deviance." *Contemporary Crises* 14(3):157–78.

Sampson, R. J. (1997). "The embeddedness of child and adolescent development: A community-level perspective on urban violence." In McCord, J., (Ed.), *Violence and Childhood in the Inner City*, (pp. 31–77). Cambridge: Cambridge University Press.

Shaw, C. R. & McKay, H. D. (1942). *Juvenile Delinquency in Urban Areas.* Chicago: University of Chicago Press.

Shaw, C. R., Zorbaugh, H., McKay, H. D. & Cottrell, L. S. (1929). *Delinquency Areas.* Chicago: University of Chicago Press.

Thrasher, F. (1927) *The Gang.* Chicago: University of Chicago Press.

CHAPTER VI

Social Ecology and Subcultural Theories

SOCIAL DISORGANIZATION THEORY

Jeffery T. Walker

A description of the history and current state of social disorganization theory is not a simple undertaking, not because of a lack of information but because of an abundance of it. From its beginnings in the study of urban change and in plant biology, research related to social disorganization theory has spread to many different fields. These areas of concentration range from simple spin-offs of the original studies (Bordua 1959; Chilton 1964; Lander 1954), to the variety of research in environmental criminology (Brantingham & Brantingham 1981), to the growing field related to crime mapping (Chainey & Rafcliffe 2005), to such far-reaching topics as the behavior of fighting dogs (Stewart 1974). Given the space limitations, this chapter limits its discussion to studies closely related to the original principles of the theory.

PRECURSORS OF SOCIAL DISORGANIZATION THEORY

The forerunners of social disorganization research are probably more varied than any other area of criminological thought. The ecological study of delinquency is the result of the unlikely combination of the study of change in France, plant biology, and the growth of the urban city.

The direct lineage of social disorganization research is found in the study of plant biology. Warming (1909) proposed that plants live in "communities" with varying states of symbiosis, or natural interdependence. Communities containing plants predominantly of the same species were more in competition with nature than with each other. Communities with several different species, however, competed for limited resources more among themselves than with the environment. Warming called this relationship a *natural economy* because of the use of resources by the plants. This natural economy was expounded on by a Haeckel (1866), who used the German word *oikos*, from which economics was formed to coin the term *ecology*.

One of the first social ecological studies was conducted by Guerry in 1833. Guerry compared the crime rates in 86 departments (counties) in France from 1825 through 1830. His study showed that crime rates had marked variation in different cities in the country. Similar studies compared different regions and cities in England (Mayhew 1862/1983), different countries in the United Kingdom (Rawson, 1839), and England and European countries (Bulwer, 1836).

The relationship between a city's central district and juvenile delinquency was first explored by Burt in 1925, who proposed that areas in London with the highest rates of delinquency were located adjacent to the central business district, and areas with the lowest rates were located near the periphery of the city.

One of the first ecological studies undertaken in the United States was conducted by Breckinridge and Abbott in 1912. They examined the geographic distribution of the homes of juvenile delinquents in Chicago. A map showing the location of these delinquents indicated that a disproportionate number of the juveniles' homes were located in a few areas of the city.

Park and Burgess (1928) used the terminology of Haeckel, the concepts of Warming, and the research of Breckenridge and Abbot to develop what they called *human ecology*. Specifically, Park and Burgess used the concept of symbiosis to describe the phenomenon in human communities where people work together for common goals and at the same time compete for resources. They also applied Warming's concepts of dominance and succession to describe a situation in which a stronger group would disrupt the community through change and eventually reestablish order by replacing (succeeding) a previously dominant group.

Park, Burgess, and McKenzie (1969) expanded on Park and Burgess's (1928) work by observing that certain characteristics of the population tended to cluster in rings set at about 1-mile increments from the center of Chicago and that the patterns changed dramatically from one ring to the next. For example, Part et al. found a zone of manufacturing enterprises immediately surrounding the central business district of the city. Outside this factory zone was an area of very low-income housing. In the third concentric ring, the dominant residential characteristic was working-class homes. The fourth and fifth rings from the center of the city were middle- and upper-class homes. Park et al. labeled this pattern the *Burgess zonal hypothesis*.

DEVELOPMENT OF THE THEORY: SHAW AND MCKAY

Shaw and McKay (1942) used the ideas of human ecology to study the association between urban ecological characteristics and juvenile delinquency. On the basis of this research they developed *social disorganization theory*. Their study of social disorganization centered around three sets of variables: (1) physical status, (2) economic status, and (3) population status.

Shaw and McKay (1942) used three variables to measure the physical status of an area: (1) population change, (2) vacant and condemned housing, and (3) proximity to industry. They proposed that areas with high delinquency rates tended to be physically deteriorated, geographically close to areas of heavy industry, and populated with highly transient residents. The primary characteristic Shaw and McKay examined was population change. They found that as population rates increased or decreased there was a corresponding increase in delinquency. They proposed that population shifts influenced delinquency because of the process of *invasion, dominance, and succession*, a term they used for disruption of the social organization of an area because members of one (typically ethnic) group moved into another group's neighborhood. The disruption in order caused a rise in crime that would get progressively worse until the invading group became the majority; then crime rates would return to near their previous level. To analyze the relationship between proximity to industry and delinquency, Shaw and McKay mapped industrial areas and the home addresses of juvenile delinquents. Borrowing from Park and Burgess (1928), they found that surrounding the central business district was a zone of manufacturing and industry. Surrounding the industrial zone was a ring characterized by high levels of the physical, economic, and population factors they were studying and a corresponding high delinquency rate. Moving toward the outskirts of the city, they found a reduction in the prevalence of these characteristics and the rate of delinquency. The final physical characteristic Shaw and McKay analyzed was the number of vacant and condemned homes in an area. They found that there was an association between the number of vacant and condemned homes in an area and its delinquency rate.

Next, Shaw and McKay (1942) analyzed the association between the economic status of an area and its delinquency rate. They used three variables for this analysis: (1) the number of families receiving social assistance, (2) the median rental price of the area, and (3) the number of homes owned rather than rented. Shaw and McKay found that, as the number of families receiving social assistance increased, there was a corresponding rise in delinquency rates. They concluded that delinquency was higher in areas with low economic status relative to areas with higher economic status. Next, Shaw and McKay analyzed the relationship between the median rental price and delinquency. They found that delinquency rates dropped as the median rental price of the area rose. Finally, Shaw and McKay examined the relationship between the percentage of residents who owned their own homes and the delinquency rate. Their findings revealed a significant negative relationship between home ownership and delinquency. Where home ownership was low, there were high rates of delinquency. As home ownership increased, even in small increments from the lowest level, the level of delinquency dropped, being lowest in areas with the highest levels of home ownership.

In explaining the influence of economic status on delinquency, Shaw and McKay (1942) suggested that economic conditions indirectly influence delinquency rates. They asserted that affluent areas offered an atmosphere of social controls, whereas areas of low affluence produced an environment conducive to delinquency because of the diversity of the residents. This diversity influenced rates of delinquency in the area because of the disparity in social norms. In areas of low delinquency, a substantial majority of people would not tolerate abnormal behavior. In areas of high rates of delinquency, however, some of the residents condoned delinquent acts, thus offering tacit support for these behaviors. Finally, Shaw and McKay proposed that economic status influenced delinquency in the case of owning one's home in that people who could afford to own their homes had a greater stake in the neighborhood where they would be permanent residents, whereas people renting would expend less effort to maintain the social organization or decrease the delinquency rate of the neighborhood.

The final analysis included in Shaw and McKay's (1942) study was the relationship between the population composition of an area and its rate of delinquency. Shaw and McKay found that areas with the highest delinquency rates contained higher numbers of foreign-born and black heads of household. They cautioned that this finding does not mean that nativity or ethnicity was the cause of crime. Delinquency rates in areas containing foreign-born and minority heads of households remained constant despite the total population shift to another group. Delinquency rates also remained constant in areas where the displaced population moved. Shaw and McKay concluded that the area of study, and not the nativity or ethnicity of its residents, was the factor contributing to delinquency.

On the basis of their findings, Shaw and McKay (1942) concluded that the ecological conditions existing in areas with high delinquency were contributing to a breakdown in the social order of the area, resulting in conditions conducive to delinquency. Shaw and McKay found that conventional norms existed in high-delinquency areas but that delinquency was a highly competitive way of life, such that there was advantage for some people to engage in delinquency and there were fewer consequences. This became the core of social disorganization theory. Shaw and McKay replicated their Chicago findings in at least eight other cities. Their research also spawned a wealth of other research, becoming one of the key theoretical seeds for most of the current criminological theories.

THE SECOND WAVE: REPLICATIONS OF SHAW AND MCKAY

Shaw and McKay's (1942) research generated several replications spanning more than a decade. Each added to the knowledge base of ecological literature by examining the relationships first considered by Shaw and McKay in slightly different ways. None of the replications, however, drew substantially different conclusions from those in the original study.

Lander (1954) correlated 8,464 juvenile delinquents tried in the Baltimore Juvenile Court from 1939 through 1942 with demographic variables taken from the 1940 census. Specifically, Lander analyzed juvenile delinquency in terms of the median years of school completed, median monthly rent, homes with 1.51 or more persons per room, homes needing substantial repairs or having no private bath, foreign-born and non-white residents, and owner-occupied homes.

Lander's (1954) findings followed the concentric ring pattern established by Shaw and McKay (1942). Lander noted, however, that the use of 1 -mile increments for the zones oversimplified the spatial distribution of delinquency because it obscured the range of delinquency rates within each zone.

Lander's (1954) findings did not support Shaw and McKay's (1942) correlation between high delinquency rates and close proximity to industry. His results indicated that the delinquency rate in census tracts with less than 50% of the area zoned for industrial purposes was lower than the city average. Lander, however, found a more pronounced relationship in Baltimore in areas zoned for commercial use. He concluded from these findings that Shaw and McKay were correct in identifying areas close to the center of the city as the highest in delinquency but that this was primarily due to ecological factors other than proximity to industry. Lander also found no support for the correlation between population change and delinquency. Lander's conclusions are not wholly contradictory to those of Shaw and McKay, however. His findings showed that the tract with the third-highest delinquency rate had a population increase of 20% and that tracts with population increases of 40% or more and decreases of 20% or more had substantially different delinquency rates than those with little or no population change. Lander found a substantial ($r = .69$) but nonsignificant relationship between delinquency and substandard housing. He added overcrowding as an additional measure of the physical status of the area and found a substantial ($r = .73$) but nonsignificant relationship between overcrowding and delinquency.

In Lander's (1954) analysis, the median rental value of housing units in Baltimore was not significantly related to delinquency. Lander reasoned that economic variables such as rental values were an unreliable predictor because they were merely indicators of where a person might live. Lander did find a significant relationship, however, between homes owned in an area and delinquency. In fact, home ownership was the most highly correlated variable in Lander's analysis.

Lander's (1954) analysis of population status followed Shaw and McKay's (1942). Zero-order correlation of the variables demonstrated that these variables were better predictors of delinquency than physical or economic variables. Although Lander's conclusions generally supported those of Shaw and McKay, there were some differences in the findings. For example, Lander found a statistically significant, inverse relationship between delinquency and number of foreign-born residents. Lauder explained this by noting that many of the foreign-born Chicago residents were recent immigrants, whereas in Baltimore most of the foreign-born residents were well integrated into the community, characterized by a high degree of home ownership. Lander also found that in areas with a moderate proportion of blacks there was a high rate of delinquency. As the percentage of blacks rose above 50%, however, the rate of delinquency dropped proportionally.

Bordua (1959) attempted to replicate part of Lander's (1954) study in an effort to clarify some of the issues that had drawn criticism. Bordua's study used delinquency data from the Detroit, Michigan, juvenile court for 1948 through 1952 and census tract data from the 1950 U.S. Census.

Bordua's (1959) physical status analysis only included substandard housing and overcrowding. His findings were generally supportive of Lander's (1954) and contradictory to Shaw and McKay's (1942). Bordua found a weaker but significant relationship between overcrowding and delinquency. Also supporting Lander and counter to the findings of Shaw and McKay, Bordua found a nonsignificant relationship between substandard housing and delinquency.

Bordua's (1959) findings regarding economic status essentially supported those of Lander (1954). Bordua found the median rental value to be nonsignificant and less substantial than Lander did. Bordua also found a significant but less substantial relationship between the percentage of homes owned and delinquency. Bordua added median income to represent economic status in the analysis and found that income was not a statistically significant indicator of delinquency.

Bordua's (1959) analysis of population variables was supportive of Shaw and McKay's (1942) research but contrary to Lander's (1954). Bordua's findings revealed that foreign birth was significantly related to delinquency but that number of black heads of households was nonsignificant. On the basis of these contradictions, Bordua chose the ratio of unrelated individuals to the total number of families as an additional measure of population status. Lander found that unrelated individuals was significantly-correlated with delinquency.

Chilton (1964) used juvenile court data from Indianapolis, Indiana, from 1948 through 1950 and data from the 1950 U.S. Census to compare the findings of Lander (1954) and Bordua (1959) with those in Indianapolis. The results of Chilton's analyses of the relationship between physical characteristics and delinquency essentially confirmed the findings of the other replications. Chilton's findings of the relationship between delinquency and substandard housing showed a substantial but nonsignificant correlation with delinquency. Chilton also found a substantial correlation between overcrowded conditions (more than 1.5 persons per room) and delinquency. Unlike the other two studies, though, the degree of overcrowding in Indianapolis was one of two statistically significant indicators of delinquency. Chilton's analyses of economic variables essentially confirmed those of Lander's and Bordua's studies. The relationship between median rental value and delinquency was found to be nonsignificant and similar to Lander's. Chilton's findings concerning home ownership also supported the other replications. His findings related to population characteristics tended to refute both Shaw and McKay (1942) and the other replications. Chilton found both percentage of foreign-born people and percentage of black people to not be significantly related to delinquency in Indianapolis. He concluded that ecological research can identify general conditions associated with delinquency but that differences between cities exist such that they cannot be addressed with traditional social disorganization theory.

The findings of Lander's (1954), Bordua's (1959), and Chilton's (1964) studies suggest that although the relationship between the physical characteristics of an area and delinquency may vary by city there appears to be a sustained relationship at some level. Shaw and McKay's (1942) findings concerning the relationship between economic characteristics and delinquency were supported by the replications, but not completely. Finally, Shaw and McKay's findings concerning population characteristics and delinquency were generally not supported by the replications.

THE LEAN TIMES: SOCIAL DISORGANIZATION IN THE 1970S AND 1980S

After the replications that followed Shaw and McKay's (1942) research, social disorganization as a theory began to decline. This was primarily a result of attacks on the use of official data in crime studies and growing criticism of theoretical problems with the theory. A few studies, however, continued to follow the principles of social disorganization. The general direction of these studies followed that of Shaw and McKay, but few followed their design closely enough to be considered replications. For example, these studies examined population status through scale measurement and analysis of change in population characteristics rather than single-variable correlations. In analyzing the association between economic status and delinquency, research in this era focused on the economic status of individuals rather than the housing conditions studied by Shaw and McKay. These studies typically measured economic characteristics through educational levels and the occupational status of residents. Because of the contradictory findings of earlier research and the growing contention that foreign birth had little to do with delinquency, these studies began to look to additional measures of population status in an effort to better measure its relationship with delinquency.

Quinney (1964) obtained data from Lexington, Kentucky, in 1960 and analyzed them with *social area analysis*. Quinney's research included three dimensions; (1) economic status, (2) family status, and (3) ethnic status. Quinney's family status was the variable most closely associated with Shaw and McKay's (1942) physical status. Quinney used census data concerning women in the workforce, fertility rates, and single-structure housing. The results of his analysis showed that family status was negatively correlated with juvenile delinquency. These findings were significant even when interaction effects of economic variables were included. Quinney used two variables to examine economic status: (1) number of school grades completed and (2) number of blue-collar workers. The results showed that juvenile delinquency was negatively correlated with economic status. Quinney used the census variable race to examine ethnic status. The racial makeup of a census tract was found to be the most highly correlated with delinquency. Quinney then conducted a second analysis to determine the degree of delinquency exhibited by each race. This analysis revealed that white delinquency rates were lowest in areas with less than 2% blacks and increased steadily as the proportion of blacks increased, peaking in the 15% to 40% black grouping. Black delinquency, however was highest in areas with less than 2% black or more than 50% black but was lowest when the racial mix was predominantly, but not completely, white. In a third analysis, census tracts were divided into areas of high and low economic status and high and low family status. In this analysis, delinquency rates varied in relation to economic status; however, the presence of high family status always lowered the rate of delinquency.

In a partial replication of Quinney's (1964) study, and to address the criticism of using official data in social disorganization research, Johnstone (1978) used self-reported data to test social disorganization theory. In this study, Johnstone administered self-reported delinquency questionnaires to 1,124 youth aged 14 through 18 living in Chicago. Johnstone also used a modified Shevsky–Bell social area analysis using "area status measures" and "family status measures." The results of a factor analysis revealed that area-status measures had a positive but nonsignificant relationship with fighting and weapon-related crimes and a negative and nonsignificant relationship with all other delinquency measures. In regard to family status measures, lower-class status was significantly associated with fighting and weapons offenses, burglary–larceny–robbery offenses, Uniform Crime Report Index offenses, and arrests.

An enduring criticism of Shaw and McKay's (1942) research was the assumption of a stable delinquency pattern in the community rather than one experiencing change. Bursik and Webb (1982) attempted to test this hypothesis by examining data from Chicago.

They used Shaw and McKay's own data and updated it to the time of their study to facilitate an examination from 1940 to 1970 in 10-year increments. Data were drawn from all male referrals to the Chicago juvenile court in the years of 1940, 1950, 1960, and 1970 and from census data for the corresponding years. A regression analysis revealed that delinquency was not associated with the indicators of change between 1940 and 1950. For the two following periods, however, this trend was reversed. Bursik and Webb also found that communities exhibiting the most rapid change were characterized by the highest increases in delinquency. The analysis showed that communities with the highest rates of population change had an average of 12 more offenses per 1,000 youth than areas with either moderate or slow change. They concluded on the basis of these findings that it was the *nature* of the change, not the *people* involved in the change, that was affecting delinquency. In explaining how their findings differed from Shaw and McKay's, Bursik and Webb concluded that the earlier study was not wrong but that it was conducted "within a specific historical context and grounded... in a model of ecological process that [has] changed dramatically since the publication of the 1942 monograph" (p. 36).

Four years later, Schuerman and Kobrin (1986) conducted a study similar to Bursik and Webb's (1982) with a 20-year historical analysis of Los Angeles County. This was accomplished by gathering data from the juvenile court for 1950, 1960, and 1970 and correlating them with measures of land use, population composition, socioeconomic status, and subculture.

Schuerman and Kobrin (1986) proposed that neighborhoods travel through three stages: (1) emerging areas, with very low delinquency rates; (2) transitional areas, with moderate levels of delinquency; and (3) enduring areas, which maintain high levels of delinquency for many years. They also proposed that deterioration preceded a rise in delinquency in early stages of transition (supporting Shaw and McKay 1942) but that as the city moved to the enduring stage, rises in the delinquency rate preceded deterioration.

In analyzing the relationship between land use (physical status) and delinquency, Schuerman and Kobrin (1986) found that the number of homes owned and land use type was inversely related with delinquency.

They also found high mobility levels in persons living in high-delinquency areas. A cross-lagged regression analysis revealed that physical deterioration was most highly associated with increases in delinquency in emerging areas. As the area continued to deteriorate and delinquency rose, however, the most significant factors shifted to economic characteristics. Schuerman and Kobrin argued that the speed of change rather than the change itself that resulted in a neighborhood moving from low to high crime rates.

In analyzing the influence of socioeconomic factors on delinquency, Schuerman and Kobrin (1986) examined the occupation, unemployment, education, and housing characteristics of census tracts. This analysis revealed expected results of a low number of professional and skilled workers and a low percentage of people with advanced education in high-delinquency areas. The trend among housing characteristics in Schuerman and Kobrin's study also supported the findings of Shaw and McKay (1942) and the replications. There was a general trend from owner- to renter-occupied housing and from single to multiple housing units as one moved from low-delinquency to high-delinquency areas. This supported Shaw and McKay's proposal that delinquency was positively correlated with the percentage of people renting and negatively correlated with the percentage of homes owned. There were also significant increases in the degree of overcrowding in high-delinquency areas, which supported the findings of Lander (1954), Bordua (1959), and Chilton (1964). Unlike physical status characteristics, economic variables were not a significant factor of delinquency in emerging areas of Schuerman and Kobrin's study. Socioeconomic status preceded increases in delinquency only in transitional and enduring stages.

Schuerman and Kobrin (1986) examined four population characteristics: (1) white and (2) non-white population and (3) white and (4) non-white female participation in the labor force. In high-delinquency areas, the percentage of blacks in the population rose slightly from 1950 through 1970, while the percentage of whites decreased dramatically in the same areas. Similar trends occurred in the female labor force participation. From 1950 through 1970, the black female participation in the labor force dropped

slightly in high-delinquency areas, but the white female labor force dropped substantially. These findings were even more substantial in the cross-lagged analysis. Schuerman and Kobrin concluded from this analysis that rapid change in population characteristics, along with high rates of deterioration and population turnover, were preceding and greatly influencing the rate of increase in delinquency.

Sampson and Groves (1989) tested social disorganization theory using data from a survey of 10,905 residents in 238 localities in Great Britain. Their rationale was that previous research had relied on census data that were not valid measures of community structure or crime. Sampson and Groves also argued that survey data were superior to Shaw and McKay's (1942) reliance on official crime. They also proposed that "low economic status, ethnic heterogeneity, residential mobility, and family disruption lead to community social disorganization, which in turn, increased crime and delinquency rates" (p. 775). On the basis of their analysis, Sampson and Groves concluded that social disorganization theory was supported, stating that "between-community variations in social disorganization transmit much of the effect of community structural characteristics on rates of both criminal victimization and criminal offending" (p. 774). Furthermore, they argued for expanded support for social disorganization theory in that "Shaw and McKay's model explains crime and delinquency rates in a culture other than the United States" (p. 776).

An ironic major drawback of social disorganization research has been the relative lack of theory to guide or explain the research (Bursik 1988). Much of the research in this area has paid tribute to social disorganization in the literature review and then simply conducted analyses with little theoretical explanation for the findings. Two authors (Sampson 1986, and Stark 1987) attempted to advance the theory itself and to provide a better link between neighborhood-oriented research and the theoretical foundation.

Responding to criticisms that ecological research lacked an intervening factor between the variables and criminality, Sampson (1986) proposed that a breakdown in informal social controls is this link. With this premise in mind, Sampson set out to show the link among ecological characteristics, social disorganization, loss of informal social control, and delinquency. The first link he attempted to make concerned the structural density of a neighborhood. In an earlier work, Sampson (1985) proposed that increases in density reduced the ability of a neighborhood to maintain surveillance and guardianship of youth and strangers. As the number of persons in a given living area increased, it was more difficult to know who lived in the area. When this occurred, residents were less able to recognize their neighbors or be concerned with their activities, resulting in an increased opportunity for delinquency. Sampson also proposed a link with residential mobility whereby he argued that neighborhoods with a high population turnover had a greater number of new faces, making it difficult to distinguish between new residents and strangers. Sampson proposed that economic status was related to delinquency through the attachment or social bond a person had to the neighborhood and the neighborhood's willingness to maintain informal social control. He also proposed that people who owned their own homes had a greater attachment and commitment to the neighborhood and took steps to maintain neighborhood networks and social control. He examined two-parent versus one-parent families and their relative ability to maintain informal social control. Sampson proposed that two-parent families provided increased supervision and that because of this they were aware of and intervened in predecessors of involvement in more serious delinquent activities.

Stark (1987) furthered Sampson's (1985, 1986) effort to add a theoretical framework to social disorganization research by formalizing some of the more important aspects of Shaw and McKay's (1942) findings in developing a set of 30 propositions. The primary focus of Stark's propositional framework was on Shaw and McKay's physical status variables. The factors Stark used to analyze population status were transience of population, mixed-use neighborhoods, and overcrowding. Stark (1987) proposed that "transience weakens voluntary organizations, thereby directly reducing both informal and formal sources of social control" (p. 900). Stark also sought to provide a basis for understanding how proximity to industry and mixed-use areas influenced delinquency. Stark argued that in areas where residents lived close to commercial

or industrial businesses there was more opportunity to commit delinquent acts (e.g., theft) because targets were readily available and close by. In purely residential areas, however, juveniles who wanted to commit such thefts might have to travel a great distance to get to a place where such acts could be committed. Stark proposed that economic status was linked to delinquency in two ways (physical status and population status). First, he proposed that homes in poor areas were typically more crowded; therefore, there was more anonymity and less supervision of children. Stark also linked economic status to delinquency through physical status in his proposition that "poor, dense neighborhoods tend to be mixed-use neighborhoods" (p. 902). In relating population status to delinquency, Stark proposed that physically unattractive areas reduced people's commitment to their neighborhood. This proposition also supported Shaw and McKay's conclusion that physically deteriorated areas in close proximity to industry and with a highly transient population cannot maintain commitment to the area by the residents and cannot maintain social control of delinquency.

A RESURGENCE: SOCIAL DISORGANIZATION THEORY IN THE 1990s

At least within criminology and criminal justice, the focus on neighborhoods experienced a resurgence in the 1990s. This was largely based on recognition of the increasing decline of American cities, increasing crime rates, and the popularity of community policing. This renewed focus produced a great deal of research on neighborhoods. Most of the research paid homage to social disorganization theory but largely abandoned it as a theoretical basis. Some studies, however (Bursik & Grasmick 1993; Sampson & Raudenbush 1999; Sampson, Raudenbush, & Earls 1997), maintained at least some of the tenets of social disorganization theory. These studies often attempted to further the understanding of neighborhoods and crime with better methodological techniques and more appropriate data.

In one of the more extensive statements of neighborhoods and crime in the 1990s, Bursik and Grasmick (1993) presented a reformulation of social disorganization theory by placing it "within a broader systemic theory of community, which emphasized how neighborhood life is shaped by the structure of formal and informal networks of association" (p. 55). Bursik and Grasmick used as a backdrop to their argument a three-level system of relationships influencing informal social control. The first level, the strength of individual relationships within a neighborhood, formed the base for the next two levels. Bursik and Grasmick argued mat strong relationships among residents would result in strong neighborhood networks, which was the second level. Bursik and Grasmick argued that when neighbors know each other, they are more likely to pay attention to events that are influencing the common good of the community. The final level of relationships were those between residents and organizations external to the neighborhood, such as local government officials or the police. This was the level at which a neighborhood would be able to marshal resources to combat invasions into the neighborhood, such as unwanted organizations (e.g., a halfway house) or crime (e.g., drug dealers).

Bursik and Grasmick (1993) found that instability greatly reduced the neighborhood residents' ability to exert social control. At the level of residents, high population turnover made it difficult to maintain ties to other residents. For example, a tenant in a public housing unit may live there for years and never form a relationship with his or her neighbors. Residents who do not know the children of the area were less likely to intervene when the children displayed unacceptable behavior. Instability also negatively influenced the security of the neighborhood because it reduced informal surveillance. A strong neighborhood network reduced the places crime could hide from surveillance, whereas weak networks increased the ability of crime to occur in the open without being detected.

A large part of research related to social disorganization in the 1990s began to fragment and examine only portions of social disorganization theory. For example, Elliott et al. (1996) analyzed the ethnic diversity of neighborhoods (measured by the number of different languages spoken) to examine the influence of crime based on differences in values and norms between the ethnic groups. Elliott et al. proposed that when there were a variety of languages being spoken,

communication could be difficult, and consensus concerning appropriate values and behaviors for the community might not be reached. There was also considerable research related to a breakdown of the family unit. Much of this research (e.g., McNulty & Bellair 2003) sought to examine the influence of single-family units (especially related to race) on crime. The research of P.-O. Wikström. and Loeber (2000, p. 1135) indicated that youth in public housing were more likely to participate in serious offending. They argued that this could be due to the serious neighborhood disadvantage of public housing and a lack of the residents' ability to collectively defend against crime (as stated by Bursik & Grasmick 1993).

By the end of the 1990s, the Project on Human Development in Chicago Neighborhoods (PHDCN) began to change the nature of social disorganization research. This project used social disorganization theory as a basis for a reexamination of neighborhood crime patterns in Chicago. This was easily the most extensive research in criminology since the work of Shaw and McKay (1942) and perhaps in the history of criminology research. It spawned a wealth of publications related to social disorganization theory but that took different conceptual paths. For example, Sampson and Raudenbush (1999, p. 627) took Bursik and Grasmick's (1993) research on the capacity of neighborhoods to control crime and introduced the concept of *collective efficacy*, defined as "cohesion among neighborhood residents combined with shared expectations for informal social control of public space" (p. 3; see also Sampson & Raudenbush 2001, p. 1).

Sampson et al. (1997) argued that collective efficacy was an intervening variable between structural conditions of neighborhoods (poverty, residential instability) and crime. They examined collective efficacy using data on 343 Chicago neighborhoods and their residents as part of PHDCN. In their analysis, Sampson et al. examined structural characteristics (disadvantage, residential stability, immigrant concentration, etc.), characteristics of residents (race, age, socioeconomic status, etc.), and collective efficacy in relation to violent crime measures. They found that collective efficacy had a statistically significant relationship to violent crime regardless of structural or individual characteristics of neighborhoods. They argued that in low-crime neighborhoods, residents used informal control to regulate the behavior of members by developing rules and collective goals for the neighborhood. For this to occur, residents must develop relationships and trust among one another. When a neighborhood's residents had a high level of social cohesion and trust among them, informal control was easier to exert, and social disorder and crime were less likely.

In addressing the influence of collective efficacy on crime, Sampson and Raudenbush (1999) followed many of the variables used in early social disorganization research. For example, they argued that a high percentage of immigrants in an area was often associated with high levels of disadvantage. This in turn increased the disorder in the neighborhood, which would lead to high levels of crime. One of the most innovative and extensive parts of the PHDCN research involved driving down selected streets using video equipment to capture measures of physical and social disorder. Sampson and Raudenbush found that both social and physical disorder were observed in neighborhoods characterized by a diverse commercial and residential use of property. They concluded that the level of crime could be explained by collective efficacy, meaning that disadvantage, not race or the ethnic composition of a neighborhood, was responsible for high levels of crime.

SOCIAL DISORGANIZATION THEORY IN THE 21ST CENTURY

By the turn of the 20th century, social disorganization theory had largely died out in its original form. It was replaced with (a) research paying tribute to the theory but straying from its original intent, (b) research focused on collective efficacy, and (c) research focused on neighborhood characteristics but using a different theoretical base (including the variety of research conducted under the term *environmental criminology*).

A number of studies acknowledged social disorganization but did not use the theory. These studies paid tribute to the theory by using the term *social disorganization* to describe neighborhoods, but they rarely used the tenets of the theory. These studies found that juveniles from socially disorganized neighborhoods were more likely to engage in aggressive and delinquent behaviors

(P.-O. Wikström & Loeber 2000), sexual activity at an early age (Browning, Leventhal, & Brooks-Gunn 2004), and violence. In addition, juveniles in these neighborhoods were more likely to witness violence and develop mental health problems. P. H. Wikström and Sampson (2003) argued that the development of antisocial and delinquent propensities among children and adolescents was influenced by community socialization and that this relationship was due to the level of collective efficacy present in the neighborhood. Neighborhoods low in collective efficacy produced children who were often unsupervised, and there was little threat of repercussions for negative behaviors.

Sampson and Raudenbush (2001) also indicated allegiance to social disorganization but strayed from its original connotation. They conceded that the ability to understand social disorganization is crucial to rally understanding urban neighborhoods. In their research, however, social disorganization consisted primarily of visual indications of neighborhood physical deterioration. They proposed that this physical deterioration was an indication of what was happening in the neighborhood, such that "disorder triggers attributions and predictions in the minds of insiders and outsiders alike, changing the calculus of prospective homebuyers, real estate agents, insurance agents, and investors" (p. 1).

Sampson and Raudenbush (2001) proposed that neighborhood structure rather than social disorganization influenced the level of disorder. Where physical and social disorder was low, high levels of collective efficacy were usually found. They proposed, however, that disorder did not produce crime. They found no relationship between disorder and homicide, suggesting that crime and disorder were both influenced by something else. They proposed that the common underlying factor comprised the characteristics of the neighborhood and the cohesiveness and informal social control of its residents (Sampson & Raudenbush 2001). This would feed into Sampson and others' research on collective efficacy.

Continuing the line of research of Sampson and Raudenbush (2001), Morenoff, Sampson, and Raudenbush (2001) made a connection between social disorganization and what they termed *social capital*. They viewed local communities as complex systems made up of friendships, kinships, and acquaintances.

They argued these groups were tied to each other through family life and other aspects of their social lives. Morenoff et al. (2001) used *social capital* to describe the social ties between people and positions. They argued social capital increases the social organization and trust within networks, which helps maintain co-operation. They proposed that neighborhoods devoid of social capital were less able to hold common values and maintain social control. This lack of control lead to an inability of the neighborhood to ward off unwanted social problems, including increases in crime. Morenoff et al. did concede that if strong expectations of social control were shared among a community, few ties were necessary among neighbors.

In one of the few articles that refocused on social disorganization, Kubrin and Weitzer (2003) stated that experimental and analytical work on the connection between crime and community characteristics has led to clarification of social disorganization theory. They argued that social disorganization theory was aided in recent research by addressing it as more of a systemic model that included both intra- and extra-neighborhood factors. They argued, however, that substantive and methodological issues remained mat needed to be overcome if social disorganization theory were to continue to advance.

The substantive improvements proposed by Kubrin and Weitzer (2003) included advancements in the operationalization of key concepts and the addition of mediating variables between neighborhood structural characteristics and crime. They argued that the primary variable that has improved the theory is collective efficacy. Kubrin and Weitzer argued that, although social control was not central to social disorganization theory, formal social control (police, code enforcement, etc.) was a critical concept in social disorganization research and should be brought into future research. Finally, Kubrin and Weitzer bemoaned the fact that the culture of the neighborhood has largely been ignored in recent research. They proposed that there should be a return to the neighborhood culture included in Shaw and McKay's (1942) original work.

Kubrin and Weitzer (2003) described recent "methodological innovation" in social disorganization theory that had helped researchers test key propositions and clarify relevant causal models. They identified these innovations as dynamic models, reciprocal effects, contextual effects, and spatial interdependence. They correctly pointed out that one of Shaw and McKay's (1942) principal findings was the changing nature of cities. They decried the research following Shaw and McKay's as dismissing urban dynamics, and they called for a return to including dynamic models of neighborhood change in social disorganization research. Kubrin and Weitzer also indicated that although the reciprocal effects of crime and community were beginning to be addressed, the inclusion of models in which community characteristics could influence crime and crime could then influence community characteristics is still not sufficient. Drawing on the current trend in multilevel modeling, Kubrin and Weitzer proposed that contextual effects addressing the connection between the neighborhood and its effect on individual outcomes should receive greater attention in social disorganization theory research. Finally, Kubrin and Weitzer argued that *spatial interdependence*, whereby spatially adjacent neighborhoods could influence one another's level of disorganization, should be more fully developed in social disorganization theory and research.

Kubrin and Weitzer (2003) concluded that more complete and more rigorous testing of social disorganization theory's propositions was possible because of methodological innovations. They conceded that although researchers continued to be challenged with the proper measurement of central concepts and methodological shortcomings, social disorganization theory could greatly increase the understanding of crime at the neighborhood level with the improvements outlined in their article.

Combining many of the developments from the previous 15 years, Warner (2007) sought to delineate the forms of social control (and collective efficacy) by examining the willingness of residents to directly intervene in a situation rather than relying on formal means of control (typically the police, but also avoidance or tolerance). Like many of the previous studies, Warner paid tribute to social disorganization theory in the introduction and literature review but did little to support the theory in the research, only including disadvantage and residential mobility as classic social disorganization variables. Other independent variables included by Warner were social ties and faith in the police.

Warner found that the relationship between neighborhood disadvantage and social control was nonlinear. She argued that this meant that both highly disadvantaged and highly advantaged people were likely to use indirect methods of control (the police) or to avoid or tolerate the situation, whereas people in the middle were more likely to take direct action. Warner stated this is in opposition to the tenets of social disorganization theory, which would hold a more linear pattern of the most disadvantaged using indirect methods and the likelihood of direct action increasing as the disadvantage of the neighborhood lessened. Warner found similar patterns for residential mobility: Mobility was significantly and positively related with the likelihood of using indirect methods of social control (police, avoidance, etc.), but it was not related to the likelihood of using direct methods. Warner found support for these results in confirming the tenets of social disorganization theory.

Overall, social disorganization theory in the first decade of the 21st century seemed to fare no better than in the last part of the 20th century. The theory still received some support from research on neighborhoods, but most of the research included only parts of the theory, a few of the variables, or simply paid tribute to the theory in the literature review and then conducted neighborhood research that was faintly consistent with the theoretical foundation of social disorganization.

FUTURE DIRECTIONS

One could argue that the future of social disorganization theory looks bleak. Although it is likely to still be considered one of the major theories, especially given a continued focus on neighborhood research, it may very well dissipate in its classic form. Other than a few articles likely to be related to dissertation work, it is likely that replications or semireplications of Shaw and McKay's (1942) work will disappear. Two directions do look promising for the vestiges of social disorganization theory, however: (1) studies using data from the PHDCN and its associated collective efficacy theory and (2) work from environmental criminology.

Life course theory and research from the PHDCN has dominated much of the theoretical work over the past 20 years. Sampson and other researchers have produced many publications detailing the intricacies of crime related to neighborhood change in Chicago. The availability of these data for other researchers and its current popularity probably means that research will be using these data for at least another decade. Furthermore, the popularity of Sampson's work on collective efficacy has probably ensured numerous publications in this area for the foreseeable future.

Beginning in the late 1970s with the work of crime prevention through environmental design (Jeffery 1971), a new area of neighborhood research was formed. This quickly developed into what is now termed *environmental criminology*. This line of research is typically based more in routine activities theory (among other theoretical foundations) than social disorganization theory, but the tenets of social disorganization theory can easily be found in much of this line of study. A recent development in environmental criminology may signal a larger place for social disorganization theory within environmental criminology. Walker (2007) used complex systems science in an effort to improve the ability of social disorganization theory to explain neighborhood change and crime. Walker termed this new theory *ecodynamics theory* after the various theoretical traditions on which it was based (social disorganization, human ecology, environmental criminology, and complex systems theory). A few conference papers at an annual meeting on environmental criminology gave rise to the argument that social disorganization theory may continue to be tested more in its classic form by these researchers than by others in criminology.

CONCLUSION

Social disorganization theory has its roots in some of the oldest research in criminological theory, dating back to the early 1800s. Studies of neighborhoods, including crime characteristics, rose almost simultaneously with the development of the field of sociology. As Park began to build the Department of Sociology at the University of Chicago, he centered on the concept of human ecology. This examination of human behavior, mostly at the neighborhood level, gave rise to Burgess's research and ultimately to the hiring of Clifford R. Shaw and Henry D. McKay, who went on to become the most influential social disorganization researchers in the first half of the 20th century.

Shaw and McKay's (1942) work resulted in the formal development of social disorganization theory as an explanation of the behavior and characteristics of neighborhoods and how changes in those characteristics could influence the level of crime. After this, social disorganization theory enjoyed a time of prominence in criminological thought, producing many replications and research through the early 1960s.

Social disorganization theory fell into disrepute in the 1970s as a result of sharp criticism of Shaw and McKay's (1942) work and because of a move away from official data concerning crime. As a consequence, not much research using social disorganization theory was conducted during this time. The research that was conducted downplayed the theory, foretelling social disorganization theory's future.

Social disorganization theory made a brief resurgence in the 1990s as the deterioration of American neighborhoods and rising crime rates produced a new interest in understanding the characteristics of neighborhoods. Even during this period, however, social disorganization theory was seldom tested in its classic form and researchers again downplayed the theory in relation to new methods and theory. By the end of the century, the PHDCN began to produce a new line of theory based on collective efficacy.

After the turn of the 20th century, most research paid tribute to the historical importance of social disorganization theory but did little to bring its tenets into modern research. Research on collective efficacy prevailed, as did research focusing on neighborhoods but doing little to further the theory itself.

The future of social disorganization theory appears close to its current status. A few criminologists are testing the theory close to its original configuration. Most of the research is likely to follow more along the lines of collective efficacy theory or to examine neighborhoods with only parts (or even none) of the tenets of true social disorganization theory.

REFERENCES AND FURTHER READINGS

Bordua, D. J. (1959). Juvenile delinquency and anomie: An attempt at replication. *Social Problems, 6,* 230–238.

Brantingham, P. J., & Brantingham, P. L. (1981). *Environmental criminology.* Beverly Hills, CA: Sage.

Breckinridge, S. P., & Abbott, E. (1912). *The delinquent child and the home.* New York: Russell Sage Foundation.

Browning, C. R., Leventhal, T., & Brooks-Gunn, J. (2004). Neighborhood context and racial differences in early adolescent sexual activity. *Demography, 41,* 697–720.

Bulwer, H. L. (1836). *France, social, literary, and political.* London: Richard Bentley.

Bursik, R. J., Jr. (1988). Social disorganization and theories of crime and delinquency: Problems and prospects. *Criminology, 26,* 519–551.

Bursik, R. X, Jr., & Grasmick, H. G. (1993), *Neighborhoods and crime: The dimensions of effective community control.* New York: Lexington.

Bursik, R. J., Jr., & Webb, J. (1982). Community change and patterns of delinquency. *American Journal of Sociology), 88,* 24–42.

Burt, C. L. (1925). *The young delinquent.* London: University of London Press.

Chainey, S., & Ratcliffe, J. (2005). *GIS and crime mapping.* West Sussex, UK: Wiley.

Chilton, R. J. (1964). Continuity in delinquency area research: A comparison of studies for Baltimore, Detroit, and Indianapolis. *American Sociological Review, 29,* 71–83.

Elliott, D., Wilson, W. J., Huizinga, D., Sampson, R., Elliott, A., & Rankin, B. (1996). The effects of neighborhood disadvantage on adolescent development. *Journal of Research in Crime and Delinquency, 33,* 389–426.

Guerry, A. M. (1833). *Essai sur la statistique morale de la France.* Paris: Crochard.

Haeckel, E. (1866). *Generelle morphologie der organismen.* Berlin, Germany: Georg Reimer Verlag.

Jeffery, C. R. (1971). *Crime prevention through environmental design.* Beverly Hills, CA: Sage.

Johnstone, J. W. C. (1978). Social class, social areas, and delinquency. *Sociology and Social Research, 63,* 49–72.

Kubrin, C. E., & Weitzer, R. (2003). New directions in social disorganization theory. *Journal of Research in Crime and Delinquency, 40,* 374–402.

Lander, B. (1954). *Towards and understanding of juvenile delinquency*. New York; AMS Press.

Mayhew, H. (1983). *London labor and the London poor* (V. Neuberg, Ed.). Mineola, NY: Dover. (Original work published 1862)

McNulty, T. L., & Bellair, P. E. (2003). Explaining racial and ethnic differences in adolescent violence: Structural disadvantage, family well-being, and social capital. *Justice Quarterly, 20,* 501–528.

Morenoff, I D., Sampson, R. J., & Raudenbush, S. W. (2001). Neighborhood inequality, collective efficacy, and the spatial dynamics of urban violence. *Criminology, 39,* 517–559.

Park, R. E., & Burgess E. W. (1928). *Introduction to the science of sociology*. Chicago: University of Chicago Press.

Park, R. E., Burgess, E. W., & McKenzie, R. (1969). *The growth of the city*, Chicago: University of Chicago Press.

Quinney, R. (1964). Crime, delinquency, and social areas. *Journal of Research in Crime and Delinquency, 1,* 149–154.

Rawson, W. (1839). An inquiry into the statistics of crime in England and Wales. *Journal of the Statistical Society of London, 2,* 334–344.

Sampson, R. J. (1985). Neighborhood and crime: The structural determinants of personal victimization. *Journal of Research in Crime and Delinquency, 22,* 7–40.

Sampson, R. J. (1986). Crime in cities: The effects of formal and informal social control. In A. J. Reiss Jr. & M. Tonry (Eds.), *Communities and crime* (pp. 271–311). Chicago: University of Chicago Press.

Sampson, R., & Groves, B. W. (1989). Community structure and crime: Testing social disorganization theory. *American Journal of Sociology, 94,* 774–802.

Sampson, R. J., & Raudenbush, S. W. (1999). Systematic social observation of public spaces: A new look at disorder in urban neighborhoods. *American Journal of Sociology, 105,* 603–651.

Sampson, R. J., & Raudenbush, S. W. (2001). *Disorder in urban neighborhoods—Does it lead to crime?* Washington, DC: US. Department of Justice.

Sampson, R. J., Raudenbush, S. W., & Earls, F. (1997, August 15). Neighborhoods and violent crime: A multi-level study of collective efficacy. *Science, 277,* 918–924.

Schuerman, L., & Kobrin, S. (1986). Community careers in crime. In A. J Reiss Jr. & M. Tonry (Eds.), *Communities and crime* (pp. 67–100). Chicago: University of Chicago Press.

Shaw, C. R., & McKay, H. D. (1942). *Juvenile delinquency and urban areas*. Chicago: University of Chicago Press.

Stark, R. (1987). Deviant places: A theory of the ecology of crime. *Criminology, 4,* 893–909.

Stewart, J. M. (1974). *Social disorganization and the control of fighting dogs*. Unpublished doctoral dissertation, Bowling Green State University.

Walker, J. T. (2007). Advancing science and research in criminal justice/criminology: Complex systems theory and non-linear analyses. *Justice Quarterly, 24,* 555–581.

Warming, E. (1909). *Oecology of plants: An introduction to the study of plant communities*. Oxford, UK: Oxford University Press.

Warner, B. D. (2007). Directly intervene or call the authorities? A study of forms of neighborhood social control within a social disorganization framework. *Criminology, 45,* 99–130.S

Wikström, P. H., & Sampson, R. J. (2003). Social mechanisms of community influences on crime and pathways in criminality. In B. L. Benjamin, T. E. Moffitt, & A. Caspi (Eds.), *Causes of conduct disorder and serious juvenile delinquency* (pp. 118–148). New York: Guilford Press.

Wikström, P.-O., & Loeber, R. (2000). Do disadvantaged neighborhoods cause well-adjusted children to become adolescent delinquents? A study of male juvenile serious offending, risk and protective factors, and neighborhood context. *Criminology, 38,* 1109–1142.

CHAPTER VII

Anomie and Strain Theories

STRAIN THEORIES

ROBERT S.
AGNEW

S train theories state that certain strains or stressors increase the likelihood of crime. These strains involve the inability to achieve one's goals (e.g., monetary or status goals), the loss of positive stimuli (e.g., the death of a friend, the loss of valued possessions), or the presentation of negative stimuli (e.g., verbal and physical abuse). Individuals who experience these strains become upset, and they may turn to crime in an effort to cope. Crime may be a way to reduce or escape from strains. For example, individuals may steal the money they want or run away from the parents who abuse them. Crime may be used to seek revenge against the source of strain or related targets. For example, individuals may assault the peers who harass them. Crime also may be used to alleviate negative emotions; for example, individuals may engage in illicit drug use in an effort to make themselves feel better. Strain theories are among the dominant explanations of crime, and, as discussed in this chapter, certain strain theories have had a major impact on efforts to control crime.

This chapter describes (a) the types of strain most conducive to crime, (b) why strains increase the likelihood of crime, and (c) the factors that increase the likelihood that individuals will cope with strains through crime. All strain theories acknowledge that most individuals cope with strains in a legal manner. For example, most individuals cope with monetary problems by doing such things as cutting back on expenses, borrowing money, or working extra hours. It is therefore critical to explain why some individuals engage in criminal coping. After presenting a basic overview of strain theories, this chapter describes how strain theories have been used to explain group differences, such as gender differences, in crime. The chapter concludes with a discussion of the policy implications of strain theories.

TYPES OF STRAIN MOST CONDUCIVE TO CRIME

Inability to Achieve Monetary Success

Merton (1938) developed the first major strain theory of crime in the 1930s. This theory was developed in the midst of the Great Depression, so it is not surprising that it focused on that type of strain involving the inability to achieve monetary success. According to Merton, everyone in the United Stated—regardless of class position—is encouraged to strive for monetary success. At the same time, lower-class individuals are frequently prevented from achieving such success through legal channels. In particular, the parents of lower-class children often do not equip them with the skills and attitudes necessary to do well in school. Lower-class individuals often attend inferior schools, and they often lack the funds to obtain college educations or start their own businesses. As a consequence, they more often find themselves unable to achieve their monetary goals through legal channels.

This goal blockage creates much frustration, and individuals may cope by engaging in crime, including income-generating crimes such as theft, drug selling, and prostitution. Merton (1938), however, emphasized that most individuals do not cope with this strain through crime. Some individuals simply endure this strain, others lower their desire for money, and still others turn to the pursuit of other goals. Merton provided some guidance as to why some individuals cope with crime and others do not. One key factor, for example, is whether individuals blame their inability to achieve monetary success on themselves or on others. Crime is more likely when the blame is placed on others.

Cohen (1955) and Cloward and Ohlin (1960) have applied Merton's (1938) theory to the explanation of juvenile gangs. Like Merton, they said that the major type of strain in the United States is the inability to achieve monetary success or, in the case of Cohen, the somewhat broader goal of middle-class status. However, they went on to state that juveniles sometimes cope with this strain by forming or joining delinquent groups, such as gangs. Strained juveniles may form gangs in order to better pursue illicit money-making opportunities, such as drug selling. They may form gangs in an effort to achieve the status or respect they desire. In particular, juveniles sometimes join gangs in an effort to feel important.

Other Strains Conducive to Crime

Beginning in the 1960s and 1970s, criminologists began to suggest that the inability to achieve monetary success or middle-class status was not the only important type of strain. For example, Greenberg (1977) and Elliott,

Huizinga, and Ageton (1979) suggested that juveniles pursue a broad range of goals, including popularity with peers, autonomy from adults, and harmonious relations with parents. They claimed that the inability to achieve any of these goals might result in delinquency. Later, Agnew (1992) drew on the stress literature in psychology and sociology to point to still other types of strain.

According to Agnew (1992), *strain* refers to events and conditions that are disliked by individuals. These events and conditions may involve the inability to achieve one's goals. As indicated earlier in this chapter, however, strains may also involve the loss of positive stimuli and the presentation of negative stimuli. In more simplistic language, strains involve situations in which individuals (a) lose something good, (b) receive something bad, or (c) cannot get what they want. These ideas formed the basis of Agnew's *general strain theory* (GST), now the dominant version of strain theory in criminology.

Literally hundreds of specific strains fall under the three broad categories of strain listed in GST. Not all of these strains are conducive to crime, however. For example, homelessness is a type of strain that is very conducive to crime. Being placed in "time out" by one's parents for misbehaving is a type of strain that is not conducive to crime. GST states that strains are most likely to lead to crime when they (a) are high in magnitude, (b) are perceived as unjust, (c) are associated with low social control (or with little to lose from crime), and (d) create some pressure or incentive for criminal coping (see Agnew 2006). Homelessness is clearly conducive to crime: It is high in magnitude, often perceived as unjust, and associated with low social control (individuals who are homeless have little to lose by engaging in crime). Furthermore, being homeless creates much pressure to engage in crime, because one must often steal to meet basic needs and engage in violence to protect oneself (see Baron 2004). Being placed in time out for misbehavior has none of these characteristics.

GST lists the strains most likely to result in crime. These include the inability to achieve monetary goals as well as a good number of other strains. In particular, the following specific strains are most likely to result in crime:

+ *Parental rejection.* Parents do not express love or affection for their children, show little interest in them, and provide little support to them.

- *Harsh/excessive/unfair discipline.* Such discipline involves physical punishment, the use of humiliation and insults, screaming, and threats of injury. Also, such discipline is excessive given the nature of the infraction or when individuals are disciplined when they do not deserve it.
- *Child abuse and neglect.* This includes physical abuse; sexual abuse; emotional abuse; and the failure to provide adequate food, shelter, or medical care.
- *Negative school experiences.* These include low grades, negative relations with teachers (e.g., teachers treat the juvenile unfairly, humiliate or belittle the juvenile), and the experience of school as boring and a waste of time.
- *Abusive peer relations.* Peer abuse includes insults, gossip, threats, attempts to coerce, and physical assaults.
- *Work in "bad" jobs.* Such jobs have low pay, little prestige, few benefits, little opportunity for advancement, coercive control (e.g., threats of being fired), and unpleasant working conditions (e.g., simple, repetitive tasks; little autonomy; physically taxing work).
- *Unemployment,* especially when it is chronic and blamed on others.
- *Marital problems,* including frequent conflicts and verbal and physical abuse.
- *Criminal victimization.*
- *Discrimination* based on race/ethnicity, gender, or religion.
- *Homelessness.*
- *Failure to achieve certain goals,* including thrills/excitement, high levels of autonomy, masculine status, and monetary goals.

Research on Strains and Crime

Researchers have examined the effect of most of the preceding strains on crime. Their studies suggest that these strains do increase the likelihood of crime, with certain of them being among the most important causes of crime (see Agnew 2006, for an overview). For example, parental rejection, harsh discipline, criminal victimization, and homelessness have all been found

to have relatively large effects on crime. The following are two examples of recent research in this area. Spano, Riveria, and Bolland (2006) found that juveniles who were violently victimized were much more likely to engage in subsequent violence. This held true even after they took account of such things as the juvenile's sex, age, prior level of violence, level of parental monitoring, and whether the juvenile belonged to a gang. Baron (2004) studied a sample of homeless street youth in a Canadian city and found that crime was much more common among youth who reported that they had been homeless for many months in the prior year. This finding was true even after a broad range of other factors were taken into account, such as age, gender, and criminal peer association.

These findings, however, test only one part of GST. GST not only asserts that certain strains increase the likelihood of crime but also describes *why* these strains increase crime. The next section focuses on this topic.

Why Strains Increase the Likelihood of Crime

Strains are said to increase the likelihood of crime for several reasons. Most notably, they lead to negative emotions such as anger, frustration, depression, and fear. These emotions create pressure for corrective action; that is, strained individuals feel bad and want to do something about it. Crime is one possible response. As indicated earlier in this chapter, crime may be a means for reducing or escaping from strains, seeking revenge against the source of strain or related targets, or alleviating negative emotions (through illicit drug use). Anger occupies a special place in GST, because it energizes individuals for action, reduces inhibitions, and creates a strong desire for revenge.

Several attempts have attempted to determine whether strains lead to negative emotions and whether these emotions, in turn, lead to crime. Most studies have focused on the emotion of anger, and they tend to find that strains increase anger and that anger explains part of the effect of strains on crime—especially violent crime (Agnew 2006). For example, Jang and Johnson (2003) asked individuals to indicate the strains or personal problems they had experienced. Many such strains were listed, including different types of financial problems, family problems, and criminal victimizations. Jang and Johnson found that individuals who experienced more strains were more likely to report feeling angry and that this anger had a large effect on crime.

A few studies also suggest that emotions such as depression, frustration, and fear may sometimes explain the effect of strains on crime (see Agnew 2006). Recently, researchers have suggested that certain strains may be more likely to lead to some emotions than others. For example, strains that involve unjust treatment by others may be especially likely to lead to anger. Also, strains that one cannot escape from may lead to depression. Furthermore, certain emotions may be more likely to lead to some crimes than others. As suggested earlier, anger may be especially conducive to violence. Depression, however, may be more conducive to drug use. Researchers are now examining these ideas.

Strains may also lead to crime because they reduce one's level of social control. Strains often involve negative treatment by people such as parents, teachers, spouses, and employers. Such negative treatment can reduce the individual's emotional bond to these conventional others. It can also reduce the individual's investment in conventional society, particularly if the negative treatment involves such things as low grades or the termination of employment. Furthermore, negative treatment can reduce the direct control exercised over individuals (i.e., the extent to which conventional others monitor the individual's behavior and sanction rule violations). This may occur if strains such as child abuse cause individuals to retreat from conventional others. Individuals who are low in these types of control are more likely to engage in crime, because they have less to lose by doing so.

Furthermore, strains may foster the social learning of crime; that is, strains may lead individuals to associate with others who reinforce crime, model crime, and teach beliefs favorable to crime. ... As Cohen (1955) and Cloward and Ohlin (1960) have suggested, strained individuals may associate with other criminals in an effort to cope with their strains. For example, abused or neglected juveniles may join gangs in an effort to find acceptance and support. Individuals who

are threatened by others may join gangs for protection. Also, individuals who are subject to those strains conducive to crime may develop beliefs favorable to crime. For example, individuals who are regularly bullied by others may come to believe that violence is a justifiable, or at least excusable, way to cope. Individuals who are chronically unemployed may come to believe that theft is sometimes justifiable or excusable.

Finally, individuals who experience strains over a long period may develop personality traits conducive to crime, including traits such as negative emotionality. Individuals high in negative emotionality are easily upset and become very angry when upset. The continued experience of strains reduces their ability to cope in a legal manner. As a consequence, new strains are more likely to overwhelm them and make them very upset. Not surprisingly, such people are then more likely to cope through crime.

Several studies have found support for these arguments; that is, strains do tend to reduce social control, foster the social learning of crime, and contribute to traits such as negative emotionality (see Agnew 2006; Paternoster & Mazerolle 1994). Strains, then, may increase the likelihood of crime for several reasons, not simply through their effect on negative emotions.

FACTORS THAT INCREASE THE LIKELIHOOD OF CRIMINAL COPING

There are a variety of ways to cope with strains, most of them legal. Juveniles who are having trouble with schoolwork, for example, might devote more time to their homework; seek help from teachers, parents, or friends; convince themselves that school is not that important; exercise or listen to music in an effort to feel better; and so on. Individuals who experience strains typically cope using legal strategies such as these. Given this fact, it is critical for strain theories to explain why some individuals choose crime as a means of coping, According to GST, criminal coping is most likely to be enacted by individuals with certain characteristics:

+ *Possess poor coping skills and resources.* Some individuals lack the skills and resources to legally cope on their own. They have poor problem-solving and social skills, including skills such as the ability to negotiate with others. They possess traits such as negative emotionality and low constraint. Individuals with these traits are easily upset and tend to act without thinking. Furthermore, they have limited financial resources. Money is a great coping resource, because it allows one to purchase needed goods and services (including the services of people such as tutors, counselors, and lawyers).

+ *Have low levels of conventional social support.* Not only are some individuals unable to legally cope on their own but also they lack others to whom they can turn for assistance. This assistance might include advice on how to cope, emotional support, financial assistance, and direct assistance in coping. For example, children who are having trouble in school might seek assistance from their parents, who may comfort them, give them advice on how to study, and arrange special assistance from their teachers. Individuals who are unemployed may obtain assistance from their friends, who may help them find work and loan them money.

+ *Are low in social control.* Some individuals also have little to lose if they engage in criminal coping. They are unlikely to be punished if they engage in crime, because their family members, neighbors, and others do not closely supervise them and rarely impose sanctions when they do misbehave. They have little to lose if they are punished, because they do not care what conventional others, such as parents and teachers, think of them. Also, they are doing poorly in school, do not plan on going to college, are unemployed or work in "bad" jobs, and do not have a good reputation in the community. They also do not view crime as wrong or immoral.

+ *Associate with criminal others.* Other criminals model criminal coping, frequently encourage individuals to engage in crime, and often reinforce crime when it occurs. Imagine, for example, a gang member who is insulted by someone. This gang member is more likely to respond with violence because that is how other members of the gang respond to similar provocations; other gang members directly encourage a violent response, and they reinforce violent responses—most often with social approval. Furthermore, they may punish nonviolent responses. For example, gang members who do not respond to provocations with violence may be called cowards (or worse) and regularly harassed.

+ *Hold beliefs favorable to criminal coping.* Some individuals believe that crime is an excusable, justifiable, or even desirable response to certain strains. For example, they believe that violence is an appropriate response to a wide range of provocation (Anderson 1999). They learn these beliefs from others, especially criminal others, Also, as indicated previously, they sometimes develop these beliefs after experiencing chronic or long-term strains (e.g., being bullied over a long period).

+ *Are in situations where the costs of criminal coping are low and the benefits high.* In particular, strained individuals are more likely to turn to crime when they encounter attractive targets for crime in the absence of capable guardians. … An individual with a desperate need for money, for example, is more likely to engage in theft if he or she comes across a valuable item that is unguarded.

In sum, individuals are most likely to engage in criminal coping when they (a) are unable to engage in legal coping, (b) have little to lose by criminal coping, (c) are disposed to criminal coping because of the people with whom they associate and the beliefs they hold, and (d) encounter attractive opportunities for crime.

Researchers have examined the extent to which certain of these factors influence the likelihood of criminal coping. The results of their studies have been mixed (see Agnew, 2006). Some have found that individuals with these factors are more likely to cope with strains through crime; for example, some research indicates that criminal coping is more likely among individuals who are high in negative emotionality or who associate with delinquent peers. Other studies, however, have not found this.

Criminologists are now trying to make sense of these mixed results (see Agnew, 2006; Mazerolle &

Maahs 2000). One possibility for the conflicting results has to do with the fact that researchers often examine the preceding factors in isolation from one another. However, it may be that individuals engage in criminal coping only when their standing on all or most of the preceding factors is favorable to such coping. Mazerolle and Maahs (2000) explored this possibility. They examined three factors: (1) low constraint, (2) association with criminal peers, and (3) beliefs favorable to criminal coping. Mazerolle and Maahs found that when all three of these factors were favorable to criminal coping, highly strained individuals were quite likely to engage in crime.

EXPLAINING GROUPS DIFFERENCES IN CRIME

Strain theories have been used primarily to explain why some individuals are more likely to engage in crime than others. Increasingly, however, they are also being used to explain group differences in crime, in particular gender, age, ethnic–racial, class, and community differences. An example of this use has already been presented.

Merton's (1938) version of strain theory has been used to explain class differences in crime. Lower-class individuals are said to engage in higher rates of crime because they have more trouble achieving their monetary goals through legal channels. Note, however, that the relationship between class and crime is not as strong as many people believe. There appears to be little relationship between class and minor crime, although lower-class individuals are somewhat more likely to engage in minor crime (see Agnew 2009). Furthermore, middle-class individuals are more likely to engage in certain types of white-collar crime, especially corporate crime. Recent versions of strain theory have attempted to explain this by noting that middle- and upper-class individuals do sometimes experience monetary strain, especially when they compare themselves with even more advantaged others (Passas 1997).

GST explains group differences in crime by arguing that the members of certain groups are more likely to (a) experience strains that are conducive to crime and (b) cope with these strains through crime. As an illustration, consider the strong relationship between gender and crime. With the exception of a few types of crime,

males have substantially higher levels of offending than females. ... Part of the reason for this is that males are more likely to experience many of the strains that are conducive to crime. This includes strains such as harsh parental discipline, negative school experiences (e.g., low grades), criminal victimization, homelessness, and perhaps the inability to achieve goals such as thrills/ excitement and masculine status. It is important to note, however, that females experience as much or more overall strain than males. Many of the strains experienced by females, however, are not conducive to crime. These include strains involving close supervision by others and the burdens associated with the care of others (e.g., children and elderly parents). Furthermore, females are more likely to experience certain strains that are conducive to crime, such as sexual abuse and gender discrimination. Overall, however, males are more likely than females to experience strains that are conducive to crime (see Agnew 2006).

Males are also more likely to cope with strains through crime. Part of the reason for this has to do with gender differences in the emotional reaction to strains. Both males and females tend to become angry when they experience strains. The anger of females, however, is more often accompanied by emotions such as guilt, shame, anxiety, and depression. This is because females more often blame themselves when they experience strains, view their anger as inappropriate, and worry that their anger might lead them to harm others. The anger of males, however, is more often accompanied by moral outrage. This is because males are quicker to blame others for their strains and to interpret the negative treatment they have experienced as a deliberate challenge or insult. These gender differences in the experience of anger reflect differences in socialization and social position. Females, for example, are more often taught to be nurturing and submissive, and so they are more likely to view their anger as inappropriate. In any event, the moral outrage of angry males is more conducive to criminal coping, especially to crimes directed against others.

Also, males are more likely to engage in criminal coping because of their standing on those factors that increase the likelihood of criminal coping. Among other things, males are higher in negative emotionality and lower in constraint. Male are lower in certain types of social support—especially emotional supports—and they are lower in many types of social control. In particular, males are less well supervised, less likely to be punished for aggressive behavior, more weakly tied to school, and less likely to condemn crime. Furthermore, males are more likely to associate with other criminals and hold beliefs favorable to crime. Males, for example, are more likely to have delinquent friends and to be gang members than are females. Finally, males are more likely to hold gender-related beliefs that are conducive to criminal coping, such as the belief that they should be "tough."

Data provide some support for these arguments. Research does indicate that males are more likely to experience many of the strains that are conducive to crime, and studies tend to suggest that males are more likely to cope with strains through crime, although not all studies have found this (see Agnew 2006; Broidy & Agnew 1997). Strain theory, then, can partly explain gender differences to crime. Strain theory has also been used to help explain ethnic–racial, age, class, and community differences in crime (see Agnew 2006 for an overview; see Agnew 1997; Eitle & Turner 2003; and Warner & Fowler 2003, for selected studies). The argument here is the same. The members of groups with higher rates of crime are more likely to experience strains that are conducive to crime and to cope with such strains through crime.

RECOMMENDATIONS FOR CONTROLLING CRIME

The early strain theories of Merton (1938), Cohen (1955), and Cloward and Ohlin (1960) had a major impact on efforts to control crime. These theories were one of the inspirations for the War on Poverty, which was developed under President Kennedy's administration and implemented under President Johnson. The War on Poverty consisted of a number of programs designed to eliminate poverty in the United States. While eliminating poverty was, of course, a desirable goal in itself, it was also felt that eradicating poverty would reduce other social problems, such as crime. Several of the programs that were part of the War on Poverty were directly inspired by strain theories. These programs were designed to help lower-income people achieve the goal of monetary success (or middle-class

status) through legal channels. Certain of these programs remain in existence.

One such program is the National Head Start Association, which sponsors a preschool enrichment program. Head Start focuses on preschool-age children in disadvantaged areas. Such children are placed in a preschool program designed to equip them with the skills and attitudes necessary to do well in school. The program also works with the parents of these children, teaching them how they can help their children do well in school. Another program, Job Corps, focuses on older juveniles and adults. This program attempts to equip individuals with the skills and attitudes necessary to obtain a good job. Some evidence suggests that both these programs are successful in reducing crime, especially when they are well implemented (see Agnew, 2009, and Agnew, in press, for further discussion),

GST suggests still other strategies for controlling crime (Agnew, 2006, in press). These strategies fall into two broad groups. First, GST recommends reducing the exposure of individuals to strains that are conducive to crime. Head Start and Job Corps fall into this category, because their primary goal is to reduce the likelihood that individuals will experience school and/or work problems, such as working in "bad" jobs or chronic unemployment. Second, GST recommends reducing the likelihood that individuals will cope with strains through crime.

REDUCING THE EXPOSURE OF INDIVIDUALS TO STRAINS THAT ARE CONDUCIVE TO CRIME

Several programs have tried to eliminate or at least reduce certain of the strains conducive to crime. For example, parent training programs attempt to reduce the likelihood that parents will reject their children and use harsh or abusive disciplinary methods. These programs target at-risk parents, such as teenage parents, or the parents of delinquent youth or juveniles believed to be at risk for delinquency. Among other things, such programs teach parents how to effectively discipline their children and how to better resolve conflicts that arise. They may also encourage family members to spend more time together in pleasurable activities. Furthermore, these programs may attempt to reduce some of the stresses or strains that parents experience, such as work and housing problems. These stresses have been found to contribute to a range of poor parenting practices.

Another program that attempts to reduce exposure to strains focuses on bullying or peer abuse at school. This program attempts to make students, teachers, parents, and administrators more aware of the extent and consequences of bullying. These individuals are then given assistance in designing an anti-bullying program. Clear rules against bullying are established, these rules are widely publicized, and teachers and others closely monitor the school for bullying. Bullies are disciplined in an appropriate manner, and the victims of bullying are offered support. Still other programs attempt to reduce strains such as poor academic performance, work and employment problems, and homelessness. Many of these programs have shown much success in reducing crime (see Agnew, 2006, 2009, in press).

Still other programs recognize that, despite our best efforts, we will not be able to eliminate all strains that are conducive to crime. Teachers, for example, will likely continue to give low grades to students. We can, however, *alter strains so as to make them less conducive to crime.* For example, teachers can be taught to assign grades in a manner that is more likely to be perceived as fair by students. Likewise, police and justice professionals can adopt techniques that are more likely to be perceived as fair by individuals who are arrested and punished. Many such techniques are embodied in the restorative justice approach. ... In addition, we can *make it easier for individuals to avoid strains that are conducive to crime.* For example, we can make it easier for students to change teachers or schools when other efforts to deal with school-related strains fail. Or we can make it easier for individuals to move from high-crime communities where they are regularly victimized.

Finally, we can *equip individuals with the traits and skills to avoid strains.* Individuals sometimes provoke negative treatment from others, including parents, peers, teachers, and employers. This is especially true when individuals are low in constraint and high in negative emotionality. As indicated, such individuals are easily upset, tend to act without thinking, and often have an antagonistic interactional style. Not surprisingly, these individuals frequently upset other people, who may then respond with negative treatment.

Parents, for example, may eventually come to reject and harshly discipline children with these traits. Several programs, however, have shown some success in teaching individuals to better manage their anger and show some restraint before acting. As such, these programs may reduce the likelihood that individuals elicit negative treatment from others.

REDUCING THE LIKELIHOOD THAT INDIVIDUALS WILL RESPOND TO STRAINS WITH CRIME

Although we can do much to reduce the exposure of individuals to strains conducive to crime, it is unlikely that we can entirely eliminate such exposure. For that reason, it is also important to reduce the likelihood that individuals respond to strains with crime. Several programs in this area have shown some success in reducing crime. One set of programs attempts to improve the coping skills and resources of individuals. For example, individuals may be taught problem-solving and social skills, thereby increasing the likelihood that they will be able to develop and implement legal methods for dealing with their strains. To illustrate, individuals may be taught how to respond in a legal manner if they are harassed by peers. On a related note, individuals may be taught methods for better managing their anger.

Individuals also may be provided with increased levels of social support. For example, they might be assigned mentors who provide assistance in coping. Also, a range of government assistance programs may be developed to help individuals cope when they face strains such as long-term unemployment, homelessness, and discrimination in the job market. Beyond that, steps may be taken to increase the level of social control to which individuals are subject. For example, parent training programs can increase the bond between parent and children and improve parental supervision. Also, school-based programs can raise academic performance and improve student–teacher relations. These programs reduce the likelihood that individuals will engage in criminal coping, because such coping is more likely to result in punishment, and individuals have more to lose if they are punished.

Programs may also be used to reduce association with criminal peers and alter beliefs that encourage criminal coping. For example, certain programs have shown some success in altering beliefs that are favorable to drug use. Unfortunately, it has been more difficult to convince individuals to quit juvenile gangs or stop associating with their delinquent friends. Some progress is being made, however.

CONCLUSION

Strain theories are based on a simple, commonsense idea: When people are treated badly, they may become upset and engage in crime. Strain theories elaborate on this idea by describing the types of negative treatment most likely to result in crime, why negative treatment increases the likelihood of crime, and why some people are more likely than others to respond to negative treatment with crime.

The strains most likely to lead to crime are high in magnitude, perceived as unjust, and associated with low social control, and they create some pressure or incentive for crime. Examples include parental rejection, harsh or abusive discipline, chronic unemployment or work in "bad" jobs, criminal victimization, homelessness, discrimination, and the inability to achieve monetary goals. These strains lead to a range of negative emotions, such as anger. These emotions create pressure for corrective action, with crime being one possible response. Crime may allow individuals to reduce or escape from strains, seek revenge, or alleviate their negative emotions (through, e.g., illicit drug use). Strains may also increase crime by reducing social control, fostering association with criminal peers and beliefs favorable to crime, and contributing to traits such as negative emotionality. Individuals are most likely to engage in criminal coping when they lack the resources to legally cope with strains, have little to lose by engaging in crime, are disposed to criminal coping, and are in situations that present attractive opportunities for such coping.

Researchers are extending strain theory in important ways. They are using the theory to help explain group differences in crime, such as gender differences in offending. Also, the implications of strain theory for controlling crime are receiving increased attention. Agnew (2006) described still other extensions. In sum,

strain theory constitutes one of the major explanations of crime and has much potential for controlling crime.

REFERENCES AND FURTHER READINGS

Agnew, R. (1992). Foundation for a general strain theory of crime and delinquency. *Criminology, 30,* 47–87.

Agnew, R. (1997). Stability and change in crime over the life course: A strain theory explanation. In T. P. Thornberry (Ed.), *Advances in criminological theory: Vol. 7. Developmental* theories in crime and delinquency (pp. 101–132). New Brunswick, NJ: Transaction.

Agnew, R. (2001). Building on the foundation of general strain theory: Specifying the types of strain most likely to lead to crime and delinquency. *Journal of Research in Crime and Delinquency, 38,* 319–361.

Agnew, R. (2006). *Pressured into crime: An overview of general strain theory.* New York: Oxford University Press.

Agnew, R. (2009). *Juvenile delinquency: Causes and control.* New York: Oxford University Press.

Agnew, R. (in press). Controlling crime: Recommendations from general strain theory. In H. Barlow & S. Decker, *Criminology and public policy: Putting theory to work.* Philadelphia: Temple University Press.

Anderson, E. (1999). *Code of the street.* New York: Norton.

Baron, S. W. (2004). General strain, street youth and crime: A test of Agnew's revised theory. *Criminology, 42,* 457–483.

Broidy, L. M., & Agnew, R. (1997). Gender and crime: A general strain theory perspective. *Journal of Research in Crime and Delinquency, 34,* 275–306.

Cloward, R., & Ohlin, L. (1960). *Delinquency and opportunity.* Glencoe, IL: Free Press.

Cohen, A. (1955). *Delinquent boys.* Glencoe, IL: Free Press.

Eitle, D. J., & Turner, R. J. (2003). Stress exposure, race, and young adult crime. *Sociological Quarterly, 44,* 243–269.

Elliott, D., Huizinga, D., & Ageton, S. (1979). An integrated perspective on delinquent behavior. *Journal of Research in Crime and Delinquency, 16,* 3–27.

Greenberg, D. (1977). Delinquency and the age structure of society. *Contemporary Crises, 1,* 189–223.

Jang, S. J., & Johnson, B. R. (2003). Strain, negative emotions, and deviant coping among African Americans:

A test of general strain theory. *Journal of Quantitative Criminology, 19,* 79–105.

Mazerolle, P., & Maahs, J. (2000). General strain theory and delinquency: An alternative examination of conditioning influences. *Justice Quarterly, 17,* 323–343.

Merton, R. (1938). Social structure and anomie. *American Sociological Review, 3,* 672–682.

Passas, N. (1997). Anomie, reference groups, and relative deprivation. In N. Passas & R. Agnew (Eds.), *The future of anomie theory* (pp. 62–94). Boston: Northeastern University Press.

Paternoster, R., & Mazerolle, P. (1994). General strain theory and delinquency: A replication and extension. *Journal of Research in Crime and Delinquency, 31,* 235–263.

Spano, R., Riveria, C., & Bolland J. (2006). The impact of timing of exposure to violence on violent behavior in a high poverty sample of inner city African American youth. *Journal of Youth and Adolescence, 35,* 681–692.

Warner, B. D., & Fowler, S. K. (2003). Strain and violence: Testing a general strain model of community violence. *Journal of Criminal Justice, 31,* 511–521.

PART
IV

Macro-Level Critical Theories

PART IV INTRODUCTION

Macro-Level Critical Theories

W e have already seen that theories about crime causation can be targeted to explain crime and behavior at different levels from micro- through meso- to macro-levels of analysis. Here we look at a cluster of seven different theories that are targeted at the macro-level of analysis but that are also "critical." According to Henry's overview (Reading 1) macro theories "assume that external forces, resulting from the configuration and organization of society as a whole, shape the nature of social institutions, and within these, channel the behavior of humans and their interaction." Thus, rather than choosing crime, or seeing crime as the outcome of biological or psychological tendencies, crime results from "criminogenic" structural, cultural and social processes. Crime then is the outcome, or more accurately, the co-production of society; societies having a lot of crime are referred to as criminogenic.

Henry (Reading 1) says that there are five ways these macro-level theories are seen as "critical." because they: (1) neither accept, nor limit themselves to state definitions of crime but instead define crime as social harm that violates human rights; (2) "do not accept that the individual offender causes crime independently of the wider social/cultural context;" (3) oppose the existing social order of capitalist, patriarchal, or race-divided society; (4) question the justice of the criminal justice, which they see as a reflection of the dominant power structure; and (5) advocate radical policy changes to society rather than just to its institutions or its individual members.

Critical theories share a similar view of humans and their relationship to society which Henry and Lanier (2006, p. 183) say "view humans as potentially active creative entities who have the ability to shape their social world, but who also recognize that the world, in the form of hierarchical power structures, shapes them." Critical theories are not structurally deterministic (meaning that the structure of society does not force individuals to act criminally) but instead recognizes a degree of individual human agency that is channeled by wider structural and cultural forces.

Critical theorists also see powerful interests at work in defining what counts as crime. This occurs when dominant groups/segments or classes define the behavior of subordinate segments or classes threatening their interests. Henry and Lanier

(2006, p. 183) explain that "Dominant groups use law as a weapon to criminalize others' behavior, and use the criminal justice system to enforce their own group's definitions of reality about what is unacceptable for the purpose of preserving their dominant positions in society." Critical theories also see crime occurring through the direct harms to subordinate segments of society by dominant segments, such as when corporations pollute the environment, or violate health and safety regulations governing the workplace.

Critical theories originally comprised two kinds: (1) conflict theory based on the idea that society was divided into competing interest groups who struggle to dominate each other and define law and crime to reflect their group's interests; and (2) radical theory whose advocates believe, based on a Marxist analysis, that the major division in society is power based on the private ownership wealth and property; the resulting class inequality allows the economically powerful elite social classes to determine laws and define what counts as crime and criminals. These radical theories tended to romanticize "street crime" and demonize corporate and white collar crime. Crime is seen as a form of resistance by subordinate segments of society, both to their own domination, and to perceived economic and social injustices. Critics point out that this "left idealism" as it is called, ignores the reality of the victims of both kinds of crime and fails to consider the harms produced by the criminal justice system to offenders and their families.

This led to a more moderate third perspective (3) known as "left realism," which saw crime as produced by social inequalities, relative deprivation and exclusion of lower classes members of society, particularly its "underclass." Left realists (e.g. Young & Matthews 1992) "believe that the polarizing effects of capitalism divide societies into the "haves" and "have nots" while simultaneously promoting competitive individualism, greed. This "exclusive society," as Jock Young has called it," marginalizes and abandons its poor; they suffer relative deprivation, frustration and anger, which they express through disrespect and violence inflicted on each other. Added to their misery and self-destruction is a class-biased criminal justice system that targets primarily lower class and minority males, the most vulnerable of the excluded, who are then also punished

by the criminal justice system" (Henry & Lanier 2006, p. 297). The left realist reform agenda looked to policies involving greater democratization of social institutions and empowerment of the lower classes, as well as democratic community control over criminal justice, and the pursuit of *social* justice: "It pushes for the immediate democratization of social institutions through the existing political structure, and it advocates for support programs to mitigate the harsh inequalities in the present system rather than waiting for revolutionary change (Henry & Lanier 2006, p. 298). Left realists want to "reintegrate the 'excluded' segments of the population through job training and education-for-work programs" (p. 298).

Parallel to this development in critical theory were those who challenged whether class alone was sufficient to explain domination and inequality. Feminist theorist formed a fourth approach (4) in critical theory that saw the bigger challenge coming from patriarchal social structure. Patriarchy is the "law of the father" in which male activities and accomplishments are more valued than those of females. Under patriarchy societal institutions, from the family to the factory, and from Main Street to Wall Street are structured to privilege men. However, feminist theorists disagreed about the source of male gender domination in patriarchal social systems: (i) "liberal feminists" saw domination through gender discrimination as a result of socialization in traditionally male-dominated institutions; (ii) radical feminists saw male domination as rooted in biological differences between males and females; these "are real physiological differences that science and observation have clarified, and these differences result in increased aggression and violence by men relative to women, illustrated by the fact that men commit 80 percent of all serious crime; (iii) socialist feminists saw male domination as a result of social structures and institutions that perpetuate male dominated hierarchical inequality differences of power between genders. In addition there were Marxist feminists, postmodernist feminists and social constructionist feminists, the latter of which saw crime as performing their masculine socially constructed identities. Feminists taking a social constructionist perspective argue that "the difference in male violence is a result of the gender-structured world and see crime as an outcome of the way males claim, build and sustain their power. For them, crime stems from and is an expression of, men's power, control, and domination over women. Crime is a manifestation of masculinity and is seen as 'doing gender'" (Henry & Lanier 2006, p. 203).

Current feminist criminological theory has adopted a more integrational stance arguing that gender is one of several divisions organizing social life. Gender, class, race, and ethnicity coalesce to oppress and channel in women's lives. The intersection of these forces also includes different cultural experience, socialization patterns, labor market situation and criminal justice experiences of women of color (Daly 2006).

Feminist criminal justice policy emphasizes the need to correct structural and institutionalized differences that expose women to victimization. For radical feminists, "the reduction of crime is dependent upon the complete removal of patriarchy and its replacement with the values of matriarchy, that is, connectedness, nurturing and creative difference" (Henry & Lanier 2006, p. 204). Other feminists question whether criminology is too narrow a field and want to broaden this to include feminist theory and social justice studies, arguing that criminology has largely been framed by men and doesn't have the capacity to transcend its masculinist limitations.

Postmodernism, including feminist postmodernism, informed a fifth (5) dimension of critical theory and transcends not only criminology but also modern disciplines. Postmodernism exposes the somewhat arbitrary nature of society norms values and institutions, through a process called "deconstruction" in which the fundamental assumptions are laid bare. Postmodernism "questions whether truth can ever be known and particularly questions the value of scientific methods as being any better at discovering truth than any other method of inquiry. Its advocates believe that rational thought is just one among several ways of thinking, and that it is not necessarily a superior way. It also believes (1) that rational thought is a form of power; (2) that knowledge is not cumulative; and (3) that there are pluralities of knowledge. It claims that all statements about knowledge are simply claims to truth rather than truth itself" (Henry & Lanier 2006, p. 221).

Postmodernist criminology is rooted in Foucault's post-structuralist critique of power and control was expressed in his 1977 book *Discipline and Punish*." Foucault saw crime as an outcome of a series of power relationships based on socially constructed differences created at multiple levels of society. Crime is thereby a coproduction of all of society, rather than the bad decisions of particular individuals or groups through whom harmful action is perpetrated. Postmodernist criminology looks toward policies that seek to empower divergent voices by including them in social change, including changing the discourse of crime talk and harm spectacles into a replacement discourse of care and reconstruction.

Since the 1990s a distinctive postmodernist criminology has emerged, the most elaborated version of which has been termed "constitutive criminology" (Henry & Milovanovic 1996). Constitutive theory recognizes that the social structures of inequality are not only the source of the harm that is crime, but are themselves crimes. Moreover, humans generate these inequalities through their use of discourse (talk), which create divisions and values. Once created, these socially constructed complex systems of inequality are self-perpetuating, and are sustained through the continued investment of energy into elaborating these inequalities.

The policy response of constitutive theory is to replace harm-producing discourse with discourse that is healthy and constructive and invest energy and build institutional structures around this. Like anarchists constitutive theorists believe in a decentralized system of restorative justice designed to reintegrate offenders, victims and community. They also believe "social judo" (turning the power of the offender back on itself), is preferable to a retributive system that adds new harms to those already present.

The postmodernist critique was one of the forerunners of a holistic approach to thinking about crime that is called "cultural criminology" (Ferrell et al. 2010) that explores the use and subversion of mass media images by those subject to the power of others' discursive practices. Crime here is seen as a mediated phenomenon, meaning that mass media and popular culture shapes and filters discourse in stories about crime. Cultural criminology, then, represents a sixth (6) area of critical theory which suggests that any individual action that produces harm is a reflection and an outcome of media communication and popular culture: "cultural criminology explores the many ways in which cultural forces interweave with the practices of crime and crime control. It emphasizes the centrality of meaning, representation, and power in the always contested construction of crime–whether crime is constructed as video-taped entertainment or political protest, as ephemeral event or subcultural subversion, as social danger or state-sanctioned violence." (Ferrell et al. 2008, p. 2). In cultural criminology crime becomes a form of play, and artistic expression and moments of resistance; a means to escape the constraint of linear and orderly social structures.

A seventh (7) critical theory of crime emanates from an anarchist perspective that opposes all forms of power and domination, and that has blossomed into two other applications: peacemaking criminology and restorative justice. It sees crime as conflict and seeks to reconcile the conflicting parties by bringing peace through restorative justice practices. Anarchist criminology first emerged in 1980 with Larry Tifft and Dennis Sullivan's *The Struggle to be Human: Crime, Criminology and Anarchism* and reappeared in the 1990s, largely through the writing of Hal Pepinsky and Jeff Ferrell (who went on to become one of the founders of cultural criminology). Anarchist criminology charges all hierarchical systems of power and authority with creating divisions and conflict between people, indeed it sees crime as an expression and embodiment of conflict.

In spite of the connotation that anarchy implies disorder and overthrow of government, it actually refers to a society without rulers (disorder is feared by supporters of hierarchical systems). Instead of the feared chaos, anarchists believe that without government, humans would organize a world through mutual aid and collaboration.

Hal Pepinsky joined with Richard Quinney and in 1991 laid out what peacemaking criminology would look like. Peacemaking, like anarchist criminology, is predicated on individual responsibility and collaborative negotiation to overcome conflict. "Instead of making 'war' on problems, peacemaking advocates believe that celebrating mutual respect and understanding are less likely to produce conflict, and when problems arise these should be approached in ways that diffuse them rather than solidify them" (Henry & Lanier 2006, p. 257). Under conventional retributive forms of justice, "The state (government) makes war on crime and suppresses crime with violence or the threat of violence. … State sanctioned violence simply perpetuates a cycle that does not reduce crime but adds its own violence to that which has already occurred" (Henry & Lanier 2006, p. 258).

Whereas anarchists call for total replacement of the existing system of state-run criminal justice with a mutual aid system of decentralized, face-to-face justice, peacemaking criminology calls for alternatives that problem solve among participants and change the structure of traditional institutions in the process. This should be a system of "restorative justice" that incorporates 1980s "peacemaking" and "abolitionist" ideas rather than war-making and fear-mongering typical of state control and punishment. The concept of restorative justice employing these principles involving offender-victim mediation, talking circles and conferencing, requires active community participation toward conflict resolution. It has been incorporated into many levels of justice, and is increasingly replacing traditional discipline in schools. In contrast to punitive justice, restorative justice involves offenders taking responsibility for the harm they cause victims and with victims developing forms of compensation and restoration. Interestingly, some of the original anarchist criminologists such as Sullivan and Tifft have become leading figures in the field of restorative justice, contributing books and editing a journal devoted to the topic. Although restorative justice has been criticized by some radical criminologists for failing to address the fundamental structural inequalities that create conflict (Shank & Takagi 2004), it argues that it makes change over time by changing the way intuitions operate their social control systems that eventually changes their structure.

REFERENCES

Daly, K. (2006). "Feminist Thinking about Crime" in S. Henry and M.M. Lanier (Eds.), *The Essential Criminology Reader*, pp. 205–213. Boulder, CO: Westview press.

Ferrell, J., Hayward, K. J. & Young, J. (2008). *Cultural Criminology: An Invitation*. London, UK: Sage.

Foucault, M. (1977). *Discipline and Punish*. Harmondsworth, UK: Allen Lane.

Henry, S. and Lanier, M. M. (Eds.) (2006). *The Essential Criminology Reader*. Boulder, CO: Westview Press.

Henry, S. & Milovanovic, D. (1996). *Constitutive Criminology: Beyond Postmodernism*. London, UK: Sage.

Pepinsky H. & Quinney, R. (Eds.). (1991). *Criminology as Peacemaking*. Bloomington: Indiana University Press.

Shank, G. &Takagi, P. (2004). "Critique of Restorative Justice." *Social Justice* 31 (3): 147–163.

Tifft, L. & Sullivan, D. (1980). *The Struggle to be Human: Crime Criminology and Anarchism*. Sanday, Orkney, UK: Cienfuegos Press.

Young, J. & Matthews, R. (Eds.). (1992) *Rethinking Criminology: The Realist Debate*. London, UK: Sage.

CHAPTER
VIII

Conflict, Radical, and
Left Realist Theories

CRITICAL CRIMINOLOGY

Stuart Henry

CRITICAL CRIMINOLOGY AS STRUCTURAL THEORY

Criminological theory can be divided into three broad kinds based on where their advocates believe or assume the source of crime is located: individual, social process, and structural. Critical criminology refers to a group of theories of the structural type. Individual-based theories assume that the causes of crime lie either in individual choice (classical and neoclassical) that may be limited by opportunity or circumstance (rational and situational choice), or in bio-psychological differences (biological, trait-based personality, or psychological), or in some combination of these choices and internal forces. Social process-based theories such as social learning, social control, and labeling theory believe that the ongoing social relations between members of groups influence the meaning of individuals' choices and actions, including whether they violate rules and laws, and what consequences follow from such violation. In contrast, social structure-based theories, such as anomie, strain, social ecology, conflict, and those grouped under the term critical criminology, assume that external forces, resulting from the configuration and organization of society as a whole, shape the nature of social institutions, and within these, channel the behavior of humans and their interaction.

Critical criminology, although a structural theory, differs in significant ways from the more reformist-oriented structural theories of strain and social ecology, although having some similarities with conflict. Moreover, although critical criminology emphasizes the crucial importance of social structure it also considers human agency to be significant, and sees society as a distinctly human product that can be changed through human actions. Thus, social structure only has the appearance of an external force; critical criminology's role is to demystify that appearance to facilitate social change.

Critical criminology (not to be confused with critical social theory of the Frankfurt School) is not one distinct theory but an umbrella term for a range of different critical structurally-oriented theories. In its most inclusive interpretation, critical criminology includes the following theories: conflict, radical, left realist, anarchist or abolitionist, peacemaking, critical feminist, critical race, queer, postmodernist, constitutive, chaos, and topology. A more restrictive interpretation would exclude the first three of these, reserving the term "critical" for theoretical developments that are post-1970s, and those primarily influenced by non-Marxist social theory.

TYPES OF CRIME

The range of theories associated with critical criminology has changed and expanded over time, although there are underlying unifying themes that cut across these differences. In its broadest interpretation, critical criminology includes all theoretical positions that see the source of crime stemming from societally generated conflict, fueled by a system of domination, based on inequality, alienation, and injustice. Critical theories are similar in their claim that crime is the direct or indirect outcome of conflict between different segments of society. They see members of society divided by their differences, and they challenge the way difference is exploited as a basis of power and interest. They typically advocate a change from criminal justice to the broader concept of social justice. Looking at the similarities among these critical criminologies, they all assume that segments of society, based on whatever difference, exist in relations of inequality to each other, meaning that some segments have more power than others, existing in a hierarchical relationship to each other. Individual humans are seen as products of these hierarchical power structures. Although theorists variously recognize a degree of individual human agency, ultimately they see humans as repressed, co-opted, and manipulated for the benefit of dominant powerful interests.

Crime, from the critical criminological perspective, is harm that comes from difference in power, and it can be manifest in several ways. One manifestation occurs when dominant groups or segments define the behavior of subordinate segments as threatening their interests. Dominant groups use law as a weapon to criminalize others' behavior, and use the criminal justice system to enforce their group's definitions of reality about what is unacceptable (this use of law can be considered as one kind of "state crime"). Groups or segments do this for the purpose of preserving their own dominant positions in the social order.

A second manifestation of crime to the critical criminologist is the direct abuse and disrespect of subordinate segments by dominant segments, such as when corporations pollute the environment, or violate health and safety regulations designed to protect employees (corporate and organizational crime, also called "suite crime"). This harm is compounded by the legal loop holes or purchased legal protection that limit the consequences to which the powerful are liable. Another version of this kind of disrespect occurs when whites, males, or heterosexuals marginalize and discriminate against blacks, women, gays, and lesbians.

Third, critical criminologists see crime as a form of resistance by subordinate segments to their domination and to perceived economic and social injustices. Resistance is manifest through such means as riots, looting, workplace theft, sabotage, and civil disobedience (also called political crime or collective crime). Crime as resistance is also seen in political action campaigns and protests.

Fourth, to the critical criminologist, crime is the harm created by a society being competitively divided such that personal, individual, and egotistic interests are pursued at the expense of social, collective, altruistic, or humanistic interests. Critical criminologists believe that many of the crimes that the structurally powerless commit on each other, such as interpersonal violence, theft, hate, and domestic abuse (called "street crimes"), are the result of this competitive individualization.

DEFINING CRITICAL CRIMINOLOGY

Critical criminology is designated "critical" for several reasons. It is "critical" because theorists neither accept nor limit themselves to state definitions of crime. They prefer to define crime as social harm or as violations of human rights. Nor does critical criminology accept that the individual offender causes crime independently of the wider social context, without also considering how offenders have themselves been "victimized." Such victimization occurs, first, by society through its inequities, dehumanization, and alienation and subsequently, by the criminal justice system, through its selective processing of the powerless for punishment. Critical criminologists are critical too, because they oppose the existing social order of inequality, facilitated through the capitalist, patriarchal, or race-divided organization of society. They question the purpose and methods of the criminal justice system, which they see as a reflection of the dominant power structure, rather than an instrument to correct injustice or achieve social justice. Finally, they are critical because the policy changes they advocate usually demand a radical transformation, not just of criminal justice, but the total social and political organization of society. Thus, instead of seeing some people as inherently "bad apples" (individual theories) or as causing other apples to go bad (social process theories), critical criminologists see the society as a "bad barrel" that will turn most of the apples bad that are put into it; the only solution is a new barrel. In seeking to understand this cluster of critical criminologies it is helpful not only to identify what they have in common, but also to outline how their analyses diverge from each other.

THEORIES OF CRITICAL CRIMINOLOGY

Critical criminological theories differ over what they take to be the nature and relative importance of the differences that are the basis of social inequality. These differences include class, race, gender, ethics or morality, ideology, religion or belief, social status, and for some, an infinite variety of yet to be constructed differences. Conflict theory, for example, challenges group power, especially elite group power. Radical criminology (both its instrumental and structural Marxist versions) - challenges class power, especially dominant class power; left realism challenges the rights of the powerful to control state institutions, especially the police; feminism (radical, Marxist, socialist, and postmodernist) challenges male power and the patriarchal social structure based on it; queer theory challenges heterosexual power and the homophobia that results from it; critical race theory challenges white power, especially white supremacy; anarchist and peacemaking criminology challenges governmental power and the power of "professionalism"; and postmodernist and constitutive theory (including varieties of chaos theory) challenge all bases of power and inequality based on known and yet to be constructed differences.

DIFFERENCES BETWEEN CRITICAL CRIMINOLOGISTS

In 1958, George Vold developed a conflict theory that was rooted in the classic late 19th century sociology of George Simmel and the 1950s reformist sociology of Ralf Darendorf, Louis Coser and Thorsten Sellin. Here society was seen as divided on several dimensions, made up of numerous groups, each defining their own interests and struggling for the power to define and control public issues. Conflict theorists recognize that crime may stem from differences in economic wealth, a clash of cultures, or from the outcome of symbolic and instrumental struggles over status, from differences in ideology, morality, religion, race, and ethnicity. Thus, Austin Turk argued that some groups, claiming an allegiance to mainstream culture, become dominant by gaining control of key resources. Dominant groups are able to criminalize the behavior of those deviating from their own cultural standards and behavioral norms. Conflict criminologists, saw crime as having both instrumental and symbolic roots in a multidimensional fragmented society, with struggles for control occurring at multiple sites of difference.

Other critical criminologists in the early 1970s, however, such as the British "new criminologists" Ian Taylor, Paul Walton, and Jock Young and American radicals such as Richard Quinney, William Chambliss, Tony Platt, and Steven Spitzer, drew on the classic works of Karl Marx and Friedrich Engels and Marxist theory's application to crime at the beginning of the 20th century by Dutch criminologist Willem Bonger. They believed that the social and symbolic dimensions of inequality were mere epiphenomenona, consequences of a deeper *economic* conflict. They saw this conflict rooted in economic power and in the appropriation and concentration of wealth by minority class interests in class-divided societies. They point to the structure of capitalism, based on the private ownership of property, which renders a society "crimogenic" by generating vast inequalities of wealth that provide the conditions for crime. But Marxist criminologists differed over the issue of whether the state is manipulated by dominant economic ruling class interests who also mystify the system that sustains their domination (instrumental Marxism), or whether the impersonal constituent forces of capitalism are responsible for its maintenance and reproduction (structural Marxism). Instrumentalists see the economic base of society as shaping the need to define behavior as crime and the intensity of enforcement strategies. Structural Marxist criminology conceptualizes a dual or many-headed power structure in which the state serves a semiautonomous role in relation to specific powerful economic interests whose position is supported by the monetary mechanism and corresponding influences from a variety of social institutions, including religion and education. Through its mediating influence, the worst excesses of economic exploitation, and the crises these create, are controlled and mitigated in the interests of legitimating the long-term maintenance of the whole capitalist system. As a result, the state and other elements of this superstructure appear as neutral elements in the power structure, allowing capitalist inequality to prevail without obvious challenge.

In contrast to conflict and Marxist theorists, critical feminist criminologists, such as Carol Smart, Meda Chesney-Lind, Kathleen Daly, and Sally Simpson, see the major division around which conflict emerges as patriarchy. This is the "law of the father" in which male activities and accomplishments are more valued than those of females, and in which societal institutions, from the family to the factory, are structured to privilege men. These critical feminist criminologists challenged the gender-structured world but have different emphases.

A similar transcendent position has also been adopted by critical race and by queer theorists. They began by observing the different ways minority groups were treated, and how the legal system obscures racial identity, resulting in white and heterosexual standards being imposed on everyone. They moved to oppose systemic discrimination, prejudice, bigotry, economic marginalization, harassment, and oppression. The ultimate challenge is to help bring social change that reduces the harms caused by these social and institutional structures of difference. Indeed, many, such as critical race theorist Katheryn Russell, now see a value in exploring the intersections of these structures of inequality and difference based on class, race, gender, and sexual preference.

Instead of class, gender, race, or sexual preference, anarchist criminologists such as Larry Tifft and Dennis Sullivan writing initially in the late 1970s and Jeff Ferrell in the 1990s, see all hierarchical systems of power and authority, whatever their configuration, as flawed. They believe that hierarchical systems of authority and domination should be opposed and that existing systems of justice should be replaced by a decentralized system of negotiated justice in which all members of society participate and share their decisions. According to Ferrell, recent anarchist criminology is an "integration" of critical approaches that seeks to relate crime as a meaningful activity of resistance to both its construction in social interaction and its larger construction through processes of political and economic authority. Anarchists call for total replacement of the existing system of state-run criminal justice with a mutual aid system of warm, living, decentralized, face-to-face justice. This should be a system of "restorative justice" that incorporates the 1980s "peacemaking" and "abolitionist" ideas of Harold Pepinsky and Richard Quinney, rather than war making and fear mongering, typical of state control and punishment.

In a polar opposition to the idealism of anarchist criminology, "left realism" was a position founded in the 1980s by Jock Young, Roger Matthews, John Lea, and Brian MacLean. Instead of what they saw as romantic celebrations of the offender as a primitive revolutionary, argued by some "idealist" Marxist theorists and anarchists, left realists focus on the reality and seriousness of harm to the powerless created by the similarly structurally powerless "street" offenders. Unlike critical perspectives, which focus on crimes of the powerful, definitions of crime, and "victimization" of powerless offenders by the state, left realism emphasizes the relationship between offenders, victims, and the criminal justice system. Left realists want to both strengthen and democratically control the criminal justice system of capitalist society, believing that the law can provide the structurally powerless with real gains, if not ideal victories.

Finally, and most recently, through the work of Stuart Henry, Dragan Milovahovic, Peter Manning, Bruce Arrigo, Gregg Barak, and T. R. Young, the 1990s saw the arrival in critical criminology of postmodernist influenced constitutive theory, which also incorporated ideas of social constructionist theory, chaos theory, semiotics, and topology theory, into an integrated critical theory.

At its simplest, constitutive theory recognizes that the social structures of inequality are not only the source of the harm that is crime, but that the inequalities themselves are crimes. Moreover, these inequalities are generated by human agents through their use of discourse (talk). Once created, these socially constructed complex systems of inequality are self-perpetuating in their own expansion, and are sustained through the continued investment of energy into a discourse that constantly elaborates the inequality.

EVALUATION

Critical criminology has fared better at providing new ways to see the world than it has at being proven through empirical research findings, or at delivering social justice. Early formulations of critical criminology lend themselves readily to the criticism that they either tend toward romanticism, as in anarchism and left idealism or to the dogmatic and doctrinal, as in instrumental Marxism or radical feminism. In either case, they embodied an unrealistic and untestable air of "conspiracy theory." Some critics have pointed out that critical criminology's class-based revelations are rather unremarkable, merely a restatement of the old Robin Hood adage that the poor steal from the rich to survive but also, like the rich, they steal for greed.

In the late 1970s, Carl Klockars attacked the weak empirical base of much Marxist criminology and argued that radicals misrepresent capitalist societies as destructively class divided, when in reality, class divisions can be beneficial, and that many divisions involve interest groups that unite people across class boundaries. The instrumental Marxist view has been criticized by outsiders and insiders alike for obscuring the diversity and conflict within both the state and corporate elites. Critics point out that not all law is designed to protect ruling capitalist class interests but is intended to protect the overall system of capitalism. Like left realists such as Jock Young, Klockars later asserted that the state actually empowers of oppressed people's rights as genuine, not as a sham or a mystification. Klockars accused early critical theorists of ignoring the contradictory facts, such as crime in socialist societies and the apparent low crime

rate in some very capitalistic societies like Switzerland and Japan. Moreover, by implicitly, if not explicitly, romanticizing socialism, early critical theorists failed to take into account the known dehumanizing conditions that socialism, as practiced in large portions of the world, produced. Furthermore, the implicit deterministic character of early versions of critical criminology minimized the self-generated uncooperative behavior of humans. Thus, these criminologists were unprepared for the wholesale rejection of socialist practice and their adoption of the crudest and more exploitative principles and practices of capitalism.

Most recently, critical and radical criminologists have been forced to acknowledge that other dimensions of social inequality such as race, gender, and sexuality are also important. Yet these other versions of critical criminology have also been subject to criticism. Stanley Cohen sees left realism's reformist turn as a reflection of both the aging of radical criminologists and the tempering of their ideas in response to broader social developments such as stable conservative governments, growing awareness of the relevance of feminism and ecology movements, and the collapse of state socialism. Left realism has been challenged for its central contradictions between the call for increased powers of the state to control crime, and their preferences for a minimalist state, subject to public scrutiny and accountability. It has been questioned for taking the spotlight off crimes of the economically powerful outside the state, especially those of corporations. The most damning criticism comes from feminist scholars who, like Phil Scraton, have argued that the construction of the realism or idealism debate has been diversionary, regressive, and purposefully misrepresentative of the advances within critical feminist criminology since the mid-1970s. Feminists claim that left realism, like radical criminology generally, has remained gender blind and as such remains part of the "male stream" ignoring activism, research, and theory drawn from women's experiences.

However, feminist criminologist positions have their own inherent weaknesses. Not the least of these stems from the very notion that gender is the central organizing theme, which some have accused of essentialism, exclusionism, and implicit racism. In spite of recognizing the socially constructed nature of "femininity" and "sexuality," there is a failure to reference the different cultural experience, socialization patterns, and experiences in the labor market and criminal justice system of black women. This does not deny a gender analysis but requires that gender include sensitivity to racial and ethnic differences. Such a sensitivity would also need to overcome the simplistic black and white distinction within a gender analysis. Different cultural experiences, such as those of Latino women, Asian women, American Indian women, and women with disabilities, would also benefit from such a broadened feminist analysis.

Though it is early to evaluate the impact of postmodernism on criminology, especially its more recent adventures into chaos theory, topology theory, and catastrophe theory, its influence is being felt in the increased questioning of traditional criminological concepts, and especially through the constitutive criminological challenge. Postmodern contributions have been criticized for their obscure language, difficult prose, and for claiming that there are no absolute standards by which to judge outcomes and effects. Critical criminology has faced considerable criticism over the years from more traditional rivals, but more recently, it is the criticism from within that has been the most devastating. The most important challenge facing critical theorists is how to develop a transcendent position that applies its critique to any criteria of difference that is used by one group to privilege themselves over others, while simultaneously recognizing the unique historical and local features of any specific differences. Moreover, how do critical criminologists problematize difference, while using difference to distinguish themselves from the mainstream? Finally, perhaps the ultimate challenge is the implementation in practical terms of their theoretical challenge. How does one realistically bring about the necessary broader changes that critical theories of crime imply in a society where by far the majority is substantially invested in reproducing the very system

that these theorists are criticizing? The hope is that humans locked in their local struggles will become aware that their specific issues are merely a facet of the underlying problem and that unless this is addressed the problems will emerge in another form. Of course, the paradox is that such a revelation requires the very identification with others' humanity that is undermined by a system based on difference and division.

REFERENCES AND FURTHER READING

Arrigo, B.A., *Social Justice/Criminal Justice: The Maturation of Critical Theory in Law, Crime and Deviance.* Belmont, CA: West/Wadsworth, 1999.

Barak, G., *Integrating Criminologies,* Boston, MA: Allyn and Bacon, 1998.

Kathleen, D. and Maher, L., *Criminology at the Crossroads: Feminist Readings in Crime and Justice.* New York, NY: Oxford, 1998.

Henry, S. and Milovanovic, D., *Constitutive Criminology: Beyond Postmodernism.* London, UK: Sage, 1996.

Lynch, M.J., Michalowski, R.J., and Groves, W.B., *The New Primer in Radical Criminology: Critical Perspectives on Crime, Power and Identity.* Willow Tree Press, 2000.

MacLean, B.D. and Milovanovic, D. (Eds.) *Thinking Critically about Crime.* Vancouver: Collective Press, 1997.

Messerschmidt, J., *Masculinities and Crime.* Lanham, MD: Rowman and Littlefield, 1993.

Martin, D.S. and Milovanovic, D. (Eds.) *Race, Gender and Class in Criminology.* New York, NY: Garland, 1996.

Milovanovic, D. (Ed.) *Chaos, Criminology and Social Justice.* New York, NY: Greenwood, 1997.

Reiman, J., *The Rich Get Richer and the Poor Get Prison: Ideology, Crime and Criminal Justice.* Boston, MA: Allyn and Bacon, 1998.

Russell, K.K., *The Color of Crime.* New York, NY: New York University Press, 1998.

Young, J. and Matthews, R., *Rethinking Criminology. The Realist Debate.* London, UK: Sage.

RADICAL CRIMINOLOGY

Michael J. Lynch and Paul B. Stretesky

C riminology textbooks tend to lump critical theories of crime together, as if all critical theories were the same. This results in a superficial examination of critical explanations of crime. To avoid this problem, this essay examines one form of critical perspective, radical criminology (on other forms see Arrigo 1995; Ferrell and Sanders 1995; Henry and Milovanovic 1996; Milovanovic 1994, 1995; DeKeseredy and Schwartz 1996; Schwartz and Friedrichs 1994).

Radical criminology examines how forms of inequality, oppression, and conflict affect crime and law. Consequently, radicals are interested in how structural inequalities evident in a society's class, race, and gender structures affect (1) participation in crime, (2) how crime is defined, and (3) the making and enforcement of laws. To answer these issues, radicals examine crime relative to the social, economic, and political structures and forms of inequality found in a given society at a particular moment in history (Lynch and Groves 1995). As a result, radical explanations pay close attention to history and culture. Thus, even though general "rules" are useful for describing the content of radical criminology, in practice, radical explanations of crime vary depending upon the historical era and cultural system to which they are applied. Taking this historical and cultural preference into account, this essay focuses primarily on modern U.S. society.

In contemporary American society, three forms of inequality—race, class, and gender—stand out. Each form of inequality has an impact on an individual's life course, the nature of power, and who holds power within society. These forms of inequality and their impact on crime are examined below.

When radicals speak about race, class and gender, they use these terms differently than traditional criminologists. For traditional criminologists, race, class, and gender tend to be interpreted as characteristics of individuals, and are used to identify subjects of study as "middle-class," "African American," or "female." For radicals, race, class, and gender are both identities and structures. As structures, race, class, and gender contain culturally and historically specific "rules" that define (1) the types of power groups possess, (2) a group's social and economic positions within society, and (3) the opportunities for success people from these groups typically possess. As identities, race, class, and gender tell us about social expectations concerning the behavior of people from different groups and the ways in which people act to construct themselves (their identities). For example, "middle-class" defines a location in U.S. social structure, which in turn defines the types of power persons can access and wield, their opportunities or pathways to success, and the forms of oppressive conditions which they control or which control them. But, being "middle-class" also defines behavioral expectations, and we expect middle-class people to behave in particular ways. We identify middle-class people by what they wear, where they live, and the schools they attend. Similarly, being African American (or white or Hispanic) or female (or male) affects a person's access to power and success and our behavioral expectations and responses. In short, a person's structural location carries with it different forms of access and different behavioral expectations. For radicals, these differences are evidence of inequality, and these inequalities help explain the probability that people located in different structural locations will engage in crime or will be labeled as criminals.

To explain this view, we first examine the nature of inequality in U.S. society. Next, we examine some background issues necessary to understand the radical view of crime. This discussion is followed by an examination of the relationship between class, race, gender, economic power, and inequality. We then examine the radical view on street crime, corporate crime, and environmental justice. The final section of this essay examines some policy implications related to this view.

CLASS, RACE, AND GENDER: SOCIAL STRATIFICATION AND ECONOMIC INEQUALITY

Radical analysis stems from the observation that societies are based on unequal social relationships characterized by a conflict between the "haves" and "have-nots" (Marx and Engels 1995, 1970). The nature and form of these conflicts vary historically and culturally. Despite the relative nature of this claim, radicals view conflict and inequality as the basis of most crime. As a result, it follows that the best way to reduce crime is to eliminate social, economic, and political inequality.

For radicals, unequal societies are characterized by a lopsided distribution of power. The more unequal a society, the greater a problem crime becomes. Inequality also has important implications for individuals living within a society. Inequality means that some people will have less (or more) access to life chances for success, and that success is a function of a person's structural position within society. Because many people occupy similar structural locations, their opportunities for success (or failure) are also similar. Radicals focus on race, class, and gender inequality to explain patterns of crime because people who occupy these structurally defined positions have similar sets of opportunities and behave or are treated in similar ways or both. Evidence of how race, class, and gender structure success and crime is examined later in this essay.

Crime and Inequality: An Overview

There are two ways to examine the influence of inequality on crime. With respect to street crime, radicals argue that those denied equal access to life chances for success will be more likely to (1) engage in crime or (2) have their behaviors defined and labeled as criminal (or both). A few brief examples illustrate this point. Studies indicate that criminal law, the most coercive form of social control society can render, tends to focus on the lower classes and minorities. Policing, for instance, is concentrated in lower-class and minority communities, and prisons primarily house people who are lower-class and minorities. Historically, crimes such as vagrancy and loitering were enacted to control the working and lower classes (Chambliss 1964; Harring 1983). Throughout history, drug laws have served similar functions, typically focusing on controlling drugs commonly used by minorities and the lower class (Brownstein 1991, 1996, 2000).

Inequality and the emphasis on acquiring power also helps explain the crimes of the powerful. Two issues are important here. First, inequality and power help explain why law focuses on the lower classes while neglecting the equally harmful behavior of the powerful (Reiman 1998). Second, our culture's emphasis on power and wealth helps explain why people with power use illegal means to obtain even more power (Friedrichs 1996; Simon 1999). In short, for radicals, the forms of inequality, power, and conflict that are part of the organization of American society can be used to explain the crime of the lower classes (and minorities and women) as well as the crimes of the upper classes.

Class Inequality and Crime: Background

In examining the relationship between inequality and crime, early radicals focused on social class, basing their views on Marx's analysis of capitalism. The emphasis on class was a defining characteristic of radical criminology, which distinguished it from all other forms of criminology. A brief overview of this position is presented below.

For Marx, the history of all societies was the history of class conflict, or the opposition of the "haves" and "have-nots." But Marx was particularly interested in examining how these conflicts played out in capitalist societies. There, conflicts revolve around the opposition of capitalists and workers. Capitalists, who own and control the machinery of production and capital, need workers to carry out their objectives of accumulating capital, and capitalists' economic power results from their ability to control and exploit the labor of workers. Capitalists also possess the ability to translate their economic power into political power. In modern societies this occurs through activities such as campaign contributions and lobbying.

Marx argued that capitalists have a particular set of interests to protect, and that their primary interest is establishing circumstances conducive to profit-making. Marx demonstrated that capitalists' profits are directly related to workers' wages, and that it was in the capitalists' best interests to keep wages to a minimum.

In contrast, workers' interests revolve around increasing wages, and in general, activities that advantage capitalists disadvantage workers. Further, whereas capitalists are relatively powerful, workers are relatively powerless, having little influence over law-making and economic processes. Nevertheless, throughout history, workers have struggled to obtain their share of society's power and wealth, demanding expanded employment opportunities, higher wages, better working conditions, and health care and retirement benefits. Workers have relied on strikes, work slowdowns, and work stoppages to achieve these goals. Sometimes, when these avenues fail or are closed off, they turn to crime as an alternative to legitimate means to success (Quinney 1980).

Law is an important method of "mediating" the conflicts between these classes. Numerous laws defining property rights, wage levels, and working conditions have been passed throughout history. Traditional criminologists argue that these laws reflect widely shared values that represent the interests of all people in society—a view commonly called consensus theory. In contrast, radicals suggest that laws generally (though not always) favor the best interests of capitalists and that most laws, even criminal laws, have a distinct advantage for the powerful, protecting the social, economic, and political organization of society that serves as the basis of the powerful's privileged position.

As noted, this class view of crime and law is unique to radical criminology. Employing this view, early radicals were acknowledged for highlighting the effects of class and inequality on crime, and for focusing attention on crimes of the powerful. But radicals were also criticized for their "singular focus" on class and crime (see Inciardi 1980). This unidimensional focus on class has, however, been addressed by radicals (e.g., Messerschmidt 1986), and they have since incorporated other important dimensions of inequality in their explanations of crime, especially racial and gender inequality (e.g., Messerschmidt 1993, 1997; Schwartz and Milovanovic 1996). Today, a radical view that fails to acknowledge the important effect each of these structures has on crime is considered inadequate (see Schwartz and Milovanovic 1996; Lynch, Michalowski, and Groves 2000).

Despite these additions, class remains an important element of radical theories of crime. Further discussion of the radical view of class is presented in the next section.

THE RADICAL ECONOMIC MODEL

For radicals, classes are defined by how people relate to a society's economic system or mode of production. The contemporary American economy is based on capitalism and is a blend of manufacturing and service sector production. In the mid-1970s, the U.S. economy shifted from a highly concentrated form of manufacturing capitalism to service capitalism. Capitalism is one example of a mode of production. Other examples include socialism, communism, and feudalism, to name a few.

Each mode of production entails specific relations to production, or more simply, a class system. People located in different classes possess different degrees of economic, political, and social power (theoretically, this distinction does not apply to communism, though in practice, self-proclaimed communist nations have been class societies). Class divisions also determine the kinds of conflicts that will emerge in society. Under capitalism, the most important conflicts are between the owners (capitalists) of the productive forces (also called the means of production) and workers.

Radicals employ a two-class model as a heuristic device. Contemporary U.S. society, however, has more than two classes (Wright 1978), which can be defined as follows: (1) capitalists or owners of large companies, (2) managers of large businesses, (3) self-employed owners of small businesses (categories two and three comprise the petty-bourgeois or small capitalists), (4) professionals, such as doctors, lawyers, or teachers, (5) workers, from those who work on mass-production lines (manufacturing workers), to clerical and fast-food employees (service workers), to construction or unskilled workers (laborers) and (6) groups that have no relationship to production, or the surplus or marginalized populations. Surplus populations consist of the unemployed, partially employed, and underemployed as well as migrant workers, the homeless, and career criminals (whom Marx called the lumpenproletariat). In U.S. society, these populations are distributed as follows: capitalists, 2 percent; the "middle class" (two, three, and four), 15 percent; workers, 65 percent; surplus population, 18 percent (Perlow 1988).

For radicals, class membership is important because it affects people's access to power. Research has shown that being born into a particular class significantly impacts a person's life chances for success and, more often than not, people remain part of the class into which they are born (Frank and Cook 1995). Most Americans don't define class in terms of a person's relationship to production, but rather with respect to income or wealth. To make our discussion relevant to the way most Americans think about class, we next review information on wealth and income.

CLASS, WEALTH, AND INCOME: INEQUALITY IN U.S. SOCIETY

Decisive evidence of social stratification and inequality in the United States emerges when examining the distribution of our nation's wealth (stored-up capital represented by savings and property holdings and other assets) and income.

One way to assess inequality is to examine the concentration of wealth—the ratio of wealth owned by the richest 20 percent of the population compared to the poorest 20 percent of the population. These data indicate that the United States has the most lopsided class system of any advanced nation in the world. It also has one of the highest rates of crime. In Japan, this ratio of inequality is four; in Germany, five; in the United States, this ratio is nine (U.N. Development Program 1993). In other words, the richest 20 percent are twice as far removed from the poor as the rich in other nations. Other measures paint a similar picture of inequality. In Britain, the richest 1 percent of the population owns 18 percent of the wealth; in France and Canada, this figure is about 25 percent; in Sweden 16 percent. In the United States, the richest 1 percent owns 39 percent of the wealth (Wolff 1995).

Faced with these facts, people argue that in America, the land of opportunity, things have improved for those at the bottom of the social structure over time, and that competition and hard work—the invisible hand of market systems—have reduced inequality. Evidence indicates otherwise: today, the wealthy have more and the poor less than they once did. Economist Edward Wolff (1995) noted that federal data "show that between 1983 and 1989 the top 20 percent of wealth holders received 99 percent of the total gain in marketable wealth, while the bottom 80 percent of the population got only 1 percent" (58). This trend was more exaggerated between 1989 to 1992 (Wolff 1995). Increasing inequality is revealed in the following as well: in the United States, the number of millionaires and billionaires increased at the same time that home-ownership and retirement savings declined for middle-income families (Wolff 1995, 1995b). Other data show a hardening of class lines and a polarization of wealth and classes in the United States over the past fifty years (Perlow 1988).

Income Inequality

Inequality is also evident in the unequal distribution of income. In 1994, the top 20 percent of income earners took home about half of all income, while the bottom 20 percent received only 3.6 percent (U.S. Census Bureau 1999). The "super rich"—the top 5 percent— took home nearly 22 percent of all income. This picture of income inequality becomes more exaggerated if we consult a broader period of time, and available evidence suggests that income inequality has widened over the past 50 years (Currie and Skolnick 1984,100–107). In recent years, the lowest 20 percent of income earners saw their share of income decline from 4.0 percent to 3.6 percent (1967–1999). In contrast, income for the top 1 percent more than doubled during a time when median income was relatively stable and the cost of living doubled (1979–1989) (Frank and Cook 1995, 5). Contrary to capitalist ideology, these facts indicate little hope for the vast majority of people within the lower class—and increasingly, the middle class—to improve their economic conditions. Wealth and income, in other words, trickle up, not down, and many of the wealthy are so well off that they are referred to as the "super rich" (Perlow 1988) or the "top-out-of-sight" (Fussell 1997).

Increasing inequality calls into question the idea that hard work gets you ahead. Frank and Cook (1995) argue that despite working harder and longer, U.S. workers are worse off today than 30 years ago, working longer hours for reduced wages, accumulating more personal debt, and having less in savings and retirement benefits (Frank and Cook 1995; Schor 1995). In short, the rich are getting much richer, while most of the rest of us are working harder and losing ground.

Many object to this depiction of American society, citing evidence of "people they know" who "made it." The big picture, however, suggests that these kinds of success stories are rare. National statistics indicate that many more people failed to achieve economic success, are in the same place they were decades earlier, or have seen their economic circumstances decline (Barlett and Steele 1992; Frank and Cook 1995). In sum, the 1980s and 1990s accelerated a growing pattern of inequality that has characterized the American class system over the past 50 years.

Inequality and the Shift from a Manufacturing to a Service Economy

The accelerated path of inequality in the United States can be explained by economic transformations that occurred over the past 25 years. In the mid-1970s, the United States began to shift from a manufacturing to a service economy. In a nutshell, this shift caused a decline in high-wage manufacturing or blue-collar employment as these jobs were shifted to nations with lower wage rates; a rise in low-wage, service sector and menial employment; declines in the quality and quantity of rewards associated with white-collar work; high levels of unemployment among minorities residing in urban areas; and decreases in leisure time (Schor 1995; Frank and Cook 1995; Wilson 1997).

To this point, we have reviewed inequality as it relates to income, wealth, and social class. In the United States, inequality is also a function of gender, race, and ethnicity.

GENDER AND ECONOMIC INEQUALITY

Economic inequality has an important gender dimension. Historically, women have less access to economic and political power than men, and this remains true today despite claims that affirmative action has eliminated discrimination against women (see Carnoy 1994; Lynch 1996; Lynch and Patterson 1996). Recent reviews of income data have generated misleading conclusions concerning gender income disparity, noting, for example, that over the past fifteen years women's incomes have increased relative to men's incomes. On its face, this statement is true. But it is true not because women are being paid more, but rather because men's wages have declined (Amott 1995, 207). The decline in men's wages can be explained relative to the shift to a service economy, which displaced men from manufacturing jobs and high-paying white-collar employment. This transformation has had little effect on women, who have traditionally been employed in low-wage service sector jobs (Figart and Lapidus 1996, 1998). On average, women earn only 73 percent as much as men (U.S. Census Bureau 1999). This gender wage disparity is evident across all forms of employment, and even women in high-status positions (physicians, lawyers, and accountants) earn significantly less than men in those fields (Ruth 1995; Figart and Lapidus 1998). Occupational and income gender inequality has numerous adverse impacts on women, which may help explain the increase in female crime over the past two decades. Contributing to gender inequality is the increasing number of women who live in female-headed households that are at or below the poverty level, a process called the feminization of poverty (Messerschmidt 1986; Kozol 1995; Rotella 1995; Sklar 1995).

RACE, ETHNICITY, AND ECONOMIC INEQUALITY: RACISM AND INEQUALITY

In the United States, economic inequality has important racial and ethnic dimensions. For example, although women are disadvantaged relative to men, not all women are equally disadvantaged; minority women suffer greater economic disadvantages than white women. The effect of race and ethnicity helps explain why minorities are more likely than whites to have lower incomes, or be part of the lower classes, and are more likely to turn to crime or to be labeled as criminals.

To be sure, relative to whites, African-Americans and Hispanics are economically disadvantaged. In 1998, for instance, median family income for whites was nearly $42,000, while black ($25,400) and Hispanic ($28,330) median family incomes were about one-third lower (U.S. Census Bureau 1999). Further, the unemployment rate for black males is more than twice that for white males (U.S. Department of Labor 1996). Employed African-American men are usually paid less tor the same work, or are more likely to be restricted to minimum wage, poorly paid service sector jobs (Carnoy 1994). Even though the middle and working classes lost ground over the past 20 years, these losses had a greater impact on blacks than whites (Carnoy 1994, 15–29).

Racism is a powerful structural force that negatively impacts African-Americans. In the United States, racism has meant that African-Americans not only hold lower-paying jobs but are also spatially segregated (Massey and Denton 1993). Segregation ensures that African Americans remain detached from economic structures that would promote their financial independence and revitalize their communities (Massey and Denton 1993).

It is commonly assumed that racism and segregation have diminished since the Civil Rights Movement. However, Massey and Denton's (1993) analysis of racial segregation in the United States shows that African-American communities have become more segregated over the past 30 years as the result of institutionalized racism, which has contributed to poor economic circumstances in African-American communities. Given these poor economic conditions, it is no surprise that crime is higher in minority communities than in white communities. Any sensible crime policy must include means of dismantling institutional discrimination and methods for revitalizing the economic base in minority communities.

The Disadvantages of Being at the Bottom

Many indicators show that the quality of life—evident in levels of illness, mental health difficulties, inadequate housing, limited access to health care, problems of self-esteem, or living in proximity to pollution and hazardous waste—declines as we descend the economic ladder. It is important to remember that these indicators are not qualities of poor people but rather result from living within a particular class and racial context that carries with it certain liabilities.

Compared to the middle and upper classes, the poor have less access to quality education, making it difficult for them to escape poverty (DiMaggio 1982; DiMaggio and Mohr 1985). Lower-income people also have less access to things the affluent take for granted, such as telephones, computers, and the Internet (e.g., Associated Press 1998) and are more likely to have hazardous waste sites in their neighborhoods, to live near polluting industries, and to suffer from environmentally induced health problems (Oilman 1995; Knox 1996, 1994, 1992a, 1992b; Knox and Gilman 1997; Stretesky and Lynch 1999). And last but not least, poor persons are more likely to be victims of violent crime. It is important to remember that these general class-linked life-chance factors are negatively enhanced for minorities.

How are the inequalities reviewed above related to crime? We will discuss these explanations in the next section.

THE CAUSES OF CRIME: A RADICAL VIEW

Crime and Social Structure

Radical criminologists locate the causes of crime within society's structure. Societies contain a variety of structural inequalities, which vary from one society to the next. The idea that crime varies with the social and economic features of a society gives rise to the claim that "a society gets the type and amount of crime it deserves" (Lynch, Michalowski and Groves 2000). In other words, the way a society is organized, the kinds of economic, racial, and gender stratification systems it contains, shapes the kinds and amounts of crime found within that society. Thus, explaining crime requires knowing about the kinds of economic, class, racial, and gender systems that operate in that society, as well as the kinds of laws and mechanisms for enforcing the law that are in operation in that society. In this view, crime is not simply the result of factors that cause crime, but is also shaped by the forms of law and the ways in which the law is enforced.

Macro versus Micro Explanations

Typically, traditional theories of crime employ a micro-level perspective to examine why individuals commit crime. In contrast, radicals employ macro-level models to examine rates of criminal offending and how the level of crime found in a society relates to its social, cultural, and economic structures. Consistent with their preference for macro-level explanations, radicals argue that it is possible to predict the level of crime in society without examining individuals' behaviors, and radical analyses of crime rates in the United States have produced very accurate predictions (Lynch, Groves, and Lizotte 1994; for review, see Lynch, Michalowski, and Groves 2000).

Connecting Structure, Inequality, and Crime

Radicals hypothesize that societies characterized by extensive networks of economic (class) and social (race and gender) inequality will have higher levels of crime than more equal societies. For radicals, crime is not the simple result of aberrant individual behavior; rather, it is caused by structural circumstances, indicating that the behavior of individuals is greatly influenced by the kinds of societies in which they live (Mills 1959).

Rather than address the broader hypothesis set out above, radicals have concentrated their efforts on explaining crime in capitalist societies (United States, England, Canada, and Australia), and most radical criminologists work in or come from these countries. As a result, radical analyses of crime explore how the inequalities and processes that characterized capitalism produce crime. This focus was inherited from the studies of crime by Friedrich Engels (Marx's friend and coauthor, who was himself a capitalist) and the Dutch criminologist Willem Bonger. We briefly review their work below, updating their view where necessary. This review is cursory and omits many subsequent studies by radical criminologists.

FRIEDRICH ENGELS

In 1845, Engels published a study of the English working class, which included his observations on crime. What follows is a description of Engels' observations and some background information needed to make sense of those observations.

As noted, capitalist society contains two primary classes: one that owns and one that labors. The working class survives by selling its labor to the capitalist class. Capitalists need to purchase labor because applied labor produces the products the capitalist class sells. The capitalist class wants to purchase labor at the lowest possible price, and it suppresses labor costs to maximize profits. Historically, and when Engels was writing, the most important means of suppressing labor costs was labor-saving technology—machinery. Machinery intensifies labor, making it more efficient, reducing the number of workers required in the manufacturing process. Technological advances benefit capitalists by lowering the cost of doing business. In contrast, technological advances negatively impact the working class. First, these advances decrease the number of jobs as machine labor replaces human laborers, generating an unemployed population that we referred to earlier as the surplus or marginal population.

Second, the generation of a surplus population increases competition for available jobs, which also contributes to a decline in wages, Engels (1973, 173) argued that job loss and declining wages can explain (in rationally understandable terms) why marginalized and even employed workers increasingly turn to crime to supplement their incomes.

This theme appears in contemporary writings of radical criminologists. Richard Quinney (1979, 1980) and David Gordon (1971), for example, argued that crime is a rational response to systems of inequitable distribution that characterize capitalism. Left with no legitimate alternatives for survival, marginalized people may turn to crime. Spitzer (1975) suggested that marginalized populations suffer a reduction in social attachments and a reduced stake in conformity that enhances the probability of criminal behavior. Because capitalism's tendency to marginalize whole groups of people is unique in the history of economic systems, capitalism is seen as responsible for the resulting levels of criminal behavior.

Under capitalist systems, competition is generally viewed as a positive force that improves products, generates innovations, and decreases prices. This view, Engels argued, neglected competition's negative consequences, which include: an increase in the surplus population, a reduction in wages, and the erosion of working-class solidarity that result from competing for a limited number of jobs. Competition also caused capitalists to violate the law to produce commodities more cheaply. Consequently, Engels viewed competition over resources as a cause of crime by the masses (1964, 224; 1973, 168–173), the businessman (1964, 201–202, 209) and the middle classes (1981, 49). In short, Engels demonstrated how capitalism generates crime. In capitalist systems, crimes are typically committed to survive and enhance profit and are the by-product of intense competition and individualism.

WILLEM BONGER

Bonger (1916), like Engels, argued that capitalism's intense competitive spirit produces crime. Bonger argued that capitalist systems socialize people to view themselves as individuals and to look out for themselves (for a modern example, see O'Connor 1985). The result is a population that does not consider how their actions might harm others. Capitalism societies, in other words, produce egoistic people, and Bonger argued that egoism generates crime among all classes. Although Bonger believed egoism was evenly distributed among all classes, he noted that the powerful's political strength enabled them to perform exploitive acts without having those acts treated/labeled as criminal. This explains why more lower-class individuals are processed by the criminal justice system than upper-class individuals.

Both Bonger and Engels emphasized an idea that came to characterize radical criminology, namely, that crime is not confined to the lower or working classes, and that many harmful acts are not treated as crimes because the people who committed them are powerful. Even though traditional criminologists focus on street crimes committed by the lower classes, radicals have concentrated on equally serious acts committed by businesses and corporations that escape legal controls, or which are defined as harms by administrative and regulatory laws. These laws are enforced by agencies, such as the Securities and Exchange Commission (SEC) which oversees stock transactions; the Occupational Safety and Health Administration (OSHA), which polices workplace safety; the Food and Drug Administration (FDA), which regulates the quality and safety of foods and drugs; and the Environmental Protection Agency (EPA), which regulates pollution and environmental laws, among others (see Frank and Lynch 1992; Friedrichs 1996; Simon 1999; Lynch, Michalowski, and Groves 2000). We examine these crimes below.

CORPORATE CRIME

In 1992, the Justice Department estimated that street crime costs approximately $18 billion. This substantial sum pales in comparison to the costs of the following in dividual corporate crimes: business frauds—$400 billion; governmental frauds—$164 billion; and EPA estimates of lost work time due to illness, diseases, and damage to buildings associated with pollution—$23 billion. Recently, Reiman (1998) estimated the total costs of corporate crime at $1 trillion, nearly 60 times the cost of all street crimes committed in the United States!

Monetarily, it is clear that corporate crime costs society much more than street crime. But corporate crimes are also more violent, causing extensive deaths and injuries (Frank and Lynch 1992). For example, the odds of workplace injures are 11 times greater than the odds of being the victim of a violent crime (Lynch, Michalowski, and Groves 2000). Unnecessary surgeries and inadequate medical care cause twice as many deaths as homicides (Reiman 1998, 78–80). Approximately 10,000 people die each year from preventable workplace accidents (injuries that could have been prevented if corporations had followed the law), while another 100,000 people die due to preventable diseases contracted in the workplace (deaths that could have been prevented if corporations had protected workers from toxic substances; see Kramer 1984). Together, these deaths, which corporations allow by their inactions, are four times higher than the number of homicides in the United States. In addition to these known deaths and injuries, countless others are caused by the marketing of unsafe foods, drugs, cosmetics, households chemicals, life-threatening herbicides and pesticides, and the aggressive advertising of tobacco and alcohol (Karliner 1997; Feagin and Lavelle 1996; Glantz et al. 1996; Gibbs 1996; Friedrichs 1996; Simon 1999; Frank and Lynch 1992).

Typically, we have assumed that the deaths and injuries corporations cause are "accidents." This excuse for corporate violence has been employed to legitimize criminological neglect of this form of violence. It is now well established, however, that corporate executives knowingly allow faulty products and dangerous chemicals to reach the marketplace. A few examples should suffice to make this point.

In the 1970s, executives at Ford Motor Company allowed Pintos to be produced even though they possessed evidence that rear-end collisions could cause gas tank leaks and explosions (Cullen, Maakestad, and Cavander 1987). The staff at CBS's *60 Minutes* recently unearthed evidence that a similar problem plagued Ford Mustangs produced during the 1960s, and that Ford had evidence of this design flaw. Similar allegations have surfaced concerning cars GM produced in the 1970s. In 1984 in Bhopal, India, Union Carbide dismantled safety equipment designed to prevent the leak of deadly gases at its production facility. A gas leak occurred at that plant, killing 2,500 and injuring as many as 200,000 people (Lynch, Nalla, and Miller 1988). Tobacco company executives have keep secret evidence of tobacco's toxicity since 1955, and in the early 1990s during testimony before Congress, they argued that to their knowledge tobacco was safe (Glantz et al. 1996). The pharmaceutical firm Wyeth-Ayerst was one of two companies to produce and sell FEN/PHEN, a diet drug, even though evidence from 30 years of research indicated severe health consequences associated with the use of the drug and its compounds (Lynch, Michalowski, and Groves 2000). Many pharmaceutical and chemical companies knowingly sell products banned in the United States (to protect public health and safety) to other countries that lack strict drug and chemical regulations (Silverman, Lee, and Lydecker 1982; Weir and Shapiro 1982). Thousands of other documented cases exist that show that corporations knowingly endanger public health in various ways (see Frank and Lynch 1992; Friedrichs 1996; Gibbs 1995; Feagin and Lavelle 1996; Karliner 1997; Simon 1999). These cases establish that corporate executives purposefully place people at risk of injury and death for the sake of economic gain. For radicals, such acts are more reprehensible than street crimes because the scope of harm is so much greater.

In the early 1970s, radical criminologists including Herman and Julia Schwendinger, Richard Quinney, William Chambliss, Paul Takagi, Tony Platt, Jock Young, Ian Taylor, and Paul Walton, among others, advanced a theoretical perspective that questioned the definition of crime, which they saw as narrowly focused on the behavior of the lower classes. These radicals sought to broaden our understanding of crime and were responsible for redirecting attention toward the kinds of corporate crimes discussed above. Traditional criminologists criticized this approach, arguing that it excluded an explanation of the crimes of the lower classes (e.g., see Inciardi 1980). This criticism was based upon a narrow reading of radical criminologists' work, which reveals that this criticism has no merit. For example, Taylor, Walton, and Young's (1973) classical book, *The New Criminology*, was devoted almost wholly to explaining street crimes; Chambliss' (1964) work on delinquency and vagrancy included clear examples of explanations of lower-class crime; and Herman and Julia Schwendinger (1970, 1985), Tony Platt (1978), and Richard Quinney (1980) also devoted significant attention to explaining lower-class crimes (see also Colvin and Pauly 1983; Greenberg 1985, 1993; Hagan 1994). It is not possible to review each of these views here. Instead, we present a unified radical explanation of crime that draws on ideas (rather than specific theories) contained in the work of radical criminologists.

THE CAUSES OF CRIME: A UNIFIED RADICAL APPROACH

Crime is not caused by one factor, but rather by many forces coming together. Thus, to explain crime, theories of crime must incorporate a wide variety of explanatory styles capable of shifting across different "levels of analysis" (Groves and Lynch 1990). Radical criminology is primarily associated with macro-level theorizing; that is, theories about how social, economic, class, racial, and gender structures affect crime rates in a given society. Macro-level theory is an example of one kind of level of analysis. Radicals, however, have also examined how other levels of analysis affect crime, including intermediary (institutional) social structures (Colvin and Pauly 1983), group structures (Schwendinger and Schwendinger 1985), cultural conditions (Ferrell and Sanders 1995), and individual level conditions (Barak 1998). Contemporary radicals rely on mixed levels of analysis to explain crime, relating each level to one another. Radicals call this kind of multilevel, relational model "contextual analysis" (Mills 1959; Groves and Lynch 1990). The term "contextual analysis" means to place crime in its context, which radicals see as a mix of macro-intermediary, and micro-level structures and conditions.

Our contextualized model of crime draws upon the insights of a number of radical criminologists. We begin with several broad observations related to America's cultural and economic system. These conditions provide the context against which we explain crime. Before beginning, we offer the following qualifying statements. First, due to space limitations, our discussion omits an important aspect of radical theories of crime, namely, how law-making and enforcement, which are also products of contextual factors, shape crime. In addition, our discussion is limited to street crime (for corporate crime, see Friedrichs 1996; Simon 1999; Lynch, Michalowski, and Groves 2000).

BACKGROUND FACTORS FOR A CONTEXTUALIZED RADICAL EXPLANATION OF CRIME

The United States is a capitalist society based on inherently unequal class divisions that translate into varying abilities to access political power and to purchase culturally valued goods. Following Merton's theory of anomie, radicals argue that cultural values are widely shared within a society, while the ability to achieve culturally valued goals is not. To paraphrase Merton, U.S. society socializes citizens to expect certain rewards and the attainment of socially desirable positions. Consequently, most Americans have similar life goals. Not all U.S. citizens, however, possess the ability to attain culturally prescribed goals. The higher the class into which an individual is born, the greater likelihood that a person will have access to wealth, power, and institutions acting as pathways to success. In the terms of another popular theory of crime, we can say that those from higher social classes have preferable life courses that maximize success and minimize the probability of engaging in crime and being labeled criminal (Sampson and Laub 1993).

Class is not the sole determinant of success. A good education is also a means to success. Here, too, the lower class is at a disadvantage, beginning with its initial entry into the public educational system. Lower-class public schools have fewer resources, such as computers, textbooks (that are likely outdated), and libraries, and physically they are in worse states of repair. In addition, where teachers can select assignments, experienced teachers are more likely to choose better schools with more facilities and are less likely to choose assignments in lower-class public schools. Not only are these schools deprived of resources and better teachers, they suffer from environments inconducive to learning. For example, evidence indicates that students attending lower-class schools are less likely to succeed in school (Rusk 1995). Empirical evidence also notes that schools in poor neighborhoods are more likely to be situated near hazardous waste sites that contain chemicals known to negatively impact cognitive processes (Lynch and Stretesky 1999).

Parental wealth has clear effects on the schools children attend, and the more wealth parents have, the greater the choice in schooling options. For example, affluent parents dissatisfied with the schools their children attend can opt to send them to private schools. Across the United States, numerous private schools cater to the children of the elite. Entry into these schools establishes a life course or pathway to success that enhances access to better educational institutions and better jobs later in life. This same kind of hierarchy characterizes U.S. universities and colleges, and only those with adequate economic resources can afford the more than $20,000 annual tuition costs at the most prestigious schools in our nation, compared to the $3,000 to $4,000 it costs to attend many state universities.

The kinds of schools children attend are a consequence of the structural location of children in society. Young children cannot choose the school they attend—that is determined by where their parent(s) can afford to live or by other factors such as redlining, a form of housing discrimination. Thus, children's life chances are intergenerational and depend upon the circumstances of their parents.

Race and ethnicity also have important impacts on life chances for success. Earlier, we noted that the United States is characterized by a system of institutionalized racism that segregates whites, blacks, and Hispanics. Institutionalized racism limits minorities' life chances for success. Proportionate to their representation in the population, more blacks and Hispanics are poor than whites, and fewer attend college or earn high school degrees. In addition, blacks and Hispanics face forms of institutionalized racism that do not impact whites. Further, although the lower classes have more limited chances for success than people from classes above them, lower-class (and within other classes as well) minorities have fewer chances for success than whites. Thus, it is not surprising that minorities are more likely to engage in street crimes compared to whites. In sum, being a member of a particular class structures (affects) the life chances a person has for success. At the same time, American culture promotes the belief that anyone can be successful. The structure of life in American society and its ideological beliefs are clearly at odds on this point. People who fail to achieve the goals promoted by our society sometimes resort to crime as an alternative means of obtaining goods society tells us are measures of success. And sometimes they resort to crime as an alternative to market mechanisms that have excluded them from participation.

Economic conditions also impact racial differences in criminal participation. As noted, minorities' chances for success have decreased over the past two decades. The decline in minorities' life chances can be traced to the mid-1970s economic restructuring in the United States. This economic transformation had its greatest impact on urban minorities who, because of past employment discrimination, were closely tied to entry-level manufacturing jobs in inner cities (Frank and Cook 1995; Wilson 1996). As the economy shifted from manufacturing to service provision and manufacturing jobs were eliminated, minorities were most hard hit. Further, the late 1970s and early 1980s were also marked by an economic recession and increased unemployment (Box 1987). That period was also accompanied by a general tendency toward inflation and a decline in relative wages (a decline in purchasing power and wages; Frank and Cook 1995). In recent years, employment has increased, but largely in low-wage sectors, and has had its greatest impact on whites. Ironically, throughout this period, black educational attainment rose, while white educational attainment remained constant (Carnoy 1994). Despite this rise in educational attainment, black employment did not expand as rapidly as white employment, while black income fell relative to white income (Carnoy 1994).

To increase profit, owners of productive forces engaged in corporate downsizing, shifting manufacturing to foreign nations and increasing the use of technology in the manufacturing sector. Each of these economic changes reduced the number of well-paying jobs and elevated unemployment. These conditions have been especially detrimental to African-Americans, and in cities like Detroit, where machine labor replaced human labor on automobile assembly lines, rates of unemployment for young black males are nearly 30 percent. Crime among this population is also high.

In the modern era, the contraction of manufacturing extended unemployment until increased employment was generated by expanding service industries. The creation of newly marginalized populations who could not find meaningful employment corresponds with the rise in crime that occurred in the 1970s and 1980s. In the broadest sense, marginalized workers find themselves in social conditions where they are detached from making a contribution to society. As Spitzer (1975) noted, these populations lack a stake in conformity, which makes crime an attractive alternative means of survival. It should also be noted that this process impacts employed workers as well, especially those whose economic status has declined due to economic transformation and increased use of technology, contributing to conditions that could propel them to commit crime (Lynch, Groves and Lizotte 1994).

It bears mention that the recent decline in crime corresponds with increased employment opportunities in the manufacturing and service industries. In contrast, traditional criminologists have suggested that these declines are due to rising rates of imprisonment. This analysis misses the mark because imprisonment rates have increased in the United States since 1972. Recent analysis suggests that there is little correlation between rising rates of incarceration and crime (Irwin and Austin 1994; Lynch 1999).

In sum, by examining patterns and trends in crime in the United States, we see that they correspond to changes in the social and economic structure of the country. Crime, whether measured by official statistics or self-reports, is higher among the lower rather than the middle or upper classes, and is higher among minorities relative to whites. Crime is also higher in urban areas, especially in regions marked by the greatest declines in capital investment and social capital, such as school resources (Hagan 1994). Empirical evidence demonstrates that crime rates are related to processes that generate high rates of profit (Lynch, Groves, and Lizotte 1994) and that unemployment, economic inequality, and poverty are also related to crime trends. Other studies indicate that the shift from a manufacturing to a service economy also had an impact on crime. Importantly, these economic conditions had their greatest negative impact on minorities, which helps explain why these groups are overrepresented in

the criminal justice system (though this cannot be done without analyzing patterns of discrimination).

TOWARDS A NEW DIRECTION: THE STUDY OF ENVIRONMENTAL JUSTICE

As noted, radical theories of crime are in a constant state of change, adapting to transformations that occur in society. The changing nature of radical criminology can be illustrated by examining green theorizing and environmental justice research.

The concept "green" is widely associated with environmentally friendly products and is often employed as an advertising gimmick. Framed more broadly, thinking green means showing concern for the connection between natural resource conservation and human welfare. At its most extreme level, being green is a political commitment to clean production practices that minimize human and environmental harms. This movement began to take shape in the early 1960s following publication of Rachel Carson's (1962) book, *Silent Spring*, and green movements grew out of more general environmental concerns that characterized the 1960s and 1970s. By the 1980s, the green movement had been formed, encompassing theoretical explanations connecting environmental pollution, race, ethnicity, class, and gender inequality—areas that also hold concerns for radical criminologists. For example, in *Dumping in Dixie*, Robert Bullard (1990) examined how racism affected the location of environmental hazards (toxic dumps). Vandana Shiva (1988) exposed the role of women as activists in green movements. More recently, economist James O'Connor (1998) called for an integration of environmental (green), class- and race-based (red) analysis. These works signaled the emergence of a perspective that exposed how the negative impacts of environmental pollution stem from oppressive and unequal race, class, ethnic and gender structures that characterize U.S. society.

In recent years, criminologists have begun to take green issues seriously (Frank and Lynch 1992; Clifford 1997; South 1998; South and Beirne 1998). One example of this concern involves the study of environmental justice (see Lynch and Stretesky 1998, 1999; Stretesky and Hogan 1998; Stretesky and

Lynch 1999). Environmental justice examines whether environmental harms (e.g., pollution, toxic waste dumping) are distributed evenly among social groups, or whether specific groups are overexposed to these harms.

Radicals are interested in four primary issues that relate to environmental justice: (1) ways in which corporate polluters maintain their power through dangerous, environmentally harmful production, distribution, and waste disposal practices; (2) the types of environmental crimes corporations engage in, and the social control responses (if any) these activities elicit; (3) patterns of environmental victimization related to race, class, and gender; and (4) solutions to the problem of environmental injustice. We explore these points below.

Corporations employ many tactics to maintain their power and protect their economic positions. Of prime importance are legislative lobbying (e.g., attempts to derail legal protections that limit harmful corporate behaviors that affect the environment and humans) and the production of scientific evidence that depicts chemical and pollution harms as minimal or nonexistent (Karliner 1997; Feagin and Lavelle 1996; Stauber and Rampton 1995). For example, between 1979 and 1995, twelve chemical companies and their employees donated nearly nine million dollars to congressional candidates (Feagin and Lavelle 1996, 124). One recipient, Representative Charles Hatcher, introduced legislation to forbid local governments from regulating pesticides. If implemented, this legislation would eliminate the additional protection local governments have traditionally applied to pesticide manufacturing above and beyond federal regulations. Representative Charles Stenholm, also a recipient of chemical industry contributions, pushed legislation to allow manufacturers to sue the U.S. Environmental Protection Agency for undue economic hardship caused by the agency. This close connection between corporations and government raises an interesting question posed by radical criminologist David Simon (1999, 122): "Who speaks for the interests of school children, minority groups, the poor, the mentally retarded, renters, migrant-workers—in short, for the relatively powerless" where environmental regulations are at issue?

Another successful industry tactic is hiring former governmental employees, especially former heads of regulatory agencies, to gain insight into regulatory

processes and to act as lobbyists and consultants on avoiding compliance with existing regulations. Between 1990 and 1995, chemical industries hired 136 former government officials (Feagin and Lavelle 1996) including John Byington, former head of the Consumer Product Safety Commission (CPSC). In his new role, Byington recommended that the chemical industry refute all studies by CPSC with its own research; use CPSC rules to sue the government for arbitrary and capricious actions; win over government personnel who are already sympathetic to claims made by industry'; use legislation and lobbying to stall CPSC's progress; and hire attorneys to attend CPSC hearings.

The chemical industry also uses lawsuits (SLAPPs: strategic lawsuits against public participants) to harass public interest groups that push for industry regulation (Rebovich 1998). In addition, many environmentally destructive industries have employed criminal tactics to influence legislation and other environmental regulatory processes. For example, in the 1970s and 1980s, several chemical and oil companies admitted making millions in illegal payments from secret funds to foreign government officials to gain a market advantage over competitors (Simon 1999). Many also engaged in various forms of illegal dumping (e.g., midnight dumping) to dispose of hazardous waste. Combined, legal and illegal chemical dump sites place an estimated 25 million people at risk of disease and death in the United States. The estimated cost for cleaning up the worst of these sites (EPA Superfund sites) is $100 million. This is an important criminological issue since the EPA estimates that 90 percent of all Superfund sites contain illegally dumped hazardous waste.

Our society has become so reliant on dangerous chemicals that nearly everyone is exposed to some type of environmental hazard in his daily life. However, minorities and the poor are disproportionately exposed to a wider variety, and higher concentrations, of toxic hazards because toxic chemical production facilities and dump sites are closer to the communities in which they live (Bullard 1990; Mohai and Bryant 1992; Moses 1993; Krieg 1995; Pollack and Vittas 1994; Ringquist 1996; Stretesky and Hogan 1998; Institute of Medicine 1998; Stretesky and Lynch 1999). Two arguments are often offered to explain this pattern of race and class bias.

One argument suggested that the poor and minorities live near hazardous waste sites by choice because properties in affected areas are inexpensive and attract the economically impoverished. A second argument holds that the placement of these facilities is unplanned. Existing evidence suggests that both explanations are wanting. Radicals (Stretesky 1996; Stretesky and Hogan 1998) have countered the choice argument, offering data demonstrating that the placement of hazardous waste sites does not alter the racial or economic characteristics of an area. Also, consider the following policy for placing waste-to-energy facilities offered by Cerrell Associates (1996) to the State of California:

> All socioeconomic group[s] ... resent the nearby siting of ... [disposal] facilities, but the middle and upper socioeconomic strata possesses better resource to effectuate their opposition [A]... great deal of time, resources and planning could be saved and political problems avoided if officials and companies look for lower socioeconomic neighborhoods that are... heavily industrialized... with little, if any, commercial activity [to place disposal facilities]... Middle and higher ... [class] neighborhoods should not fall within the one-mile and five-mile radius of the proposed site. (43, 117)

Cerrell's siting advice illustrates how race and class affect the placement of hazardous waste facilities. Given this advice, it should come as no surprise that these facilities are disproportionately found in lower-class and minority communities. Because hazardous waste siting decisions disproportionately affect the poor, they are also likely to disproportionately affect minorities. Interestingly, studies funded by the toxic waste industry find no relationship between race and hazardous waste siting (e.g., Anderton et al. 1994). Our own independent assessments of this relationship, utilizing several different data sets (hazardous waste production; waste disposal; chemical accidents) and locales (Tampa, Florida; the State of Florida; the United States), however, demonstrated a consistent race effect.

Studies of environmental justice are important for a number of reasons. First, proximity to hazardous waste production and disposal sites increases the likelihood of contracting certain diseases and illnesses. Because facility proximity is linked to the geography of race and class, the health consequences associated with hazardous chemicals in the United States are not evenly distributed among the population. In short, because adverse health consequences can be predicted by knowing the race and class of an area, an institutionalized system of injustice exists. Second, some of the chemicals found in hazardous waste sites also have adverse impacts on behavior. Many hazardous waste disposal facilities contain high levels of heavy metals, such as lead, which have detrimental impacts on children's learning abilities and behavior. In brief, this means that some portion of minority and lower-class children's poor school performance may be a result of the unequal distribution of hazardous substances and may, in turn, affect their progress through life, enhancing the probability that these children will turn to crime as they grow up. In addition, hazardous waste facilities also have high levels of pesticide contaminants. It is well known that overexposure to pesticides (and lead) produces aggression, which may explain why rates of violent crime (assaults and homicides) are higher in lower-class and minority communities.

Finally, the study of environmental justice underscores the need for social transformation as an appropriate mechanism for dealing with crime and injustice. To a large degree, the production and disposal of hazardous waste is the result of the way things are currently produced. In many manufacturing areas, alternative production methods that generate less (or even none) of the toxins that result from current production practices already exist. But, corporations avoid these alternatives because they are more costly, and show little concern for the general public's health. In short, the problem is that corporations make hazardous waste production and disposal decisions based on profit margins. These profit margins exclude calculations of the human and environmental harms these practices generate. There is a clear need to de-emphasize profit as the basis for decision making, a difficult task within the current profit-oriented social and economic structure that characterizes the United States.

Stauber, John and Sheldon Rampton. (1995). *Toxic Sludge is Good For You!* Monroe, ME: Common Courage.

Stretesky, Paul B. (1996). "Environmental Equity?" *Social Pathology*, 2(3): 293–298.

Stretesky, Paul and Michael Hogan. (1998). "Environmental justice: An analysis of superfund sites in Florida." *Social Problems*, 45:268–287.

Stretesky, Paul and Michael J. Lynch. (1999). "Environmental justice and the predictions of distance to accidental chemical releases in Hillsborough County, Florida." *Social Science Quarterly*, 80:830–843.

Taylor, Ian, I.P. Walton and J. Young. (1973). *The New Criminology*. London: Routledge and Keegan Paul.

United Nations Development Program. (1993). *Human Development Reprot.* New York: United Nations.

U.S. Bureau of the Census. (1999). *Wealth and Income in the United States,* 1998. http:// www.census.gov.

U.S. Department of Labor. (1996). *Employment and Unemployment in the U.S.* http://www.dol.gov.

Weir, and Shapiro. (1982). *Circle of Poison.* San Francisco: The Food Institute.

Wright, Erik Olin. (1978). *Class, Crisis and the State.* London: New Left.

Wolff, Edward N. (1995). *Top Heavy: A Study of the Increasing Inequality of Wealth in America.* New York: Twentieth Century Fund Press.

CHAPTER
IX

Feminist and Gender Theories

FEMINIST CRIMINOLOGY

Susan F. Sharp

C riminology has traditionally been one of the most androcentric (male-centered) fields of study in the social sciences. The majority of the research and theory have been based on the study of male criminality and criminal justice system responses to male offenders. Women, when considered at all, have been represented in negative and stereotypical ways, with a focus on their failure to adhere to "traditional" models of appropriate female behavior, as in W. I. Thomas's (1923) paternalistic view of women. Furthermore, in its quest to be recognized as a scholarly field, criminology has focused on objective empirical research, using official records and large national surveys. The result has been a failure to consider important differences in male and female pathways into crime, types of crime, victimization, and punishments. Feminist criminology seeks to address this limitation by enhancing our understanding of both male and female offending as well as criminal justice system responses to their crimes.

Feminist criminologists seek to place gender at the center of the discourse, bringing women's ways of understanding the world into the scholarship on crime, criminality, and responses to crime. In the following sections, the focus will be on the emergence of feminist criminology; the range of perspectives and methods used in feminist criminological research; and the maturing of feminist criminology, both in scholarship and in visibility.

THE SCOPE OF FEMINIST CRIMINOLOGY

It is readily apparent that males do indeed commit far more offenses, especially those deemed important to criminology, than females do (see Daly & Chesney-Lind 1988). This focus has been in part due to the relationship of criminology with legislative and corrections systems. The field developed in part to help improve understanding of why people commit crimes so that policies could be enacted to reduce those crimes. Not only do women commit fewer crimes, but also they commit crimes that are of less interest to those concerned about public safety. Thus, women were largely ignored until the 1970s.

Additionally, the Weberian value-free approach to the study of criminology has failed to recognize that the experiences of the researchers themselves shape and formulate their own approaches to their research. This has resulted in an unreflective supposition that data and theories about boys and men would be generalizable to girls and women. Researchers and theorists have assumed that the study of male crime was the generic study of crime and that women who engaged in crime were more of an aberration than a subject to be studied in and of itself. Ultimately, the feminist approach to criminology emerged from the critique of this practice.

It has been only in the last 30 years that feminist criminology has developed into a recognized perspective in criminology. However, the term *feminist criminology* is somewhat misleading; it might perhaps be better to speak of *feminist criminologies*. Feminist criminology encompasses a wide range of theoretical perspectives and methodologies that place the ways in which gender shapes experience at the center of scholarly inquiry. It focuses on a broad range of issues related to women and crime, including theoretical explanations of crime, responses to female offending, programming in women's prisons, women as workers in the field of corrections, and the special needs of women prisoners. Feminist thought is not a homogeneous approach; it incorporates the liberal feminist focus on equal opportunities for women, the Marxist feminist focus on class relations and capitalism as the source of women's oppression, socialist feminists' blending of male domination with political and economic structures in society as the source of inequality, and the radical feminist focus on patriarchal domination of women, to name the most well-known branches. However, these feminist approaches have in common their focus on the ways in which the gendered structure of society is related to crime.

EMERGENCE OF FEMINIST CRIMINOLOGY

Until the latter half of the 20th century, most criminological work focused on male offenders and criminal justice system responses to male crime. The lack of attention to female offending stemmed from the fact that most crime was committed by males. However, by the last two decades of the 20th century, female incarceration rates were skyrocketing, leading to a surge in research on girls, women, crime, and the criminal justice system. Many scholars point to the "war on drugs" and the federal sentencing reforms of the 1980s as the primary explanations of the large increase in female prisoners as well as of the emergence of feminist criminological scholarship. Clearly, the war on drugs and federal reforms are the driving forces behind the tremendous increase in the incarceration of women. However, the roots of feminist criminology predate these changes. They are instead found in second-wave feminism as well as in the radical criminology of the 1960s and the 1970s.

The Gender Equality Argument

In the 1960s, scholars began to argue that women were ignored in criminological theorizing and research. This early interest come not from within the United States but instead from Canada and Great Britain (see Bertrand 1969, and Heidensohn 1968). According to these scholars, the role of gender had been largely ignored, other than noting that males committed more crime. Thus, theories had been developed that could explain the gender gap in crime but that were sorely lacking in being able to equally well explain female crime. The second-wave feminism of the mid-20th century led to a renewed interest in female offenders. Two important books were published in the early 1970s, derived from second-wave liberal feminism's focus on gender equality: (1) Adler's (1975) *Sisters in Crime* and (2) Simon's (1975) *Women and Crime*. Although they focused on different aspects of the issue and reached somewhat different conclusions, both argued that the mid-20th-century women's movement changed both female participation in crime and *perceptions of* female participation in crime. Indeed, the central thesis of these two works was that women would engage in more crime as a result of women's liberation. Also, with the focus on equal treatment, the criminal justice response to female offending would become harsher and less "chivalrous."

Both books were important in bringing more attention to female crime and the criminal justice system's response to female crime, but the focus on increased criminal opportunities for women coming out of the push for equality has been critiqued by feminist criminologists. Among the criticisms, two broad themes emerged. First, scholars questioned whether lower-class female offenders were acting out of a desire to achieve equality with male offenders or whether increases in female crime might be due to the "feminization of poverty," because the composition of families in poverty became increasingly dominated by female-headed households. In addition, these scholars pointed out that lower-income female offenders tended to have more traditional and stereotypical views of women's roles, calling into question the idea that these offenders were trying to compete with men in the realm of crime (Daly & Chesney-Lind 1988). Second, careful analysis of data failed to support the contention that the gap between male and female offending was narrowing (Steffensmeier & Allan 1996). The focus of feminist criminological thought began shifting to the ways in which social and economic structures shaped women's lives, as well as their participation in crime.

The Influence of Critical Criminology

The second major factor in the rise of feminist criminology during the 1970s was the emergence of the "new criminologies," or the radical, conflict approaches to the study of crime. With intellectual roots grounded in conflict and Marxist theory, these perspectives viewed crime as the result of oppression, especially gender, race, and class oppression. Both radical criminology and feminist criminology emerged during the highly political, socially conscious 1960s and 1970s. In the United States and much of the Western world, this was an era of rapid social change and political unrest. Existing ideologies and power structures were challenged, and social movements emerged, including the anti-war movement, the civil rights movement, and the women's liberation movement.

However, feminist criminologists quickly became somewhat disenchanted with what was perceived as the overly idealistic and still male-centered approach of critical/radical criminology. The "new criminology" view of the offender as a noble warrior engaged in a struggle with a powerful state (Young 1979) also

angered radical feminists working to end intimate violence and rape. Feminist criminology began instead focusing on the ways in which a patriarchal society enabled the abuse of women. Radical feminism, with its focus on the consequences of patriarchy, contributed to the burgeoning body of feminist criminological scholarship.

Radical Feminism and Feminist Criminology

During the early 1970s, radical feminist scholars and activists labored to reform the public response to crimes such as rape and intimate violence. Prior to the revision of policies and laws, rape victims were often blamed for their victimization. Two seminal works during the mid-1970s brought the victimization of women by men into the forefront of feminist criminology and were extremely influential in the development of feminist criminological thought. Susan Brownmiller's (1975) *Against Our Will* was a searing analysis of the role of male dominance in the crime of rape. Similarly, Carol Smart (1976) critiqued mainstream criminological theories, not only for their failure to look at crime through a gendered lens but also for their assumption that victimization was a similar experience for all victims. Smart argued that mainstream theories failed to recognize how the patriarchal structure of society contributed to and shaped the victimization of women.

The contribution of radical feminism to the development of feminist criminology is important for two reasons. First, in collaboration with community activists, radical feminist scholars were able to effect social change. Violence against women became a matter of public concern. Shelters for battered women began emerging throughout the country, and rape laws were reformulated to protect the victims from undue scrutiny. Until the mid-1970s, victims of rape were essentially placed on trial themselves. Proof of rape required evidence that the victim had resisted as well as corroborating evidence. Also, the victim's past sexual conduct could be introduced as evidence by the defense. The feminist approach to rape incorporated the perspective of the victim, and ultimately rape shield laws were enacted that barred introduction of the victim's past sexual behavior into evidence.

Second, the feminist scholarship on rape and intimate violence impacted mainstream criminology. This
has led to a revised understanding of the complexities
of victimization. Statistics support the feminist position that women's victimization is intrinsically and
fundamentally different than that of men. For example,
women are far more likely to be victimized by someone
close to them. From the radical feminist perspective,
this is because social institutions and norms facilitate
the victimization of women.

Much like the feminist scholarship on sexual
violence, feminist criminological research has helped
reshape our understanding of violence within the home
and between partners. Much of the early research on
intimate violence stems from work using the Conflict
Tactics Scale developed by Straus and Gelles (1986).
Feminist scholars have pointed out that although this
scale measures the *incidence* of a wide range of aggressive
tactics, it fails to place them in *context*. Stanko's (1990)
examination of *everyday violence* provided evidence
that women's victimization was frequently unreported.
Thus, research conducted by feminist criminologists, in
conjunction with activism, impacted not only laws but
also police practices. Eventually, the National Crime
Victimization Survey was reformulated to address the
experiences of female victims. Questions about rape
and sexual assault were added, as were questions about
violent victimization in the home (Britton 2000). By
1994, the Federal Violence Against Women Act was
passed. Prevention and intervention programs were
developed, aggressive prosecution was pursued, and
funding for research became available. More recently,
the International Violence Against Women Act has
carried this focus on the rights of women to safety into
the international arena.

In summary, feminist criminological thought gained
prominence during the highly political era of the 1960s
and 1970s. At first, the field focused on the missing
information on girls and women in criminological
scholarship. As the field grew, the focus shifted to
include violence against women as well as the development of feminist criminological theories and feminist
ways of approaching existing theories. A broad base of
scholarship has been amassed from the women's liberation movement, critical theories, and radical feminism.
The following section focuses on feminist approaches

to theoretical explanations of crime and criminality.
This is followed by a summary of the subject matter of
feminist scholarship.

CRIMINOLOGICAL THEORIES FROM A FEMINIST PERSPECTIVE

As suggested earlier in this chapter, feminist criminological theorizing is not limited to one approach.
Feminist criminologists have adopted many different
perspectives, the most noteworthy of which are a feminist approach to mainstream criminological theory,
feminist pathways theory, socialist feminist theory, and
the most recent development: multiple marginalities/
intersectionality theories.

Mainstream Theories and Feminist Criminology

A major thrust of feminist criminology has been the
critique of the development of mainstream theories
based on research with boys and men. The "add women
and stir" approach of mainstream criminology has
meant that gender, if considered at all, has frequently
been used only as a control variable. Although this
has provided confirmation that males are indeed more
criminal than females, virtually no information about
female criminality can be garnered through this type of
research. There are two unspoken assumptions inherent in this approach with which feminist criminologists
take issue. First is the tacit assumption that, because
males are far more likely than females to engage in
criminal behavior, females are somehow unimportant
to the field. Second, mainstream criminology assumes
that males and females are alike and that what works
to explain male criminality will work equally well to
explain female criminality.

In particular, theories like Merton's (1938) *strain
theory* have been criticized by feminist criminologists
for their focus on economic goals and their failure to
consider how personal relationships may contribute to
criminality. Merton argued that crime was largely the
result of having the American dream as a goal but lacking opportunities to achieve this goal in a legitimate
manner. Feminist criminologists argued that Merton's
theory was obviously not equally applicable to women.

They pointed out that, although women were certainly more financially blocked than men, they committed far less crime (Belknap & Holsinger, 2006). Likewise, social learning and differential association theories, with their focus on peer attitudes and behaviors, have been criticized for the failure to take into account the gendered nature of peer relationships. Whereas male delinquency is strongly linked to having peers with delinquent behaviors and attitudes, this is far less true for females. Actually, females who are intimately involved with older delinquent males may be introduced to crime and delinquency by these intimate partners rather than by their peers. Although this is certainly not an exhaustive list of mainstream theories critiqued by feminist criminologists, it does give an idea of the male-dominated approach taken by purportedly gender-neutral theories.

However, other feminist criminologists have argued that mainstream theories may still be used if they are restructured and operationalized in a manner that is more sensitive to the predictors of crime in both men and women. In particular, Agnew's (1992) *general strain theory* attempts to be gender sensitive. By incorporating a broader range of sources of strain in the theory, he has attempted to address the concerns voiced by feminists. In his theory, he has explicitly focused on relationship strains as well as on negative life experiences, both of which are important predictors of female delinquency. Also, he has pointed out that men and women tend to have different emotional reactions to strain, possess different coping skills and resources, and commit different types of offenses (Broidy & Agnew 1997). A feminist operationalization of general strain theory could explicitly examine the role of abuse histories in predicting female crime. Agnew has argued that it is not strain per se but rather negative emotional responses to strain that lead to crime. Again, a thoughtful and gendered analysis would focus on how emotional responses and coping resources are gendered and how this would help explicate the different relationships between life experiences of males and females and their subsequent participation in crime. Indeed, general strain theory lends itself more to a gendered analysis than most, if not all, of the mainstream criminological theories.

Likewise, life course theories may offer an opportunity for a gendered exploration of women's criminality.

These theories not only look at factors important in the initiation of criminal behavior but also examine occurrences that may change the pathways from criminal to noncriminal, or vice versa. In a broad sense, life course theories suggest that it is the salience of an event or reason that determines the likelihood that someone engaging in criminal behavior will cease. In the case of men, this may be marriage or career. However, for women, it may be important to examine other reasons. In particular, the birth of a child may provide sufficient motivation for a woman engaging in criminal behaviors to change her trajectory to a noncriminal one.

Overall, the gendered use of mainstream theories is not particularly well received by feminist criminologists. Many argue that these theories fail to explore in detail the ways in which the experiences of girls and women shape their lives. In contrast, feminist pathways theory focuses explicitly on the relationship between life experiences and future criminality, arguing that one must consider the role, of patriarchal society if one truly wishes to understand female crime and criminality.

Feminist Pathways Theory

Perhaps the greatest breakthrough in feminist criminological theory and research has come by means of the feminist pathways model. In the effort to demonstrate how female crime is inextricably linked to the life experiences of women and girls, this theory focuses on the ways in which women's place in society leads them into criminal lifestyles. In numerous articles and books, Meda Chesney-Lind (see Chesney-Lind & Pasko 2004) has laid out how childhood abuse and a patriarchal juvenile justice system shape the opportunities of girls, ultimately forcing them into criminal lifestyles. She argues that, unlike boys, girls' initial encounters with the juvenile justice system are largely the result of status offenses, such as running away or engaging in sexual activity. The patriarchal double standard means that girls engaging in these behaviors are seen as immoral and in need of "correction." Girls and women have historically faced institutionalization for engaging in behaviors that were at the most mildly frowned on in males. Indeed, girls suspected of sexual "misconduct" have often been treated more harshly than either boys or girls engaging in criminal activity. It is this patriarchal, paternalistic approach to the social control of the behavior of females that pushes them into contact with the juvenile justice system. Furthermore, there has been a failure to recognize that early sexual behaviors, as well as running away from home, are frequently the result of abuse within the home. Instead of intervening in the lives of abused girls, society has reacted with a double standard that labels these girls as incorrigible and/or immoral. By punishing these girls for behaviors that may actually be self-preserving (e.g., running away from abusive or neglectful homes), society may be further limiting then life chances by identifying them as delinquents. This perspective also examines the relationship between abuse and substance abuse, the number one offense leading to women's imprisonment. Substance abuse is seen as a coping mechanism. Girls and women often use alcohol and drugs to self-medicate their trauma that has resulted from abuse they have experienced. This is an important point, because the majority of incarcerated girls and women have substance abuse problems. Likewise, the majority of these "offenders" have histories of physical, sexual, or emotional abuse. Feminist pathways theory seeks to illuminate the connections between the abuse and exploitation of young females and their subsequent offending. It is arguably the dominant approach in contemporary feminist criminology.

Socialist Feminist Criminology

It would be remiss in any treatise on feminist criminology to exclude a discussion of how feminist criminology has led to examination of masculinity and crime. As discussed earlier, part of the feminist critique of criminology is the *ungendered* examination of crime. Feminist criminological scholarship has led to efforts to incorporate a clearer understanding of the experiences of both males and females. Messerschmidt (1986) focused on the ways in which patriarchal capitalism structures the experiences of both males and females. He laid out a theory that seeks to explain both male and female crimes of various types and argued that one cannot ignore either economic structures or gender relationships in any true explanation of crime. His theory suggests that marginalized lower class and minority males engage in street crimes because of their

blocked opportunities and their roles as males in a patriarchal capitalistic society. In contrast, the structure of gender relations in society tends to relegate women's crime to low-level larceny and fraud.

In keeping with the feminist focus on crimes against women, Messerschmidt (1986) also explored the sexual exploitation of women in the sex trade in third world countries, showing how both patriarchy and capitalism place these women in desperate situations where they submit to exploitation in order to survive. In addition, he drew links between economic inequality and male-dominated family patterns in his discussion of male violence against women. Finally, he provided a masterful blending of theories about male privilege as well as theories about capitalism in his examination of higher level white-collar and corporate crimes, which are committed primarily by males. His work is extremely important to the development of feminist criminology because he directly addresses the feminist criticism that most criminology ignores how gender relations structure crime. His theory illustrates that the feminist approach is cognizant of both men's and women's experiences, seeking to illuminate how gender is intrinsically related to crime.

Feminist Criminology and Multiple Marginalities

As in many of the social sciences, early feminist criminological scholarship has been criticized for its assumption that the experiences of all women are similar. This has led to scholarship that acknowledges the intertwined effects of gender, race, class, and sexual identity. In many ways, the critical race critique of feminist criminology has been similar to the feminist critique of mainstream criminology. The charge is that feminist criminologists have in many ways essentialized the experiences of women, assuming that all women are alike. Proponents of intersectionality and multiple marginality argue that race, class, and gender are each impacted by the social structure and in turn impact individuals. Furthermore, these impacts interact. It is not simply being female, being African American, being lesbian, or being poor that matters; neither are the effects cumulative. Instead, there is an interaction that evolves from the intersection of statuses. One's actions and opportunities are structured by one's placement along each of these dimensions. Thus, the experiences of, for example, Hispanic women are different from those of Hispanic men as well as white or African American women (Burgess-Proctor 2006).

METHODOLOGY IN FEMINIST CRIMINOLOGY

Not only does feminist criminology encompass many topics, but it also uses many methodologies. Like their mainstream counterparts, feminist criminologists use both quantitative and qualitative methods, often triangulating or combining them to draw on the strengths of each. On the quantitative side, they may examine official data and use large-scale surveys to explore both the relationships between women's experiences and their offending and official responses to women and how those may be colored by gender. In qualitative research, feminist scholars use a broad range of methodologies. In particular, focus groups, in-depth interviews, and life histories provide information to help tease out the complexity of relationships between victimization and offending. Often, a combination is used, with information from surveys or official data suggesting questions to be explored qualitatively and qualitative research informing the statistics (see Owen 1998).

One final aspect of feminist scholarship and research should be addressed. We have seen that mainstream criminology places emphasis on the researcher taking a value-free stance, detaching himself or herself from the subject matter of the research. From the feminist perspective, however, this is an impossibility. The argument is that we are never free of our own beliefs and values, that those shape our research. In addition, the feminist criminological approach suggests the need for *praxis* or *participatory action research*. In contrast to the value-neutral approach of much social science research, participatory action research and praxis-driven methodologies stress the importance of research that is geared toward social change. In feminist criminology, this has meant working toward changes in laws, policies, and prisons. In feminist criminology, as in most areas of feminism, activism and scholarship are intrinsically intertwined.

FEMINIST CRIMINOLOGICAL SCHOLARSHIP

The subject matter of feminist criminology, as in the discipline of criminology overall, includes a broad range of topics. As described earlier, feminist approaches to criminological theorizing have been an important focus. Also, it is evident that violence against women is part of the puzzle. Feminist criminology recognizes that there is not a clear-cut dichotomy of victims and offenders; instead, female offenders are quite likely to also be victims, whether of childhood abuse or abuse as adults (Belknap 1996). Furthermore, the motherhood role must be taken into account, and numerous feminist criminologists have explored the effects of large-scale female incarceration on both the women and their children (Sharp 2003).

Extensive research has examined the offending of women and girls. The bulk of feminist criminological scholarship since the mid-1980s has focused on the criminal justice system's response to female offending. The war on drugs and the federal sentencing guidelines of the 1980s resulted in massive increases in the number of women sent to state and federal prisons. Changes designed to reduce the inequities of indeterminate sentencing resulted in mandatory sentences for lower level female offenders. In particular, aggressive prosecution of drug offenses has impacted women, especially women of color. By the end of 2007, more than 100,000 women were incarcerated for felony convictions on any given day.

This has led to extensive research on the arrest, prosecution, conviction, and incarceration of female offenders. Feminist criminologists also have focused on the conditions in women's prisons and the programs available to female inmates (see Sharp 2003). Two major characteristics of feminist criminological scholarship are evident in the research. First, feminist scholars have consistently argued that the treatment of girls and women in society helps shape then criminal behavior. However, this focus does not end with pointing out the female pathways into crime but instead leads to the second characteristic: Feminist scholars point out that because women and men have essentially different life experiences as well as motivations for crime and types of crime, the criminal justice system should not be designed to treat women the same as men.

Thus, considerable recent scholarship has focused on both the problems of incarcerated women and difficulties with how the system is serving them. Some have gone as far as to challenge the gender equity of the corrections systems, arguing that applying the punitive approach designed for men is a form of "vengeful equity," a sort of backlash against women demanding equality. (For a detailed discussion of this argument, see Chesney-Lind 1999, cited in Sharp 2003.)

This emphasis by feminist criminologists may be better understood by looking at an example. Perhaps a young girl is being physically or sexually abused in the home. Eventually, she may run away, may start using drugs, and may engage in sexual behaviors, perhaps for money or drugs in order to survive. She is eventually caught and remanded back to the custody of her parents. As a result of her behavior, conditions in the home may become worse, with more abuse or unreasonable rules. She again runs away, perhaps getting arrested for drug possession this time. Depending on the location, her status, and perceived resources of her family, she may be placed into a juvenile facility and deemed incorrigible. While there, she experience more abuse. Upon release, returning to her community she finds that she is now labeled as a "bad" girl. She may be behind academically in school; she may have difficulty finding peers with whom she can spend time; and she begins hanging out with an older, tougher crowd. She meets a young male, several years older, who seems to have ready access to drugs. They eventually become intimate, and she becomes pregnant. By this time, she may be old enough that her parents no longer report her as a runaway. She drops out of school and has the child. The boyfriend leaves, whether through boredom or choice. Now she is a poorly educated single mother, with low self-worth, probably with a drug problem. She has difficulty finding and holding a job. She may steal to support herself, her child, and her drug use. Eventually, she may find another male to help support her. This relationship is likely to be abusive. Her self-esteem becomes even lower, her drug use progresses, and eventually she is charged with felonies and sent to prison. She may or may not have sought drug treatment prior to incarceration. With a dependent child, her options have been limited. She may have been on probation, but her inability to stay off drugs

as well as her inability to hold a job and to pay fees makes her a noncompliant probationer. Once she arrives in prison, she finds that there are few programs there to help her with her greatest needs: drug abuse, victimization issues, low self-esteem, education, job training, and planning how to successfully reintegrate into society on her release. Thus, once she is released, she quickly falls into the same behaviors that sent her to prison. She is rearrested, her parole is revoked, and she finds herself in prison again. Her situation is further complicated by the fact that she is a single mother. Her child may be with her family, or social services may have intervened and placed the child in foster care. When men go to prison, the children's mother usually remains with the children, but when women are incarcerated, the majority of the time there is no father present to care for the children, creating hardship for the child as well as the mother. Because women's prisons are often in remote areas, she is rarely if ever able to see her child. If the child is with family members, he or she may be abused, just as the prisoner was as a child. If the child is in state custody, her parental rights may be terminated. Now the woman is more depressed and feels like she has failed at motherhood. The cycle then continues. Without effective interventions that can help her deal with past traumas and resulting mental health issues, the likelihood that she will remain off drugs is low. Without assistance in improving her educational and job skills, building a healthy support network, and finding a safe place to live on release, there is small chance she will be successful when released again.

This scenario illustrates the complexity and interwoven nature of feminist criminology. Theories that illuminate the victimization and experiences of women may help explain their criminal behavior where mainstream theories cannot. Also, the plights of the hypothetical woman just described, and thousands like her, have driven feminist criminologists into the criminal justice system to examine its structure. Awareness of women's pathways into crime points to the need for prisons and prison programs that are geared to the needs of female offenders. Thus, the prison system and programming in women's prisons have become major foci of feminist criminological research as well. Because the correctional system arose in response to male offending, the needs and abilities of women are often not taken into account. Feminist criminologists demonstrate, through their research on the characteristics of female prisoners, what types of programs would be most beneficial for women as well as which ones might not be effective.

Even substance abuse treatment, vocational rehabilitation, and therapy in prisons are viewed through a gendered lens. During the 1990s, the therapeutic communities and boot camp program became common forms of rehabilitation in US. prisons. However, these programs are not equally well suited to males and females. Among other issues, women respond less positively to confrontation, a staple of both types of programs (Marcus-Mendoza, Klein-Saffran, & Lutze 1998). Also, female prisoners tend to have health problems that may preclude their participation in physically demanding activities (Sharp, 2003). Finally, to increase the likelihood of successful reentry, motherhood must be taken into account. With two thirds of female prisoners mothers to minor children, it is readily apparent that this is a serious social issue.

As the field moved into a focus on the criminal justice system and its response to women, scholarship related to women working within that system began emerging as well. Both the need for more workers and the increasing number of female prisoners have contributed to an increase of women working in law enforcement, as attorneys, and in the corrections industry. The entire field of criminal justice has long been dominated by men, in part because most criminals were men. With the rapid increase in both feminist criminological scholarship and of female prisoners, there is a burgeoning body of work by feminist criminologists that takes a gendered approach to studying policing, corrections, and the law. This approach has primarily focused on two aspects of the gendered nature of criminal justice employment. First, it looks at how women and men differ in the practices of then jobs. Feminist criminology asks what characteristics women working in criminal justice bring to their jobs and how these impact their work. Second, some feminist scholars have examined the ways in which the structure of law enforcement, corrections, and courts continues to lead to gender inequality (Britton 2000).

FEMINIST CRIMINOLOGY IN THE 21ST CENTURY

Gaining widespread acceptance of feminist criminological scholarship has been a daunting task. Given the fact that the field of criminology has been dominated by scholars who are more wed to mainstream theories and research, approaches challenging the mainstream perspective have met with disdain or simply with disinterest. This has led to considerable difficulty getting feminist scholarship published as well as marginalization of the work that has been published. Indeed, there was not even a session on women and crime at the annual American Criminology Society meetings until 1975.

Publication in criminology journals has also been difficult, and much feminist scholarship was relegated to smaller, and not very prestigious, criminology journals. In 1989, the journal *Women & Criminal Justice* was launched, specifically devoted to the publication of scholarly research on all aspects of women's and girls' involvement in the criminal justice system. Then, in 1995, *Violence Against Women* was launched to publish peer-reviewed scholarship on gender-based violence and female victims. Since the early 1990s, a wide range of books about women, crime, and criminal justice have been published. In 2006, Sage Publications introduced the first issue of *Feminist Criminology*, the official publication of the Division on Women and Crime of the American Society of Criminology. This journal has taken a broad focus on feminist scholarship, publishing peer-reviewed articles on feminist criminological theories, female offending, victimization of women, and the treatment of women and girls in the justice systems.

FEMINIST CRIMINOLOGY FROM A GLOBAL PERSPECTIVE

Feminist criminology has arguably had more impact outside of the United States than within. This is because of the focus on violence against women that is a hallmark of feminist criminology as well as a recognized problem internationally. Research has focused on the abuse of women in Muslim countries and in India, female circumcision/genital mutilation, and female infanticide, to name a few topics.

Because international attention has been drawn to the plight of women and girls in various parts of the world, research that takes a feminist slant on women's victimization has been welcomed (Maidment, 2006). At the international level, considerable attention has been paid to the exploitation of women and girls in the global sex industry. In addition, feminist criminologists study the ways in which laws and criminal justice policies around the world may victimize women, sanctioning them for violating traditional gender norms, in particular in regard to sexuality. For example, in some Muslim countries, women who are raped may be viewed and treated as offenders instead of as victims because they have violated the expectations regarding women's sexuality.

Some feminist criminologists have recently argued that there has been a global backlash against feminist attempts to improve the situations of girls and women, not only in third world countries but also in the industrialized West. A 2008 issue of *Feminist Criminology* was devoted to articles on how crime and victimization initiatives by feminists have led to a countermovement.

CONCLUSION

Although progress in the publication of feminist scholarship has been made, it remains somewhat marginalized in the overall discipline. Not only do mainstream journals publish only limited feminist scholarship, but also textbooks give scant attention to feminist criminological theory. Thus, new generations of criminologists are educated and yet given little if any information about feminist criminology. This is reflected in their research as well as in their teaching and mentoring of new scholars. The cycle therefore remains self-perpetuating, with new criminologists receiving scant education on feminist criminology (Renzetti 1993).

However, feminist criminology remains alive and well. The Division on Women and Crime is one of the largest sections of the American Society of Criminology, several major publishers have book series focusing on women and crime, and new scholars continue to emerge. The Division on Women and Crime, which started with a small group of scholars in the mid-1980s, has now existed almost a quarter of

a century, and feminist scholars have been recognized as Fellows by the American Society of Criminology. Current feminist criminological scholarship includes theory building and theory testing, as well as research on violence against women; women's crime; and women in the criminal justice system, both as offenders and workers. The defining characteristics of feminist criminology are the emphasis on how social structures affect men and women differently, the relationship between research and activism, and the interrelatedness between victimization and offending among women.

REFERENCES AND FURTHER READINGS

Adler, F. (1975). *Sisters in crime: The rise of the new female criminal.* New York: McGraw-Hill.

Agnew, R. (1992). Foundation for a general theory of crime and delinquency. *Criminology, 30,* 47–87.

Belknap, J. (1996). *The invisible woman: Gender, crime and justice.* Belmont, CA: Wadsworth.

Belknap, J., & Holsinger, K. (2006). The gendered nature of risk factors for delinquency. *Feminist Criminology, 1,* 48–71.

Bertrand, M. A. (1969). Self-image and delinquency: A contribution to the study of female criminality and women's image. *Acta Criminologia, 2,* 71–144.

Britton, D. M. (2000). Feminism in criminology: Engendering the outlaw. *Annals of the American Academy of Political and Social Science, 571,* 57–76.

Broidy, L. M., & Agnew, R. (1997). Gender and crime: A general strain theory perspective. *Journal of Research in Crime and Delinquency, 34,* 275–306.

Brownmiller, S. (1975). *Against our will: Men, women and rape.* New York: Simon & Schuster.

Burgess-Proctor, A. (2006). Intersections of race, class, gender, and crime: Future directions for feminist criminology. *Feminist Criminology, 1,* 27–47.

Chesney-Lind, M. (1986). "Women and crime": The female offender. *Signs, 12,* 78–96.

Chesney-Lind, M., & Pasko, L. (2004). *The female offender: Girls, women and crime* (2nd ed.). Thousand Oaks, CA: Sage.

Chesney-Lind, M., & Shelden, R. G. (1992). *Girls, delinquency and juvenile justice.* Belmont, CA: Wadsworth.

Daly, K., & Chesney-Lind, M. (1988), Feminism and criminology. *Justice Quarterly, 5,* 497–538.

Flavin, J. (2001). Feminism for the mainstream criminologist: An invitation. *Journal of Criminal Justice, 29,* 271–285.

Goodstein, L. (1992). Feminist perspectives and the criminal justice curriculum. *Journal of Criminal Justice Education, 3,* 165–181.

Heidensohn, F. (1968). The deviance of women: A critique and an *enquiry. British Journal of Sociology, 19,* 160–176.

Maidment, M. (2006). Transgressing boundaries: Feminist perspectives in criminology. In W. S. DeKeseredy & B. Perry (Eds.), *Advancing critical criminology: Theory and application* (pp. 43–62). Lanham, MD: Lexington Books.

Marcus-Mendoza, S., Klein-Saffran, J., &. Lutze, F. (1998). A feminist examination of boot camp prison programs for women. *Women &. Therapy, 21,* 173–185.

Merton, R. K. (1938). Social structure and anomie. *American Sociological Review, 3,* 672–682.

Messerschmidt, J. W. (1986). *Capitalism, patriarchy and crime: Toward a socialist feminist criminology.* Totowa, NJ: Rowman & Littlefield.

Naffire, N. (1996). *Feminism and criminology.* Philadelphia: Temple University Press.

Owen, B. (1998). *"In the mix": Struggle and survival in a woman's prison.* Albany: State University of New York Press.

Potter, H. (2006). An argument for black feminist criminology: African American women's experience with intimate partner abuse using an integrated approach. *Feminist Criminology, 1,* 106–124.

Rafter, N. H. (1985). *Partial justice: Women in state prisons, 1800–1935.* Boston: Northeastern University Press.

Renzetti, C. M. (1993). On the margins of the malestream (or, they still don't get it, do they?): Feminist analyses in criminal justice education. *Journal of Criminal Justice Education, 4,* 219–234.

Richie, B. (1996). *Compelled to crime: The gendered entrapment of black battered women.* New York: Routledge.

Sharp, S. F. (2003). *The incarcerated woman: Rehabilitative programming in women's prisons.* Upper Saddle River, NJ: Prentice Hail.

Sharp, S. F., & Hefley, K. (2006). This is a man's world … or at least that's how it looks in the journals. *Critical Criminology, 15,* 3–18.

Simon, R. J. (1975). *Women and crime.* Lexington, MA: Lexington Books.

Smart, C. (1976). *Women, crime and criminology: A feminist critique.* Boston: Routledge and Kegan Paul.

Smart, C. (1997). Criminological theory: Its ideology and implications concerning women. *British Journal of Sociology, 28,* 89–100.

Stanko, E. (1990). *Everyday violence.* London: Pandora Press.

Steffensmeier, D., & Allan, E. (1996). Gender and crime: Toward a gendered theory of female offending. *Annual Review of Sociology, 22,* 459–488.

Straus, M. A., & Gelles, R. J. (1986). Societal change and change in family violence from 1975 to 1985 as revealed by two national surveys. *Journal of Marriage and the Family, 48,* 465–479.

Thomas, W. I. (1923). *The unadjusted girl.* Boston: Little, Brown.

Young, J. (1979). *Capitalism and the rule of law.* London: Hutchinson.

CHAPTER
X

Postmodern and Critical
Culture Theories

POSTMODERNISM AND CONSTITUTIVE THEORIES OF CRIMINAL BEHAVIOR

Stuart Henry and Dragan Milovanovic

Postmodernism is a movement among social theorists and philosophers that is skeptical of science and the scientific method and its promise to deliver progress. Postmodernism transcends disciplinary boundaries, and indeed began in the arts and the humanities before arriving in the social sciences. It did not reach criminology until the late 1980s. The basic position of those termed postmodernist is found in a cluster of ideas, which include the following: truth is unknowable; rational thought is merely one way of thinking, and not necessarily a superior way; rational thought is a form of power; knowledge is not cumulative; facts are merely social constructions that are supported by various claims to truth that constitute a discourse or way of talking about phenomena; and criticism assumes an alternative truth and should be replaced by "critique" or "deconstruction," which is the continuous attempt to expose the constructed nature of knowledge by revealing the assumptions on which it is based. In criminology, this cluster of postmodernist ideas was seen as valuable but too "skeptical." An alternative version, called "affirmative postmodernism" accepted the basic tenets of postmodernism but argued that deconstruction also implies "reconstruction." In other words, if the world was socially constructed through discourse, it is possible to reconstruct it through different discourse. Such reconstruction or "replacement discourse" is no more truthful, and no less contingent, but can be attended to in such a way that the consequences for those investing their energy in the construction of the social world could be less harmful and less painful. Such reconstruction implies a continuous ongoing societal process of struggle to replace harmful social constructions with less harmful ones.

The affirmative postmodern position in criminology draws on several other strands of social theory including Ferdinand de Saussure's semiotics, Jacques Lacan's psychoanalysis, Alfred Schutz's sociological phenomenology, Harold Garnnkel's ethnomethodology, Michel Foucault's poststructuralism, Peter L. Berger and Thomas Luckmann's social constructionism, Anthony Gidden's structuration theory, Paulo Freire and Henry A. Giroux's critical pedagogy, and it also incorporates the diverse ideas from the mathematics of Benoit Mandlebrot, as well as topology theory and chaos and catastrophe theory. Leading theorists introducing aspects of postmodernist theory into criminology include

Bruce Arrigo, Gregg Barak, Stuart Henry, Ronnie Lippens, Dragan Milovanovic, Peter Manning, Rob Schehr, and T. R. Young, however, the fullest development of these ideas into an integrated theoretical perspective is with Stuart Henry and Dragan Milovanovic's *Constitutive Criminology*.

CONSTITUTIVE CRIMINOLOGY

Constitutive criminology, consistent with its postmodernist roots, believes that crime and its control cannot be viewed separately from the historical, cultural, and social contexts within which it is generated. Constitutive theory rejects the arguments in mainstream criminology that see crime and offenders as disconnected from the wider society or the result of individuals acting independently from the context of which they are a part. Constitutive criminologists argue that it is relationships of power, constructed by humans through their discourse, that provide the motivation, the scripts, and the props for the play that creates the harms that are labeled "crime." Humans, they argue, are active coconstructors of their worlds. They construct their worlds by transforming their surroundings through social interaction, not least via discourse or language use. Through language and symbols humans identify differences, construct categories, and share a belief in the reality of their world that gives apparent order to otherwise chaotic states. It is toward these social constructions of reality that humans act. Insofar as our world is socially produced by our collective actions, we also coproduce the harm in our world. Thus constitutive criminology shifts the criminological focus away from narrow dichotomized issues focusing either on the individual offender or on the social environment. Crime is not parasitic behavior on our social world perpetrated by evil individuals, nor is it the result of uncontrollable forces of our social environment. Rather it is an integral part of our relationships with the world we create.

Constitutive criminology thus takes a holistic conception of the relationship between the "individual" and "society" that examines their mutuality and interrelationship. In the process of investing energy in socially constructed categories of order, humans not only shape their social world, but are also shaped by it. They are coproducers and coproductions of their own and others' agency. Constitutive criminology is about how some of this socially constructed order, as well as the humans constituted within it, can be harmed, impaired, and destroyed by both the process and by what is built during that process: ultimately by each other as fellow humans.

Constitutive theorists argue that the coproduction of harmful relations occurs through society's structure and culture, as these are energized by human actions. Constitutive criminologists look at what it is about the psychosocial-cultural matrix that provides the medium through which humans construct "meaningful" harms to others. They find that this medium is to be found in relations of inequality and power.

Constitutive criminologists argue that relationships of inequality established throughout the whole of society and reflected in its organizational and cultural arrangements translate into specific harmful relationships between the powerful and the powerless. Social processes of inequality not only produce directly harmful outcomes, but they also provide a blueprint for how all relationships operate. To the constitutive criminologist, human relationships in hierarchically ordered societies as different as those in the U.S., Europe, China, or India are first and foremost relationships of power and relationships about power.

The power that frames human relationships may be formal and stabilized in social institutions, such as corporations, government agencies, marriage, and the family. This power may be traditionally established as part of a historical and cultural context, as in relations between different races, ethnicities, and genders. It may be informal and fluctuating, as in subcultural groups or within interpersonal relationships among otherwise similar individuals. In any of these frames of power, and particularly in the interrelations of all three, harm is either a manifest or dormant outcome. Harm is not so much caused by inequality as it is embedded in relations of inequality. Thus, rather than identifying specific causes of crime, constitutive criminology seeks to demonstrate the ways in which harm is the frequent outcome of unequal power relationships , and to demonstrate the ways that some of this harm is labeled as crime.

Constitutive criminology sees crime as the outcome of humans investing energy in harm producing, socially constructed relations of power, based on inequalities constructed around differences. Crimes are nothing less than people being disrespected for being different. People are disrespected in numerous ways, but all have to do with denying or preventing us from becoming fully social beings. What is human is to make a difference to the world, to act on it, to interact with others, and together to transform the environment and ourselves. If this process is prevented or limited we become less than human; we are harmed. Thus constitutive criminologists define crime as "the power to deny others their ability to make a difference." The paradox of constitutive criminology is that although the making of difference constitutes what it is to be human, the use of difference to deny others the right to be different and make a difference constitutes the harm that is crime.

Constitutive criminology divides crime into two types: "crimes of reduction" and "crimes of repression." Crimes of reduction occur when those offended experience a loss of some quality relative to their present standing. They could have property stolen from them, but they could also have dignity stripped from them as in hate crime. Crimes of repression occur when people experience a limit, or restriction, preventing them from achieving a desired position or standing or realizing an accomplishment as occurs in sexism or racism. Considered along a continuum of deprivation, crimes of reduction or repression may be based on an infinite number of constructed differences.

In Western industrial societies such crimes or harms cluster around familiar socially and discursively constructed differences: economic (class, property), gender (sexism), race and ethnicity (racism, hate), political (power, corruption), morality, human rights, social position (status or prestige, inequality), psychological state (security, well-being), self-realization or actualization, biological integrity, etc. Whatever the construction, actions are harms either because they move an offended away from a position or state they currently occupy, or because they prevent them from occupying a position or state that they desire, the achievement of which does not deny or deprive another. However, actions and processes are not considered harms of repression when they limit the attempts by some person or social process to make a difference that themselves limit others' attempts to do the same. Where attempts to achieve a desired position or standing are themselves limiting to others, then the repression of these attempts might be more correctly called control. Such control is to some extent also always a crime of repression, but the manner in which control is achieved can be more or less harmful or more or less justified.

This reconception of crime, offender, and victim leads to a different notion of crime causation. To the constitutive criminologist crime is not so much caused as discursively constructed through human processes of which it is one. However, there is something uniquely concentrated about those designated as criminals. Whether single human beings or human groups, constitutive criminology sees such people as "excessive investors" in the power to impose order (i.e., discursive constructions) on others. The offender is viewed as an "excessive investor" in the power to dominate others. Excessive investors put energy into creating and magnifying differences between themselves and others. This investment of energy disadvantages, disables, and destroys others' human potentialities. The investor's "crime" is to limit others' freedom. Their crime is that they act toward others as objects for domination such that, in the process, the victim loses some of their humanity, or the ability to make a difference or to be different. Victims, from this perspective, are disabled by the excessive investor and suffer loss. Victims suffer the pain of being denied their own humanity. The victim of crime is thus rendered a nonperson, a nonhuman, or a less complete being.

Constitutive criminology envisions criminal justice, as it is traditionally practiced, as part of the very problem it claims to control. Its practitioners act toward the discursively constructed categories of crime and crime control as if they were real. Criminal justice is an exercise in the investment of energy that perpetuates further harm. Criminal justice is a major excessive investor in harm. Both the discursive fear of the victimized and the system of criminal justice thus feed crime. Both fuel the energies that drive our notions of crime. Indeed, as indicated above, agencies of law and criminal justice, the official social control institutions of society, are themselves organizations that exercise power (and, therefore, harm). Agencies of justice and law not only accomplish both crimes of reduction (of liberty, of property, of life) and repression (incapacitation), they also deepen the problem by labeling and categorizing only some harmful behavior of power relationships as "crime," leaving other harmful behavior unlabeled, as though it were acceptable, legal, legitimate, or "not crime." In this process of societal social control, harmful behavior and those who produce it become colonized by criminal justice; they become subject to justice's own powerful relations. The results are amplification, concentration, and multiple layering of powerful relations and from these emerge multiple possibilities for harm.

Contributing further to the excessive investment in harm are crime shows, crime dramas, crime documentaries, crime news, crime books, crime films, crime precautions, agencies of criminal justice, lawyers, and academic criminologists. Each contributes to the continuous coproduction of crime by exploiting the relations of power and by perpetuating the discourse of crime (domination).

Language is a key ingredient in the coproduction of the relations of power that produce harm. It is through discourse (language and symbol use) that we conceive of and act to produce our world. Therefore, discourse is a major means of achieving social change, changes in structures of powerful relations and, through this, crime (harm) reduction. Constitutive criminology suggests alternative ways to deal with the harm that is "crime" that build on the central role of language. This involves reorganizing society to minimize the harm that is based on differences of power. Part of this reorganization comes from a deconstruction of the language or "discourse" of power. To help bring about such reorganization and social change, constitutive criminologists suggest developing "replacement discourses." These are alternative ways of describing the world that do not perpetuate existing relations of power, nor create new relations of power, but help constitute relationships founded on human interconnectedness. Here difference is the basis for greater understanding rather than a foundation for inequality. Developing such replacement discourses will be a key practical action in the reconstruction of human relations toward minimizing harm.

Given the continuous coproduction of crime, and its compounding by the criminal justice process, and the mass media's discursive reproduction of the very relations of power that affirm their reality, what can be done? Constitutive criminology suggests that crime must be deconstructed as an ongoing discursive process, and that reconstruction must take place. The emphasis is on creating replacement discourses that provide the linguistic materials out of which new conceptualizations of being human in society may appear.

The new constructions are designed to displace crime as moments in the exercise of power and as control. They offer an alternative medium by which social constructions of reality can take place. Beyond resistance, the concept of replacement discourse offers a celebration of unofficial, informal, discounted, and ignored knowledge through its discursive diversity. In terms of diminishing the harm experienced from all types of crime (street, corporate, state, hate, etc.), constitutive criminology talks of "liberating" replacement discourses that seek transformation of both the prevailing political economies and the associated practices of crime and social control. Constitutive criminology thus simultaneously argues for ideological as well as materialistic changes; one without the other renders change only in part.

Replacement discourse can be implemented through attempts by constitutive criminologists to reconstruct popular images of crime in the mass media through engaging in what Barak (1998) has called "newsmaking criminology." It can also be induced through what Parry and Doan (1994) call "narrative therapy." Narrative therapy developed as part of family therapy to enable offenders (excessive investors in power) to construct more liberating life narratives and through these reconstitute themselves.

EVALUATION

Constitutive criminology has raised much discussion in recent literature and several arguments have been levied against it, although most share Thomson's (1997) view that this theory is stimulating, "raising issues that must be confronted by scholars in the empirical, romantic, and Marxist traditions of modern theorizing."

Several of the criticisms of constitutive criminology relate to its postmodernist leanings. For example, a central theme is that postmodern or constitutive prose is excessively complex, difficult and "esoteric." Constitutive theorists counter that it is only difficult because of the narrow range of discourse that mainstream criminologists are exposed to. A second issue is to challenge the value of using integrative methodology. The general charge here is that constitutive theorizing attempts artificial integration of incompatible theoretical positions such as modernism and postmodernism or idealism and materialism. Constitutive theorists believe that these positions are interrelated, and the mistake is to separate and prioritize one over the other. Unlike much of modernism's dualisms such as "free will versus determinism," "conflict versus consensus" and "order versus chaos," constitutive theory sees that each of these is operative. Indeed, according to the insights generated by chaos theory, we can have order and disorder in the same system.

Third, some critics disparage constitutive criminology's embrace of social constructionist concepts. They assume that because of constitutive criminology's claim that crime is socially constructed, advocates also believe crime does not have any real consequences. However, constitutive theorists believe that real harm comes from people acting toward constructions as if they are realities, as is clearly demonstrated in the example of crimes committed in the name of religion.

Fourth, others have criticized the constitutive redefinition of crime as harm, saying that this expands crime beyond its real scope, but constitutive theorists point to the arbitrary nature defining only some harm as crime.

Fifth, questions have been raised over whether a set of causal assumptions still really underlie the analysis, and if so whether this can be measured. For example, critiques have been levied against constitutive criminology's use of nonlinear logic, especially the use of chaos theory rather than conventional causal analysis. Leading mainstream modernist theorists like Ron Akers complain that "constitutive criminology has not yet offered a testable explanation of either crime or criminal justice."

Sixth, given the various forms of repressive practices in society, the question of what to do about crime that we address above through replacement discourse has also led to significant reaction. Here critics often feel that they have the last word against constitutive criminology, claiming that such theorizing "can too easily lead toward nihilism, cynicism, and conservatism." Others challenge the policy of constitutive criminology for being naïve in believing changes in discourse can change power structures. Some point out that there is nothing sacrosanct about the idea of "replacement discourse" as a form of reconstruction that limits its strategic use to progressive and harm reducing objectives. Nor is replacement discourse the prerogative of one particular political persuasion. Indeed, even some sympathetic supporters indicate that replacement discourse may itself be harm producing, and that while affording a means of resistance it can also allow new negative constructions to occur. Finally, there are critics who believe that the constitutive approach to social change implies a vanguard of intellectuals rather than workers, which they claim, embodies a pacifism that is likely to be ineffective against the powerful excessive investors. The problem for constitutive theorists, however, is not to remove existing institutional and social structures that reproduce the differences whose investment with power results in oppression and inequality. Instead, the problem is how to cease our nonreflexive rebuilding of these social forms and structures while reinvesting energy in alternative, connective, interrelational social forms. They suggest that structures that are extremely sensitive to their environment and its perturbations and consequently undergo continuous change while still providing provisionally stable horizons for social action may become the basis of political action and social policy. Whether these reconstructed contingent orders will be able to replace existing more harmful ones is the challenge to constitutive criminology.

FURTHER READING

Barak, G. (1998). *Integrating Criminologies*, Boston, MA, Allyn and Bacon.

Henry, S. & Milovanovic, D. (1999). *Constitutive Criminology at Work: Applications to Crime and Justice*, Albany, NY, SUNY Press.

Henry, S. & Milovanovic, D. (1996). *Constitutive Criminology: Beyond Postmodernism*, London, Sage.

Milovanovic, D. Ed., (1996a). *Chaos, Criminology and Social Justice,* Westport, CT, Praeger.

Milovanovic, D. (1998). Postmodern Criminology, New York, Garland.

Parry, A. & Doan, R. E. (1994). *Story Re-Visions: Narrative Therapy in the Postmodern World,* New York, Guilford Publications.

Rosenau, P. M. (1992). *Postmodernism and the Social Sciences,* Princeton, NJ, Princeton University Press.

The Journal of Postmodern Criminology. Red Feather Institute website.

Thomson, A. (1997). *Post-Modernism and Social Justice,* Paper presented at the Annual Meeting of the Society of Socialist Studies, St. John's, Newfoundland. Also available at: A shorter version is published in *Canadian Journal of Sociology,* 23, 109–113 (1998).

CULTURAL CRIMINOLOGY

Jeff Ferrell

Over the past two decades, cultural criminology has emerged as a distinctive perspective on crime and crime control. As the name suggests, *cultural criminology* emphasizes the role of *culture*—that is, shared styles and symbols, subcultures of crime, mass media dynamics, and related factors—in shaping the nature of criminals, criminal actions, and even criminal justice. Cultural criminologists contend that these factors must be considered if we are to understand crime in any of its forms: as a moment of victimization in the street or in the home, as a collective or group activity, or as a social issue of concern to politicians or the public.

Cultural criminologists, for example, study the ways in which criminal subcultures recruit and retain members through secretive shared experiences, distinctive styles of clothing, and exclusive ways of talking. They examine the ways in which police officers display their power and authority through police uniforms and special language and the ways in which the authority of criminal justice is symbolized in the court or the prison. Cultural criminologists often focus on media technology and the mass media and the process by which television shows, popular films, and newspaper reports communicate particular images of crime, criminals, and criminal justice and so affect public perceptions of them. Similarly, they look at the ways in which politicians and lawmakers define some crimes as more important than others and then encode these definitions in laws and enforcement policies. This broad focus on culture and communication, cultural criminologists argue, allows scholars, students, and the public to develop a deeper and more critical understanding of crime and criminal justice. From this view, the subject matter of criminology cannot simply be criminals and what they do; instead, it must include the ways in which crime is *perceived* by others; the particular *meanings* that crime comes to have for criminals, victims, crime control agents, and everyday citizens; and the consequences of these meanings and perceptions for criminal activities, crime control policies, and even the politics of contemporary society.

It is significant that cultural criminologists intend this perspective to expand the subject matter and analytic approach of conventional criminology—but they also intend for cultural criminology to provide a distinct alternative to conventional criminology and at times to directly confront what they see as its current weaknesses and limitations. As already suggested, this divergence between cultural criminology and more conventional forms of criminology is partly one of subject matter; over the past few decades, conventional criminology has largely dismissed from analysis the very components of social life—media, style, symbolism, meaning—that cultural criminologists argue are essential for a fully developed criminology. In this sense, cultural criminologists push to incorporate these elements—or, as discussed in this chapter, reincorporate them—into criminology.

But, as we will also see, the tension between cultural criminology and conventional criminological perspectives runs deeper than simply subject matter. Cultural criminologists contend that many of the more popular contemporary criminological theories are inadequate for explaining crime precisely because they exclude any understanding of culture, communication, and meaning. They likewise argue that the most widely used research methods in conventional criminology are designed in such a way that they inevitably ignore the most important features of crime, culture, and social life. And they point out that many of these current failings are the result of conventional criminology's overidentification with criminal justice, and its overreliance on governmental grants and legalistic definitions of crime. In this sense, cultural criminology is designed not only to study crime, but to study and critique the taken-for-granted practices of contemporary criminology.

THEORY

Cultural criminology has developed from a synthesis of two primary theoretical orientations, one largely British, the other primarily American. In the 1970s, scholars associated with the Birmingham School of cultural studies, the National Deviancy Conference, and the "new criminology" in Great Britain (S. Cohen 1972; Taylor, Walton, & Young 1973) began to explore the distinctive cultural dynamics through which power was exercised and maintained. In this context they also examined the ideological dimensions of crime and crime control—that is, the ways in which crime issues and concerns often tapped into larger political agendas—and they linked all of this to emerging patterns of social and economic inequality. Reconceptualizing the nature of social control and resistance to it, these scholars documented the cultural practices associated with social class, investigated leisure worlds and illicit subcultures as sites of stylized defiance to authority, and recorded the mediated campaigns and ideologies essential to social and legal control. In this way they began to conceptualize some of the many links between cultural and criminal processes. During roughly this same time, a second starting point for cultural criminology was emerging among American sociologists and criminologists who used symbolic interactionist theory and labeling theory in their study of crime and deviance (Becker 1963). These scholars argued that the nature and consequences of crime were not inherent to an individual criminal act; instead, they were largely determined by others' reactions to an act or person—that is, by others' perceptions and by the meanings they attributed to the act or individual. Killing another person, for example, can mean many things to many people: murder, self-defense, heroism, or insanity. Likewise, politicians or police officers or the family of the victim can subsequently make the killing into a symbol of something else: the decline in morality, the dangers of guns, or the need for stronger laws. The social reality of crime—fears about it, models for confronting it, social harms engendered by it, even the visceral experience of it as perpetrator or victim—is therefore seen to be part of an ongoing cultural and political process. Like their counterparts in Great Britain, American symbolic interactionists and labeling theorists were beginning to link crime, culture, and power. Significantly, they were also beginning to document these linkages through ethnographic research inside the worlds of drug users, pool hustlers, and other "outsiders" (Becker 1963), producing a series of case studies that revealed how criminals and anti-crime crusaders alike constructed meaning and negotiated symbolic communication.

In the following decades, these two orientations co-evolved, with British cultural theorists and "new criminologists" providing American scholars with sophisticated theoretical critiques of ideological control and American interactionists offering ethnographic inspiration to British scholars. In the mid-1990s, the two orientations were synthesized for the first time into a distinct "cultural criminology" (Ferrell & Sanders

1995) that, while building primarily on these twin foundations, also integrated the work of subcultural researchers, postmodern theorists, cultural geographers, and progressive political theorists. Exploring further the symbolic components of crime, this new cultural criminology focused especially on two dynamics: (1) the ways in which criminal enterprises incorporate cultural components of style, dress, and language and (2) the ways in which cultural enterprises such as art and music are often criminalized by legal authorities and moral entrepreneurs (Becker 1963). Honoring the informal history of trans-Atlantic co-evolution, this more formalized cultural criminology has also continued to integrate scholarly work from the United States, Great Britain, and beyond.

Cultural criminologists today use a variety of theoretical models that incorporate and expand on these intellectual orientations. Among the more influential of these is the concept of *edgework*, as developed by Steve Lyng (1990, 2005), Jeff Ferrell (1996), and others (Ferrell, Milovanovic, & Lyng 2001). These theorists argue that acts of extreme and often illegal risk taking—graffiti writing, street racing, BASE (building, antenna, span, earth) jumping (i.e., jumping off a fixed object with a parachute) from cliffs or buildings—can best be understood not as moments of out-of-control self-destruction but as situations in which participants reclaim a sense of self through an exhilarating mix of risk and skill. This sort of edgework allows participants to develop the sort of finely crafted skills that are today often absent from the tedium of daily life and daily work, and it forces them to test these skills in meaningful situations that matter profoundly. This mix of skill and risk in turn spirals participants closer to the edge; after all, the more polished one's skills as a street racer or graffiti writer, the more risk one can take—and the more risk one takes, the more polished those skills must become. In this way, cultural criminologists attempt to go inside what Jack Katz (1988) called the immediate *seductions of crime*—that is, inside its experiential meaning and allure for participants—while also seeing this edgework experience as a response to larger, dehumanizing social forces. The edgework concept also helps explain another, ironic dynamic between crime and criminal justice. Given that edgework generates a seductive adrenalin rush as participants mix skill and

risk, aggressive law enforcement strategies designed to stop illegal edgework often serve only to heighten the risk and so to force the development of further skills—thereby amplifying the very experience that participants seek and legal authorities seek to prevent.

Two other cultural criminological theories likewise address the links among experience, emotion, perception, and larger social conditions. Mike Presdee (2000) posited that contemporary crimes such as drug taking, gang rituals, arson, and joyriding in stolen cars can be understood through a theory of *carnival*. Carnival has in many human societies historically been a time of dangerous excess, ridicule, and ritualized vulgarity; yet since it was ritualized, and so confined to particular periods and places, it also served to contain dangerous desires, to serve as a sort of temporary emotional safety valve after which normalcy was restored. Now, Presdee argued, carnival has been for the most part destroyed, outlawed in some societies and converted into legally regulated and commercialized spectacles in others. As a result, some remnants of carnival are now bought, sold, and consumed in the form of sadomasochistic pornography or degrading reality television shows, but others are enacted as crime, all the more dangerous because now cut loose from their containment within a community ritual.

Jock Young (1999) widened this focus in addressing contemporary economic and cultural dynamics and their connections to criminality. His theory of *exclusion/ inclusion* notes that contemporary society is defined by the increasing economic and legal exclusion of large portions of the population from "respectable," mainstream society. The loss of millions of jobs, the prevalence of low-wage work, the economic decay of many inner cities, the mass incarceration rates in the United States—all serve to exclude many among the poor, ethnic minorities, and even the formerly middle class from the comforts of mainstream society. Yet at the same time, these and other groups tend to be increasingly culturally included; through the power of the mass media and mass advertising, they learn to want the same consumer goods and symbols of lifestyle success as do others. Increasing levels of frustration, resentment, insecurity, and humiliation are the result—and with them, Young pointed out, crimes of retaliation and frustration as well. Echoing Robert K.

Merton's (1938) famous formulation of adaptations to socially induced strain, Young argued that this heightened strain between economic exclusion and cultural inclusion helps us understand all manner of crimes, from those of passion to those of economic gain.

A final theoretical model focuses especially on the interplay of the media, crime, and criminal justice in contemporary society. Ferrell, Hayward, and Young's (2008) theory of *media loops and spirals* argues that we are now well beyond simple questions of how accurately the media report on crime or whether media images cause copycat crimes. Instead, they argued, everyday life is today so saturated with media technology and media images that a clear distinction between an event and its mediated image seldom exists, and so criminologists are confronted by a looping effect in which crime and the image of crime circle back on one another. When gang members stage violent assaults so as to record them and post them on the Web, when reality television shows entrap their participants in actual assaults and arrest, when police officers alter their street enforcement strategies because of their own police car cameras or the presence of news cameras, then crime and media have become inherently entangled. Moreover, these loops often reproduce themselves over time, spawning an ongoing spiral of crime, criminal justice, and media. Videotapes of police activities, for example, often become the basis for later court cases, which are then covered in local or national media; similarly, images of criminality often function over time as legal evidence, marketed entertainment, and fodder for news reporting. Because of this, cultural criminologists argue, any useful criminology of day-to-day crime and violence must also be a cultural criminology of media and representation.

METHODS

Cultural criminology's theoretical orientations intertwine with its methods of research. As already seen, cultural criminology and its various theories focus on the meaning of crime, as constructed in particular situations and more generally; on the emotions and experiences that animate crime and criminal justice; and on the role of mediated representation and cultural

symbolism in shaping perceptions of crime and criminals. To conduct research that is informed by these theories, then, cultural criminologists need methods that can get them inside particular criminal situations and experiences and that can attune them to emotion, meaning, and symbolism. They also need methods that can penetrate the dynamics of media technology and the mass media and that can catch something of the loops and spirals that entangle crime and its image. Cultural criminologists argue, though, that the research methods conventionally used by criminologists are ill-suited to this task, and so cultural criminologists regularly adopt alternative methods of research.

From the view of cultural criminology, for example, survey research and the statistical analysis of survey results—the most widely used methods in conventional criminology—preclude by their very design any deep engagement with meaning, emotion, and the social processes by which meaning and emotion are generated. Such methods force the complexities of human experience and emotion into simplistic choices prearranged by the researcher and so reduce research participants to carefully controlled categories of counting and cross-tabulation. Such methods remove the researcher from the people and situations to be studied, creating a sort of abstract, long-distance research that excludes essential dynamics of crime and justice—ambiguity, surprise, anger—from the process of criminological research (Kane 2004). Worse yet, cultural criminologists argue, such methods are often used precisely because they do produce safe findings and abstract statistics in the service of political agencies or criminal justice organizations, thereby forfeiting the critical, independent scholarship that cultural criminologists see as necessary for good criminological research and analysis.

Instead of relying on such methods, then, cultural criminologists often turn to *ethnography*: long-term, in-depth field research with the people to be studied.

Cultural criminologists who are deeply immersed in the lives of criminals, crime victims, or police officers can become part of the process by which such people make meaning and can witness the ways in which they make sense of their experiences through symbolic codes and shared language. Sharing with them their situations and experiences, and vulnerable to their tragedies and triumphs, cultural criminologists

similar critique of criminological models that would ignore, or simply assume, the subtleties of meaning, symbolism, and style that shape criminal subcultures.

Other criminological approaches more explicitly share cultural criminology's critical stance toward mainstream criminology and criminal justice. *Convict criminology* has emerged primarily from scholars who were themselves once imprisoned and who have transformed their own incarceration into a critique of the criminal justice system; it uses ethnographic research and other approaches to construct a critical, cultural analysis of mass incarceration, the criminal justice policies that have produced it, and the sorts of mainstream prison research and media stereotypes that support it (Richards & Ross 2001). Feminist criminology likewise shares with cultural criminology an analysis of the sorts of cultural assumptions that tilt both criminology and criminal justice toward privileged groups, as well as a critique of media distortions of female criminals and crime victims (Chesney-Lind & Irwin 2008). More generally, cultural criminology, convict criminology, and feminist criminology all find common ground in that large subfield of criminology generally labeled *critical criminology*—an approach oriented toward a critical investigation of the many ways in which power and inequality shape crime, victimization, and criminal justice.

FUTURE DIRECTIONS

Among the current trends in cultural criminology are those that are expanding the substantive range of cultural criminological analysis, especially in the direction of greater diversity and inclusivity. Originally, for example, the cultural criminological concept of edgework developed from the experiences and ethnographic research of male scholars involved in predominantly masculine forms of illicit risk taking. Now, though, the concept is increasingly being explored in the context of women's lives, with a focus on the distinctive ways in which women experience and make sense of high-risk activities. Recent research by female and male scholars has investigated women who lead BASE jumping underground, women who are members of search-and-rescue teams or whitewater rafting expeditions—even women who hone their skills so as to push the dangerous, outer boundaries of anorexia and bulimia. Similarly, cultural criminology has from its origins incorporated in equal part scholarship from both the United States and Great Britain—and now this international sensibility is widening. Cultural criminologists are now studying, for example, illegal street racing in Finland, immigration cultures and criminal law in the Netherlands, violence against Filipino women in Australia, crime discourse in Japan, the culture of Russian prisons, and the international affiliations of urban street gangs.

Cultural criminologists are also developing new methodologies designed to mirror cultural criminology's particular theoretical orientations and to resonate with the particular nature of contemporary social and cultural life. For example, ethnographic research and the quest for criminological *verstehen* have traditionally been defined by the researcher's long-term participation with the individuals being studied, on the assumption that the more time a researcher spends inside a group or situation, the more deeply he or she can understand its cultural dynamics. Although this can certainly still be the case, the rapid-fire pace of contemporary crime and culture—as embodied in virtual crime and communications, instant news and entertainment, and short-term employment—have suggested to cultural criminologists new possibilities for ethnographic research. Their theoretical models have suggested this as well; concepts such as "edgework" and the "seductions of crime," for example, focus attention on the immediate, situated dynamics that shape criminal experiences and emotions. Consequently, cultural criminologists have developed the notion of *instant ethnography* (Ferrell et al. 2008)—a researcher's immediate and deep immersion in fleeting moments of criminality or transgression—and have begun to use the method in studying BASE jumpers and other groups.

The new notion of *liquid ethnography* (Ferrell et al. 2008) has developed from a similar rethinking of ethnographic research. Ethnography typically has focused on a single, definable group or subculture that occupies a distinct location as well. Today, though, groups and subcultures are often on the move, migrating into new locations or mixing with new groups as global economies and global migration blur distinct boundaries and identities. Moreover, as already seen with the concept of media loops and spirals, social groups are today more and more likely to be confounded with their own image, as representations of the group come to shape the group itself and to flow among alternative media, the mass media, and other institutions. Liquid ethnography, then, is a type of ethnography attuned to these circumstances—that is, it is ethnography sensitive to the dynamics of transitory communities; immersed in the ongoing interplay of images; and aware of the ambiguous, shifting nature of contemporary social life.

Using this sort of approach, cultural criminologists are now beginning to explore, for example, the ways in which urban street gangs move beyond crime to intermingle political resistance, community empowerment, and religious practice in their shifting collective identities. These cultural criminologists (Kontos et al. 2003) are also finding that global forces regularly intersect with local dynamics, with gangs embodying multiethnic identities, responding to the effects of immigration and mediated communication, and forming global alliances with other groups. Likewise, British cultural criminologists are now conducting liquid ethnographies with prostitutes, immigrants, asylum seekers, and others who are pushed to the legal margins of the global economy, and in this research they are using alternative media, such as art, photography, and street performance (O'Neill, Campbell, Hubbard, Pitcher, & Scoular 2007). Such research allows cultural criminologists to collaborate with even the most transitory and contingent communities in defining their meaning and identity, developing the *verstehen* of shared emotional knowledge, and working toward a holistic sense of social justice.

Appropriately enough for cultural criminology, a final trajectory focuses not so much on subject matter, theory, or methodology but on representation and style. Cultural criminologists argue that issues of crime, violence, and criminal justice lie at the very heart of contemporary society and its challenges and that because of this, criminologists must find ways to disseminate their scholarship, contribute to public debate, and so help to work toward a safer and more just society. Yet conventional, mainstream criminology, they contend, is poorly equipped to meet this challenge;

too often, criminologists talk and write only for each other, and they do so through dry and confusing language, needlessly abstract concepts, and impenetrable graphs and tables. As a result of this off-putting and exclusionary style, criminology's potential contribution to the larger society is lost, with criminologists and their scholarship often left on the sidelines of public debate and efforts at social progress.

Aware of this problem, and sensitive to issues of style and representation, cultural criminologists are in response increasingly experimenting with new styles of scholarship and alternative modes of communication, with the intention of making criminology more engaging for students, policymakers, and the public. In place of lengthy reports, they at times issue *manifestos*—short, sharply written texts that can communicate succinctly key ideas and issues. Instead of relying on traditional forms of academic writing, they on occasion write short stories that embody cultural criminological themes, or craft *true fiction*—that is, stories that blend a number of actual, existing crime issues into a narrative form that is more appealing to the reader. Responding to a world awash in media images, they also increasingly turn to the analysis of these images as visual documents, and they produce their own photographs, photographic collections, documentary films (Redmon 2005), and Web sites as a way of making criminology conversant with this world.

CONCLUSION

Cultural criminology emphasizes the essential role of symbolism, meaning, and emotion in shaping the complex reality of crime and crime control for all involved: criminals, victims, crime control agents, politicians, the media, and the public. Cultural criminology is in this way designed to operate as a double challenge: to simplistic public assumptions about crime and criminal justice and to the theories and methods of mainstream criminology that exclude analysis of cultural forces. Today more than ever, cultural criminologists argue, there can be no useful study of crime that is not also the study of culture.

REFERENCES AND FURTHER READINGS

Altheide, D. (1987). Ethnographic content analysis. *Qualitative Sociology, 10,* 65–77.

Becker, H. (1963). *Outsiders: Studies in the sociology of deviance.* New York: Free Press.

Chesney-Lind, M., & Irwin, K. (2008). *Beyond bad girls.* New York: Routledge.

Cohen, A. (1955). *Delinquent boys.* New York: Free Press.

Cohen, S. (1972). *Folk devils and moral panics.* London: MacGibbon and Kee.

Cultural Criminology Team: http://www.culturalcriminology.org

Ferrell, J. (1996). *Crimes of style.* Boston: Northeastern University Press/University Press of New England.

Ferrell, J. (1999). Cultural criminology. *Annual Review of Sociology, 25,* 395–418.

Ferrell, J. (2001). *Tearing down the streets.* New York: Palgrave/MacMillan.

Ferrell, J. (2006). *Empire of scrounge.* New York: New York University Press.

Ferrell, J., & Hamm, M. (Eds.). (1998). *Ethnography at the edge.* Boston: Northeastern University Press/University Press of New England.

Ferrell, J., Hayward, K., Morrison, W., & Presdee, M. (Eds.). (2004). *Cultural criminology unleashed.* London: Glasshouse/ Routledge.

Ferrell, J., Hayward, K., & Young, J. (2008). *Cultural criminology: An invitation.* Thousand Oaks, CA: Sage.

Ferrell, J., Milovanovic, D., & Lyng, S. (2001). Edgework, media practices, and the elongation of meaning. *Theoretical Criminology, 5,* 177–202.

Ferrell, J., & Sanders, C. (Eds.). (1995). *Cultural criminology.* Boston: Northeastern University Press/University Press of New England.

Hamm, M. (1997). *Apocalypse in Oklahoma.* Boston: Northeastern University Press/University Press of New England.

Hamm, M. (2002). *In bad company.* Boston: Northeastern University Press/University Press of New England.

Hayward, K. (2004). *City limits: Crime, consumer culture and the urban experience.* London: GlassHouse/Routledge.

Hayward, K., & Young, J. (2004b). Cultural criminology: Some notes on the script. *Theoretical Criminology, 8,* 259–273.

Hayward, K. J., & Young, J. (Eds.). (2004a). Cultural criminology [Special issue]. *Theoretical Criminology, 8*(3).

Kane, S. (2004). The unconventional methods of cultural criminology. *Theoretical Criminology, 8,* 303–321.

Katz, J. (1988). *Seductions of crime.* New York: Basic Books.

Kontos, L., Brotherton, D., & Barrios, L. (Eds.). (2003). *Gangs and society: Alternative perspectives.* New York: Columbia University Press.

Lyng, S. (1990). Edgework: A social psychological analysis of voluntary risk taking. *American Journal of Sociology, 95,* 851–886.

Lyng, S. (Ed.). (2005). *Edgework.* New York: Routledge.

Merton, R. (1938). Social structure and anomie. *American Sociological Review, 3,* 672–682.

O'Neill, M., Campbell, R., Hubbard, P, Pitcher J., & Scoular, J. (2007). Living with the Other: Street sex work, contingent communities and degrees of tolerance. *Crime, Media, Culture, 4,* 73–93.

Presdee, M. (2000). *Cultural criminology and the carnival of crime.* London: Routledge.

Redmon, D. (Producer/Director). (2005). *Mardi Gras: Made in China* [Motion picture]. New York: Carnivalesque Films.

Richards, S. C., & Ross, J. I. (2001). The new school of convict criminology. *Social Justice, 28,* 177–190.

Snyder, G. (2009). *Graffiti lives.* New York: New York University Press.

Taylor, L, Walton, P., & Young, J. (1973). *The new criminology.* New York: Harper & Row.

Wilson, L, & Kelling, G. (2003). Broken windows: The police and neighborhood safety. In E. McLaughlin, J. Muncie, & G. Hughes (Eds.), *Criminological perspectives* (pp. 400–411). Thousand Oaks, CA: Sage. (Original work published 1982)

Young, J. (1999). *The exclusive society.* Thousand Oaks, CA: Sage.

Advancing Critical Criminology Through Anthropology

Avi Brisman

Since its genesis, critical criminology has been committed to a critique of domination and to developing and exploring broader conceptions of "crime" to include "harms" that are not necessarily proscribed by law. Without diminishing the contributions of early or current critical criminologists, this article suggests that critical criminology can further its goals by looking to anthropology. Such a recommendation is not without risk. Early "criminal anthropology" regarded criminality as inherited and contended that individuals could be "born criminal" (e.g., Fletcher 1891). Subsequent anthropological investigations of crime were and have continued to be sporadic, and the discipline's approach to crime has not been particularly unified. (Anthropology has often considered crime within broader explorations of law, for example, or through related, albeit different, examinations of sorcery and witchcraft.) Despite these limitations or shortcomings, this article presents three ways in which anthropology can speak to, and engage with, critical criminology's "insistence that criminological inquiry move beyond the boundaries imposed by legalistic definitions of crime" and its critique of domination (Michalowksi 1996:11): 1) anthropology can help reveal processes of domination that are pervasive; 2) anthropology can remind us that what constitutes "crime" is culturally specific and temporal; and 3) anthropology can help provide paradigms for better living—allowing critical criminologists to be not just critical, not just prescriptive, but aspirational. A wide range of ethnographic accounts is considered.

Introduction

As a subject, "crime" has not generated significant interest in the field of cultural anthropology.[1] While one could point to an anthology here or a review essay there, one would be hard-pressed to support the contention that anthropology has approached crime in a coherent, unified, or sustained way—or that it has even generated substantial, ongoing debates about crime.[2] Most often, crime appears in the context of some other inquiry, such as disorder (Comaroff and Comaroff 2004, 2006), violence (e.g., Betzig et al. 1988; Knauft et al. 1991), witchcraft and sorcery (Favret-Saada 1980; Geschiere 1997), primitive law (Driberg 1928), the nature of the relationship between law and conflict (Collier 1975), or labor, employment, social stratification, and the effects of deindustrialization (e.g., Bourgois 1996; Phillips 1999; Sullivan 1989), rather than on its own and as the primary subject of anthropological attention (see Parnell and Kane 2003; Schneider and Schneider 2008).

This phenomenon may be due, in part, to sociology's near hegemony over all matters crime-related (before criminology became its own discipline or sub-discipline, depending on one's perspective).[3] But cultural anthropology's lack of attention to crime may also be attributed, at least in part, to the regrettable subfield of criminal anthropology (also known as anthropological criminology), which Fletcher (1891:204), in his famous address to the Anthropological Society of Washington, defined as "the study of the being who, in consequence of physical conformation, hereditary taint, or surroundings of vice, poverty, and ill example, yields to temptation and begins a career of crime." Although such efforts to "biologize law-breaking" (Rafter 2007:808) were later discredited and abandoned because of concerns for their racist and eugenicist policy implications (Cullen and Agnew 2006:22; see also Brennan et al. 1995:65; Raine 2002:43), the experience may have left anthropology reluctant to venture into the world of crime.[4]

Such unwillingness is unfortunate for a number of very basic reasons: 1) anthropology shares sociology's and criminology's forefathers (e.g., Durkheim, Marx, Weber) and canonical figures (e.g., Foucault)—individuals who contemplated issues of conflict and cooperation, power and punishment, which lie at the heart of or are integral to understandings of crime;[5] 2) while all cultures possess proscribed behaviors, "crime" is still culturally-specific and peoples differ (over time) over what behavior is to be condemned and condoned (see, e.g., Betzig et al. 1988; Brisman 2006; Cullen and Agnew 2006:266–67; Daly and Wilson 1997:53; Ellis and Walsh 1997:230; Fletcher 1891:204; Herrnstein 1995:40), rendering crime ideal for longitudinal and comparative anthropological study; and

3) relatively few ethnographies of crime exist—"thick" accounts (in the Geertzian sense) of the experience of committing crimes or participating in a subculture of crime, of being a victim, of residing in a community that fears crime, or of migrating to a particular community because of its low crime rate.

This last point merits some clarification. I do not mean to suggest that researchers have not employed ethnographic field methods in their study of crime. Many fine ethnographies of crime have improved and shaped our understanding of the convergence of cultural and criminal processes in various societies (e.g., Adler 1985; Becker 1963; Ferrell 1993; Ferrell and Hamm 1998; Humphreys 1975). But only a small percentage have been written by anthropologists or with an anthropological perspective (e.g., Malinowski 1959; Merry 1981). While ethnography does not and should not reside solely under the dominion of anthropology (see Kratz 2007), given anthropology's strength with this methodology and the fact that the study of crime has been increasingly dominated by "shallow survey research" and "abstract statistical analysis" (Ferrell 1999:402),[6] there is a tremendous need for more anthropologically-oriented studies of crime (see generally Betzig et al. 1988; Burawoy et al. 1991; Hagedorn 1990; Polsky 1969; Van Maanen 1995; and Sampson and Groves 1989).

Furthermore, while sociology is often focused on *social structures* (and while criminology tends to focus either on how *individual characteristics* influence actors' propensity for aggression, violence, and crime based on biological or social psychological antecedents, or on individuals in relation to their *larger social environments*, such as schools, neighborhoods, and nation states (Griffiths, Yule, and Gartner 2011), anthropology appreciates these structures, characteristics, and environments, but realizes that much of what makes humans "human" lies in *cultural ideation* (Donovan 2008:xiv). In other words, because anthropology casts a wider net than its sister discipline, sociology—because anthropology extends beyond *society* and *social structures*—because anthropology considers elements of culture, such as beliefs, ideas, symbols, and other internal dimensions of group living (Donovan 2008:xviii)—anthropology can provide further avenues for understanding how "crime" is, has been, or might be defined, prevented, and controlled, as well as its meaning for offenders, victims, cultural groups, and society, more generally. As such, anthropology should be more heavily invested in issues of, and matters pertaining to, crime and criminology, or can, at the very least, and as this article suggests, contribute to criminologist's study of crime.

Despite anthropology's inattention to crime as a singular subject matter—or, at least, anthropology's sporadic interest in crime—there is much that criminology as a whole could gain from a consideration of anthropological approaches, insights, and perspectives on crime. For example, Collier (1975:125) provides anthropological support for both labeling theory and Quinney's (1969, 1974) Marxist criminology. There may still be fruitful linkages between criminology and biological and evolutionary anthropology (see, e.g., Brisman 2010c). To offer a third example: anthropologists, because of the time spent in the field, and the scope of their inquiries, can consider the distinctions and relationships between "norms" and "institutions," "legal formalities" and "legal realities," and "rules" and "behaviors" (Donovan 2008:14, 18, 23–24)—all of which could have bearing on criminological studies and explorations. In this article, I consider ways that anthropology can help or advance *critical criminology*—or reasons why critical criminologists might look to some of the work of anthropologists. More specifically, I identify three ways in which anthropology can speak to, and engage with, critical criminology's "insistence that criminological inquiry move beyond the boundaries imposed by legalistic definitions of crime" and its critique of domination—for "unapologetically" embracing "a commitment to confronting racism, sexism, working class oppression and US neo-colonialism" (Michalowksi 1996:11, 12):

1. Anthropology can help reveal processes of domination that are pervasive.
2. Anthropology can remind us that what constitutes "crime" is culturally specific and temporal (a point alluded to above).
3. Anthropology can help provide paradigms for better living—allowing critical criminologists to be not just *critical*, not just *prescriptive*, but *aspirational*.

These categories or types of intersections between anthropology and critical criminology are but the tip of the iceberg. The discussion that follows offers representative examples for each, rather than an exhaustive account of relevant anthropological inquiries. My hope is that this article will prompt further investigations into the nature of, and extent to which, anthropological-critical criminological linkages exist—so that the typology becomes both more elaborate and more robust.

ANTHROPOLOGY CAN HELP REVEAL PROCESSES OF DOMINATION THAT ARE PERVASIVE

European anthropologists in the early twentieth century were more likely to be complicit in, rather than challengers of, processes of domination. Much fieldwork and ethnography at this time was undertaken by anthropologists at the behest of, and with funding from, European powers with colonialist and imperialist objectives in Africa and Asia—and, as Bodley (2008:21) explains, "anthropologists were quick to stress the presumed deficiencies of tribal cultures for externally imposed change or a rejection of proposals that tribals be granted political autonomy." British social anthropologists of this era, in particular, have been criticized for implicitly and explicitly supporting British foreign policy, which utilized ethnographic knowledge to govern through indirect rule (Erickson & Murphy 2003; Kottak 2008).

Nineteenth-century American anthropology should also be considered in a less-than-positive light—individuals such as Samuel George Morton and Josiah Clark Nott promoted racial polygenism (the doctrine that races are immutable, separately created species), which was used to defend slavery in the ante-bellum American South (see Erickson & Murphy 2003). But many American anthropologists in the early twentieth century operated in the spirit of critical criminologists today. Franz Boas, often considered the father of American cultural anthropology, rejected racial polygenism and argued that cultural differences are influenced by environment, rather than heredity. Ruth Benedict, Boas' student, worked with other anthropologists for the United States Office of War Information to promote cultural relativism, combat ethnocentrism and racism, and help defeat Nazism and the Axis powers (see Erickson and Murphy 2003).[7]

Thus, while early anthropology (British social anthropology and American cultural anthropology) may not have possessed the most laudatory goals or "findings"—and were often "agents of colonial governments" (Bodley 2008:1)—anthropologists from the mid-twentieth-century onward were, and have continued to be, "instrumental in bringing to the world's attention the wide variety of cultures extant on the planet we all share" (Donovan 2008:198). Bodley acknowledges that "[a]nthropologists may justifiably take credit for exposing the ethnocentrism of nineteenth-century writers who described indigenous peoples as badly in need of improvement," but he is less effusive than Donovan. Bodley points out that until recently, anthropologists "overlook[ed] the ethnocentrism that ... commonly occurred in the professional literature on economic development"—writing that often "mistakenly attributed to [small-scale cultures] the conditions of starvation, ill health, and poverty, which actually may be related to the inequalities that often accompany industrialization and commercialization" (2008:21, 24).[8] Notwithstanding Bodley's well-founded concerns about anthropological inattention to ethnocentric economic development writing, anthropological knowledge and insights frequently have and will continue to contest ethnocentrism, which is and should persist in being vital to the critical criminological endeavor.

To take matters one step further, Knauft asserts that one of the goals of anthropology is, or should be, "to expose, analyze, and critique human inequality and domination" (1996:50)—a position that is very close to Michalowski's description of, and prescription for, critical criminology above. What I would like to suggest in this section is that critical criminology might further achieve its (shared) goal of critiquing domination *through* anthropology. More specifically, I wish to propose that by looking at anthropological accounts, critical criminologists might be able to better locate instances of domination that we may not see in our day-to-day lives (either in the U.S. or elsewhere), and to discover the extent to which particular instances of domination are more widespread —the extent to

which they are rampant and raging, rather than unique or isolated occurrences.

For example, mainstream criminologists frequently limit their study of "violence" to behavior by an individual that threatens or causes physical, sexual, or psychological harm and resist critical criminologists' desire to look beyond legal definitions of violence (i.e., those defined by criminal statute). Critical criminologists, seeking to generate additional support for their more capacious view, might turn to Taussig (2005:134–35), who writes:

> [W]hen I look at my diaries [from Colombia] for 1970–1972, I get a shock. I see first of all that my definition of 'violence' is quite different. Instead of in-your-face knives and guns and corpses alongside the roads just outside of town, I see another class of violence ... the violence of the economy with its unemployment, miserable pay, and humiliating working conditions ... The violence of the economy ... gives way to the blatantly political and criminal violence, which in turn gives way to routine and numbness punctuated by panic.

Taussig's treatment of unemployment, underpayment, and disastrous working conditions as violence can bolster critical criminologists' broad conception of "violence;" that his example is from Colombia illustrates that this type of violence occurs outside of North America, Western Europe, and Australia—the usual loci for criminological research.

Taussig could also prove helpful for critical criminologists interested in state crime—specifically extra-judicial domination and violence—and linkages between various economic interests and state crime and violence. Criminologists who research state crime[9] often study "political criminality" (i.e., corruption and manipulation of the electoral process); criminality associated with economic and corporate activities (such as violations of health and safety regulations); criminality at the social and cultural levels (such as institutional racism); and genocide, ethnic cleansing, terrorism, torture, and other security or police force criminality (McLaughlin 2001). While anthropology has the potential to contribute to critical criminological discourse on all of these categories of state crime.[10] I will confine my comments here to the fourth category.

If Vincent (1989:156) contends that "lawmaking in the hands of members of the ruling class serves their interests," Taussig and others show that law*breaking* in the hands of members of the ruling class serves their interests. Taussig describes how the Colombian paramilitaries (*limpieza*) function as a "clandestine wing of the army and police," meaning that they "lie beyond the reach of law, human rights, and the restrictions imposed by the U.S. government on its aid to the Colombian armed forces" (2005:xii). Linger (2003), Scheper-Hughes (1992, 2006), and Pinheiro (2000) have all extensively documented the ways in which and the potential reasons why acts of abduction, torture, and murder have continued to occur throughout Brazil, in spite of democratic governance and long after the formal end of authoritarian rule. Scheper-Hughes (2006:157) describes how the middle class in northeastern Brazil are "complicit" in unleashing death squads to "sweep the streets of … social garbage." Pinheiro records "a continuation of the death squads and other repressive clandestine organizations and practices that prevailed during the dictatorship" and explains that "[t]he police tend to see the rule of law as an obstacle rather than as an effective guarantee of public security" (2000:121, 127). Pinheiro details how police violence (including torture and taking place both in prisons and on the streets) is largely directed toward "dangerous classes"—who do not view the state as a/the defender of rights or protector of security (2000:126).

While Pinheiro's account, like that of Linger and Scheper-Hughes, and that of Taussig in Colombia—as well as those of state crime critical criminologists, illustrates how contempt for the penal code by state-level or quasi-state-level authorities may still exist in countries with democratic governance, what is particularly compelling about his work is that he posits that the rule of law is far from being effectively established because a "certain tolerance for violence continues in government organizations and in society in general" (2000:136). Essentially, while Pinheiro places the larger onus on state institutions (and calls for, among other things, constitutional amendments to reform the judicial court system and the institution of the police), he recognizes

that "violence is deeply rooted in the wide gap between the elites and the general population, the longevity of slavery, racial discrimination, and profound social inequalities" (2000:139), and that a democratic civil society is both a product of, *and necessary for,* a democratic state. In other words, anthropology can contribute to critical criminology's study of state crime by offering examples that fall within the above-mentioned categories. Work like that of Pinheiro can help uncover various processes, trends, and features of *civil* society that may play a role in, or exacerbate, state crime, thereby affording critical criminologists the opportunity to expand their critique and offer more holistic recommendations for reform and change.

Aside from a more capacious conception of violence and more pervasive examples of extrajudicial violence and state crime, we might consider how critical criminology maintains that crime stems from relations of power and selective processes of criminalization (Chadwick and Scraton 2001). Similarly, albeit through a comparative and historical perspective, anthropology has exposed processes of criminalization—ways in which state authorities, media, and "citizen discourse" (which may or may not be separate entities/phenomena) define particular groups and practices as criminal, with prejudicial consequences—"selectively ignor[ing] or sponsor[ing] some illegal activities while vigorously prosecuting others" (Schneider and Schneider 2008:351, 352). Critical criminologists who are interested in such state-level examples of domination and who are seeking interdisciplinary and cross-national examples of such "institutionalized forms of power" (Ortner 1995:174)[11] might consider Collier's (1989:201) broad observations about the relationship between the forms that laws take and the impact of laws at the local level. Or they might review Borneman (1997:25), discussed in greater detail below, who asks (in the context of formerly communist states attempting to transition to democratic governance): "which crimes are the state's business to punish? And what are the justifications for these criminalizations?" Others might find Merry (1998; 2000) instructive for her description of how European colonizers attempted to criminalize the everyday practices of their colonial subjects, applying the unfamiliar legal framework of "harm to society" as distinct from harm to specific others punishable through compensation, and for her illustration of a shift from the criminalization of "vice" to the severe interdiction of "work violations" as British and U.S. planters set up the sugar economy in Hawaii. Those seeking a more contemporary example might find Sharff (1987:47) useful for description of the ways in which the War on Drugs was carried out in the early-to-mid 1980s in New York City:

> Early in 1984, the city launched a massive, military-type campaign on drug dealing in the neighborhood with regular, housing, and transportation police and undercover agents. They were supported by mounted police as well as motorcycle, canine, and helicopter units. During the next two years, over 17,000 young men were arrested in the neighborhood, of whom the majority were street dealers. Many of them now languish in city jails, state prisons and federal penitentiaries. The fact that these institutions are so overcrowded means that most of the prisoners cannot be reached by training or rehabilitative programs. The stressful life in prisons with its chicanery and debasement of every detail of daily life ensures that very few lucky and persistent men will profit from the existing educational programs. And most of the men, once caught in the wheels of criminal justice, are certain to stay hooked up to the system. The women remain, raising children and hoping.

While there have been numerous critiques of the "militaristic" War on Drugs (see, e.g., Austin, et al. 2001; Ferrell 2002; Robinson 2001; see also Merolla 2008; Preson and Roots 2004), Sharff's account offers another instance of what has been criminalized and who have been the objects of such processes of criminalization, and lends further support to research on the ongoing effects of such "military-type campaigns" on both those arrested and their families.[12]

Before turning from the ways in which anthropology can help reveal processes of domination that are pervasive—and the ways in which anthropology can assist critical criminology in making its claims about and

critiques of domination—I would like to offer one final comment and caveat. Anthropology can help reveal how domination is or can be resisted (see, e.g., Abu-Lughod 1986; Ong 1987; see also Abu-Lughod 1990:53 n.1 and Ortner 1995:183).[13] That said, while there has been significant attention to resistance in anthropological literature, resistance as a subject of inquiry and representation has been a matter of contention, and critical criminologists seeking to undertake studies of resistance should be familiar with these anthropological debates.

Writing about the state of the discipline of anthropology and the relationships between theoretical perspectives and approaches since the 1960s, Ortner (1984) expressed concern about the growing interest in, and attention to, domination in the field of anthropology. While acknowledging that "to penetrate into the workings of asymmetrical social relations is to penetrate to the heart of much of what is going on in any given system," Ortner voiced her unease with "the centrality of domination," arguing that "such an enterprise, taken by itself, is one-sided. Patterns of cooperation, reciprocity, and solidarity constitute the other side of the coin of social being" (1984:157).

Ten years later, the concern had shifted to "the theoretical hegemony of resistance" (Brown 1996:729). According to Brown "[r]esistance, as well as its myriad refinements and mutations (such as 'subversion,' 'transgression,' and so forth), has become a central, perhaps even a dominant, theme in the study of social life. Selecting a recent issue of the *American Ethnologist* (February 1994) more or less at random, one finds that 'resistance' appears in the title or internal subheads of about half the essays offered; still others mention it in passing" (1996:729). Brown decries "[t]he discovery of resistance almost everywhere," worrying that anthropology's "concern with multiple layers of resistance [can] blind us to certain features of the story that are potentially of great interest" (1996:730, 731). Brown's intention is not to "disparage the struggles of the downtrodden," but rather to make the case there is often more to interlocutors' social life than just resistance/ resisting and that "[a] myopic focus on resistance ... can easily blind us to zones of complicity and, for that matter, of sui generis creativity" (1996:730, 733). Brown (1996:734) concludes:

All social life entails degrees of dominance and subordination, which mirror the hierarchy intrinsic to the family and to the socialization process itself. Resistance to such power can no more explain the myriad forms of culture than gravity can explain the varied architecture of trees.

The task of cultural anthropology remains, as it always has been, to illuminate how human beings use their emotional, intellectual, aesthetic, and material resources to thrive in a range of social settings. Domination and subordination are, of course, key elements of this process. But so are reciprocity, altruism, and the creative power of the imagination, forces that serve to remind us that society cannot be relegated to the conceptual status of a penal colony without impoverishing anthropological theory and, worse still, violating the complex and creative understandings of those for whom we presume to speak.

Abu-Lughod's perspective on anthropology's heightened interest in resistance is more nuanced than that of Brown. She recognizes a shift in the way in which resistance has been studied: "what one finds now is a concern with unlikely forms of resistance, subversions rather than large-scale collective insurrections, small or local resistances not tied to the overthrow of systems or even to ideologies of emancipation" (1990:41). While she seems to value the attention paid to "such previously devalued or neglected forms of resistance"—to such "minor defiances"—she asserts that the focus on resistance has been undertaken at the expense of an analysis of power, and fears that there is now a "tendency to romanticize resistance, to read forms of resistance as signs of the ineffectiveness of systems of power and of the resilience and creativity of the human spirit in its refusal to be dominated" (1990:41, 43, 42). Put differently, Abu-Lughod states that the most interesting thing to come out of the work on resistance "is a greater sense of the complexity of the nature and forms of domination," but that "[d]espite

the considerable theoretical sophistication of many studies of resistance and their contribution to the widening of our definition of the political, it seems … that because they are ultimately more concerned with finding resistors and explaining resistance than with examining power, they do not explore as fully as they might the implications of the forms of resistance they locate." Urging scholars to consider the implications of studies of resistance for our theories of power, Abu-Lughod calls for "a small shift in the way we look at resistance" so that resistance is used as a "diagnostic of power" so that it can, among other things, identify historical shifts in configurations or methods of power (1990:42).

Focusing on the Awlad 'Ali Bedouins in Egypt, Abu-Lughod endeavors to describe not only "the rich and sometimes contradictory details of resistance," but also how such details can reveal "the complex workings of social power" (1990:42). Essentially, Abu-Lughod uses resistance as a lens: contemplating various forms of resistance in Bedouin society (e.g., women's minor defiances of restrictions enforced by male elders, such as secrets and silences, collusion in the hiding of knowledge, covering for each other in minor matters, smoking in secret; resistance to (arranged) marriage; sexually irreverent discourse, such as making fun of men and manhood; folktales, jokes, and poems/songs—*ghinnāwas*—that are recited in public in the midst of ordinary conversations and that function as "subversive discourse") enables her to bring to light the ways in which power relations are historically transformed (1990:42–48). But her larger point—and one that is relevant for critical criminologists—is that "we should learn to read in various local and everyday resistances the existence of a range of specific strategies and structures of power. Attention to the forms of resistance in particular societies can help us become critical of partial or reductionist theories of power" (1990:53). To do otherwise, Abu-Lughod suggests, may essentialize power (in as much as it runs the risk of oversimplifying or idealizing resistance).

In "Resistance and the Problem of Ethnographic Refusal," Ortner (1995) expresses her displeasure with studies of resistance, exhibiting much of the same trenchant criticism that she showed in her comments about domination in her 1984 article, discussed above. Ortner begins by discussing various ways in which resistance has been conceptualized. She explains that resistance was initially "a relatively unambiguous category, half of the seemingly simple binary, domination versus resistance. Domination was a relatively fixed and institutionalized form of power; resistance was essentially organized opposition to power institutionalized in this way" (1995:174). She then acknowledges Foucault's success in shifting attention to less institutionalized, more omnipresent and quotidian forms of power, and Scott's (1985) illumination of less organized, more enveloping and persistent everyday forms of resistance.[14] Ortner notes how some have addressed the question of intentionality (i.e., whether an act can be deemed one of resistance if the actor does not possess the conscious objective to resist), before stating that while resistance may be ambiguous and may present problems as a category, it is still "a reasonably useful category, if only because it highlights the presence and play of power in most forms of relationship and activity.... [W]e are not required to decide once and for all whether any given act fits into a fixed box called resistance" (1995:175).

With this backdrop, Ortner proceeds with her key concern—resistance studies' ethnographic thinness. Ortner refers to this as the problem of "ethnographic refusal"—"a refusal of thickness, a failure of holism or density which itself may take various forms"—and presents a number of issues that arise as a result of this "ethnographic refusal" (1995:174). First, Ortner asserts that studies of resistance do not contain enough analysis of the *internal* politics of the resistors. Ortner claims that "resistors are doing more than simply opposing domination" and that ignoring the dynamics, tensions, and conflicts among subalterns produces a romanticized picture of the resistors—a point Abu-Lughod (1990) makes to which I alluded above. Ortner (1995:179) stresses that "individual acts of resistance, as well as large-scale resistance movements, are often themselves conflicted, internally contradictory, and affectively ambivalent, in large part due to these internal political complexities," and she emphasizes that in order to conduct an adequate examination of resistance, one must observe the prior and ongoing politics within resistance groups. In other words, Ortner feels that resistance studies have devoted too much attention to the politics

in the oppressor-resistor relationship and have neglected to scrutinize the politics in the relationships of resistors to each other.

In a similar vein, Ortner alleges that resistance studies frequently do not attend to, or even recognize, the "cultural richness" of the resistors (1995:183). Here, Ortner urges scholars to pay attention to cultural dynamics—such as religion—which may reveal some of the beliefs and values behind resistance movements, and which will help avoid the depiction of resistors' responses to domination as ad hoc and springing solely from specific situations or instances of domination. Ortner maintains that recognizing a subaltern group's cultural processes, practices, and features will also help show the depth and range of the group's own notions of order, justice, and meaning—and the basis for and vision of their world without the oppressors.

Finally, Ortner reminds us that "subaltern" is not a "monolithic category ... who is presumed to have a unitary identity and consciousness" (1995:183). She criticizes the "poststructuralist move ... to de-essentialize the subject"—or the "de(con)struction of the subject" (1995:185, 186)—and argues that ethnographic subjects need to "retain powerful voices"—that they should not "representationally disappear" (1995:187). Part of the purpose of providing better representation of subjects is to create "better portraits of subjects in and of themselves" (1995:187). Doing so also uncovers "the projects that they construct and enact. For it is in the formulation and enactment of those projects that they both become and transform who they are, and that they sustain or transform their social and cultural universe" (1995:187). I would add that while retaining and representing the subject can help scholars to depict the internal politics and cultural complexity of the resistors—issues alluded to above—an adequate treatment of the individual subject can also reveal how domination and resistance is experienced personally (as well as collectively), and can disclose transformations in consciousness, awareness, and identity.

To conclude, anthropology can help expose instances of domination as reflections of widespread processes. Anthropology can also provide some models for the study of resistance (however conceived). But because of critical criminology's anti-positivism and the left-leaning political perspectives of its adherents, critical criminologists should be aware of, contemplate, and engage the anthropological debates surrounding studies and accounts of resistance so as not to romanticize it.

ANTHROPOLOGY CAN REMIND US THAT WHAT CONSTITUTES "CRIME" IS CULTURALLY SPECIFIC AND TEMPORAL

In "A Sociological Analysis of the Law of Vagrancy," William J. Chambliss laments the "severe shortage of sociological relevant analyses of the relationship between particular laws and the social setting in which these laws emerge, are interpreted, and take form" (1964:67). Examining the law of vagrancy in Anglo-American jurisprudence, Chambliss finds support for the Weberian contention that " 'status groups' determine the content of the law" (1964:77, citing Rheinstein 1954)—a position inconsistent with the perspective that the law is a reflection of "'public opinion'" (1964:77, citing Friedmann 1959).

Chambliss further develops his ideas about the disparities between the "law in action" and the "law in the books" in *Law, Order, and Power*, where he and his co-author, Robert B. Seidman, argue that "[t]he legal order —the rules which the various law-making institutions in the bureaucracy that is the State lay down for the governance of officials and citizens, the tribunals, official and unofficial, formal and informal, which determine whether the rules have been breached, and the bureaucratic agencies which enforce the law—is in fact a self-serving system to maintain power and privilege" (1971:4). Chambliss and Seidman examine the creation of formal rules of law, general principles of criminal law, and the implementation of law. Towards the end of their treatise, in a chapter on poverty and the criminal process, Chambliss and Seidman set forth a number of propositions regarding the decision to enforce the laws against certain persons and not against others. Two of the propositions are as follows: "In complex societies, political power is closely tied to social position. Therefore, those laws which prohibit certain types of behavior popular among lower-class persons are more likely to be enforced, while laws restricting

the behavior of middle- or upper-class persons are not likely to be enforced" (1971:475).

Chambliss reworks many of his ideas from his 1964 article and his 1971 book in his chapter, "Toward a Radical Criminology," in the first edition of *The Politics of Law: A Progressive Critique*—a work of "critical legal theory" and part of both the anthropology of law and critical criminology canons. In the spirit of his earlier work, Chambliss asserts that traditionally, criminology has asked "Why is it that some people commit crime while others do not?" (1982:230). In the wake of 1960s civil rights demonstrations, anti-Vietnam War protests, and blatant criminality by political leaders and giant corporations, Chambliss suggests that the more salient question is "Why are some acts defined by law as criminal while others are not?" (1982:230). The former question treats "crime" as a constant and takes "the definition of behavior by the state as a given" (1982:233). The latter question recognizes that "many acts come to be defined as criminal because of the interplay of power and political struggles reflecting economic conditions" (1982:230–31). To support this position, Chambliss (1982:233) states:

> Historical analyses [have] revealed the political and economic forces behind the creation of criminal law. … [T]he law of theft arose to protect the interests and property of mercantilists against the interests and property of workers; vagrancy laws reflected the tensions in precapitalist England among feudal landlords peasants, and the emergent capitalist class in the cities; 'machine smashing' in rural England was a rational response to workers seeking to defy the trend toward boring, monotonous industrial production, but the state came down on the side of the capitalist class and criminalized such acts; rights of rural village dwellers to hunt, fish, and gather wood were retracted and such activities became acts of criminality punishable by death as a result of the state's intervention on the side of the landed gentry in opposition to the customs, values, and interests of the majority of the rural population; indeed, even murder came

234 CRIME AND BEHAVIOR

to be defined as an act against the state (that is, as a crime) as a result of political and economic struggles in which the majority of the people were simply powerless to have their views represented at law. Laws that were acknowledged by everyone as serious violations of personal freedom and security —laws prohibiting murder, rape, vandalism, and theft—were found, on closer scrutiny, to be based on contradictory values and to have emerged as a result of political and economic forces.

Essentially, what is defined as "criminal" changes over time and history can reveal the political and economic forces behind the creation of criminal law. Chambliss contends that when one adopts this perspective and considers revelations of white-collar, corporate, governmental and organized crime in the 1960s and 1970s, as well as findings that "crime waves" and "soaring crime rates" frequently distort or misrepresent the actual danger of crime and the seriousness of offenses, criminology cannot continue with "business as usual" (1982:234). Chambliss describes and calls for a "paradigm revolution"—one that defines crime not as a criminal justice problem or as a social-psychological problem—but as a cultural phenomenon. Chambliss argues that criminology should not try to answer the impossible question of "why some people commit crime while others do not" and should instead try to "understand and explain the entire range of phenomena called crime" (1982:239). According to Chambliss (1982:239):

> We must understand the political, economic, and social forces leading to differences in crime rates in different historical periods as well as differences between countries in the same period. We must explore the differences between crime in capitalist and socialist societies. We must look carefully at the historical roots of criminal laws and the legislative and appellate court processes that define acts as criminal to understand the larger issues and enlighten the public as to exactly what crime is and what kind of threat it

poses to their well-being. We must continue to examine the legal process to see why some laws are enforced and others are not; why some people are arrested, prosecuted, and sentenced, while others are not.

Writing twenty years later, anthropologist Laura Nader (2003) describes how in 1990, eight years after Chambliss' chapter, the second edition of *The Politics of Law* replaced Chambliss' chapter with Elliott Currie's "Crime, Justice, and the Social Environment"—a chapter that discusses a "conservative revolution" in the United States marked by a rapid rise in incarceration and the privatization of new and old prisons. The third edition of *The Politics of Law* (published in 1998), Nader explains, also omits Chambliss' chapter and includes instead an updated chapter by Currie, "Crime and Punishment in the United States: Myths, Realities and Possibilities," that further details the growth of incarceration in the United States. Currie's chapters pay little attention to "crime as a category," Nader (2003:57) explains. "So much for paradigm revolutions," she laments. "It appears that we are now back to business as usual."

Although an anthropologist, Nader accepts Chambliss' challenge for criminology and attempts to illustrate via cross-cultural examination how "crime is a category arbitrarily applied in relation to social configurations expressed in law" (2003:57). Drawing on a range of examples—from natural resource plundering in Indonesia and Papua New Guinea, to toxic tort litigation in the United States, to her own research among the Zapotec on the seriousness of endangering the interests of the Commons—Nader illustrates how the very distinctions between "civil" and "criminal" that we take for granted in Western law and that more or less help to circumscribe the field of *crimi*nology (efforts of critical criminologists notwithstanding) either do not exist or exist in very different configurations in many of the non-Western places that anthropologists study. According to Nader (2003:58), "the question of native categories forces us to address the two powerful categories of Western law—'civil' and 'criminal'—that are ipso facto part of our cultural baggage when we go elsewhere to work." As Nader (2003:58) explains, "when anthropologists work in non-Western contexts we cannot simply accept the categories civil and criminal as given. In developing nation states they are clearly cultural constructs, the legacy of a specific Western tradition." She continues: "Although crimes, from the Western perspective, are violations of the law, violations of the law from the cross-cultural perspective are not necessarily crimes. The concept of crime, an idea related to Western jurisprudential history, becomes problematic when applied cross-culturally" (2003:59). Following Chambliss and extending his line of thinking, Nader calls for continued inquiries as to why some acts are defined by law as criminal while others are not, and suggests that such examinations might "shift the current civil and the criminal paradigm toward consequence thinking rather than rigid adherence to categories" (2003:71).

Despite its omission from subsequent editions of *The Politics of Law*, Chambliss' chapter remains an important tract for both legal anthropologists and critical criminologists. As well it should. Chambliss' appeal is as relevant now as in 1982 (or in 1971 or 1964, for that matter), and perhaps more so. Nader should be commended for responding to Chambliss' plea and for persuasively arguing that "crime" is a culturally-constructed category that loses its moorings when subjected to cross-cultural (and historical) examination. Indeed, anthropology is particularly well-suited to illustrating that while all cultures possess (some form of) proscribed behaviors, "crime" is still culturally-specific and location-specific, and that people(s) differ (over time) over what behavior is to be condemned and condoned, and how we should respond to the former.

For example, Fletcher, his ideas regarding criminal anthropology (noted at the outset of this article) notwithstanding, comments that:

> we are met with the difficulty of deciding what constitutes crime. True, the criminal law of every country answers the question; but that which is a crime under one government is not so regarded under another. Duelling, for example, which, if fatal, is punished as murder in many countries, is not cognizable by law at all in others if the encounter has been fairly conducted. So, also, what was formerly regarded as a crime becomes diminished in its gravity or

may disappear altogether as public opinion changes. Sorcery, sacrilege, heresy, and blasphemy have practically disappeared from the penal codes of the civilized world (1891:204).

Whereas Fletcher writes about crime from a somewhat meta-analytical level—i.e., as a reflection on and prescription for the discipline of anthropology—Oberg (1934) approaches crime as merely one issue among many in a culture's wide social milieu. His account of "Crime and Punishment in Tlingit Society" is purely descriptive, rather than comparative or theoretical. For instance, when Oberg (1934:146) states that "crime against an individual did not exist. The loss of an individual by murder, the loss of property by theft, or shame brought to a member of a clan, were clan losses and the clan demanded an equivalent in revenge," he does so for purposes of using crime and punishment to illuminate the relation of the individual to the clan more generally. He is not interested in making larger statements about anthropological approaches to crime, nor does he wish to comment on crime in Tlingit society in relationship to crime in U.S. society. But the critical criminologist interested the relationship of economic and political power to enforcement and punishment who reads Oberg today might be interested in Oberg's finding that "[h]ow crime is to be punished depends largely upon the rank of the criminal. Men of high rank could often escape death through a payment of goods" (1934:152).

In her review, "Law and Anthropology," written almost eighty years after Fletcher and thirty-five years after Oberg, Moore explains that anthropologists believe that "law is incomprehensible outside of its social context," and that while most (if not all) peoples distinguish between serious and trivial breaches of legal rules "not all formalize these into named categories like 'felony' and 'misdemeanor'" (1969:289, 266)—categories that have tremendous legal and practical importance in U.S. jurisprudence, but that are hardly as fixed as we sometimes imagine them to be and which carry little currency *qua* categories in cross-cultural contexts. Similarly, Borneman (1997), in his study of transitional justice in the former East Germany (with some select comparisons with other formerly communist states in Europe), addresses the question of how societies deal with the abuses of power, crimes, and human rights violations of the previous regime. In so doing, Borneman demonstrates how taken-for-granted categories (such as criminality and the rule of law, perpetrator and victim, reconciliation and vindication) are socially and politically constructed: "*Crime* is a socially constructed category of wrong and unjust deeds; such acts are by definition both socially disapproved of and legally prohibited. Needless to say, definitions of crime vary by place and over time" (1997:62). This is not to suggest that because Borneman, like Moore and Nader (or Fletcher and Oberg, for that matter), views categories such as "crime" to be culturally- or situationally-constructed, that he also regards such categories as insignificant or meaningless. Nor does Borneman wish to downplay or diminish violence and atrocities by quibbling over terminology. To the contrary, Borneman states that "although both criminals and victims are culturally and historically variable categories ... who in periods of intensive change can easily switch places, it will nonetheless be necessary in a legal regime of the rule of law type to reaffirm the distinction between the two" (1997:144). In other words, because such categories are malleable, ductile, and impermanent, what becomes imperative is the *response* to various abuses and injustices. Borneman's specific argument is that "accountability" (established in part through retributive justice) is of central importance to (the legitimacy of) emerging democracies. But his concern for how harm is conceptualized and perpetrated, and, more notably, how states respond to and rectify state-level crime is, and should continue to be, consistent with the critical criminological endeavor.

Other anthropologists support the proposition that crime is culturally, temporally, and geographically specific, but do so almost in passing or in the context of a broader inquiry. Greenhouse (1986:165), for example, notes that "associating in the nighttime in the town of Hopewell [GA] with [one's] negro slave woman" was a capital offense in the 1860s. Although Greenhouse's focus is on the development of social structure in the town of Hopewell, Georgia, and the meaning of conflict for Hopewell residents, rather than on capital crimes before the 13th Amendment's

prohibition of slavery, her account not only adds support to the notion of the impermanence of criminal law, but could prove insightful for critical criminologists interested in the range and scope of anti-miscegenation laws before *Loving v. Virginia* (which struck down a Virginia statute prohibiting interracial marriage), in drawing comparisons between anti-miscegenation laws and sodomy laws prior to *Lawrence v. Texas* (which invalidated Texas's law classifying consensual, adult homosexual intercourse as illegal sodomy), as well as for critical criminologists interested in informal means of conflict resolution.

In sum, anthropology can provide broad and substantial support for the notion that "crime" is a cultural construct incomprehensible outside of its social, temporal, and geographic context—an inquiry unto itself—and can offer useful examples for critical criminologists interested in investigating such matters as: 1) why some acts are defined by law as "criminal" while others are not (Chambliss's and Nader's question); 2) the relationship of economic and political power to enforcement and punishment (noted above in the context of Oberg); 3) why some crimes are labeled "felonies" and others "misdemeanors" (noted above in the context of Moore); 4) how to respond to and make amends for state crimes committed by oppressive regimes (noted above in the context of Borneman); and 5) the relationship of race and crime (noted above in the context of Greenhouse). For Nader (and for Chambliss), the real goal of considering crime as a cultural construct and asking why some acts are defined by law as "criminal" while others are not, is to help shift our analyses to the consequences of various acts and omissions, however they may be categorized (e.g., "civil" or "criminal").

I would take the additional step of proposing that contemplating and exposing the consequences of various acts and omissions (whether "civil" or "criminal," whether "legal" or "illegal") could enable critical criminologists to push for regulation of social harms—harms that are not (necessarily) proscribed by law, but that are nonetheless injurious—as well as for the decriminalization of certain types of behavior that cause little detriment or may actually be beneficial (see Brisman 2010e). In other words, anthropology can provide a lens with which to examine how other cultures have delineated permissible and proscribed behaviors.

Given that criminology reifies the category of "crime" (efforts of critical criminologists notwithstanding), turning to anthropological examples (and engaging in ethnological study) might help to reduce the supremacy of the "crime" category so that we consider the effects of a wider range of acts and omissions (however defined) rather than confining our study to that which falls within the "crime" grouping. For example, such an endeavor could help critical criminologists push for regulation of (or better regulation of) activities, behaviors, patterns, and practices on the corporate- and state-level that lead to environmental degradation and natural resource destruction (e.g., amending the Resource Conservation and Recovery Act to include E-waste material—electronic devices (or parts of electronic devices)—that are currently exempt under the legislation's definition of "hazardous" waste[15]). Conversely, treating crime as a cultural construct and shifting our analyses to the consequences of various acts and omissions could help critical criminologists push for the repeal of statutes that criminalize certain behaviors (e.g., possession of marijuana) or laws that have a disproportionate impact on certain groups of people (e.g., sentencing disparities for crack and powder cocaine).

Finally, if anthropology can offer examples of and lend support to critical criminologists' position that what constitutes "crime" is culturally specific and temporal, anthropology might also offer a paradigm for how to apply this knowledge in the criminal justice arena—an issue that has been a challenge for critical criminologists who, as Michalowski (2010:5) has explained, have been "politically marginalized," have received few "invitations to sit at the councils of government or to dine at the trough of government-funded research," and who have often encountered obstacles to achieving progressive reform, let alone social justice. Although an in-depth discussion is outside the scope of this article, I would also like to suggest that critical criminologists might examine the ways in which anthropologists have served as expert witnesses in cases involving cultural differences (e.g., Sutherland 1994). To explicate, anthropologists have occasionally testified in cases involving the "culture defense"—"characterized as a claim that when ascertaining guilt or setting a penalty the court should consider relevant features of the defendant's cultural

background" (Donovan 2008:217). In such cases, which have ranged from those involving animals, attire, and children to drugs, homicide, and death/the dead (see Renteln 2005), the defendants have asserted that their "their cultural background properly negated the intent required to be held responsible for committing a crime" (Goldstein 1994:143) and anthropologists have testified to the cultural heritage or tradition and to the individual's membership in the group or culture. For example, Sutherland, an anthropologist who has conducted extensive fieldwork with Gypsies in the United States, participated in a case in which a nineteen-year-old Gypsy man was charged with using a false social security number (that of his five-year-old nephew) to obtain credit to purchase a car. She testified for the defense that the defendant lacked the intent to defraud because Gypsies (nomadic people by tradition) frequently borrow each others' American names and social security numbers because they consider them as "corporate property" of their kin group (or *vitsa*) and that secretiveness and concealing identity is a long-established pattern of Gypsies who have been persecuted around the world for centuries (1994:75).[16] Cultural differences have also been at stake in cases involving child marriage,[17] polygamy,[18] *oyako-shinju* (parent-child suicide),[19] and "marriage-by-capture,"[20] as well as in homicide cases involving defenses based on culture-bound syndromes,[21] diminished capacity,[22] and provocation[23] (although not all of these cases have involved testimony from anthropologists).[24]

Essentially, I could envision a role for critical criminologists that is akin to that of anthropologists in cases involving cultural differences (see Brisman 2010b). Because critical criminologists accept that "crime" is a cultural construct that differs based on context, circumstance, geography, and time, they might be willing and able to serve in this capacity—especially if they have conducted extensive fieldwork. In addition, because legal systems tend to reify their own cultural assumptions—to treat them as "normal" or even "natural" and to dismiss, condemn, and criminalize others' cultural beliefs and practices (see Donovan 2008:225)—critical criminologists, who, as noted above, are committed to a critique of domination, might embrace the opportunity to assist in the defense of an individual who has been charged with a crime and whose non-dominant culture is, effectively, on trial. That said, critical criminologists would need to be careful that their endorsement of the culture defense does not result in support for or acceptance of various cultural practices that are themselves oppressive—a position taken by Koptiuch (1996:228, 229), who has argued that the "culture defense" does not reflect "multicultural sensitivity," but rather sustains racist, sexist, and colonialist forms of knowledge.[25] Notwithstanding such concerns, critical criminologists might agree with Starr and Collier (1989:7) that the "legal system does not provide an impartial arena [for] contestants from all strata of society" and find inspiration in Renteln's (2005) reasoning that for "litigants to be treated equally under the law [they must be] treated differently"—something that the culture defense has the potential to offer and which critical criminologists might provide.

ANTHROPOLOGY CAN HELP PROVIDE PARADIGMS FOR BETTER LIVING—ALLOWING CRITICAL CRIMINOLOGISTS TO BE NOT JUST CRITICAL, NOT JUST PRESCRIPTIVE (IN THE SENSE OF OFFERING RECOMMENDATIONS), BUT ASPIRATIONAL (HOW ONE OUGHT TO BEHAVE)

Critical criminology challenges the assumptions and content of orthodox or traditional criminology. It contests this "administrative criminology," which treats crime as a "value free" concept and non-reflectively accepts the prevailing definitions of what constitutes the problem of crime, and which possesses a lack of interest in the structural forces and social and economic causes of crime (see Presdee 2004). In the process of confronting the goals, knowledge base, and theories of orthodox or traditional or "administrative" criminology, critical criminology has also asserted that the concepts of inequality (economic and racial, as well as gender) and power are integral to understanding crime and crime control, and has maintained that the criminal justice system, which defends the existing social order, reflects the power structure in society and protects the interests of the capitalist class. As Maguire (1988:134) explains, critical criminology contends "(1) that conflict, domination and repression are characteristic elements

of capitalist society; (2) that the majority of crime in capitalist societies is the result of the inherent contradictions of capitalist social organization; (3) that laws and the criminal justice system generally protect the interests of the powerful to the disadvantage of the powerless."[26] Similarly, Michalowski (1996:12) explicates that critical criminologists have "fram[ed] the class structure and the institutional arrangements of 20th century corporate capitalism as causal forces in the labeling of crime and criminals" and have "linked social constructionism with a critique of domination as manifest in the political-economic framework of the nation and the world. At its best, this analysis helped reveal the subtle dynamics of race, class, and gender oppression in the making of laws and the administration of justice."

Because critical criminology has been both critical of the discipline of criminology and critical of capitalism as an economic system,[27] one might be inclined, then, to view critical criminology in purely oppositional terms—as *against* certain approaches, concepts, orders, and systems, rather than *for* anything in particular. But Michalowski (1996:9) states that critical criminologists are "concerned with the political, economic, and cultural forces that shape the definition and character of crime, and that frame the public and academic discourse *about how we might achieve justice*" (emphasis added). Similarly, Maguire (1988:134, 138) observes that critical criminologists hold fast to the notion that "criminal justice makes sense only in the larger context of social justice," and that "criminal justice reforms need to be married to social justice reforms." Likewise, Young (1985:552) asserts: "The conservative solution [to crime] is more prisons, more police, faster trials, harsher sentences, and closer surveillance. The radical policy is more social justice and less criminal justice." Thus, critical criminologists do stand for something—*social justice*—and have taken additional steps to propose and promote specific policy proposals. This is, by no means, a new development. In as much as it is a critique of advanced capitalist society, Quinney's *Class, State, and Crime* contains a Marxist-based call for "popular justice"—where people "attempt to resolve conflicts between themselves in their own communities and workplaces [and] [o]utside the legal institutions of the capitalist state" (1977:162–63). Young (1985: 567–74) presents an "agenda for critical criminology" to transform criminal justice into social justice, and to move from "production for profit" to "production for human need, for community, and for praxis." And in his survey of radical criminologists, Maguire (1988:145) found that for radical criminologists, "the etiology of crime has to do with social structural arrangements and institutional opportunities and constraints. Work education, health care and the distribution of wealth and income are social justice foci that … have an influence on criminal behavior." Beyond this macro-emphasis, respondents in Maguire's (1988:145) survey identified a number of specific criminal justice recommendations:

> the professionalization and humanizing of police training and work (e.g., sabbaticals and job rotation plans [reduce police burnout and mitigate the tendency for police officers to think in us/them terms]); the formulation of laws and legal procedure to reflect a social harms standard (e.g., the commission of an overhaul of the FBI's Uniform Crime Reports, or an increase in funds to combat corporate crime); the guarantee of equal legal representation (e.g., national legal insurance); and the development of community-based retrospective justice (e.g., the establishment of neighborhood tribunals for disposition of many, if not most, criminal offenses).

An in-depth examination of programs and recommendations promulgated by critical criminologists is unattainable in this "era of interdisciplinarity," to use Ortner's (1995:176) phrase. Even a cursory overview of critical criminologists' proposed programs and recommendations is outside the scope of this article. Instead, I wish to take the more modest step of suggesting that because "most anthropologists today are rarely satisfied to accrue … knowledge for its own sake, hoping instead to be able to use these insights to improve the conditions of the original ethnographic informants, if not all persons and cultures" (Donovan 2008:xi)—a perspective that critical criminologists likely share (even if their methodology does not involve ethnography and informants)—critical criminologists might build upon and expand their ideas for an "imagined future"

(Cover 1986:1604) or "world-that-might-be" (Cover 1984:181) by looking to anthropological accounts of justice, dispute resolution, and the like.

For example, anthropology can help critical criminology narrow the gap between the existing world (and current criminal justice paradigms) and the imagined world by providing models and arguments for greater/increased governmental (and corporate) accountability (Borneman 1997:16) and for a form of justice that seeks to compensate victims for moral injuries (agreed-upon wrongs that do not necessarily result in specific harm), thereby helping to reestablish victims' dignity (Borneman 1997:7). When proposing penalties for environmental crimes, such as water pollution and other damage to the Commons (e.g., the Deepwater Horizon oil spill in the Gulf of Mexico?), critical criminologists might look to Nader's study of the Zapotec, who considered pollution of the water supply and endangering the public health of communities to be more serious than murder (1969, 1980, 2003; Nader and Todd 1978). Those critical criminologists interested in progressive, rather than regressive fines—ones that penalize the rich more heavily than the poor—might consult Barton's (1919) description of fines among the Ifugao of the Philippines, whose system was organized according to the ability of each class to pay, as well as Rosen's (2006) comments about Scandinavian courts issuing traffic fines based on one's income.[28] Finally, Chagnon's (1992) description of Yanomami village headmen, who must lead by example and persuasion, and who must be more generous than any other villager, could provide a paradigm for the type of characteristics and qualities our leaders and public figures should possess.

Of course critical criminologists would need to be careful. "Cross-disciplinary raids on theories and theoreticians run significant risks," Lave and Fernandez caution, and individuals conducting interdisciplinary cross-fertilization should be wary of "precisely what kind of anthropology and what kind of history they bring together" (1992:261, citing Comaroff 1982). More on point, critical criminologists will need to be careful not to romanticize the peoples described in anthropological accounts. As Ortner reminds us, every group has its "own politics"—e.g., "local categories of friction and tension" between men and women, parents and children, seniors and juniors; conflicts among brothers over inheritance; struggles for supremacy between religious sects (1995:177). Even the simplest societies, she continues, contain a politics that may be as complex and "sometimes every bit as oppressive, as those of capitalism and colonialism" (Ortner 1995:179). Thus, critical criminologists will need to be mindful of the context in which appealing models of dispute resolution, justice, and the like appear. While anthropology can provide some ideas, before importing any broad or specific approaches, models, perspectives, rules or penalties, critical criminologists will need to study the circumstances that have taken place in those particular cultures that have given rise to such ideas (so that we do not romanticize these cultures and/ or ignore instances of oppression and domination there). That said, whereas some disciplinary divisions are tenaciously sustained, South (2010:228) suggests that "criminology as a field has always been shaped by the influence of, and borrowings from, many other academic disciplines." In other words, given that criminologists have been open to influence from other disciplines and have been willing to poach theories and approaches from other fields, provided critical criminologists pay attention to context and circumstances, politics and history, there is little reason they should not look to anthropology for prescription, inspiration, and aspiration.

CONCLUSION

I wish to conclude this article with three points and a word of caution as I look ahead to future endeavors involving the intersections and exchanges between critical criminology and anthropology.

First, at the outset of this article, I stressed that critical criminology has been committed to a critique of domination and to developing and exploring broader conceptions of "crime" to include harms that are not necessarily proscribed by law. By titling this article, "Advancing Critical Criminology through Anthropology," I do not wish to diminish the contributions of early or current critical criminologists who have admirably undertaken (and succeeded in) the task of expanding the boundaries of criminology beyond "legalistic definitions of crime" and "confronting

racism, sexism, working class oppression and US neo-colonialism" (Michalowski 1996:11, 12). I do not want to ignore the early calls for "trans-societal comparisons" (Young 1985:567) of anti-social behavior and crime (however defined by different societies)—as well as the different contexts and social formations in which such behavior and crime appears and the responses to them. Nor do I intend to disregard the more recent work of *comparative criminologists*, who have urged criminologists, in general, to engage in the systematic and theoretical comparison of crime, crime prevention, and crime control in two or more cultural states (see Barak 2000a, 2000b), and who have recommended that professors introduce comparative criminology into their teachings. As Johnson (2009:15) explains,

> [g]iven the chance, many students get interested in comparative criminology because it scratches their itch to know about other peoples and cultures and because it reveals assumptions and raises questions about patterns that are taken for granted in America but that do not get much attention when the preoccupation is the United States. One important purpose of comparative criminology is to deepen understanding of what is distinctive and problematic about crime and punishment in one's own country.

Critical criminology is a vibrant division/perspective within criminology, and comparative criminological undertakings have become increasingly more popular; neither critical criminology nor comparative criminology can be considered flailing, stagnant or in need of resuscitation from another discipline. My goal in this article has been to generate further avenues of inquiry for current and future critical criminologists—inquiries that will also benefit the discipline of anthropology—rather than to find fault with critical criminology or identify a deficiency.

Second, at the beginning of this article, I distinguished anthropological and sociological contributions to the field of criminology and to the study of crime and criminality. In particular, I noted that anthropology and sociology share common ancestors, but that their unit of study and history with respect to crime, criminality, and criminology has been different. I made only passing reference to the issue of methodology and then proceeded to focus on the "results generated" by anthropology (see Donovan 2008:vii), rather than the process by which anthropologists have arrived at them. It bears mention that the reason that I have neglected a consideration of the ways in which criminology (in general) and critical criminology (in particular) could benefit from anthropological insights into qualitative methods is that I firmly believe that many others (e.g., Ferrell 1993, 1999; Ferrell and Hamm 1998; Sullivan 1989) have persuasively argued for greater use of ethnographic methods and that the discipline of criminology is attuned to this debate, even if its researchers and scholars have not responded as enthusiastically as they might.

Third, this article has focused on the ways in which anthropology can help critical criminology expose processes of domination and illuminate the contingent nature of crime—that what constitutes "crime" is culturally specific and temporal. This article has also endeavored to demonstrate how anthropology can present paradigms for better living—allowing critical criminologists to be not just *critical*, not just *prescriptive*, but *aspirational*. While this article has stressed the ways in which critical criminology can advance through anthropology, this article has devoted less attention to the ways in which anthropology might advance through critical criminology. The emphasis on the benefits that anthropology might provide for critical criminology should not be interpreted as an indication that critical criminology has little to offer to anthropology. To the contrary, I see anthropology and critical criminology in a *mutualistic* relationship—where each provides benefits to the other—rather than a *commensalist* relationship where anthropology is neither helped nor harmed.[29] And this article has proposed that anthropology could profit from more direct or comprehensive ethnographic study of crime and has implied that there is much that anthropology could gain from the theoretical orientations of critical criminology. While I leave for another day a more in-depth examination of what anthropologists might learn from critical criminologists (for example, how to expand ethnography into different regions)—or how both anthropology and critical criminology might overcome

disciplinary and subdisciplinary parochialism and insularity—this article's emphasis on the benefits to critical criminology should not be understood as a suggestion that anthropology is, or would be, unaffected or harmed by collaboration or cross-fertilization with critical criminology (to mix biological metaphors).

Finally, while this article has argued that anthropology can help expose processes of domination that are repeated elsewhere (i.e., outside of the major loci of criminological attention) and are pervasive, and while anthropology can offer paradigms for better living, we need to be careful. As Nietzsche famously warned: "He who fights with monsters should be careful lest he thereby become a monster. And if thou gaze long enough into an abyss, the abyss will gaze into thee" (1886:52). Critical criminologists should battle monsters—racism, sexism, misogyny, homophobia, xenophobia, working class oppression, environmental degradation and natural resource destruction, economic exploitation, U.S. neo-colonialism and imperialism. And anthropology can be helpful in these fights—its rejection of ethnocentrism (which underpins racism and xenophobia, and which at its worst, can lead to genocide) and its promotion of cultural relativism should prove instructive for critical criminology, and its examination of the discourse of human rights (see, e.g., Brisman 2011a, 2011b; Goodale and Merry 2007; Merry 2006; Riles 2006) can help critical criminology further develop its thinking in this regard. But in the process, we should be careful not to become monsters ourselves; regardless of our interests and influences, we should be mindful that in critiquing domination, we, ourselves, do not become domineering. For example, one of the ways in which the British justified their own dominance in colonial India was to point to what they considered barbaric practices, such as sati (widow burning), and to claim they (the British) were engaged in a civilizing mission that would save Indian women from these practices (see Ortner 1995:178; see also Jain, Misra, and Srivastava 1987; Mani 1987)—a situation that Spivak (1988:296) described as one in which "white men are saving brown women from brown men." This is not to suggest that critical criminologists have become British colonialists/ imperialists. But a critique or challenge to domination can (and often does) result in replacing "old prejudices with new ones" (Omi and Winant 1994:198n.9)—one *form* of domination with another. In as much as we need to critique domination, we need to "exercise vigilance" over our critique (Rosse 1993:290)—or employ a "cautious discernment among commitments" (Cover 1984–85:196). Anthropology can provide the theory, history, and context to help mitigate such risks.

ENDNOTES

1. I specify "cultural anthropology" because "crime" has been explored from a biological anthropological and evolutionary anthropological vantage point in arguably a more substantive way than it has been from a cultural anthropological perspective. Indeed, "forensic anthropology" is the application of the science of physical anthropology and human osteology to the legal process, usually in criminal cases where the victim's remains have been burned, mutilated, are in the advanced stages of decomposition, or are otherwise unrecognizable (see Kottak 2008).

2. Although well outside the scope of this article, it is worth noting that some would ask whether cultural anthropology has *ever* approached *anything* in a unified way. Writing in the mid-1980s, Ortner claimed that the field of anthropology had become "a thing of shreds and patches, of individuals and small coteries pursuing disjunctive investigations and talking mainly to themselves" (1984:126). Although Ortner acknowledged that "there was at least a period when there were a few large categories of theoretical affiliation, a set of identifiable camps or schools," she denied that anthropology was ever "actually unified in the sense of adopting a single paradigm" (1984:126).

3. Note, however, that according to Barak (2003:218), because criminology's "interests are too wide ranging, its practices too diverse, and its theories too interdependent, no single discipline has ever been able to monopolize criminology successfully. Sociology had appeared to do so until its collapse and the meteoric rise of cultural studies and criminologies in their own right during the last quarter of the 20th century."

4. "Crime"—an act or omission that the law makes punishable—is quintessentially the product of states and state law (see Henry and Lanier (2001) for a presentation of classic/legalistic definitions of "crime," as well as new directions in defining "crime" and integrating approaches to the study of "crime"). Not all societies have had "law"—in the sense of possessing a formal legal code, an enforcement mechanism, and a judiciary system—and, indeed, classical anthropologists tended to conduct fieldwork in non-state and protostate societies or among peoples technically within the borders of a state, but subject to very limited state influence (see Chambliss and Seidman 1971 for a discussion). Accordingly, they did not—or *could not*—study "crime," which was contingent on states and state law.

   While not all societies have had "law," all have had some form of social control—i.e., beliefs and practices that operate to maintain norms, ensure compliance, and regulate conflict—and some classical anthropologists did study deviation from cultural norms. Indeed, as Schneider and Schneider (2008:354) explain, "until the 1950s, anthropological research was oriented toward small-scale societies in which deviance had a moral rather than legal status, and violators of norms were shamed, ridiculed, held up for retribution, or punished as witches or sorcerers." But this is as close as classical anthropologists came to studying "crime."

   Today, all political entities exist within nation-states and are subject to state control. As a result, anthropologists cannot investigate bands, tribes, or chiefdoms as self-contained forms of political organization. While this fact of political organization (and the real or perceived presence of the state) should (or, at least, *could*) make "crime" an appropriate subject of inquiry for anthropologists, anthropology has been slow to contemplate "crime" (including its definition, prevention, control, and meaning to offenders, victims, and society, more generally). In addition, I would suggest that the fact that cultural anthropology traditionally focused on small-scale, non-state and protostate societies (and has been less interested than sociology in promoting grand theories or models to explain/understand social phenomena) may have made it more difficult for anthropology to overcome the regrettable endeavor of criminal anthropology/anthropological criminology than it was for sociology to move past the shortcomings of positivist theories of crime (e.g., Lombroso).

5. See, e.g., Ortner (1984) for a discussion of the role and impact of such figures in anthropology. Readers who are interested in the shared epistemological foundations

and complementary objectives of anthropology and history might consult Levi-Strauss (1963), Lewis (1968), Sahlins (1981), Schapera (1962), and Worsley (1968).

6. Writing ten years earlier, Sullivan (1989:6–7) lamented the "shift in research methods away from ethnographic studies toward analyses of self-report survey data and of aggregate social statistics on crime on unemployment," claiming that such "quantitative methods do not portray … local-level processes very well."

7. It bears mention that *ethnocentrism*—the belief in the superiority of one's own culture—"is vital to the integrity of any society" (Bodley 2008:21) and "contributes to social solidarity, a sense of value and community, among people who share a cultural tradition" (Kottak 2008:196). Where ethnocentrism becomes problematic—and potentially deadly—is when it "becomes the basis for forcing irrelevant standards upon another culture" (Bodley 2008:21).

8. Bodley further indicts economic development writers in the 1960s for lumping tribal peoples indiscriminately with underdeveloped peoples, and takes such writers to task for "referring explicitly to economic underdevelopment as a 'sickness,' speaking of the 'medicine of social change,' and comparing change agents to brain surgeons" (2008:25, citing Arensberg and Niehoff 1964). According to Bodley (2008:25), "[i]t appears that the attitudes of some modern cultural reformers were unaffected by the discovery of ethnocentrism."

9. It bears mention that state crime is a subject that has broad appeal and is of interest to criminologists who do not hold critical criminological perspectives, as well as to legal scholars. I thank Dawn L. Rothe for reminding me of this.

10. I do not wish to imply here that criminology, in general, and critical criminology, more particularly, has somehow been deficient in its investigations of state crime. Fredrichs (1998), Ross (2000), Rothe (2009), and Rothe and Mullins (2010) are but a few examples of the breadth and depth with which criminology has considered state crime. I merely wish to suggest—as I have endeavored to do throughout this paper—that critical criminology could strengthen its positions (and improve the range and detail of its examples) by looking to anthropological accounts and perspectives.

11. I leave for another day a consideration of how critical criminologists might explore anthropological examples of "less institutionalized, more pervasive, and more everyday forms of power" *à la* Foucault (Ortner 1995:175).

12. For a discussion of the gendered impact of the United States' War on Drugs abroad, see, e.g., Norton-Hawk (2010).

13. As with my discussion of state crime, *supra* n.10, I do not wish to imply here that criminology, in general, and critical criminology, more particularly, has somehow been lacking in its investigations of resistance. To the contrary, criminologists working in critical or cultural veins have closely examined how power has been defied, opposed, and subverted (see, e.g., Ferrell 1993, 2001; Snyder 2009). Nor do I want to insinuate that scholars studying resistance have not already toggled back and forth between anthropology and critical criminology (see, e.g., Kane 2009). (My own work on resistance has also been cross-disciplinary in this regard; see, e.g., Brisman 2007, 2008a, 2008b, 2009a, 2009b, 2009c, 2010d, 2010f.) Rather, I merely wish to suggest—as I have endeavored to do throughout this article—that critical criminology could strengthen its positions (and improve the range and detail of its examples) by looking to anthropological accounts and perspectives on resistance.

14. For an argument that the domination-resistance binary obscures an understanding of postcolonial relations, see Mbembe (1992).

15. See Gibbs, McGarrell, and Axelrod (2010) for a discussion.

16. As Sutherland (1994:75, 81) explains, by using the social security number of a relative, the defendant was following "a time-honored tradition to remain anonymous and separate from non-Gypsy society" and that "[i]dentification—a serious legal issue in a bureaucratic society composed of people with fixed abodes and a written language—has virtually no meaning for the nomadic Gypsies who consider descent and extended family ties the defining factor for identification."

17. People v. Benu, 87 Misc.2d 139, 385 N.Y.S.2d 222 (N.Y.City Crim.Ct. 1976).

18. People v. Ezeonu, 155 Misc.2d 344, 588 N.Y.S.2d 116 (N.Y.Sup. Ct. 1992).

19. People v. Kimura, No. A-091133 (Santa Monica Super. Ct. Nov. 21, 1985); see also Bryant (1990); *Harvard Law Review* (1986); Pound (1985); Rosen (2006:171–75); Woo (1989).

20. People v. Moua, No. 315972–0 (Fresno County Super. Ct. Feb. 7, 1985).

21. State v. Ganal, 81 Hawai'i 358, 917 P.2d 370 (Haw. 1996).

22. People v. Poddar, 26 Cal.App.3d 438, 103 Cal.Rptr. 84 (Cal.App. 1 Dist. 1972).

23. People v. Aphaylath, 68 N.Y.2d 945, 502 N.E.2d 998, 510 N.Y.S.2d 83 (N.Y. 1986).

24. It bears mention that in these cases, courts have not uniformly permitted or disallowed cultural testimony. Furthermore, those cases where courts have allowed such cultural testimony have not always resulted in acquittal or sentencing mitigation for the defendant.

25. In her examination of "the cultural debate over the applicability of U.S. criminal law to select groups of recent immigrants in America's diaspora," Koptiuch "track[s] the historical genealogy of the unacknowledged colonial shadow that darkly haunts uncritical exuberance about the liberatory potential of 'multiculturalism' within the law," and argues that "[i]n the culture defense, gender violence ordinarily criminalized by U.S. legal science is redefined as 'ritual' by authority of anthropological science" (1996:217, 216). Readers interested in the debates regarding the pros and cons of the culture defense might consult, for example, Choi (1990); Gallin (1994); Magnarella (1991); Renteln (1993); Rimonte (1991); Rosen (1991); Sams (1986); Sherman (1986); Sheybani (1987); Thompson (1985); and Volpp (1994).

26. It bears mention that Maguire (1988:134) employs the term, "radical criminology," but indicates that the label encompasses "conflict," "critical," and "Marxist" perspectives, among others. Michalowski (1996:14) also notes that there exist multiple "critical criminologies" and that "critical criminology" encompasses "broad social theories such as feminism, political-economy, poststructuralism and postmodemism, as well as its own distinct hybrid theories such as anarchist criminology, constitutive criminology, cultural criminology, newsmaking criminology, peacemaking criminology, and left realist criminology." In this paper, I primarily employ the term, "critical criminology" (or "critical criminologist"), using "radical criminology" (or "radical criminologist") only in the context of discussing Maguire in order to maintain consistency with his writing.

27. Maguire (1988:146) explains that in addition to attempting to influence and reshape the field of criminology and "the powerful in society," critical criminologists also target elected representatives, administrators, and functionaries in the criminal justice system, and public opinion.

28. Rosen (2006:192) notes that Finnish police gave a speeding ticket in the amount of $216,900 to a millionaire, based on his income tax information. It bears mention that Scandinavian countries are not the only ones in which traffic offenders have been fined according to their income. In January 2010, a Swiss court fined a speeder with an estimated wealth of over $20 million $290,000 for driving thirty-five miles an hour (fifty-seven kilometers an hour) faster than the fifty-mile-an-hour (eighty-kilometer-an-hour) limit (Huffington Post 2010).

29. In biology, symbiosis refers to any intimate relationship or association between members of two or more species. The concept includes mutualism, where different species living in close association provide benefits to each other, commensalism, an association between two different species in which one benefits and the other is unaffected, and parasitism, in which one organism benefits and the other is adversely affected.

REFERENCES

Abu-Lughod, Lila. 1986. *Veiled Sentiments: Honor and Poetry in a Bedouin Society*. Berkeley: University of California Press.

Abu-Lughod, Lila. 1990. "The Romance of Resistance: Tracing Transformations of Power through Bedouin Women." *American Ethnologist* 17:41–55.

Adler, Patricia A. 1985. *Wheeling and Dealing: An Ethnography of an Upper-Level Drug Dealing and Smuggling Community*. New York: Columbia University Press.

Arensberg, Conrad M. and Arthur H. Niehoff. 1964. *Introducing Social Change: A Manual for Americans Overseas*. Chicago: Aldine.

Austin, James, Marino A. Bruce, Leo Carroll, Patricia L. McCall, and Stephen C. Richards. 2001. "The Use of Incarceration in the United States." *Critical Criminology* 10(1):17–41.

Becker, Howard S. 1963. *Outsiders: Studies in the Sociology of Deviance*. New York: Free Press.

Barak, Gregg. 2000a. "Comparative Criminology: A Global View." *The Critical Criminologist* 10(2):8–10.

Barak, Gregg (ed.). 2000b. *Comparative Criminology: A Global View.* Westport, CT: Greenwood Press.

Barak, Gregg. 2003. "Revisionist History, Visionary Criminology, and Needs-Based Justice." *Contemporary Justice Review* 6(3):217–225.

Barton, R. F. 1919 [1969]. *Ifugao Law.* Berkeley: University of California Press.

Betzig, Laura, Robert Know Dentan, Bruce M. Knauft, Keith F. Otterbein. 1988. "On Reconsidering Violence in Simple Human Societies." *Current Anthropology* 29(4):624–636.

Bodley, John H. 2008. *Victims of Progress 5/e.* Lanham, MD: AltaMira.

Borneman, John. 1997. *Settling Accounts: Violence, Justice, and Accountability in Postsocialist Europe.* Princeton: Princeton University Press.

Bourgois, Philippe. 1996 [2003]. *In Search of Respect: Selling Crack in El Barrio.* 2nd edition. Cambridge: Cambridge University Press.

Brennan, Patricia A., Sarnoff, A. Mednick, and Jan Volavka. 1995. "Biomedical Factors in Crime." pp. 65–90 in *Crime,* edited by James Q. Wilson and Joan Petersilia. San Francisco: ICS Press.

Brisman, Avi. 2006. "Meth Chic and the Tyranny of the Immediate: Reflections on the Culture-Drug/Drug-Crime Relationships." *North Dakota Law Review* 82(4):1273–1396.

Brisman, Avi. 2007. "Sabotage, Interventionism, and the Art of Disruption." Paper presented at On the Edge: Transgression and The Dangerous Other: An Interdisciplinary Conference. John Jay College of Criminal Justice and The Graduate Center, City University of New York (CUNY), New York, NY, Aug. 10.

Brisman, Avi. 2008a. "'Docile Bodies' or Rebellious Spirits?: Issues of Time, Power, and Spectacle in the Withdrawal of Death Penalty Appeals." Paper presented at the 35th Annual Conference, Western Society of Criminology, Sacramento, CA, February 16.

Brisman, Avi. 2008b. "Fair Fare?: Food as Contested Terrain in U.S. Prisons and Jails." *Georgetown Journal on Poverty Law and Policy* 15(1):49–93.

Brisman, Avi. 2009a. "Direct Action as Conceptual Art: An Examination of the Role of the Communiqué for Eco-Defense and Animal Liberation." Paper presented at the 2009 American Society of Criminology Annual Meeting, Philadelphia, PA (Nov. 5, 2009).

Brisman, Avi. 2009b. "'Docile Bodies' or Rebellious Spirits: Issues of Time and Power in the Waiver and Withdrawal of Death Penalty Appeals." *Valparaiso University Law Review* 43(2):459–512.

Brisman, Avi. 2009c. "Resisting Speed." Paper presented at the First Annual International Crime, Media, and Popular Culture Studies Conference: A Cross Disciplinary Exploration, Indiana State University, Terre Haute, IN, October 7.

Brisman, Avi. 2010a. "Animal Cruelty, Free Speech, and the Parameters of Critical Criminology." Paper presented at The Poetics of Pain: Aesthetics, Ideology, and Representation, Annual Interdisciplinary Graduate Student Conference, The Graduate Center-City University of New York, Department of Comparative Literature, New York, NY, Feb. 26.

Brisman, Avi. 2010b. "Appreciative Criminology and the Jurisprudence of Robert M. Cover." Paper presented at the American Society of Criminology Annual Meeting, San Francisco, CA, Nov. 20.

Brisman, Avi. 2010c. "Déjà vu All Over Again: Preliminary Notes on Reconceptualizing Evolution and Crime". Paper presented at the 37th Annual Conference, Western Society of Criminology, Honolulu, HI, Feb. 5.

Brisman, Avi. 2010d. "'Creative Crime' and the Phytological Analogy." *Crime Media Culture* 6(2):205–225.

Brisman, Avi. 2010e. "The Indiscriminate Criminalisation of Environmentally Beneficial Activities." Pp. 161–92 in *Global Environmental Harm: Criminological Perspectives,* edited by Rob White. Devon, UK: Willan Publishing.

Brisman, Avi. 2010f. "The Waiver and Withdrawal of Death Penalty Appeals as 'Extreme Communicative Acts.'" *Western Criminology Review* 11(2):27–41.

Brisman, Avi. 2011a. "Probing the Parameters of Critical Criminology: What Kinds of Domination Should Critical Criminology Not Critique?" Paper presented at the Critical Criminology and Justice Studies Mini-Conference, hosted by the Criminology and Justice Studies Program in the Department of Sociology at

California State University San Marcos, in conjunction with the San Diego State University School of Public Affairs, and the School of Urban and Public Affairs University of Texas-Arlington, Vancouver, B.C. Feb. 3.

Brisman, Avi. 2011b. "Probing the Parameters of Critical Criminology: When Does the Critique of Domination Become Domination Itself?" Paper presented at the 38th Annual Conference, Western Society of Criminology, Vancouver, B.C., Feb. 4.

Brown, Michael F. 1996. "On Resisting Resistance." *American Anthropologist* 98(4):729–35.

Bryant, Taimie. 1990. "*Oya-ko Shinju*: Death at the Center of the Heart." *UCLA Pacific Basin Law Journal* 8(1):1–31.

Burawoy, Michael, Alice Burton, Ann Arnett Ferguson, Kathryn J. Fox, Joshua Gamson, Nadine Gartrell, Leslie Hurst, Charles Kurzman, Leslie Salzinger, Josepha Schiffman, and Shiori Ui. 1991. *Ethnography Unbound: Power and Resistance in the Modern Metropolis*. Berkeley: University of California Press.

Chadwick, Kathryn, and Phil Scraton. 2001. "Critical Criminology." Pp. 70–72 in *The Sage Dictionary of Criminology*, edited by Eugene McLaughlin and John Muncie. London: Sage.

Chagnon, Napoleon A. 1992 [1983]. *Yanomamo: The Fierce People* 4/e. New York: Harcourt Brace.

Chambliss, William J. 1964. "A Sociological Analysis of the Law of Vagrancy." *Social Problems* 12(1):67–77.

Chambliss, William J. 1982. "Toward a Radical Criminology." Pp. 230–41 in *The Politics of Law: A Progressive Critique*, edited by New York: Pantheon.

Chambliss, William J. and Robert B. Seidman. 1971. *Law, Order, and Power*. Reading, MA: Addison-Wesley.

Choi, Carolyn. 1990. "Application of a Cultural Defense in Criminal Proceedings." *UCLA Pacific Basin Law Journal* 8(1/2):80–90.

Collier, George A. 1989. "The Impact of Second Republic Labor Reforms in Spain." Pp. 201–22 in *History and Power in the Study of Law: New Directions in Legal Anthropology*, edited by June Starr and Jane F. Collier. Ithaca, NY: Cornell University Press.

Collier, Jane 1975. "Legal Processes." *Annual Review of Anthropology* 4:121–44.

Comaroff, John L. 1982. "Dialectical systems, history and anthropology: units of study and questions of theory." *Journal of Southern African Studies* 8:143–72.

Comaroff, Jean and John Comaroff. 2004. "Criminal Obsessions, After Foucault: Postcoloniality, Policing, and the Metaphysics of Disorder." *Critical Inquiry* 30(Summer):800–24.

Comaroff, Jean and John Comaroff, eds. 2006. *Law and Disorder in the Postcolony*. Chicago: Univerity of Chicago Press.

Cover, Robert M. 1984–85. "The Folktales of Justice: Tales of Jurisdiction." *Capital University Law Review* 14:179–203.

Cover, Robert. 1986. "Violence and the Word." *Yale Law Journal* 95:1601–29.

Cullen, Francis T. and Robert Agnew. 2006. *Criminological Theory: Past to Present*. 3rd edition. Los Angeles, CA: Roxbury.

Daly, Martin and Margo Wilson. 1982. "Homicide and Kinship." *American Anthropologist* 84(2):372–378.

Derrida, Jacques. 1990. "Force of Law: The 'Mystical Foundation of Authority.'" *Cardozo Law Review* 11:919–1046.

Donovan, James M. 2008. *Legal Anthropology: An Introduction*. Lanham, MD: AltaMira.

Driberg, Jack Herbert. 1928. "Primitive Law in East Africa." *Africa* 1: 63–72.

Ellis, Lee and Anthony Walsh. 1997. "Gene-Based Evolutionary Theories in Criminology." *Criminology* 35(2):229–276.

Erickson, Paul A. and Liam D. Murphy. 2003. *A History of Anthropological Theory* 2nd edition. Orchard Park, NY: Broadview.

Favret-Saada Jeanne. 1980. *Deadly Words: Witchcraft in the Bocage*. Cambridge, UK: Cambridge Univ. Press.

Ferrell, Jeff. 1993. *Crimes of Style: Urban Graffiti and the Politics of Criminality*. Boston, MA: Northeastern University Press.

Ferrell, Jeff. 1999. "Cultural Criminology." *Annual Review of Sociology* 25:395–418.

Ferrell, Jeff. 2001. *Tearing Down the Streets: Adventures in Urban Anarchy*. New York: Palgrave Macmillan.

Ferrell, Jeff. 2002. "Speed Kills." *Critical Criminology* 11(3):185–198.

Ferrell, Jeff and Mark S. Hamm eds. 1998. *Ethnography at the Edge: Crime, Deviance, and Field Research.* Boston: Northeastern Univ. Press.

Fletcher, Robert. 1891. "The New School of Criminal Anthropology." *American Anthropologist* 4(3):201–36.

Foucault, Michel. 1978. *The History of Sexuality*, R. Hurley, trans. New York: Pantheon.

Fredrichs, David O. ed. 1998. *State Crime*, vols 1 and 2. Aldershot, Gower.

Friedmann, Wolfgang Gaston. 1959. *Law in a Changing Society.* Berkeley and Los Angeles: University of California Press.

Gallin, Alice. 1994. "Cultural Defense: Undermining the Policies Against Domestic Violence." *Boston College Law Review* 35(3):723–45.

Geschiere, Peter. 1997. *The Modernity of Witchcraft: Politics, and the Occult in Postcolonial Africa.* Charlottesville: Univiversity of Virginia Press.

Gibbs, Carole, Edmund F. McGarrell, and Mark Axelrod. 2010. "Transnational white-collar crime and risk: Lessons from the global trade in electronic waste." *Criminology and Public Policy* 9(3):543–60.

Goldstein, Taryn F. 1994. "Cultural Conflicts in Court: Should the American Criminal Justice System Formally Recognize a 'Culture Defense'?" *Dickinson Law Review* 99:141–68.

Goodale, Mark, and Sally Engle Merry, eds. 2007. *The Practice of Human Rights: Tracking Law Between the Global and the Local.* Cambridge: Cambridge University Press.

Greenhouse, Carol J. 1986. *Praying for Justice: Faith, Order, and Community in an American Town.* Ithaca, NY: Cornell University Press.

Griffiths, Elizabeth, Carlyn Yule, and Rosemary Gartner. 2011. "Fighting Over Trivial Things: Explaining the Issue of Contention in Violent Altercations." *Criminology* 49(1):61–94.

Hagedorn, J.M. 1990. "Back in the field again: gang research in the nineties." Pp. 240–59 in *Gangs in America*, edited by CR Huff. Newbury Park, CA: Sage.

Harvard Law Review. 1986. "The Culture Defense in the Criminal Law." *Harvard Law Review* 99 (April):1293–1311.

Henry, Stuart, and Mark M. Lanier, eds. 2001. *What Is Crime? Controversies over the Nature of Crime and What to Do about It.* Lanham, MD: Rowman and Littlefield.

Herrnstein, Richard J. 1995. "Criminogenic Traits." Pp. 39–63 in *Crime*, edited by James Q. Wilson and Joan Petersilia. San Francisco: ICS Press.

Huffington Post. "Swiss Court Fines Speeding Millionaire $290,000." 2010. Retrieved January 7, 2010 (http://www.huffingtonpost.com/2010/01/07/swiss-court-fines-speedin_n_414644.html).

Humphreys, Laud and Lee Rainwater. 1975. *Tearoom Trade: Impersonal Sex in Public Places.* New York: Aldine de Gruyter.

Jain, Sharada; Nirja Misra; and Kavita Srivastava. 1987. "Deorala Episode: Women's Protest in Rajasthan." *Economic and Political Weekly*, XXII:45(November 7): 1891–1894.

Johnson, David T. 2009. "Teaching Tip: Teaching Comparative Criminology." *The Criminologist* 34(6):15–16.

Kane, Stephanie C. 2009. "Stencil graffiti in urban waterscapes of Buenos Aires and Rosario, Argentina." *Crime Media Culture* 5:9–28.

Knauft, Bruce M. 1996. *Genealogies for the Present in Cultural Anthropology.* New York: Routledge.

Knauft, Bruce M., Thomas S. Abler, Laura Betzig, Christopher Boehm, Robert Knox Dentan, Thomas M. Kiefer, Keith F. Otterbein, John Paddock, and Lars Rodseth. 1991. "Violence and Sociality in Human Evolution [and Comments and Replies]." *Current Anthropology* 32(4):391–428.

Koptiuch, Kristin. 1996. "'Cultural Defense' and Criminological Displacements: Gender, Race, and (Trans)Nation in the Legal Surveillance of U.S." Pp.215–33 in *Displacement, Diaspora, and Geographies of Identity*, edited by Smadar Laview and Ted Swedenburg. Durham, NC: Duke University Press.

Kottak, Conrad Phillip. 2008. *Window on Humanity: A Concise Introduction to Anthropology* 3rd edition. New York, NY: McGraw-Hill.

Kratz, Corinne A. 2007. Personal communication. Dec. 7.

Lave, Jean, Paul Duguid, Nadine Fernandez, and Erik Axel. 1992. "Coming of Age in Birmingham: Cultural Studies and Conceptions of Subjectivity." *Annual Review of Anthropology* 21:257–282.

Levi-Strauss, Claude. 1963. "Introduction: History and Anthropology." Pp.3–28 in *Structural Anthropology*. Claude Levi-Strass, trans. by Claire Jacobson and Brooke Grundfest Schoepf. Garden City, NY: Anchor Books.

Lewis, I.M. ed. 1968. *History and Social Anthropology*. London.

Linger, Daniel T. 2003. "Wild Power in Post-Military Brazil." Pp. 99–124 in *Crime's Power: Anthropologists and the Ethnography of Crime*, edited by Philip C. Parnell and Stephanie C. Kane. New York: Palgrave Macmillan.

Magnarella, Paul. 1991. "Justice in a Culturally Pluralistic Society: The Cultural Defense on Trial." *Journal of Ethnic Studies* 19(3):65–84.

Maguire, Brendan. 1988. "The Applied Dimension of Radical Criminology: A Survey of Prominent Radical Criminologists." *Sociological Spectrum* 8:133–151.

Malinowski, Bronislaw. 1959. *Crime and Custom in Savage Society*. Totowa, NJ: Littlefield, Adams and Co.

Mani, Lata. 1987. "Contentious Traditions: The Debate on Sati in Colonial India." *Cultural Critique* 7(Fall):119–56.

Mbembe, Achille. 1992. "The Banality of Power and the Aesthetics of Vulgarity in the Postcolony." Janet Roitman, trans. *Public Culture* 4(2):1–30.

McLaughlin, Eugene. 2001. "State Crime." Pp. 289–90 in *The Sage Dictionary of Criminology*, edited by Eugene McLaughlin and John Muncie. London: Sage.

Merolla, David. 2008. "The war on drugs and the gender gap in arrests; a critical perspective." *Critical Sociology* 34(2):255–270.

Merry, Sally Engle. 1981. *Urban Danger: Life in a Neighborhood of Strangers*. Philadelphia: Temple University Press.

Merry, Sally Engle. 1998. "The Criminalization of Everyday Life." Pp. 14–40 in *Everyday Practices and Trouble Cases*, edited by A. Sarat, M. Constable, D. Engel, V. Hans, S. Lawrence. Evanston, IL: Northwestern University Press.

Merry, Sally Engle. 2000. *Colonizing Hawai'i: The Cultural Power of Law*. Princeton: Princeton University Press.

Merry, Sally Engle. 2006. "Transnational Human Rights and Local Activism: Mapping the Middle." *American Anthropologist* 108 (1):38–51.

Michalowski, Raymond J. 1996. "Critical Criminology and the Critique of Domination: The Story of an Intellectual Movement." *Critical Criminology* 7(1):9–16.

Michalowski, Raymond J. 2010. "Keynote Address: Critical Criminology for a Global Age." *Western Criminology Review* 11(1):3–10.

Moore, Sally F. 1969. "Law and Anthropology." *Biennial Review of Anthropology* 6:252–300.

Nader, Laura. 1969. "Styles of court procedure: To make the balance." Pp.69–91 in *Law in Culture and Society*, edited by Laura Nader. Chicago: Aldine.

Nader, Laura. 1980. "Preface." Pp. xv-xix in *No Access to Law: Alternatives to the American Judicial System*, edited by Laura Nader. New York: Academic Press.

Nader, Laura. 2003. "Crime as a Category—Domestic and Globalized." Pp. 55–76 in *Crime's Power: Anthropologists and the Ethnography of Crime*, edited by Philip C. Parnell and Stephanie C. Kane. New York: Palgrave Macmillan.

Nader, Laura and Harry F. Todd, Jr. 1978. "Introduction." Pp. 1–40 in *The Disputing Process: Law in Ten Societies*, edited by Laura Nader and Harry F. Todd. New York: Columbia University Press.

Nietzsche, Friedrich. 1886 (1997). *Beyond Good and Evil: Prelude to a Philosophy of the Future*. Helen Zimmern, trans. Mineola, N.Y.: Dover Publications, Inc.

Norton-Hawk, Maureen. 2010. "Exporting Gender Injustice: The Impact of the U.S. War on Drugs on Ecuadorian Women." *Critical Criminology* 18(2):133–146.

Oberg, Kalervo. 1934. "Crime and Punishment in Tlingit Society." *American Anthropologist* 36(2):145–56.

Omi, Michael and Howard Winant. 1994. *Racial Formation in the United States: From the 1960s to the 1990s*. 2nd edition. New York: Routledge.

Ong, Aihwa. 1987. *Spirits of Resistance and Capitalist Discipline: Factory Women in Malaysia*. Albany, NY: State University of New York Press.

Ortner, Sherry B. 1984. "Theory in Anthropology since the Sixties." *Comparative Studies in Society and History* 26(1):126–66.

Ortner, Sherry B. 1995. "Resistance and the Problem of Ethnographic Refusal." *Comparative Studies in Society and History* 37(1):173–193.

Parnell, Philip C. and Stephanie C. Kane (eds.). 2003. *Crime's Power: Anthropologists and the Ethnography of Crime*. New York: Palgrave Macmillan.

Phillips, Susan A. 1999. *Wallbangin'—Graffiti and Gangs in L.A.* Chicago: University of Chicago Press.

Pinheiro, Paulo Sérgio. 2000. "Democratic Governance, Violence, and the (Un)Rule of Law." *Daedalus* 129(2):119–43.

Polsky, N. 1969. *Hustlers, Beats, and Others.* Garden City, NY: Anchor.

Pound, Leslie. 1985. Mother's Tragic Crime Exposes a Cultural Gap. *Chicago Tribune.* June 10. Retrieved July 30, 2011 (http://articles.chicagotribune.com/1985-06-10/features/8502060678_1_first-degree-murder-suicide-fumiko-kimura).

Presdee, Mike. 2004. "Cultural criminology: The long and winding road." *Theoretical Criminology* 8(3):275–85.

Preston, F. W., and Roots, R. I. 2004. "Law and its unintended consequences." *American Behavioral Scientist* 47(11):1371–1376.

Quinney, Richard. ed. 1969. *Crime and Justice in Society.* Boston: Little, Brown.

Quinney, Richard. ed. 1974. *Criminal Justice in America: A Critical Understanding.* Boston: Little, Brown.

Quinney, Richard. 1977. *Class, State, and Crime: On the Theory and Practice of Criminal Justice.* New York: David McKay.

Rafter, Nicole. 2007. "Somatotyping, Antimodernism, and the Production of Criminological Knowledge." *Criminology* 45(4):805–833.

Raine, Adrian. 2002. "The Biological Basis of Crime." Pp. 43–74 in *Crime,* edited by James Q. Wilson and Joan Petersilia. Oakland: ICS Press.

Renteln, Alison Dundes. 1993. "A Justification of the Cultural Defense as Partial Excuse." *Southern California Review of Law* 2(2):437–526.

Renteln, Alison Dundes. 2005. *The Cultural Defense.* Oxford: Oxford University Press.

Rheinstein, Max. 1954. *Max Weber on Law in Economy and Society.* Cambridge, MA: Harvard University Press.

Riles, Annelise. 2006. "Anthropology, Human Rights, and Legal Knowledge: Culture in the Iron Cage." *American Anthropologist* 108(1):52–65.

Rimonte, Nilda. 1991. "A Question of Culture: Cultural Approval of Violence Against Women in the Pacific-Asian Community and the Cultural Defense." *Stanford Law Review* 43(6):1311–27.

Robinson, Matthew B. 2001. "Wither Criminal Justice? An Argument for a Reformed Discipline." *Critical Criminology* 10(2):97–106.

Rose, Nikolas. 1993. "Government, Authority, and Expertise in Advanced Liberalism." *Economy and Society.* 22(3):283–299.

Rosen, Lawrence. 1991. "The Integrity of Cultures." *American Behavioral Scientist.* 34(5):594–617.

Rosen, Lawrence. 2006. *Law as Culture: An Invitation.* Princeton: Princeton University Press.

Ross, Jeffrey Ian. 2000. *Controlling State Crime* 2nd edition. New York: Transaction Publishers.

Rothe, Dawn L. 2009. *State Criminality: The Crime of All Crimes.* Lexington.

Rother, Dawn L., and Christopher W. Mullins (eds.). 2010. *State Crime: Current Perspectives.* New Brunswick, NJ: Rutgers University Press.

Ruddick, Sue. 2003. "The Politics of Aging: Globalization and the Restructuring of Youth and Childhood." *Antipode* 35:351–73.

Sahlins, Marshall. 1981. *Historical Metaphors and Mythical Realities.* Ann Arbor, MI: University of Michigan Press.

Sampson, Robert J. and W. Byron Groves. 1989. "Community Structure and Crime: Testing Social-Disorganization Theory." *American Journal of Sociology* 94(4):774–802.

Sams, Julia P. 1986. "The Availability of the 'Cultural Defense' as an Excuse for Criminal Behavior. *Georgia Journal of International and Comparative Law* 16(Spring):335–54.

Schapera, Isaac. 1962. "Should Anthropologists be Historians?" *Journal of the Royal Anthropological Institute* 92(2):143–56.

Scheper-Hughes, Nancy. 1992. *Death Without Weeping: The Violence of Everyday Life in Northeast Brazil.* Berkeley: University of California Press

Scheper-Hughes, Nancy. 2006. "Death squads and democracy in Northeast Brazil." Pp. 150–88 in *Law and Disorder in the Postcolony: An Introduction,* edited by Jean Comaroff and John L. Comaroff. Chicago: University of Chicago Press.

Schneider, Jane, and Peter Schneider. 2008. "The Anthropology of Crime and Criminalization." *Annual Review of Anthropology* 37:351–73.

Scott, James C. 1985. *Weapons of the Weak: Everyday Forms of Peasant Resistance.* New Haven: Yale University Press.

Sharff, Jagna Wojcicka. 1987. "The Underground Economy of a Poor Neighborhood." Pp. 19–50 in *Cities of the United States: Studies in Urban Anthropology*, edited by Leith Mullings. New York: Columbia University Press.

Sherman, Spencer. 1986. "When Cultures Collide." *California Lawyer* 6(1):33–36, 60–61.

Sheybani, Malek-Mithra. 1987. "Cultural Defense: One Person's Culture is Another's Crime." *Loyola of Los Angeles International and Comparative Law Journal* 9(3):751–83.

Snyder, Gregory J. 2009. *Graffiti Lives: Beyond the Tag in New York's Urban Underground.* New York: New York University Press.

South, Nigel. 2010. "The ecocidal tendencies of late modernity: transnational crime, social exclusion, victims and rights." Pp. 228–47 in *Global Environmental Harm: Criminological Perspectives*, edited by Rob White. Cullompton, Devon, UK: Willan.

Spivak, Gayatri Chakravorty. 1988. "Can the Subaltern Speak?" Pp. 271–316 in *Marxism and the Interpretation of Cultures*, edited by C. Nelson and L. Grossberg. Urbana, IL: University of Illinois Press.

Sullivan, Mercer L. 1989. *"Getting Paid": Youth Crime and Work in the Inner City.* Ithaca: Cornell University Press.

Sutherland, Anne. 1994. "Gypsy Identity, Names and Social Security." *PoLAR* 17(2):75–83.

Taussig, Michael. 2005. *Law in a Lawless Land: Diary of a Limpieza in Colombia.* Chicago: University of Chicago Press.

Thompson, Mark. 1985. "The Cultural Defense." *Student Lawyer* 14(1):24–29.

Van Maanen, John. 1995. *Representation in Ethnography.* Thousand Oaks, CA: Sage.

Vincent, Joan. 1989. "Contours of Change: Agrarian Law in Colonial Uganda, 1895–1962." Pp. 153–67 in *History and Powr in the Study of Law: New Directions in Legal Anthropology*, edited by June Starr and Jane F. Collier. Ithaca, NY: Cornell University Press.

Volpp, Leti. 1994. "(Mis)identifying Culture: Asian Women and the 'Cultural Defense.'" *Harvard Women's Law Journal* 17: 57–101.

Woo, Deborah. 1989. "*The People v. Fumiko Kimura*: But Which People?" *International Journal of the Sociology of Law* 17:403–28.

Worsley, Peter. 1968. *The Trumpet Shall Sound.* New York.

Young, T.R. 1985. "Social Justice vs. Criminal Justice: An Agenda for Critical Criminology." *Journal of Sociology and Social Welfare* 12:552–75.

Cases

Lawrence v. Texas, 539 U.S. 558, 123 S. Ct. 2472, 156 L. Ed. 2d 508 (2003).

Loving v. Virginia, 388 U.S. 1, 87 S. Ct. 1817, 18 L. Ed. 2d 1010 (1967).

People v. Aphaylath, 68 N.Y.2d 945, 502 N.E.2d 998, 510 N.Y.S.2d 83 (N.Y. 1986).

People v. Benu, 87 Misc.2d 139, 385 N.Y.S.2d 222 (N.Y.City Crim.Ct. 1976).

People v. Ezeonu, 155 Misc.2d 344, 588 N.Y.S.2d 116 (N.Y.Sup. Ct. 1992).

People v. Kimura, No. A-091133 (Santa Monica Super. Ct. Nov. 21, 1985).

People v. Moua, No. 315972–0 (Fresno County Super. Ct. Feb. 7, 1985).

People v. Poddar, 26 Cal.App.3d 438, 103 Cal.Rptr. 84 (Cal.App. 1 Dist. 1972).

State v. Ganal, 81 Hawai'i 358, 917 P.2d 370 (Haw. 1996).

CHAPTER
XI

Anarchist, Peacemaking, and Restorative Justice Theories

PEACEMAKING CRIMINOLOGY

Michael Braswell,
John Fuller, and
Bo Lozofff

Major wisdom traditions and religions of the world have incorporated the principles of peace, love, and social justice into their messages. The peacemaking perspective is first and foremost a personal philosophy that starts in the heart of the individual. This chapter, however, extends the peacemaking perspective beyond the individual to the institutional and the cultural context. It is argued that for the peacemaking perspective to be effective, we need an overarching philosophy that allows individual goodness and integrity to be carried on in collective actions, and gives us hope that our institutions and society can be transformed and come to a point of more effectively addressing the problems of crime, the criminal justice system, and corrections. The individual is the necessary starting point. Personal change, however, must lead to social and institutional transformation to achieve our goals of peace and social justice.

Fortunately, we do not have to fashion institutional and societal change from a vacuum. There is a rich history of attempts to induce social change at all levels of society. In this chapter, we will review some of these ideas and theories and suggest how they relate to the peacemaking perspective, particularly as it applies to corrections. Central to our investigation here is the efforts of feminists and critical theorists who have addressed the problems of crime and social justice. By adding these two types of voices to that of the individual transformation outlined in Chapter 2, we hope to show how the peacemaking perspective has a long, diverse, rich, and productive tradition, and that peacemaking can be a lens through which the corrections system can be viewed in a new light. The religious and humanist, feminist, and conflict traditions need not be viewed in isolation from each other. There are scholars and practitioners who incorporate more than one of these traditions and would feel constrained if we were to label them as subscribing to only one tradition. Nevertheless, for our purposes here, it is useful to consider how each contributes to the peacemaking perspective.

FEMINIST TRADITIONS

At first glance it may seem presumptuous for three men to discuss feminism. We take this step without trepidation, however, because we believe to be fully human is to include the feminist perspective. Feminism is not an ascribed status available only to females. Feminism is a philosophy that argues that men and women should be politically, economically, and socially equal. While many men have not embraced this idea because it challenges their source of dominance, other men have come to recognize that, not only is feminism a fairer way to distribute rewards and opportunities, but that in a patriarchal society, there are costs to men as well as women. The costs of patriarchy to women are, obviously, much more extensive and severe than those to men, and we do not want to deny the oppression of women, but such a way of organizing society is harmful to everyone. Men live shorter lives, are susceptible to more stress, are alienated from their families, and are living lives made dysfunctional by the unrealistic and oftentimes unhealthy demands of the contemporary masculine role.

This simple idea that men and women should be treated equally by society's institutions, has far-reaching implications for societies around the globe. The United States has long been an arena engaged in the struggle for gender equity and can be contrasted with other cultures where the struggles are more entrenched and often more deadly. Looking at this issue from a cross-cultural and a historical perspective can demonstrate how peacemaking is concerned with ideas that have a broader context than simply the American criminal justice system. Gender roles are embedded into the very social fabric of cultures. It is impossible to examine how women are treated in the Middle East without an understanding of the Islamic religion. It is futile to look at the way women are treated in China without an appreciation for the ancient and recent history of that country. It is problematic to consider the role of women in the United States without grasping the impact capitalism has on efforts of social change. In short, feminism cannot be linked to the peacemaking perspective without a deep appreciation of how cultural, economic, and social systems have shaped and constrained the relationships between women and men. Therefore, our comments here need to be qualified as only suggestive of the impact of gender roles. A full understanding of feminism takes more space than available for our present purposes of simply identifying the issues.

In order to understand feminism, we must expand our way of thinking to realize that schools of thought can sometimes require fundamental life-changing challenges. For example, in defining feminism M. Kay Harris argues:

> Feminism offers and is a set of values, beliefs, and experiences—a consciousness, a way of looking at the world. Feminism should be seen not merely as a prescription for granting rights to women, but as a far broader vision. There are a number of varying strands within feminist thought, but there are some core values that transcend the differences. Among the key tenets of feminism are three simple beliefs—that all people have value as human beings, that harmony and felicity are more important than power and possession, and that the personal is the political ...[1]

Feminism, therefore, is not simply a political theme, but rather, a new way of looking at the relations between women and men as those relations exist in the context of social, economic, and political systems. The exact way those relations are envisioned is linked to the type of feminism that is adopted. The differences between types of feminism are significant, but, as Harris points out, there are key tenets that cut across all the variations.

Feminism can be envisioned in many ways. One method to differentiate between the variations is to look at the 12 types of feminism identified by Lorber.[2] Each type presents questions, issues, and concerns that guide its underlying feminist philosophy. For example, developmental feminism is concerned with the problems of women in developing countries, which are in many ways different than those in the United States. Lorber suggests:

> For *developmental feminism*, the theoretical emphasis on universal human rights is reflected in developing countries in political pressure for the education of girls,

maternity and child health care, and economic resources for women who contribute heavily to the support of their families. However, when feminist gender politics calls for wives and husbands to be equal, and for women to have sexual autonomy, developmental feminism frequently has to confront traditional cultural values and practices that give men power over their daughters and wives. The women's own solution to this dilemma is community organizing around their family roles.[3]

Clearly, when it comes to feminism, one size does not fit all. The state of development of the country, the religious context of the culture, the social status of the family, and the differences in the level of education between husband and wife and father and daughter all mediate the types of opportunities and roles that are afforded women. Equally important are the conscious decisions women make in deciding to become involved in conventional society. These types of feminism argue that conformity is too high a price to be paid for fundamental human rights. There should be tolerance for diversity in societies that are just, and that put the welfare of all citizens, particularly the "least of those," above the religious or moral systems of those who happen to be in power.

In this light, feminism can be seen as a natural tradition from which criminology peacemaking is derived. The concern for the individual caught up in the power of the dominant society speaks to both the fight against paternalism and such policies as the war on crime. When the state sanctions policies that deny equality to individuals, it is only reasonable for citizens to complain. In that complaint, however, new ways of relationships are suggested by both the many forms of feminism and peacemaking criminology. For instance, they converge on issues such as rape, domestic violence, gender discrimination in employment in the criminal justice system, and treatment of sex offenders. Additionally, problems such as the international trafficking in women and girls have been addressed by both feminists and peacemaking criminologists. The concern for both nonviolence and social justice are cornerstones of feminism and peacemaking criminology. Using domination to eliminate domination is an oxymoron. It's like the old 1960s saying about "fighting for peace." Feminism argues for new ways of knowing based on cooperation instead of conflict. The same can be said for peacemaking criminology.

There are a number of women whose work in peacemaking criminology flows from their commitment to feminist values and practices. M. Kay Harris is a university professor who has had extensive experience working in agencies that form crime control policies. She writes:

> A feminist orientation leads to greater awareness of the role and responsibility of society, not just the individual, in the development of conflict. This suggests that individuals, groups, and societies need to accept greater responsibility for preventing and reducing those conditions, values, and structures that produce violence and strife. Removing the idea of power from its central position is key here, and this requires continually challenging actions, practices, and assumptions that glorify power, control, and domination, as well as developing more felicitous alternatives.[4]

Another feminist who can be considered a peacemaking criminologist is M. Joan McDermott. McDermott argues that there is a link between one's personal life and social awareness and responsibility. To her, peacemaking at the personal level should be extended to the institutional and global levels. The connectedness of both peacemaking criminology and feminism are seen in her work:

> Ethical concerns and priorities of criminology as peacemaking are similar to those of feminist ethics, and these include … : We are all tied to other human beings and also the environment. To achieve peace and justice, we need loving and compassionate individuals. We also need equality. From love and compassion flow understanding, service, and justice. The nonviolent ethic assumes that human action is motivated by emotion as well as reason, and that knowledge is both rational and emotional.[5]

Peacemaking criminology shares many of its values, perspectives, and practitioners with the feminist perspective. Many would hesitate to make a distinction between them and would object to being identified as one and not the other. They are not mutually exclusive points of view. In many ways, peacemaking criminology can be expressed as feminism that is applied to the problem of crime and the criminal justice system. But while they share many characteristics, peacemaking and feminism are not the same concept. Peacemaking criminology includes ideas from feminism, but does not mimic it. In fact, feminism draws much of its evolution from secular and humanist traditions. Peacemaking criminology also includes ideas from other intellectual traditions. Peacemaking criminology, in addition to feminism, looks to religious and humanist intellectual traditions for inspiration and guidance. There is a third intellectual tradition identified by Pepinsky and Quinney that gives life to peacemaking criminology: the critical intellectual tradition.[6]

CRITICAL TRADITIONS

The critical intellectual tradition that informs peacemaking criminology covers a wide range of issues, theories, and perspectives. In the introductory essay of his book of readings titled, *Social Justice, Criminal Justice*, Bruce Arrigo does an excellent job not only of listing, but of showing the relationships between, the various strains of critical theory in law, crime, and deviance.[7] While recognizing that there are countless variations of critical criminology, Arrigo's book details 12 important and distinct types: Marxism, social feminism, peacemaking, prophetic criticism, anarchism, postmodern feminism, semiotics, constitutive criminology, critical race theory, chaos, catastrophe/topology, and queer theory.

Each of these critical perspectives examines ways in which individuals are oppressed by society and how this oppression is related to the problems of crime. Critical criminology is very much a macro-level analysis of society's contribution to the formulation of the crime problem and just as importantly, of the implications of how society responds to crime. As the criminal justice system is a tool of the powerful to maintain their interests, crime control can be looked at as an instrument of repression. The critical analysis of how the state uses the criminal justice system to selectively protect the interests of some individuals while selectively oppressing others, is at the heart of the critical intellectual tradition in criminology.

Arrigo situates the emergence of critical criminology in the works of Karl Marx. Marxism as a social philosophy is the intellectual father of all 11 variations of critical criminology in his book. While peacemaking criminology is not as indebted to Marxism as other critical traditions, it does owe some of its orientation to this way of analyzing crime and conflict. Before we detail just how peacemaking criminology is related to Marxism, it is useful to understand just how fundamental Marxism is to the understanding of how crime and social control are problems located at the level of society and institutions rather than only at the level of the individual. For example, David Greenburg writes:

> To study crime in relation to the way societies organize their economic and political institutions is to ask different sorts of questions about crime than have typically been asked in non-Marxist criminology. Marxists do not deny that social-psychological processes and face-to-face interactions may have some importance for understanding crime and criminal justice, but they try to see these as shaped by larger social structures. And in characterizing these structures, they give particular attention to the organization of economic activity, without neglecting the political and ideological dimensions of society. Thus the Marxist perspective directs criminological theory "outward" rather than "inward."[8]

Critical criminology as it follows its Marxist heritage will look at how the economic arrangements and social organizations of a society will contribute to its crime problems. Marx was interested in the contradictions of capitalism and how the workers were exploited by those who owned the means of production. While many contemporary criminologists take capitalism as an unexamined background assumption, the critical criminologist will examine the economic system as a structural feature that mediates how the individual relates to society. Peacemaking criminology does not emphasize the economic dimension as much as some of the other variations of critical criminology, but views it as a genuine concern. Peacemaking criminologists are interested in the causes of suffering and in ways of relieving the pain of both victims and offenders, and the economic system is an important variable that can shed light on the constraints and possibilities of social and individual change.

For peacemaking criminology, however, the economic system is just one factor in the struggle for justice. Arrigo points out the distinction between *instrumental* and *structural* Marxism. Instrumental Marxists do see the economy as the primary factor in the development of crime and society's response to crime. Critical criminology perspectives such as left realists, social feminists, and postmodern criminologists are influenced by the emphasis on the economy of instrumental Marxism. On the other hand, structural Marxists see other forces such as politics, education, personal beliefs, and morality to be underlying structures that influence how a society develops definitions about crime, deviance, and law. Here, according to Arrigo, peacemaking criminology shares its heritage with other critical perspectives such as critical race theory and anarchist criminology.

Peacemaking criminology is sometimes faulted for drawing some of its heritage from Marxism that is associated with revolution.[9] The question is asked, how can peacemaking criminology arise out of a perspective that advocates violence as a way of seeking justice? This confusion arises from a misunderstanding about how intellectual traditions influence peacemaking. The idea of violence as a justified action is not supported by peacemaking criminology. For example, Gandhi and Martin Luther King, Jr., were both revolutionaries of a sort, but they stubbornly met violence with nonviolence. Just because some ideas are derived from Marxism doesn't mean that all of Marxism applies to peacemaking criminology. The Marxist tradition is just one area from which peacemaking criminology draws inspiration, and there are other intellectual traditions such as the religious and feminist that offer different proscriptions on the efficacy of violent behavior. One should not confuse Marxism with peacemaking criminology simply because they sometimes travel on the same road.

For some students, the term Marxism has extremely negative connotations. It is associated with communism, which we have been taught is evil. In our capitalistic state we are socialized to believe that other economic systems are not only inferior, but that the people who choose those systems are somehow bad people. Without getting into an extended debate about the relative merits of capitalism, socialism, and communism, we would like to suggest that a critical analysis of the problems of crime and the criminal justice system would be incomplete without recognizing that the economic organization of a society is a legitimate and important area to study. To exclude capitalism from the study of crime would be like playing football and saying that no one may tackle the quarterback. Marxist thought looks at the contradictions in the capitalist system that contribute to crime. Critical criminology perspectives, including peacemaking criminology, look at capitalism, as well as a host of other features of society, in their attempts to understand crime and formulate criminal justice policy. An intellectually honest football player must tackle anyone who has the ball, even if it is sometimes his own quarterback.

A PEACEMAKING CRIMINOLOGY PERSPECTIVE

Just as we have seen that there are many ways that Marxist thought can be used to examine the issues of crime and the criminal justice system, so too, are there many ways that peacemaking criminology can be constructed. What we present here is just one way that makes sense to us. As peacemaking is relatively new to the study of crime, it is still evolving. We do not claim that what we present here will be definitive. Our conception of peacemaking criminology is only suggestive of one way of looking at the important issues. We present here the structure of peacemaking criminology used by Fuller in his book, *Criminal Justice: A Peacemaking Perspective*.[10] In a later chapter we will apply this perspective to the field of corrections.

Fuller envisioned peacemaking criminology as a pyramid of ideas. He calls this model the Peacemaking Pyramid Paradigm. At the base of the pyramid is the foundation of nonviolence. Following the ideas of Christ, Tolstoy, Gandhi, and Martin Luther King, Jr., and other saints and sages, any proposal that advocates or tolerates violence as a response to infractions of the law cannot be considered a peacemaking perspective. State violence such as excessive use of police force,

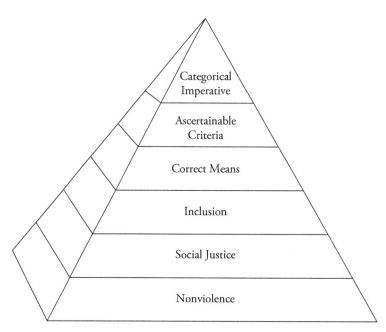

Figure 17.1   Peacemaking Pyramid Paradigm

capital punishment, corporal punishment, or any such idea that citizens can be punished into conformity is outside the bounds of peacemaking criminology. A state that models the violence it is trying to prevent is engaged in a vicious, self-perpetuating cycle of pain and suffering for all concerned. Violence begets violence and as a social and criminal justice policy, violence is doomed to failure and carries with it far-reaching consequences.

After nonviolence, the next criteria necessary for a peacemaking perspective, is social justice. Even when cases are resolved in a nonviolent manner, if the underlying social justice that gave rise to the problem remains, the solution can't be considered to be in keeping with the peacemaking perspective. Peacemaking should not be confused with peacekeeping. Peacemaking is a more comprehensive concept that attempts to resolve the underlying issues that gave rise to the conflict. For example, in the case of a juvenile who continually bullies his classmates, it would not be enough to simply move the young man to another classroom. Peacemaking would entail repairing the relationship between the bully and his victims. The bully must learn to understand how his behavior causes suffering, and the victims must have their concerns addressed and not act out

bullying behaviors on other younger and weaker victims. Peacemaking strives to solve the problem through social justice, not simply sweep it under the rug. This idea is currently being expanded as demonstrated in the restorative and community justice movement.

A third principle of the peacemaking perspective is inclusion. All who are affected by a criminal justice system decision should be included in its making. This means not just the state, but the victim(s), the offender, the community, and even some more tangentially affected parties, such as the offender's family or school officials. All who are harmed by the violation or are significant agents for positive change in the offender's life should be eligible for inclusion in the resolution of the case. This means the offender should have some input into the sentence. In order for the sentence to be more than simple punishment, and for it to help transform and rehabilitate, the offender needs to have his or her voice heard. There is an added benefit of this concept of inclusion and that is the dividends accrued from community participation in the process. Fuller puts it this way:[11]

> From a peacemaking perspective, this involvement of the offender and the victims in the process can do much toward

revitalizing the trust citizens have in their ability to govern themselves. When the victim and the offender are pawns in the games played by the courtroom work group they become disenfranchised. When mandatory sentences are decided by the legislature, the criminal justice system practitioners become also become distanced and alienated from the process. In our rush to remove discretion from the criminal court system, we have also removed the attachments that bond individuals to the process and the outcomes. From a peacemaking perspective, what is needed is a way to bring people back into the system.

The next step on the pyramid is the concept of correct means. This idea is found in many religious traditions and argues that the end, however desirable, does not justify immoral means. Applied to the criminal justice system, this idea of correct means would include the principle that the offenders be given their constitutional and human rights. Law enforcement officers should adhere to the procedural law that dictates how they detect crime and arrest offenders. Correct means entails the idea that the determination of outcomes is as important as the outcomes themselves. The process should be a model of the desired outcome. Gandhi was a champion of the notion of "correct means" and supported the idea that we must "become" the change that we want to see in our community and our world. This is no less true for the criminal justice system. Correct means requires the criminal justice system to be the paragon of fairness and virtue. This is a difficult concept for some criminal justice practitioners to accept. Because offenders often lie in addition to committing their other crimes, it is believed by some that trickery and subterfuge are acceptable means to use in the criminal justice system. The procedural law that dictates how law enforcement officers do their jobs is crafted to prevent abuse of the means of enforcement. The law is sometimes viewed as "getting in the way" or "tying the hands of the police." The procedural law protects all citizens from overzealous police officers. While dealing fairly and justly with criminals is a difficult and challenging task, the vast majority of police officers are conscientious professionals. There are, however, some who are not professional in the way they administer justice, but may be so negligent of the procedural law that they violate the legal, and sometimes human, rights of citizens. The arrest of Rodney King in Los Angeles is a good example of incorrect means.

The fifth step in the Peacemaking Pyramid Paradigm is ascertainable criteria. This idea is taken from a useful book on negotiating conflict titled *Getting to Yes*.[12] One of the principles of the book is that of using objective criteria. This means that if there is a dispute about the price of a house, an independent appraisal can be conducted to fix a price upon which everyone can agree. In the Peacemaking Pyramid Paradigm, ascertainable criteria expands on this idea by ensuring the means of justice are not only objective, but are actually understood by all concerned. The legal jargon of the criminal justice system is not understood by many. Individuals are processed through the system with little understanding of how or when they agreed to give up legal rights. It is useful to the criminal justice system as well as other professions, to employ complicated criteria and unintelligible parlance. Those who do not understand cannot object to incorrect means. If all offenders were lawyers, the use of highly technical and legal language would not be a problem. In the criminal justice system, however, most of the offenders do not understand what is happening, and it is desirable to educate them to the process so they can feel they have been treated fairly.

Finally, the Peacemaking Pyramid Paradigm advocates the Kantian concept of the categorical imperative. Simply put, the categorical imperative says that every action should be considered as if it would become a universal law. In other words, I cannot be willing to have something done to you that I would not be willing to have done to myself. This would ensure a certain consistency to how our laws are enforced and give individuals a clear idea of where the boundaries of appropriate behavior are drawn and enforced. Additionally, the categorical imperative can be applied to the peacemaking perspective according to the following:

> From a peacemaking perspective, this means that solutions to particular criminal justice

problems should entail underlying moral reasoning so that the solution would be applicable in other times and places. Kant's categorical imperative attempts to establish principles that transcend the particular circumstances of individual cases and can serve as guides to moral behavior.[13]

As can be seen, the Peacemaking Pyramid Paradigm attempts to include a number of peacemaking principles and organize them in a way that demonstrates a comprehensive process of envisioning peace in the criminal justice system. There are certainly other ways of conceptualizing a peacemaking philosophy that can be applied to the criminal justice system, but we find the Peacemaking Pyramid Paradigm sufficient for our needs to explore how peacemaking can be applied to corrections. In fact, corrections is one of the areas of the justice system that has tremendous potential for adopting the peacemaking perspective.

LEVELS OF PEACEMAKING

One of the strengths of the peacemaking perspective lies in its applicability and integration to many levels of analysis. The peacemaking perspective can be envisioned at the intrapersonal, interpersonal, institutional/societal, and the international/global levels. While our focus on corrections is on the first three of these levels, there is certainly an opportunity to link peacemaking to the international/global level as we consider how we should proactively respond to correct problems with other countries and how other countries choose to deal with offenders. Briefly, the levels of analysis of the peacemaking perspective are important because of the way they form a seamless web of thought and action for the problems of crime, social order, and justice.

The intrapersonal dimension is concerned with how individuals think about themselves. Their sense of who they are is a powerful contributor to their behavior. Thoreau said, "most men lead lives of quiet desperation." For some offenders, their lives are not so quiet and are punctuated by acts of extreme violence. It is the opinion of one psychiatrist who has worked extensively with violent inmates that an underlying problem is their feelings of shame.

> I have yet to see a serious act of violence that was not provoked by the experience of feeling shamed and humiliated, disrespected and ridiculed, and that did not attempt to prevent or undo this "loss of face"—no matter how severe the punishment, even if it includes death. For we misunderstand these men at our own peril, if we do not realize that they mean it literally when they say they would rather kill or mutilate others, be killed or mutilated themselves, than live without pride, dignity, and self-respect. They literally prefer death to dishonor.[14]

This intrapersonal dimension is a key and a possible starting point to the understanding of how we might approach the rehabilitation of offenders. While some critics of the peacemaking perspective might contend that we should not care if offenders see potential value or worth in themselves or not, but that we should only worry about their behavior, the peacemaking perspective argues that how individuals feel about themselves in relation to others is a primary determinant of their behavior.[15]

The interpersonal dimension deals with how we relate to each other in our daily lives. The peacemaking perspective has relevance here as a guide for harmony, togetherness, and intimacy. Whether it is a spouse, child, coworker, fellow inmate, or total stranger, the peacemaking perspective suggests that your interactions be based on trust, fairness, kindness, and compassion. For too many of us, the pressures of competition in a perceived zero-sum game prevent us from interacting in a positive and co-operational way with others.

The institutional/societal level of the peacemaking perspective includes the criminal justice system and, of course, corrections. It also includes many other arenas of potential conflict such as the family, school, and workplace. The way we structure our social institutions can have profound effects on how people behave. When we allow racism or sexual (or other kinds of) harassment to be tolerated in our schools and businesses, we invite reactions that may be violent. When we do not allow equal opportunity and social justice, we invite fraud and deceit. In the corrections system, we invite violence and conflict for offenders and correctional staff alike, when we allow inmates to be brutalized by correctional officers and each other. We model killing for society when we employ capital punishment. By changing the way we operate our institutions, we can began to have a more positive impact on how we relate to each other. It is a reciprocal process.

At the international/global level the peacemaking perspective has a well-recognized tradition. The prevention and resolution of armed international conflicts is a major concern for organizations like the United Nations. While some might claim there are still plenty of wars in the world, it seems clear that there could be even more but for the efforts of organizations and individuals who actively work to resolve conflicts. The Camp David Accord is an example of peacemaking that has maintained the peace between Israel and Egypt for many years. The international/global level of the peacemaking perspective can also be applied to the environment (as can the other levels). Human beings must learn to live in harmony with the environment for their long-term survival. There are concerns by many that the environment is being destroyed in many parts of the world with the results being unsafe air, water, and scarcity of food. Additionally, there are longer-term, complex problems such as global warming and the destruction of important resources such as the Amazon rain forest that have more than just a local or regional impact. It was Buckminster Fuller who coined the term spaceship earth to illustrate how interdependent we all have become.

CRIME AND PEACE

It has been our intention in this chapter to demonstrate the applicability of the peacemaking perspective to the criminal justice system. We have done this by outlining two intellectual traditions from which the peacemaking perspective draws inspiration. The feminist and critical traditions challenge the power structures of contemporary society. Crime and criminal justice are very much about how power is distributed and used in this society, as we will demonstrate in a following chapter.

A peacemaking perspective that presents a comprehensive paradigm of how peace principles can be applied at many levels of analysis has also been outlined. This perspective, while just one way to envision how peacemaking can be focused on the criminal justice system, has the advantage of illustrating how interconnected the personal and political realms of life actually are.

Finally, we would suggest that peacemaking criminology is increasingly becoming a major perspective in our thinking about crime. We will demonstrate how through processes such as alternative dispute resolution and restorative justice, that peacemaking criminology is more than just an academic curiosity. In the real world of crime, criminals, and society's response to issues of social control, the peacemaking perspective is a viable and powerful choice.

NOTES

1. Harris, M. Kay "Moving into the New Millennium: Toward a Feminist Vision of Justice." In Harold Pepinsky and Richard Quinney (eds.) (1991). *Criminology as Peacemaking*. Bloomington, IN: Indiana University Press, pp. 83–97.
2. Lorber, Judith (1998). *Gender Inequality: Feminist Theories and Politics* Los Angeles: Roxbury Publishing Company. Lorber identifies 12 types of feminism: liberal, Marxist and socialist, developmental, radical, lesbian, psychoanalytic, standpoint, multiracial, men's, social construction, and postmodern and queer theory.
3. Lorber, p. 16.
4. Harris, p. 93.
5. McDermott, M. Joan. "From a Peacemaking Perspective, Is Personal Change More Important Than Social Change? No." In John R. Fuller and Eric W. Hickey (eds.) (1999). *Controversial Issues in Criminology*. Boston, MA: Allyn and Bacon, pp. 119–126.
6. Pepinsky, Harold and Richard Quinney (eds.) (1991). *Criminology as Peacemaking*. Bloominton, IN: Indiana University Press.
7. Arrigo, Bruce A. (1999). *Social Justice, Criminal Justice: The Maturation of Critical Theory in Law, Crime, and Deviance*. Belmont, CA: West/Wadsworth.
8. Greenburg, David F. (1981). *Crime and Capitalism: Readings in Marxist Criminology*. Palo Alto, CA: Mayfield Publishing, p. 18.

9. Akers, Ronald L. (1997). *Criminological Theories: Introduction and Evaluation*, Second Edition. Los Angeles, CA: Roxbury Publishing Company.

10. Fuller, John R. (1998). *Criminal Justice: A Peacemaking Perspective*. Boston, MA: Allyn and Bacon.

11. Fuller, p. 121.

12. Fisher, Roger, William Ury and Bruce Patton (1995). *Getting to Yes*, Second Edition. New York, NY: Penguin Books.

13. Fuller, p. 57.

14. Gilligan, James (1996). *Violence: Reflections on a National Epidemic* New York, NY: Vintage Books.

15. These critics include, Gendreau, Paul (1996). "Offender Rehabilitation: What We Know and What Needs to Be Done." *Criminal Justice and Behavior*, 23:144–161. Ross, R. and Gendreau, P. (1980). *Effective Correctional Treatment*. Toronto, CN: Butterworth.

RESPONSIBILITY AND RESTORATIVE JUSTICE

*John Braithwaite
and Declan Roche*

Restorative justice owes part of its growth in popularity to its broad political appeal, offering something to politicians of varying stripes. In particular, "getting offenders to take responsibility for their actions" has been part of the political appeal of restorative justice. So has "getting families to take responsibility for their kids." While it may seem appropriate to exploit such political appeal, restorative justice must have a more meaningful sense of responsibility than this. Restorative justice cannot sell itself in these terms yet simultaneously distance itself from similar sounding neoconservative ideas of responsibility, without clearly articulating its own conception of responsibility. As O'Malley says, "Discourses of responsibility for crime and crime prevention are … not possessions of the political Right, and they do not imply only a punitive response to offending" (O'Malley 1994:22). Responsibility is a fundamental and contestable part of any scheme of justice, including restorative justice.

The purpose of this chapter is to explore the concept of responsibility within a restorative justice framework. As a starting hypothesis, let us see if restorative responsibility might be conceived as that form of responsibility most likely to promote restoration—of victims, offenders, and communities. Given that framework, we will first find a useful distinction between active responsibility and passive responsibility. Then we show how that distinction maps onto distinctions between active and passive deterrence, rehabilitation, and incapacitation. We then seek to develop the rudiments of a jurisprudence of active responsibility. Finally, we consider some worries about the restorative conception of responsibility we have developed.

ACTIVE AND PASSIVE RESPONSIBILITY

Carol Heimer (1999:18) makes a distinction between being held accountable for the wrong one has done in the past and taking responsibility for the future. Mark Bovens (1998:27) makes a similar distinction between passive responsibility and active responsibility. Twentieth-century Western retributive justice has been mostly concerned with passive responsibility. Restorative justice, we will argue, shifts the balance toward active responsibility.

Bovens says that in the case of passive responsibility "one is called to account after the event and either held responsible or not. It is a question of who *bears* the responsibility for a given state of affairs. The central question is: 'Why *did* you do it?'" (Bovens 1998:27). Bovens sees passive responsibility as requiring transgression of a norm, a causal connection between conduct and damage, blameworthiness, and sometimes a special relationship of obligation toward the person(s) harmed (Bovens 1998:28–31). The literature is full of debates about the best way to conceive of passive responsibility (see, for example, Mulgan 1997; Thomas 1998). We will not add to those debates here. While we have some doubts about Bovens's conception of passive responsibility, we will not discuss them, as our interest is to move on to the special appeal for restorative justice theory of his concept of active responsibility.

First, however, it must be said that restorative justice cannot do without some concept of passive responsibility. For example, a restorative justice conference is held after the commission of a crime ("after the event," in Boven's terms) and in light of the admission of guilt by the offender (which determines "who bears responsibility"). Furthermore, a conference, at least in its early stages, will often involve asking the offender why he or she did it. Our argument is not that restorative justice abandons passive responsibility, but that restorative justice uses passive responsibility to create a forum in which active responsibility can be fostered. Restorative justice, then, is about shifting the balance from passive responsibility toward active responsibility.

So what is active responsibility, according to Bovens? He sees active responsibility as a virtue, the virtue of taking responsibility when something needs to be done to deal with a problem or put things right: "[T]he emphasis lies much more on action in the present, on the prevention of unwanted situations and events ... The central question here is: 'what *is* to be done?'" (Bovens 1998:27).

To interpolate in a restorative justice frame, active responsibility entails seeking to take responsibility to repair harm, and especially to restore relationships. According to Bovens, active responsibility requires:

(1) an adequate perception of threatened violations of a norm, (2) consideration of consequences, (3) autonomy, and (4) taking obligations seriously. Restorative dialogue, in which the problem rather than the person is put in the center of the circle (Melton, 1995), and in which respectful listening is a central value, seems well designed to cultivate Boven's virtue of active responsibility. As Heimer and Staffen (1998:369) put it, "it is the humanity of other people that inspires responsibility." Bovens also sees active responsibility as requiring "conduct based on a verifiable and consistent code"(Bovens 1998:36). This seems to be an excessively positivist requirement; families can nurture active responsibility through restorative dialogue without codifying their norms.

We argue that restorative justice reconceptualizes responsibility, so that when people claim that restorative justice offers *better* responsibility than traditional court sentencing,[1] they are impliedly making a claim about what is accomplished by active responsibility.

Those who favor retribution are concerned with passive responsibility because their priority is to be just in the way that they hurt wrongdoers. The shift in the balance toward active responsibility occurs because the priority of restorative justice proponents is to be just in the way that they heal.

While it is clear that a backward-looking, deontological theory such as retributivism is clearly concerned more with passive than active responsibility, the influence of passive responsibility also permeates forward-looking, consequentialist theories. Utilitarians along the lines of Jeremy Bentham are equally preoccupied with hurting rather than healing, and with passive rather than active responsibility. We will argue that utilitarians have an inferior theory of deterrence, rehabilitation, incapacitation, and crime prevention to that of restorative justice theorists. At the root of this inferiority is the utilitarian's obsession with passive responsibility to the exclusion of active responsibility.[2] First, we will show how under the restorative alternative, while passive responsibility maps onto passive deterrence, active responsibility maps onto active deterrence—and the latter is more powerful. Then we will do the same for rehabilitation and incapacitation.

Passive and Active Deterrence

Deterrence is not an objective of restorative justice. In fact, to make deterrence of wrongdoing a value would destroy restorative justice for the same reason that making shaming a value would destroy it. As Kay Pranis (1998:45) puts it, "An intention to shame [we add deter] is not respectful. An intention to help a person understand the harm they caused and to support them in taking full responsibility for that harm is respectful."[3] However, this is not to deny that theories of shame and deterrence can help us understand why restorative processes might have more preventive potential than retributive/deterrent processes.

Most deterrence literature in criminology indicates that the severity level of punishment rarely has a significant deterrent effect. While a criminal justice system with no passive deterrence would clearly be one with a lot of crime, the data give utilitarians reason to be discouraged that increasing the quantum of passive deterrence will reduce crime (or that reducing passive deterrence will increase crime). Active deterrence, we will suggest, is a different story.

Ayres and Braithwaite (1992:19–53) have argued that deterrence theory in criminology is primitive compared to deterrence theory in international relations because it is excessively passive. When the United States seeks to deter a form of international behavior, it does not announce in advance that the punishment if states do X will be Y, if they do 2X, it will be 2Y, and so on with a passive deterrence tariff. Instead, its deterrence strategy is active in two important senses. First, the United States uses its power to persuade other states on whom the rogue state is dependent for some reason (for example, trade) to intervene (actively) to persuade the rogue state that it should refrain from the rogue action. What is being mobilized by this kind of active deterrence is a web of complex interdependency (Keohane 1984). Second, the United States' strategic deterrence is active in the sense of being dynamic rather than passive. The deterrent threat does not just sit there as a passive promise of punishment; deterrence is escalated up and down an enforcement pyramid in response to the level of cooperative response and the concessions made by the rogue state.

International relations theory has escaped the shackles of Benthamite thinking about certain response with punishments calibrated to be passively optimal.

Restorative Justice and Deterrence

How could restorative justice theory do better than legal deterrence theory? Let us illustrate with some restorative justice analogies to active webs of complex interdependence. Consider the restorative approach that has been developing in Australian business regulation. First, the regulator meets with the agents in the corporation who seem most passively responsible for the lawbreaking, along with some victims (where appropriate). Because the corporate actors most directly responsible have the most to lose from a criminal conviction of the corporation, they will be hard targets, difficult to deter. They are likely to fight passive deterrence by denial of responsibility. For Benthamite corporate crime fighters, that is the end of the story—another contested court case that they do not have the resources to fight, another defeat at the hands of those who control corporate power. However, what we know is that causal and preventive power over corporate crime is, as the philosophers say (Lewis 1986), overdetermined. So what we do is move up the organization, widening the circle of dialogue, convening another conference to which the boss of the passively responsible agent of the corporation is invited. Often the boss will turn out to be a hard target as well. When that fails, we convene another conference and invite her boss. Fisse and Braithwaite (1993:230–232) have described one restorative justice experience in which the process led right up to the Chief Executive Officer, who was the "toughest nut" of them all. After that, though, the Australian Trade Practices Commission widened the circle to include the Chair of the Board, who was shocked at this recalcitrant unwillingness to restore the victims' losses and reform the corporation's compliance systems. The Chair actually fired the CEO. (Not very restorative! A case of active deterrence leading to passive deterrence.)

In other more extended treatments of the deterrence theory of restorative justice, Braithwaite (1997a, 1999) has argued that corporate crime is not different from common crime in that it is mostly a collective, or at least a socially embedded, phenomenon, in which there are many actors with preventive capabilities. For example, one interpretation for the success of whole-school anti-bullying programs in reducing bullying up to 50 percent (Olweus 1993) is in these terms. Whenever a fourth grader is bullying another child, many children in the school (particularly from the fifth grade up) are in a position to intervene to prevent the bullying. From a deterrence theory perspective, therefore, whole-school anti-bullying programs work because the deterrence target shifts from the bully (a hard target to deter passively) to active deterrence of responsible peers of the bully.

One reason that empowerment is a central value of restorative justice is that it encourages people to take active responsibility—and active responsibility delivers, among other things, active deterrence. The environmentally conscious citizen of the corporation intervenes to stop the environmental crime even though she has no passive responsibility for causing it. A school friend intervenes to stop bullying even though she bears no passive responsibility for it. An ideal of the design of restorative institutions is to create democratic spaces for the nurturing of the virtue of active responsibility among citizens, young and old.

In the context of violence against women, Braithwaite and Daly (1994) have argued that restorative justice is more likely to be attempted, taken seriously, and to actually work, if it is located within a dynamic enforcement strategy in which the upshot of repeated failure of restorative conferences will be escalation to deterrence and incapacitation. This is not to advocate restorative justice transacted on the basis of threat. Rather it is to say that powerful criminals are more likely to succumb to the entreaties of restorative justice when deterrence is threatening in the background instead of threatened in the foreground (for the theory, see Ayres and Braithwaite 1992:47–51). The idea is not that deterrence is there as an ever-present passive threat but that everyone knows it is democratically available as an active possibility if dialogue fails or is spurned. Because "everyone knows" this, there is no need to make threats; indeed, to do so is counterproductive. So an offender who chooses not to participate in a conference knows the alternative is an appearance in court, where he or she will be subject to passive responsibility.

THE RESTORATIVE JUSTICE PROCESS AND RESPONSIBILITY

Conferences and circles provide opportunities to nurture active responsibility. If you empower citizens in a punitive society to decide how to put right a wrong, many choose to do so punitively against the wrongdoer. Kathleen Daly suggests that restorative justice does deliver a deal of retribution (Daly 2000). Moreover, because restorative justice processes of confronting victims and their own families are often grueling even for hardened offenders, and because we know that "the process" in all systems is usually the greater part of punishment (Feeley 1979), restorative justice also delivers a lot of process-related passive deterrence.

However, the empirical experience of restorative justice is that victims and other citizens are not as punitive as we expected they would be, and not as punitive as they are in the context of adversarial courtroom justice. When courts do intervene to overturn decisions of restorative justice conferences, it is rarely to make them less punitive; instead, it is usually to increase punishment (Maxwell and Morris 1993). So it seems that while people have the opportunity to pursue punitiveness and passive responsibility, they choose to do so far less than we might expect.

A conference convened by one of the authors of this chapter provides an example. A middle-aged married couple came to the conference to meet the young person who had stolen and damaged beyond repair the car the husband had spent three years and thousands of dollars restoring. In the conference, it was explained to the offender that he had done great damage to the car, probably without realizing it. After the man explained that, his wife shared that her stoic husband had been privately shattered about the loss of the car that he had hoped to display at car shows—and that since the offense, he did not have the heart to start over. She also explained that their daughter was in the advanced stages of a difficult pregnancy and the loss of the car made it difficult to help with tasks such as collecting their grandchildren from school and doing grocery shopping. Yet, despite the harm, the couple declined offers of physical labor from the offender, insisting that the only outcome that would help them was one that helped him (in this case, taking small steps to resume his education). In Boven's terms, the couple was concerned that the young person exercise his active responsibility in respect to this incident in a way that nurtured the virtue of active responsibility in him for the future.

A process that allows victims to meet the offender and his or her family often generates compassion for the offender and a better understanding of his or her actions. Compassion contributes to the pursuit of restoration and active responsibility more than it does to the pursuit of punishment. However, there is not always compassion in conferences and there often is retribution. How can this be an alternative model of justice if citizens often choose to deter or seek revenge? One response is to draw an analogy to democracy. If you set up a democracy, citizens often vote for candidates with anti-democratic values. What is happening there is that we honor the institution (democracy) that conduces to a shift to democratic values rather than honoring the values themselves. To take democracy away from people as soon as they chose to manifest anti-democratic values would be not only perverse but a prescription for historically unsustainable democracy. What we do instead is write constitutions that put limits on anti-democratic action.

Likewise, restorative justice must be constitutionalized so that limits are placed on the pursuit of deterrence. Thus, people can (if they insist) pursue anti-democratic or anti-restorative aims to the extent to which those systems allow.[4] We think these limits should constrain restorative justice conferences against any incarcerative or corporal punishment, any punishment that is degrading or humiliating,[5] and any punishment in excess of that which would be imposed by a court for the same wrongdoing.[6]

Active and Passive Rehabilitation

"Support without accountability leads to moral weakness. Accountability without support is a form of cruelty."
—Harriet Jane Olsen,
The Book of Discipline of the United Methodist Church (1996)

Having outlined in some detail the story of active and passive deterrence, we hope we can briefly state how to apply the same principles to active and passive

rehabilitation (for more detail, see Braithwaite 1998, 1999). There is much evidence that the least effective way of delivering rehabilitation programs is for the state to decide what is best and to require criminals to be passive recipients of that benevolence. In the most empowering restorative justice programs, such as one described by Burford and Pennell (1996), which is designed to deal with family violence, the victims, offenders, and their communities of care are not subjected to rehabilitative prescription but are empowered with knowledge. Experts come into the conference to explain the range of rehabilitative options available. State monopolies of provision of rehabilitative services are replaced by a plurality of service providers from civil society, private enterprise, and the state. More radically, resourcing can be available for professional help for communities of care to craft and operate their own rehabilitative interventions.

The two variables in play here that we know are associated with superior rehabilitative outcomes are: (1) active choice as opposed to passive receipt, and (2) embedding of that choice in networks of social support (Cullen, 1994) rather than choice by isolated individuals. We suspect that the reason for active rehabilitation being superior to passive rehabilitation goes beyond the documented effects of commitment and social support. We also suspect that communities of care empowered with good professional advice will actually make technically superior choices from among a smorgasbord of rehabilitative options, because of the richer contextual knowledge they have of the case (Bazemore, 1999). This is particularly plausible in a world in which, for example, psychotherapy often seems to work but in which there is no consistent evidence showing that one school of psychotherapy works better than another. The hope is that contextually informed community-of-care choices (assisted by professional choice brokers) will be better on average than individual or state choices (Braithwaite 1998).

Active and Passive Incapacitation

In Braithwaite and Daly's (1994) family violence enforcement pyramid, most of the options for escalation are in fact more incapacitative than deterrent. They include options like "a relative or other supporter of the woman moving into the household," "the man moving to a friend's household," and imprisonment. Once we move beyond a passive conception of incapacitation, which is statically linked to confinement in state prisons, we can see that *capacitation of victims* can be theoretically equivalent to *incapacitation of offenders*. Hence, in a family violence enforcement pyramid, giving a victim the capacity to leave by putting a bank account or funding for alternative accommodation at her disposal (victim capacitation) can be functionally equivalent to removing the offender from the home (offender incapacitation).

Court-ordered incapacitation is notoriously less effective than it would seem. Violent men continue to perpetrate assault and rape in prison. Drug dealers continue to entice vulnerable young people.

Judges incapacitate drunk drivers by canceling their licenses only to find that a majority of them continue to drive (Barnes 1999).

By contrast, the active intervention of communities of care evokes alternative modalities of incapacitation. If the problem is that it is only on Friday and Saturday nights that the offender gets out on the town, Uncle Harry can take responsibility for holding the keys to the car on Friday and Saturday nights and ensuring that the car stays in the garage. Alternatively, the girlfriend can volunteer to call a taxi every time. Or the drinking mates can sign a designated driver agreement at the conference. Or the owner of the pub or club where the offender drinks can agree to train the staff to intervene so that someone else in the bar drives the offender home. We have seen all these forms of active incapacitation negotiated at restorative drunk driving conferences. All of them require cultivation of the virtue of active responsibility. We never see them in drunk driving court cases, which last an average of seven minutes in Canberra, compared with 90 minutes for conferences (Barnes 1999).

Active Crime Prevention, Active Grace

Braithwaite (1998, 1999) has argued that crime prevention programs mostly fail for four reasons: (1) lack of motivation, (2) lack of resources, (3) insufficiently plural deliberation, and (4) lack of follow through. He argued that making restorative justice conferences a site of crime

prevention deliberation in the community can help remedy those four reasons for the failure of crime prevention programs. Motivation, resources, and follow-through on crime prevention have more momentum when coupled to the mainstream processing of criminal cases than when ghettoized into specialized crime prevention units. We will not reiterate the four sets of arguments here, but one way of summarizing them is that they are concerned with the way restorative justice deliberation nurtures the virtue of active responsibility. Active responsibility does not come naturally in response to a plea to attend a Neighborhood Watch meeting. It comes more naturally in reply to a plea from a neighbor who has been a victim of crime to support them in a conference/circle. Similarly, an occupational health and safety poster in the workplace proclaiming "Reporting (accidents) is everyone's responsibility" does not foster a sense of active responsibility in the way that conferences held to discuss specific workplace injuries do.

Serious crime is an opportunity to confront evil with a grace that transforms human lives to paths of love and care. Desmond Tutu would want us to evaluate his Truth and Reconciliation Commission less in terms of how it prevents crimes of violence and more in terms of how its healing lays the foundation of a more humane South Africa.

While we can never expect restorative justice institutions to be the most important institutions of community building, they can play their part in the nurturing of active responsibility that is the indispensable ingredient of community development.

If we believe that reintegrative shaming is what is required to deal with the wrongdoing of a Winnie Madikizela-Mandela and a P.W. Botha alike,[7] no one is required to take active responsibility for saying "shame on you" for the killings and the racism under an evil regime. The testimony of the victims and the apologies (when they occur, as they often enough do) are sufficient to accomplish the necessary shaming of the evil of violence. However, there can never be enough citizens active in the reintegration part of reintegrative shaming. If is true that reintegrative shaming prevents crime, and if it is true that it is the reintegration part that is always in short supply, then the particular, if limited, kind of integration into communities of care that is transacted in restorative justice rituals has a special humanitarian significance.

TOWARD A JURISPRUDENCE OF ACTIVE RESPONSIBILITY

So far, we have conceived of active responsibility as the essential element for securing restoration. At the same time, we have argued that without passive responsibility there is risk of injustice. For example, a minimum requirement for punishing an offender for doing wrong would be an inquiry to demonstrate causal responsibility for the wrong.

Now we will complicate this picture by arguing that while passive responsibility remains indispensable to justice in this way, restorative justice propels us to develop a more just notion of criminal liability, on which passive responsibility depends. That is, the emphasis on active responsibility is not only a matter of the jurisprudence of restoration but also of the normative theory of justice.

We turn to Brent Fisse's (1983) theory of reactive fault (further developed in Fisse and Braithwaite 1993) for key insights here. All criminal justice systems incorporate notions of causal fault and reactive fault. Causal fault is about being causally responsible, while reactive fault is about how responsibly one reacts after the harm is done. The balance between the two varies enormously from system to system. Western criminal justice systems (such as that of the United States) are at the causal end of the continuum; Asian systems (such as that of Japan) tend to be at the reactive end. Yet, even in the West, reactive fault sometimes dominates causal fault, as evidenced in our intuition that with hit-and-run driving, the running is the greater evil than the hitting. Early guilty pleas in court and "remorse" also result in sentence reductions. In *Crime, Shame and Reintegration*, Braithwaite (1989:165) told two stories to illustrate the extremes in the cultural balancing of causal and reactive fault, the first from Haley (1982:272), the second from Wagatsuma and Rosett (1986:486):

> The first is of two American servicemen accused of raping a Japanese woman. On Japanese legal advice, private reconciliation with the victim was secured; a letter from the victim was tabled in the court stating that she had been fully compensated and that she absolved the Americans completely. After hearing the evidence, the judge leaned forward and asked the soldiers if they had anything to say. "We are not guilty, your honor," they replied. Their Japanese lawyer cringed; it had not even occurred to him that they might not adopt the repentant role. They were sentenced to the maximum term of imprisonment, not suspended.
>
> The second story is of a Japanese woman arriving in the U.S. with a large amount of American currency which she had not accurately declared on the entry form. It was not the sort of case that would normally be prosecuted. The law is intended to catch the importation of cash which is the proceeds of illicit activities, and there was no suggestion of this. Second, there was doubt that the woman had understood the form which required the currency declaration. After the woman left the airport, she wrote to the Customs Service acknowledging her violation of the law, raising none of the excuses or explanations available to her, apologizing profusely, and seeking forgiveness. In a case that would not normally merit prosecution, the prosecution went forward *because* she has confessed and apologized; the U.S. Justice Department felt it was obliged to proceed in the face of a bald admission of guilt. (emphasis in original)

These are stories about how the United States justice system creates disincentives for reactive fault, while the Japanese justice system requires it. Fisse (1983) advocates "reactive fault" as the core criterion of criminal fault. In its most radical version, this would mean in a case of assault, the alleged assailant would go into a restorative justice conference not on the basis of an admission of criminal guilt but on the basis of admitting responsibility for the *actus reus* of an assault ("I was the one who punched her").[8] Whether the mental element required for crime was present would be decided reactively, on the basis of the constructiveness and restorativeness of his or her reaction to the problem caused by the act (Braithwaite 1998). If the reaction were restorative, the risk of criminal liability would be removed; only civil liability would remain. However, if reactive criminal fault were found by a court to be present,[9] that would be insufficient for a conviction; the mental element for the crime would also have to be demonstrated before or during its commission.[10] However, reactive fault would be a more important determinant of penalty than causal fault.

This gives us an answer to the retributivist who says: "Where is the justice with two offenders who commit exactly the same offense: one apologizes and heals a victim who grants him mercy; the other refuses to participate in a circle and is punished severely by a court." The answer is that while the two offenders are equal in causal fault, they are quite unequal in reactive fault. Viewed in terms of passive responsibility, they might be equal; in terms of active responsibility, though, they are not.[11]

The Major Worry about Active Responsibility

In restorative justice conferences, sometimes victims say they are responsible for their own victimization or others blame them for it. This is not a worry when victims blame themselves for leaving open the window through which the burglar entered; indeed, it can be a good thing if it motivates victims to invest in target hardening to protect them from a repeat victimization.[12] Similarly, a victim of a schoolyard fight may reflect on the provocation of the offender that led to the assault. It is a different matter, though, if a girl who is a victim of sexual assault is blamed for wearing a short skirt. What is the difference? It is that this type of victim-blaming is connected to a history of subordination of young women, and the denial of their freedom, which has been much exacerbated by victim-blaming.

Restorative justice implies a grave risk of the occurrence of oppressive victim-blaming. The hope is that when it occurs, participants in the circle will speak up in defense and support of the victim—that there will be reintegrative shaming of victim-blaming. The fact

that we cannot guarantee that this will occur is deeply troubling.

Defenders of formal legal processes might further protest that criminal trials do incorporate formal guarantees against victim-blaming. Most of these, however, come into play at the level of proving that sexual assault occurred—guarantees not relevant to normal restorative justice processes that are not concerned with the adjudication of guilt. In any case, it is hard to argue that victim-vilification does not occur in criminal trials.[13] As Hogg and Brown put it, "Police, lawyers and judges have often been derisory in their treatment of complainants who have acted in ...'sexually provocative' ways" (1998:65). Indeed, restorative justice advocates argue that the problem with the criminal trial is that it creates incentives for the prosecution to vilify defence witnesses, and vice versa. This is what puts the vulnerable most at risk of stigmatization. The problems that formal legal guarantees against victim-blaming seek to redress are in part problems created by the formal adversarial process.

In terms of the impact of victim-blaming on traditional adversarial justice, we should not confine our examination to trials and sentencing. Ngaire Naffine suggests that in light of the statistics on the extent of unreported rapes, rapes without active resistance (and we would suggest, rapes involving other types of victim-blaming) are "much less likely to find their way into a court of law ... (and) are more likely to be filtered out of the criminal justice system" (Naffine 1992:761). Hence, it is clear that victim-blaming is a problem at every level.

What can be said in favor of restorative justice is that while the criminal trial assembles in one room those capable of inflicting maximum damage on the other side, the restorative justice conference assembles in the room those capable of offering maximum support to their own side—be it the victim or the offender side. It is in this structural difference, and in the ethic of care and active responsibility that it engenders, that restorative justice places its hope against victim vilification.

It will be a hope that will continue to be disappointed from time to time, we fear. There are few higher priorities for research and development than to improve the micro-design of conferences/circles.

Videos shown to participants before they go into their first conference could not only show how conferences work and how participants can be actively responsible citizens within them, but perhaps they could also warn against victim-blaming and urge a responsibility to speak out against victim-blaming should it occur. Training for convenors should also address this risk. For both court and conference processes, research should be able to test a variety of innovations in order to discover which procedures best protect victims from stigmatization.

Restorative Justice—Beyond Responsibilization

In its traditional criminological forms, utilitarianism tended to objectify and infantilize offenders. In contrast, many writers see newer crime prevention and community policing as involving a new form of subjectification and responsibilization (Crawford 1997; Garland 1997; O'Malley 1992). Garland, for example, identifies a new mode of governing crime, which he characterizes as a "responsibilization strategy": "This involves the central government seeking to act upon crime not in a direct fashion through state agencies (police, courts, prisons, social work, etc.) but instead by acting indirectly, seeking to activate action on the part of non-state agencies and organizations" (Garland 1996:452). Garland says that this is a response to the predicament that "having taken over control functions and responsibilities which once belonged to the institutions of civil society, the state is now faced with its own inability to deliver the expected levels of control over criminal conduct"(Garland 1996:449). The recurring message of this approach, as Garland puts it, "is that the state alone is not, and cannot effectively be, responsible for preventing and controlling crime" (Garland 1996). Clearly, it is possible to read our account of restorative justice in this frame.

There are some distinctions that must be drawn, however. Responsibilization strategies vary in their approaches to achieving responsibility. Foucault's work is the theoretical influence underlying the responsibilization literature. Subjects are "taught to become 'responsible'" (Garland 1997:191) by "techniques of the self" for cultivating a security-conscious *homo prudens*. This Foucauldian interpretation is

contrasted with one in which individuals are assumed to be "'naturally' capable" of responsible action (Garland 1997:191). Our conception of restorative responsibility is closer to the end of the continuum that assumes a natural capability for responsibility. At least we assume that the simple process of human beings talking through the consequences that have been suffered as a result of wrongdoing is all that is needed to elicit spontaneous proffering of active responsibility. At the same time, though, however natural and unforced the dialogue within it, we must concede that the creation of the institution of a restorative justice conference is itself a regulatory move designed to cultivate this "natural capability" for responsibility.

There are many unattractive features of responsibilization trends from which restorative justice must keep its distance. We see the worst manifestation of responsibilization in laws that hold parents legally liable for the delinquencies of their children. The normative theory of restorative justice should make it clear that only individual actors who are passively responsible (causally responsible) for crime should be held legally or morally responsible for it. Active responsibility of all kinds, including offers of help and support, forgiveness, care, compassion, love, and participation—all the things on which restorative justice most depends for success, should be conceived as gifts rather than moral duties, and certainly not as legal duties. They are supererogatory,[14] to put the claim formally. The legal system rightly recognizes parents as having duties of care to their children. In the context of a restorative justice conference for a criminal offense, though, a decision by parents to refuse to attend (or do anything the conference asks) should not be viewed as a breach of any duty.[15] No one, including the offender, has a duty even to attend.[16]

Restorative justice works because people are prepared to assume an active responsibility (particularly when they have a personal involvement) beyond any allocated passive legal or moral responsibility. Active responsibility often involves an assumed collective responsibility that can provide restoration and crime prevention in ways that courts restricted to allocating passive responsibility (enforced responsibility) cannot. A more structural worry about responsibilization is that it passes gender-related burdens of care down to individuals. This worry is that what is going on is a move by the state to slough off some of its social welfare obligations. A comparable concern arises with using restorative justice to deal with regulatory offenses; it may be part of a state's strategy to walk away from its obligations to regulate in areas such as environment (where it has clear responsibilities) by delegating them to civil society.

Christine Parker's (1999) work is a useful corrective here (see also Braithwaite and Parker 1999). Parker sees a need for two-way communication. She wants institutions in which the justice of the law filters down into the justice of the people as manifest in restorative justice processes (so that, for example, respect for fundamental human rights constrains informal justice). Obversely, Parker wants a restorative justice that gives the justice of the people an opportunity to percolate up to influence the justice of the law. In terms of active and passive responsibility, we want the active responsibility to have an influence on the passive responsibility. The same theme is apparent in recent writings of Clifford Shearing (1995) and Jurgen Habermas (1996) on how the state can open itself up to "the input of free-floating issues, contributions, information, and arguments circulating in a civil society set apart from the state" (Habermas 1996:183–184). According to Habermas (1996:442), the theory is clear:

> [T]he public sphere is not conceived simply as the back room of the parliamentary complex, but as the impulse-generating periphery that *surrounds* the political center: in cultivating normative reasons, it affects all parts of the political system without intending to conquer it. Passing through the channels of general elections and various forms of participation, public opinions are converted into a communicative power that authorizes the legislature and legitimates regulatory agencies, while a publicly mobilized critique of judicial decisions imposes more-intense justificatory obligations on a

judiciary engaged in further developing the law.

The theory sounds fine, but it all seems rather romantic to imagine the day-to-day work of conferences bubbling up to influence the law. Cumulatively and potentially, though, this is not necessarily romantic. In communities in which conferencing is widespread, justice dilemmas that arise in conferences are discussed in civil society (at dinner parties, for example, including those attended by judges).[17]

We can already cite specific conferences in New Zealand that have had an impact, albeit small, on the law. In the Clotworthy case, the decision of a conference for community service and victim compensation to fund cosmetic surgery needed as a result of a vicious knife attack was overruled by the Court of Appeal.[18] To the disappointment of restorative justice advocates, the Court of Appeal ordered a custodial sentence. However, the sentence was reduced in response to the wishes of the victim as articulated in the conference. Moreover, the Court did recognize the principle that the demands of restorative justice can affect sentences in very serious cases. Put another way, conferencing is in a position not dissimilar to the routine processing of cases in the lowest courts. Although what happens in the lowest courts might be the bulk of the law in action (and therefore "is" the law), rarely does it have any impact on the law in the books, or formal law. In rare strategic cases, though, the Magistrates "bubble up" the Clotworthy case.

One can imagine how restorative justice processes might achieve this task in a variety of contexts. A conference for schoolgirls caught smoking marijuana could communicate to school principals that passive responsibility such as expulsion is excessive and inappropriate. Conferences can and do also "bubble up" community disapproval of certain investigative techniques by the police, which tend to be suppressed in court. This capacity can be reinforced by making an inquiry of how fairly participants have been treated by the police in this formal part of the restorative justice process. Where there is a concern, the police, as a signatory of the conference agreement, can commit to report back to the participants about the results of an internal or ombudsman investigation of their conduct.

Fisse and Braithwaite (1993:232–237) have documented how a series of conferences exposed the victimization of Australian Aboriginal people in remote communities through fraudulent practices by major insurance companies. One of the decisions of the meetings between offending companies, regulators, victims, and Aboriginal Community Councils was to call a press conference. The abuses exposed were so systemic and shocking that the Prime Minister asked to be briefed by the regulatory agency. Significant change to regulatory law and practice ensued.

While it would be overly optimistic to hope that conferences would often be the transmission vehicle to percolate the justice of the people into the justice of the law, such cases show this is a possibility that can be realized. The Aboriginal insurance cases show that just as restorative justice can serve to responsibilize individuals in a way that relieves the state of burdens, so is it possible for powerless individuals to use restorative justice to responsibilize the state when the state is failing in its regulatory or welfare obligations.

Restorative justice is empowering in that it takes a ball away from the feet of a judge and puts it at the feet of a group of citizens. The type of responsibilizing that then goes on depends on how those citizens decide to exercise their political imagination in the use of that little piece of power. To use a soccer analogy, many will kick their own goals by taking responsibility for awesome burdens of care for which the state should be giving them more help. Others will learn from the example of those Aboriginal Community Councils from far North Queens-land and kick the goals of state responsibilization.

CONCLUSION

A neglected part of the restorative justice research agenda has been the development of a restorative conception of responsibility— the kind of responsibility that will maximise restoration of victims, offenders, and communities. We have seen that restorative responsibility will be very different from traditional conceptions of criminal responsibility. It will involve a balance between passive and active responsibility with a substantial shift toward the latter.

We have seen that restorative responsibility has:

1. An important political rationale;
2. A strong philosophical foundation in responsibility for action and responsibility as a virtue;
3. A promising jurisprudential future through development of Fisse's notion of reactive fault; and
4. Practical promise in its links to theories of crime prevention.

At the same time, there remain unsolved worries about responsibilization, such as the risks of blaming victims of sexual assault and foisting unreasonable expectations on single parents who already are expected to do too much with too little support.

NOTES

1. The recent Canadian Supreme Court decision *R v. Glaude* (1999) provides an example of such a comparison: "Central to the (restorative justice) process is the need for offenders to *take* responsibility for their actions. By comparison, incarceration obviates the need to *accept* responsibility" (emphasis added) (at 72)

2. Some readers might question whether an approach that aims to prevent future events can be characterised as passive responsibility. After all, active responsibility is about the prevention of unwanted events. But it is our contention that one can seek to avoid future events using passive responsibility or active responsibility. At the heart of the difference between the active and passive forms of these theories is the distinction between people taking responsibility (the active form) and risking being held accountable (the passive form).

3. The normative force of Pranis's assertion arises in our view from the normative claim that respectfulness (Braithwaite, 1989) ranks beside non-domination (Braithwaite and Pettit, 1990; Pettit, 1997) and empowerment (Braithwaite, 1999b) as central restorative values.

4. Some critics might argue that punitiveness on one hand, and active responsibility and restorative justice on the other, are not mutually exclusive: that is, if active responsibility is the taking of responsibility to restore harm, and a punitive outcome is what is required to restore some victims' harm (by satisfying their desire to punish), then punitive outcomes can involve active

responsibility. However we would say if a punitive outcome is imposed on an offender without their consent
it in no way involves active responsibility. If an offender
does seek or actively consent to a punitive outcome,
then it may involve active responsibility, but we would
nevertheless seek to impose limits on such outcomes.

5. For instance, the International Covenant on Civil and
Political Rights prohibits inhuman or degrading treatment or punishment (Article 7).

6. For example, under the legislation governing one
conferencing scheme in Australia, the outcome must
"not (be) more severe than those that might have been
imposed in court proceedings for the offence" (Section
52(6)(a) Young Offenders Act 1997 (NSW)).

7. The allegations against Winnie Madikizela-Mandela
included the murder of a child in her pursuit of political
objectives on behalf of the African National Congress.
  P.W. Botha was the South African head of state during
a period when his Cabinet is alleged to have authorized
murder and other atrocities against those opposed to
Apartheid.

8. Functionally, New Zealand law already accomplishes
this result by putting cases into family group conferences not on the basis of an admission of criminal guilt,
but on the basis of formally "declining to deny" criminal
allegations.

9. An example of this would be if a report from a conference said that the offender simply cursed the victim and
refused to discuss restitution.

10. Brent Fisse takes the more radical view that if criminal
liability is about punishing conduct known to be harmful and if failure to respond responsibly is harmful, then
such reactive fault can be sufficient to establish criminal
liability.

11. This is not the whole answer, however. The other part of
it is that the just deserts theorist is seen as morally wrong
to consider equal justice for offenders a higher value than
equal justice for victims (Braithwaite, 1999).

12. Having just been a victim of burglary is the single big-
gest predictor of burglary victimisation (Pease)

13. In Victoria, Australia, a man who raped a woman
received a sentence that took into account that the
woman's experience as a prostitute meant it was reasonable to assume that she suffered less psychological
harm than would have been suffered by other victims of
sexual assaults [*Hakopian*, 1991, unreported, Victorian

County Court (see Cass 1992 for case summary and
comment)].

14. See Mellema, 1991; Heyd, 1982.

15. Of course, this would not be the position with care and
protection as opposed to a criminal justice conference,
where the legal subject of the conference is whether parents are meeting their legal duty to care for and protect
their child.

16. The only duty here rests with the police and prosecutor,
who have a duty to take sufficiently serious cases to court
when the opportunity for voluntary acts of responsibility
in a restorative framework are spurned.

17. Indeed judges will attend conferences during their life-
times as supporters of victims or of their own children
who get into trouble as offenders.

18. *The Queen v. Clotworthy* (CA 114/98, 29 June 1998,
NZ Court of Appeal) allowing appeal from sentence of
District Court Judge Thorburn, 24 April 1998

REFERENCES

Ayres, I., and J. Braithwaite (1992). *Responsive Regulation: Transcending the Deregulation Debate*. Oxford, England: Oxford University Press.

Barnes, G. (1999). "Procedural Justice in Two Contexts: Testing the Fairness of Diversionary Conferencing for Intoxicated Drivers." Ph.D. dissertation, University of Maryland.

Bazemore, G. (1999)."After Shaming, Whither Reintegration: Restorative Justice and Relational Rehabilitation." In *Restorative Juvenile Justice: Repairing the Harm of Youth Crime*, edited by G. Bazemore and L. Walgrave. Monsey, NY: Criminal Justice Press.

Bazemore, G., and M. Dooley (2000). "Restorative Justice and The Offender: The Challenge of Reintegration," this volume.

Bovens, M. (1998). *The Quest for Responsibility*. Cambridge, England: Cambridge University Press.

Braithwaite, J. (1989). *Crime, Shame and Reintegration*. Cambridge, England: Cambridge University Press.

Braithwaite, J. (1997a)."On Speaking Softly and Carrying Sticks: Neglected Dimensions of Republican Separation of Powers." *University of Toronto Law Journal* 47:1–57.

Braithwaite, J. (1998). "Linking Crime Prevention to Restorative Justice." In *Conferencing: A New Response to Wrongdoing*. Proceedings of the First North American Conference on Conferencing, August 6–8, Minneapolis.

Braithwaite, J. (1999). "Restorative Justice; Assessing Optimistic and Pessimistic Accounts." In Michael Tonry (ed.) *Crime and Justice: A Review of Research*.

Braithwaite, J., and K. Daly (1994). "Masculinities, Violence and Communitarian Control." In *Just Boys Doing Business*, edited by T. Newburn, and E. Stanko. London and New York: Routledge.

Braithwaite, J., and C. Parker (1999). "Restorative Justice is Republican Justice." In *Restoring Juvenile Justice: Repairing the Harm of Youth Crime*, edited by Gordon Bazemore and Lode Walgrave. Monsey, NY: Criminal Justice Press.

Braithwaite, J., and P. Pettit (1990). *Not Just Deserts: A Republican Theory of Criminal Justice*. Oxford, England: Oxford University Press.

Burford, G., and J. Pennell (1996). "Family Group Decision Making: New Roles for 'Old' Partners in Resolving Family Violence." *Implementation Report Summary*. St. Johns, Newfoundland: Family Group Decision Making Project.

Cass, D. (1992). "Case and Comment: Hakopian." *Criminal Law Journal* 16:200–204.

Crawford, A. (1997). *The Local Governance of Crime: Appeals to Community and Partnerships*. Oxford, England: Clarendon Press.

Cullen, F.T. (1994). "Social Support as an Organizing Concept for Criminology: Presidential Address to the Academy of Criminal Justice Sciences." *Justice Quarterly* 11(4):527–559.

Daly, K. (2000) "Revisiting the Relationship Between Retributive and Restorative Justice." In *Restorative Justice: Philosophy to Practice*, edited by H. Strang and J. Braithwaite, 33–54. Aldershot, England: Dartmouth.

Eckel, M.D. (1997). "A Buddhist Approach to Repentance." In *Repentance: A Comparative Perspective*, edited by A. Etzioni and D.E. Carney. New York: Rowman and Littlefield.

Feeley, M. (1979). *The Process is the Punishment*. New York: Russell Sage.

Fisse, B. (1983). "Reconstructing Corporate Criminal Law: Deterrence, Retribution, Fault, and Sanctions." *Southern California Law Review* 56:1141–1246.

Fisse, B., and J. Braithwaite (1993). *Corporations, Crime and Accountability*. Cambridge, England: Cambridge University Press.

Garland, D. (1996). "The Limits of the Sovereign State: Strategies of Crime Control in Contemporary Society." *The British Journal of Criminology* 36(4):445–471.

Garland, D. (1997). "'Governmentality' and the Problem of Crime: Foucault, Criminology, Sociology." *Theoretical Criminology* 1:173–214.

Habermas, J. (1996). *Between Facts and Norms: Contributions to a Discourse Theory of Law and Democracy*. London: Polity Press.

Heimer, C. (1999). "Legislating Responsibility," unpublished manuscript.

Heimer, C., and L. Staffen (1998). *For the Sake of the Children: The Social Organization of Responsibility in the Hospital and the Home*. Chicago: The University of Chicago Press.

Heyd, D. (1982). *Supererogation: Its Status in Ethical Theory*. Cambridge, England: Cambridge University Press.

Hogg, R., and D. Brown (1998). *Rethinking Law and Order*. Sydney: Pluto Press.

Keohane, R. (1984). *After Hegemony: Cooperation and Discord in World Politics*. Princeton, NJ: Princeton University Press.

Lewis, D. (1986). "Causation" and "Postscript: Redundant Causation." In *Philosophical Papers*, Vol. II. Oxford, England: Oxford University Press.

Makkai, T., and J. Braithwaite (1994a). "Reintegrative Shaming and Regulatory Compliance." *Criminology* 32(3):361–385.

Maxwell, G.M., and A. Morris (1993). *Family, Victims and Culture: Youth Justice in New Zealand*. Social Policy Agency and Institute of Criminology, Victoria University of Wellington, New Zealand.

Mellema, G. (1991). *Beyond the Call of Duty: Supererogation, Obligation and Offence*. Albany: State University of New York Press.

Melton, A.P. (1995). "Indigenous Justice Systems and Tribal Society." *Judicature* 79:126–133.

Mulgan, R. (1997). "The Processes of Public Accountability." *Australian Journal of Public Administrion* 56(1):25.

Naffine, N. (1992). "Windows on the Legal Mind: The Evocation of Rape in Legal Writings." 18 *MULR* 741.

Olweus, D. (1993). "Annotation: Bullying at School: Basic Facts and Effects of a School Based Intervention Program." *Journal of Child Psychology and Psychiatry* 35:1171–1190.

O'Malley, P. (1992). "Risk, Power and Crime Prevention." *Economy and Society* 21:252–275.

O'Malley, P. (1994). "Responsibility and Crime Prevention: A Response to Adam Sutton." *The Australian and New Zealand Journal of Criminology* 27:21–24.

Parker, C. (1999b). *Just Lawyers.* Oxford, England: Oxford University Press.

Pease, K. (1998). "Repeat Victimization: Taking Stock." Crime Detection and Prevention Series, Paper 90. Police Research Group, London.

Pettit, P. (1997). *Republicanism.* Oxford, England: Clarendon Press.

Pranis, K. (1998). "Conferencing and the Community." In *Conferencing: A New Response to Wrongdoing.* Proceedings of the First North American Conference on Conferencing. August 6–8, Minneapolis.

Shearing, C. (1995). "Reinventing Policing: Policing as Governance." In *Privatisierung staatlicher Kontrolle: Befunde, Konzepte, Tendenzen. Interdisziplinare Studien zu Recht und Staat* 3:69–88.

Thomas, P. (1998). "The Changing Nature of Accountability." In *Taking Stock: Assessing Public Sector Reforms*, edited by G. Peters and D. Savoie. Montreal: McGill-Queen's University Press.

Conclusion

CONCLUSION

The Challenges of Integrating Criminological Theories*

Stuart Henry

Integrative theory in criminology can be traced back to 1979 (Elliott, Agerton, & Canter, 1979; Johnson, 1979) with continuing work in the 1980s (Colvin & Pauly 1983; Elliott et al. 1979; Hagan 1989; Hawkins & Weis 1985; Jeffrey 1990; Messner, Krohn, & Liska 1989; Pearson & Weiner 1985), extending to more recent developments (Agnew 2011; Akers 1994; Barak 1998a, 1998b, 2006, 2009; Bernard 2001; Colvin 2000; Fishbein 1998; Muftić 2009, Robinson 2004; 2006; Robinson & Beaver 2009; Shoemaker 1996; Tittle 1995).

Integrative theory, as its name suggests, involves not one theory but many which are integrated or combined to produce a comprehensive analytical framework that transcends the explanatory power of any of its constitutive theories and moves us toward developing more holistic policies to address crime (Einstadter & Henry 2006, p. 310). Instead of seeing crime through a single disciplinary framework, or even through multiple perspectives, integrative criminological theorists take an interdisciplinary approach defined as: "the combination of two or more pre-existing theories, selected on the basis of their perceived commonalities, into a single reformulated theoretical model with greater comprehensiveness and explanatory value than any one of its component theories" (Farnworth 1989, p. 95). For example, in explaining juvenile delinquency, one theory may focus on a child's personality development, another on the interactive learning process, a third on the impact of social control and parental and school bonding, and a fourth on the way the intersection of class, race and gender shape these different processes. Integrative theory combines each of these explanatory components into one theoretical explanation.

* This Reading draws on Henry, S. (2012). "The challenges of integrating criminology: A commentary on Agnew's toward a unified criminology" *Journal of Theoretical and Philosophical Criminology*, 4(2): 10–26, and Henry, S. & Bracy, N.L. (2012). "Integrative theory in criminology applied to the complex social problem of school violence" In A. Repko, W. Newell and R. Szostak (eds.) *Case studies in interdisciplinary research* (pp. 259–282). Thousand Oaks, CA: Sage.

Advocates of integrative theory see distinct advantages in integrating the insights from existing discipline-based theories. Barak (1998b) summarizes these advantages, arguing that criminologists engaging in integration do so: (1) because of a desire to develop central concepts that are common to several theories; (2) to provide coherence to a bewildering array of fragmented theories, and thereby reduce their number; (3) to achieve comprehensiveness and completeness, and thereby enhance their explanatory power; (4) to advance scientific progress and theory development; and (5) to synthesize ideas about crime causation and social control policy.

While the advantages of integrative theory seem to supersede the limits of the traditional mono-disciplinary theories that we have explored in this book, Robert Agnew (2011) in *Toward a Unified Criminology: Integrating Assumptions about Crime, People and Society*, points out that none of the integrated theories have attracted wide support, not least because the integrations have been selective and partial, reflecting the division and politics of the discipline (p. 191). But this lack of theoretical traction may also reflect the variety of ways to accomplish integration, and the number of different integrative theories that have emerged as a result. Finally, some theoretical perspectives defy integration because they are incompatible.

So the first important question is "what is to be integrated?" Is it theoretical concepts or a theory's propositional statements about the relations between events and factors? A related question is how do we know that the meanings of the elements integrated are the same? The way different theories are integrated and what precisely is integrated has been the subject of much discussion (for a recent review see Henry & Bracy 2012). In the literature on integrative theories of crime, there are four different ways that theories can be integrated: (1) conceptual integration; (2) propositional integration; (3) causal integration; and (4) cross-level integration (Einstadter & Henry 2006; Hirschi 1979; Liska, Krohn, & Messner 1989).

Conceptual integration is the simplest idea when combining theories. It involves finding concepts "that have similar meanings in different theories and merging them into a common language" (Einstadter & Henry 2006, p. 316). This has also been called

finding "common ground" (Henry & Bracy, 2012; Repko, 2008). If theoretical concepts are merged but they are different, how far does that merger distort the original concepts? A related issue is when individual concepts are distilled, do they lose their integrity in the new emergent synthesis of common ground?

Propositional integration entails meaningfully "linking the propositions and not just the concepts of two or more theories into a combined theory … or relate the propositions of different theories into the new theory" (Paternoster & Bachman 2001, p. 307). A key issue in generating a comprehensive understanding through integrating theory is to consider how theoretical propositions are logically related (Liska et al. 1989, pp. 5–15). Three types of relationships between propositions have been identified: (i) end-to-end or sequential integration, which implies a sequential causal order; (ii) side-by-side or horizontal integration, which implies overlapping influences; and (iii) up-and-down or vertical integration, which "refers to identifying a level of abstraction or generality that encompasses much of the conceptualization of the constituent theories" (Bernard & Snipes, 1996; Messner et al., Krohn, & Liska, 1989, pp. 5–15). Integrating propositions rather than concepts has its own challenges, since the propositions derived from just two theories, for example, differential association and social control, amount to at least 13 and if other theories are included "the number of potential variables in the analysis would soon approach 50!" (Shoemaker 1996 p. 254).

Causal integration recognizes that there are at least four different kinds of causes that describe the relationships between crime variables: (i) linear causality, which takes the form of a sequential chain of events resulting in crime; (ii) multiple causality, which sees crime as the outcome of several different independent causes; (iii) interactive causality, in which the effects of one event or factor influence other events or factors, which then influences the crime event; and (iv) dialectical or reciprocal causality, in which causes and events are not discrete entities but are overlapping, and interrelated, and codetermining of the crime event (Barak 1998a; Einstadter & Henry 2006; Henry & Milovanovic 1996). If a combination of these types of causes is used, how is that configured and how does the combination vary by level of analysis and type of crime?

Cross-level integration involves integrated theorists explicitly paying attention to whether theories to be integrated address a micro-, meso-, or macro-levels of analysis, or whether these theories are integrated across all levels, which is called "cross-level integration" (Liska et al. 1989; Muftić 2009). The integrational levels to be considered in cross-level integration include: "(1) kinds of people, their human agency, and their interactive social processes (micro); (2) kinds of organization, their collective agency, and their organizational processes (meso); and (3) kinds of culture, structure, and context (macro)" (Einstadter & Henry 2006, p. 319). This raises a further question of whether integrative theorists should combine only theories that operate at one level of analysis, such as micro-, for example integrating rational choice, with biological and psychological causes? Similarly, should theories at the meso-level addressing the relationships between groups, organizations and institutions be integrated; and finally, should different macro-level theories be integrated such as Marxism and Structural-Cultural Feminism as in "power-control" theory (Hagan, Simpson & Gillis 1987)?

Alternatively, should integrative theories integrate across analytical levels? An example of such cross-level (macro-micro) integration in criminology is Colvin & Pauly's (1983) attempt to combine Marxist, conflict, and strain (macro-level), with subculture, social learning, and social control (micro-level) theories. Intuitively, it seems that if comprehensiveness is the goal, then all three levels (and even a fourth global level) need to be addressed simultaneously in what has been called "multilevel" integration (Paternoster & Bachman 2001, p. 305). (See also Henry 2009; and Muschert et al 2013, multi-level integrated application to school violence). As Henry and Bracy (2012) point out, without an explicit awareness that macro-micro level interactions occur, it might be seductive to believe that an integration of a range of theories is adequate, without realizing that macro-level theories have been omitted. For example, the 16 different integrated theories identified by Lanier and Henry (2010, pp. 385–89) draw on micro-level theories in greater numbers (66%) than they draw on macro-level theories (33%). Put simply, integration of discipline-based theories in criminology has typically been biased toward same-level rather than cross-level analyses.

If multi-level integration is adopted, then how do the levels relate to each other and do we need a bridging concept as in Bronfenbrenner's (1979) ecological systems theory of childhood development in which the concept of "exosystem" is used to comprehend the connection between micro-, meso-, and macro-systems, as well as the concept of "chronosystem" to explain the dynamic of changes in the relationships and their effects over time, such as the lifecourse, or over historical periods (For an example of this multi-level application to school violence see Hong et al, 2013; Benbenishty & Astor, 2005).

Because of the different ways theories can be integrated, and because if the number of different disciplinary-based theories in the field, as we mentioned above, there are many combination or integrated packages. In the 2006 edition of *Criminological Theory*, Einstadter and Henry (2006) identify 16 different integrated theories, each drawing on two or more discipline-based theories, the most popular being: social learning (micro) and social control (micro), followed by strain (meso and macro) and conflict (macro). Hunter and Dantzker (2002) went even further identifying 21 integrated or "holistic" theories. Thus, "we now no longer bob from theory to theory in our failure to transcend one-sided interpretations of reality, but scamper from one integrated theory to another in an attempt to transcend the transcenders" (Einstadter and Henry 2006 pp. 330–31).

Finally, as Henry and Bracy (2012) point out, a critical question for those favoring integrative theory is how to assess the relative contribution of each theoretical explanation to the totality of an integrated explanation of crime. In explaining a particular crime or criminal behavior, what is the relative explanatory strength of each theory, at each level, to the overall integrated explanation, and does that change for different crimes, or different crime types, or different contexts? Indeed, Agnew acknowledges "most theories have some merit, explaining a portion of the variation of some crime" (Agnew 2011, p. 191). The key question is how much is explained and to what extent does each explain the phenomenon?

Related to this, if an effective policy is developed it would seem that the components of the policy should be included to the extent that they address the strength of causal explanations. If this varies across crimes, populations and contexts, that presents challenges unless policies are adapted and multi-variegated. Indeed, some integrative theorists adopt what appears to be a multi-level integrational approach but then differentiate between constitutive theories that have "proximate influence" and those that have "distal influence" (Hong et al. 2013). Paradoxically, this gives priority to the micro- and meso-levels, and abandons the macro-level. So, how far does Agnew's recent "unified criminology" overcome or side-step some of these challenges to integration?

AGNEW'S UNIFIED CRIMINOLOGY

Agnew argues that recent developments in science and social science knowledge make it easier for criminologists to assess the relative contribution of each theory's underlying assumptions, though he notes that criminologists have not done this. He points out that while all underlying assumptions have some empirical support, even though they are different and often oppositional, "there is some truth to each of the underlying assumptions ... but that each assumption only captures part of the truth ... Each theory or perspective typically has some support but falls far short of providing a complete explanation of crime" (Agnew 2011, pp. 193–94). Moreover, since many theories make assumptions that are contradictory, these cannot be integrated unless the differences in underlying assumptions are first resolved. It is toward just such a resolution that Agnew's work is directed.

Agnew's first task is to review and integrate definitions of crime and in doing so he arrives at an integrated definition of crime that contains three elements. Crimes are acts that: (1) cause blameworthy harm; (2) are condemned by the public and (3) are sanctioned by the state. As he acknowledges, this goes a little, but not much, further than Hagan's (1977; 1985) original statement in his "pyramid of crime," and not quite as far as our own "prism of crime" (Henry & Lanier 1998; 2001), with the exception that it draws on international law to define blameworthy harm. However, as far as addressing the issue of what is to be integrated, all we have with Agnew's restatement of Hagan is an end-to-end

list of elements rather than one integrated definition. What is problematic about this is the relativity of the definition, and its failure to define crime other than by political process. Determining harm is anchored to the variable politics of a legal process, albeit international. Public condemnation can be mediated by so many factors, from mass media to knowledge of harm, to perception of loss; its relativity is reflected in its changing assessment depending on *who* is the perceiver and *what* is their social context, cultural and spatial location and historical period. Finally, acts determined by the state are part of a power mediated political process, which hardly addresses the harms created by corporations or the state, or those omitted from criminalization because of the interests of those with lobbying power over that process.

Such an integrated definition takes account of both street crimes, where property is taken from another through theft, force or deception (economically reducing a person from what they were) or crimes of violence (such as rape or murder that reduces a person, socially and biologically). But such an integrated definition also includes "suite" crimes by corporations and crimes by governments and state agencies who exercise power over others, including deprivations administered through the criminal justice system. The integration of mainstream and critical criminologies is hereby integrated, in ways that do not diminish either, but nor do they privilege one over another because of the current structure of the political process. The point here is to point out that an integrated definition needs to go beyond simply stringing together elements of other different definitions and to become transcendent and inclusive.

The next dimension tackled by Agnew is whether crime (or for that matter other action) is determined by forces or voluntarily chosen by active human agents. This is a version of the classic "free will versus determinism" debates, applied to crime. Agnew argues that recent research does not settle this issue but suggests that "behaviors fall along a continuum, ranging from fully determined to somewhat agentic" (p. 195). As rational choice theorists say, human agents are not fully free but have limited or bounded rationality, what Agnew calls "bounded agency." Agnew says that although research does not prove the existence of agency it shows that, "humans exercise greater agency when they: (a) are motivated to alter their behavior, (b) believe they can produce change, (c) have the traits and resources to exercise agency ... and (d) are in environments that have weak or countervailing constraints, provide numerous opportunities for agency and encourage agency" (Agnew 2011, p. 195). Moreover, he says the exercise of agency is subject to guidance and influence and that "we would expect behavior to be more unpredictable and somewhat more likely to involve crime when conditions favor the exercise of agency" (Agnew 2011, p. 195). Apart from this being somewhat tautological in that the evidence for agency is the very definition of agency: acting freely is stated to be more likely occur when there is less constraint, it also begs the question of causality. If agency is more likely when there is motivation to make behavioral change and belief that change can occur, and that this is facilitated by resources, then what explains the motivation and belief, and are those subject to internal or external forces, and if so, how much agency is left? If lack of controls or confusion about controls and availability of resources to make change are factors, then the presence or absence of these can be seen as contributing causes of action, so again, how free is the agency to act, and how much is a part of the overall equation? Moreover, from the policy perspective, if agency is subject to this amount of influence or the absence thereof, how can a person seen to be acting agentically and thus be held accountable for his or her actions? Clearly they cannot be held fully accountable, since the definition here does not leave agency free from a variety of conditions. However, an even more disturbing part of this agency versus determinism picture is that the very conditions that result in highest agency are the same ones that produce the highest levels of creativity, innovation and art; they are the hallmarks of think tanks, and the substance of "positive deviance." Indeed, rather than being more likely to produce crime, they are as likely, or even more likely to be expressions of the very essence of humanity. The problem with this integration of agency and determinacy, then, is that it assumes agency acting freely is dangerous and harmful, and that constraint and control and influence produces conformity, stability and reduced deviance. However, as we know, some of the worst atrocities of humanity have been produced by the exercise of control under the guise of producing stability. What this integration doesn't help us explain is how some exercising agency relatively freely do so creatively and positively, and others do so in ways that harm others and negatively impact humanity; nor does it explain how some conditions of constraint and control limit others excesses, and yet other systems of constraint, guidance and influence are themselves harm producing. Integrating agency and determinism and recognizing there is a continuum in which some of both are present is certainly an advance over mono-theoretical positions. But until we know in what proportions, and what kinds produce negative outcomes, we will not only be unable to prevent such outcomes. However, we will have raised serious questions about a criminal justice system that, with a few exceptions, holds individuals as though they are fully accountable, even when the conditions were contributing factors. Yet we do not, except is some restorative justice processes, ensure that the producers and systems that contributed to the behaviors are also held accountable.

In turning to the issue of human nature (though some of the previous discussion is embodied in this) Agnew points out that research supports the view that humans are not discretely classifiable but are constituted by more or less degrees of: (1) self-interest and rationality, (2) social concern for others, especially those members of an in-group, with whom they empathize, protect, cooperate and engage in reciprocal activities mutual support, and (3) capacity for social learning: "So people show evidence of social concern, self-interest and social learning--with the strength of these traits varying across individuals and social circumstances" (Agnew 2011, p. 196). Along with other integrative criminologists Agnew holds a more complex view of human nature suggesting that "all theories of crime are relevant, including those that focus on the constraints to crime and on the motivations for crime ... [and] that criminologists need to pay much attention to bio-psychological factors, since the underlying traits that cause crime vary across individuals for reasons that are in part biologically based" (Agnew, 2011, p. 196). This seems to privilege some components over others, not least because there is no explanation of the ways that concepts are linked and no analysis of causal type or direction, nor a recognition that biology (or psychology) does not stand separately from the more meso- and macro-levels within which it is enmeshed. Agnew recognizes these levels affect or impact one another, but not that they are or can be mutually constitutive, implying an interactive rather than a dialectical or even dialogical coproduction. For example, are the biological and psychological traits independent of the culture and structure of a society, and if so why do societies have very different rates and kinds of crimes? Can individual biology and psychology be, in part, a product of the kind of group, place in organizations, kind of culture and social structure, and even the discursive patterns that characterize a people's way of life? When Agnew says criminologists should pay attention to the ways social concern and social interest affect crime, and how social circumstances that foster them affect crime, this must also refer to how these elements are interrelated with each other and coproduce the very human agents whose behavior becomes manifest as "individuals" identities and human subjects in the total social matrix.

An integrative theorist would want to know the relationship, not just of these elements to crime, but to each other over time. They would want, in the words of Gregg Barak (2003; 2006) to know the "reciprocal interactive effects" at different levels of the structure and culture over the life course and over time. For example, in his analysis of pathways to violence and non-violence Barak points out that in spite of clear evidence that violence is cumulatively interrelated across a range of societal levels, most analyses are "un-reflexive," tending to "focus on one particular form of violence, without much, if any reflection on the other forms." He argues "these fragmented and isolated analyses seek to explain the workings of a given form of violence without trying to understand the common threads or roots that may link various forms of violence together" (Barak 2003, p. 39). He argues that pathways to violence (and nonviolence) range "across the spheres of interpersonal, institutional and structural relations as well as across the domains of family, subculture and culture" and that these pathways "are cumulative, mutually reinforcing, and inversely related" (Barak 2003, p. 169). Unifying criminology then requires more than a simple additive or even interactive process; it requires us to examine the interrelated complexity of the multiple ways we are constituted as human agents and to explore ways to reconstitute our social, cultural, biological and psychological production to be a less harmful species.

This leads us to consider what an integrative view of society looks like. While it is important to recognize that societies have a core consensus and a common condemnation of personal theft and violence and "beyond that the extent and nature of consensus and conflict vary" (Agnew 2011 p. 197) there is an assumption, based on research, that harms and crimes are accentuated by conflict and that "Group conflict generally increases crime among oppressors and oppressed, although certain types of conflict might reduce crime among the oppressed" (Agnew 2011, p. 197). What is neglected here is not just the harm produced by some kinds of conflict such as discrimination, that Agnew acknowledges needs more research, but research on the ways consensus imbued with power produce harms, and the ways that conflict can be productively healthy in reducing power differentials and balancing opposing interests. A consensus about the value of a power hierarchy, legitimated by the fear of a chaos of competing interests in its absence, is likely to produce numerous harms of repression of the very subjects it claims to be protecting, as we have seen too often in regimes around the globe. So it is not enough to say consensus is good and conflict is bad (not that Agnew is this simplistic), but rather to examine the distribution of power in a society and to assess what harms are created by different distributions of power, both those subject to it and those expressing it, which is a point which Agnew makes.

Agnew then attempts to integrate the conflict or consensus in society with theories of causation recognizing that it is important to examine not only a range of macro- and micro- causes, but also "the relationship between these causes, thereby providing a better sense of why they vary and how they work together to cause crime" (Agnew 2011, p. 162). He states that whereas conflict theory tends to focus on the larger social environmental causes, it often neglects individual or micro-level mechanisms. In contrast mainstream theories, including those rooted in a consensus perspective focus on individual-level causes, neglecting the ways these are impacted by the wider social environmental causes. He says since "integrative theory draws on both conflict and consensus perspectives, it provides a good vehicle for cross-level integration" (Agnew 2011, p. 162).

Importantly, Agnew also recognizes that causes do not necessarily apply to all people and all types of crime, but that an integrative approach suggests that "the applicability of the causes sometimes depends on the nature of society, the groups to which people being and the type of crime being explained … societies differ in the extent and nature of consensus/conflict. And this difference has *some* effect on the causes of crime that are most applicable" (Agnew 2011, pp. 162–163). Indeed, he says causes differ across groups, particularly across more or less advantaged groups, across types of group affiliation, and vary depending on the type of crime. He says integrated theory needs to pay more attention to the role of context in facilitating or mitigating crime causation and how this varies across different societies. He emphasizes too, that integrative theory needs to recognize that not all causes of crime increase its likelihood, since crime is only one response to these causes and, indeed, the motives for such action may be not to harm others as much as reduce their own pain, frustration, or oppression: "The response taken is shaped or conditioned by a range of factors. . [I]ntegrative theory should describe those factors that condition the responses to the causes of crime" (Agnew 2011, p. 163).

Insofar as the research on crime, human agents and society is subject to the assumptions about whether social reality can be measured, raises questions about the extent of its socially constructed nature. Agnew sees this as a problem of designing more effective measurement techniques to take account of both objective and subjective features of reality, since both affect the way crime is produced and the effectiveness of prevention and intervention. Importantly, he recognizes the value of tapping multiple knowledge producers, seeing these not only as objective disciplinary based knowledge by criminologists in organized academia, but also spontaneous and less organized professional and subjective knowledge produced by practitioners and professionals in communities, in order to reduce the bias of existing measures. (See Henry 2012 on moving from interdisciplinary to transdisciplinary producers of knowledge in criminology).

CONCLUSION

Overall, the goal of Agnew's integrated criminology "is to lay the foundation for a unified theory of crime, one that examines a broad range of crimes and incorporates the key arguments of all major theories and perspectives" because all have some relevance (p. 201). How far he succeeds in this endeavor is open to interpretation. What is new, and is to Agnew's great credit is that he marries two approaches, mainstream criminological theories and critical theories, using the core assumptions as a vehicle for theoretical integration. This has not been done before and represents a major innovation in criminological thinking. However, because he fails to systematically review the previous literature on integrative theory Agnew does not address the core questions raised by this previous work, but rather side-steps them. Nonetheless, as a mainstream theorist responsible for one of the central theories in criminology, general or revised strain theory, *Toward unifying criminology* represents a major shift recognizing not only the value of the mainstream contribution, but also the contribution by critical criminology to the field. Ironically, that Agnew does not tell us precisely what concepts and propositions should be integrated, in what ways, and at what level, or how much contribution each theoretical explanation makes to the overall causal explanation of what kinds of crimes or offenders, and in what ways this combination varies for different agencies, entities or peoples, may be less significant to the field than the symbolic impact that one of its leading single-theory advocates has made the integrative turn.

On balance, Agnew's unifying criminology restates the need for integration, raises many of the same questions other integrationalists have raised, and although he does not answer them, he lays out a research agenda for how they may be answered, and does all this in a unique and accessible way.

REFERENCES

Agnew, R. (2011). *Toward a unified criminology: Integrating assumptions about crime, people and society.* New York: New York University Press.

Akers, R. (1994). *Criminological theories: Introduction, evaluation and application.* Los Angeles: Roxbury.

Athens, L. H. (1992). *The creation of dangerous violent criminals.* Champaign: University of Illinois Press.

Barak, G. (Ed.). (1998a). *Integrated criminology.* Aldershot, UK: Ashgate.

Barak, G. (1998b). *Integrating criminologies.* Boston: Allyn & Bacon.

Barak, G. (2003). *Violence and nonviolence: Pathways to understanding.* Thousand Oaks, CA: Sage.

Barak, G. (2006). "Applying integrative theory: A reciprocal theory of violence and nonviolence." In Stuart Henry and Mark M. Lanier (eds). *The essential criminology reader,* (pp. 336-346). Boulder, CO: Westview Press.

Barak, G. (2009). *Criminology: An integrated approach.* New York: Rowman and Littlefield.

Benbenishty, R., & Astor, R. A. (2005). *School violence in context: Culture, neighborhood, family, school and gender.* New York: Oxford University Press.

Bernard, T. J. (2001). "Integrating theories in criminology." In R. Paternoster & R. Bachman (Eds.), *Explaining criminals and crime* (pp. 335–346). Los Angeles: Roxbury Press.

Bernard, T. J., & Snipes, J. B. (1996). Theoretical integration in criminology. In M. Tonry (Ed.), *Crime and justice: A review of research* (Vol. 20, pp. 301–348). Chicago: University of Chicago Press.

Bronfenbrenner, U. (1979). *The ecology of human development: Experiments by nature and design.* Cambridge, MA: Harvard University Press.

Colvin, M. (2000). *Crime and coercion: An integrative theory of chronic criminality.* New York: Palgrave Press.

Colvin, M. & Pauly, J. (1983). "A critique of criminology: Toward an integrated structural-Marxist theory of delinquency production." *American Journal of Sociology, 89,* 513–551.

Einstadter, W. J., & Henry, S. (1995. 2006). *Criminological theory: An analysis of its underlying assumptions.* New Boulder, CO: Rowman and Littlefield.

Elliott, D., Agerton, S., & Canter, R. (1979). "An integrated theoretical perspective on delinquent behavior." *Journal of Research on Crime and Delinquency, 16,* 3–27.

Farnworth, M. (1989). "Theory integration versus model building." In S. F. Messner, M. D. Krohn, & A. Liska (Eds.), *Theoretical integration in the study of deviance and crime: Problems and prospects* (pp. 93–100). Albany: State University of New York.

Fishbein, D. (1998). "Biological perspectives in criminology." In S. Henry & W. J. Einstadter (Eds.), *The criminology theory reader* (pp. 92–109). New York: New York University Press.

Hagan, J. (1977). *The disreputable pleasures.* Toronto: McGraw-Hill Ryerson.

Hagan, J. (1985). *Modern criminology: Crime, criminal behavior and its control.* New York: McGraw-Hill.

Hagan, J. (1989). *Structural criminology.* New Brunswick, NJ: Rutgers University Press.

Hagan, J., Simpson, J. &A. R. Gillis. (1987). "Class in the household: A power-control theory of gender and delinquency." *American Journal of Sociology* 92:788–816.

Hawkins, J. D., & Weis, J. G. (1985). "The social development model: An integrated approach to delinquency prevention." *Journal of Primary Prevention, 6(2),* 73–97.

Henry, S. (2009). "School violence beyond Columbine: A complex problem in need of an interdisciplinary analysis." *American Behavioral Scientist, 52(9),* 1246–1265.

Henry, S. (2012). "Expanding our thinking on theorizing criminology and criminal justice? The place of evolutionary perspectives in integrative criminological theory." *Journal of Theoretical and Philosophical Criminology* 4(1): 62-89.

Henry, S. & Lanier, M. (1998). "The prism of crime: Arguments for an integrated definition of crime." *Justice Quarterly* 15: 609-27.

Henry, S. & Bracy, N. L. (2012). "Integrative theory in criminology applied to the complex social problem of school violence" In A. Repko, W. Newell & R. Szostak (eds.) *Case Studies in Interdisciplinary Research* (pp. 259-282). Thousand Oaks, CA: Sage.

Henry, S. & Lanier, M. (eds.). (2001). *What is crime?* Boulder, CO: Roman and Littlefield.

Henry, S. & Milovanovic. D. (1996) *Constitutive criminology: Beyond postmodernism.* London: Sage.

Hirschi, T. (1979). "Separate and equal is better." *Journal of Research in Crime and Delinquency, 16,* 34–38.

Hirschi, T. (1989). "Exploring alternatives to integrated theory." In S. F. Messner, M. D. Krohn, & A. E. Liska (Eds.), *Theoretical integration in the study of deviance and crime* (pp. 37–49). Albany: State University of New York Press.

Hong, J. S., Espelage, D. L., Ferguson, C. J. & Allen-Meares, P. (2013). "Violence prevention and intervention." In G. W. Muschert, S. Henry, N. L. Bracy, & A. A. Peguero, (Eds.). (2013). *Responding to school violence: Confronting the Columbine effect* (pp. 139-156). Boulder, CO: Lynne Rienner.

Hunter, R. D., & Dantzker, M. L. (2002). *Crime and criminality: Causes and consequences.* Upper Saddle River, NJ: Prentice Hall.

Jeffrey, C. R. (1990). *Criminology: An interdisciplinary approach.* Englewood Cliffs, NJ: Prentice-Hall.

Johnson, R. E. (1979). *Juvenile delinquency and its origins.* Cambridge, UK: Cambridge University Press.

Lanier, M. M., & Henry, S. (2004; 2010). *Essential criminology.* Boulder, CO: Westview.

Liska, A. E., Krohn, M. D., & Messner, S. F. (1989). "Strategies and requisites for theoretical integration in the study of deviance and crime." In S. F. Messner, M. D. Krohn, & A. E. Liska (Eds.), *Theoretical integration in the study of deviance and crime* (pp. 1–19). Albany: State University of New York Press.

Messner, S. F., Krohn, M. D. & Liska, A. E. (Eds.) (1989). *Theoretical integration in the study of deviance and crime: Problems and prospects.* Albany: State University of New York Press.

Muftić, L. R. (2009). "Macro-micro theoretical integration: An unexplored theoretical frontier." *Journal of Theoretical and Philosophical Criminology, 1*(2), 33–71.

Muschert, G. W., Henry, S., Bracy, N., L., & Peguero, A. A. (Eds.). (2013). *Responding to school violence: Confronting the columbine effect.* Boulder, CO: Lynne Rienner.

Paternoster, R., & Bachman, R. (Eds.). (2001). *Explaining criminals and crime.* Los Angeles: Roxbury.

Pearson, F. S., & Weiner, N. A. (1985). "Toward an integration of criminological theories." *Journal of Criminal Law and Criminology, 76*(1), 116–150.

Repko, A. F. (2008). *Interdisciplinary research: Process and theory.* Thousand Oaks, CA: Sage.

Ritzer, G. (1975, August). Sociology: A multi-paradigm science. *American Sociologist,* 15–17.

Robinson, M. B. (2004). *Why crime? An integrated systems theory of antisocial behavior.* Upper Saddle River, NJ: Pearson Prentice Hall.

Robinson, M. B. (2006). "The integrative systems theory of anti-social behavior." In S. Henry & M. M. Lanier (Eds.), *The essential criminology reader* (pp. 319–335). Boulder, CO: Westview Press.

Robinson, M. B., & Beaver, K. (2009). *Why crime? An interdisciplinary approach to explaining criminal behavior.* Durham, NC: Carolina Academic Press.

Shoemaker, D. J. (1996). *Theories of delinquency: An examination of explanations of delinquent behavior* (3rd ed.). New York: Oxford University Press.

Tittle, C. R. (1995). *Control balance: Toward a general theory of deviance.* Boulder, CO: Westview.

CREDITS

Derek B. Cornish and Ronald V. Clarke, "The Rational Choice Perspective," *The Essential Criminology Reader*, ed. Stuart Henry and Mark M. Lanier, pp. 18–29. Copyright © 2006 by Perseus Books Group. Reprinted with permission.

Marie Skubak Tillyer and John E. Eck, "Routine Activities," *21st Century Criminology: A Reference Handbook*, ed. J. Mitchell Miller, pp. 279–287. Copyright © 2009 by Sage Publications. Reprinted with permission.

Angela D. Crews, "Biological Theory," *21st Century Criminology: A Reference Handbook*, ed. J. Mitchell Miller, pp. 184–201. Copyright © 2009 by Sage Publications. Reprinted with permission.

Gina Lombroso-Ferrero, *The Criminal Man*. Copyright in the Public Domain.

John W. Clark, "Psychological Theories of Crime," *21st Century Criminology: A Reference Handbook*, ed. J. Mitchell Miller, pp. 271–278. Copyright © 2009 by Sage Publications. Reprinted with permission.

Edwin H. Sutherland and Donald R. Cressey, "A Theory of Differential Association," *Principles of Criminology*, ed. Jean McGloin. Copyright © 1955 by Estate of Donald R. Cressey.

Ronald L. Akers and Wesley G. Jennings, "Social Learning Theory," *21st Century Criminology: A Reference Handbook*, ed. J. Mitchell Miller, pp. 323–331. Copyright © 2009 by Sage Publications. Reprinted with permission.

Travis Hirschi and Michael R. Gottfredson, "Self-Control Theory," *Explaining Criminals and Crime: Essays in Contemporary Criminological Theory*, ed. Raymond Paternoster and Ronet Bachman, pp. 81–96. Copyright © 2000 by Oxford University Press. Reprinted with permission.

Jeffrey Walker, "Social Disorganization Theory," *21st Century Criminology: A Reference Handbook*, ed. J. Mitchell Miller, pp. 312–322. Copyright © 2009 by Sage Publications. Reprinted with permission.

Robert S. Agnew, "Strain Theories," *21st Century Criminology: A Reference Handbook*, ed. J. Mitchell Miller, pp. 332–339. Copyright © 2009 by Sage Publications. Reprinted with permission.

Stuart Henry, "Critical Criminology: An Overview," *Encyclopedia of Criminology*, ed. Richard Wright and J. Mitchell Miller, pp. 347–351. Copyright © 2005 by Taylor & Francis Group LLC. Reprinted with permission.

Stuart Henry, "Critical Criminology: An Overview," *Encyclopedia of Criminology*, ed. Richard Wright and J. Mitchell Miller, pp. 347–351. Copyright © 2005 by Taylor & Francis Group LLC. Reprinted with permission.

Michael J. Lynch and Paul B. Stretesky, "Radical Criminology," *Explaining Criminals and Crime: Essays in Contemporary Criminological Theory*, ed. Ronet Bachman and Raymond Paternoster, pp. 267–286. Copyright © 2000 by Oxford University Press. Reprinted with permission.

Sue Sharp, "Feminist Criminology," *21st Century Criminology: A Reference Handbook*, ed. J. Mitchell Miller, pp. 245–252. Copyright © 2009 by Sage Publications. Reprinted with permission.

Stuart Henry and D. Milovanovic, "Postmodern and Constitutive Criminology," *Encyclopedia of Criminology*, ed. Richard A. Wright and J. Mitchell Miller, pp. 1245–1249. Copyright © 2005 by Taylor & Francis Group LLC. Reprinted with permission.

Jeff Ferrell, "Cultural Criminology," *21st Century Criminology: A Reference Handbook*, ed. J. Mitchell Miller, pp. 219–227. Copyright © 2009 by Sage Publications. Reprinted with permission.

Avi Brisman, "Advancing Critical Criminology Through Anthropology," *Western Criminology Review*, vol. 12, no. 2. Copyright © 2011 by Western Criminology Review. Reprinted with permission. Provided by ProQuest LLC. All rights reserved.

Michael Braswell, John Fuller, and Bo Lozoff, "Peacemaking Criminology," *Corrections, Peacemaking and Restorative Justice*, pp. 29–42. Copyright © 2001 by Elsevier Science and Technology. Reprinted with permission.

John Braithwaite and Declan Roche, "Responsibility and Restorative Justice," *Restorative Community Justice*, ed. Gordon Bazemore and Mara Schiff, pp. 63–84. Copyright © 2001 by Elsevier Science and Technology. Reprinted with permission.

ABOUT THE COVER

"Distorted Perceptions" by Cassandra Marie Fait

Artist's explanation of work:

The painting presented represents the types of things one may run into in a "distorted" community and the struggles faced by those growing up on the dark side of town, what people know as the "ghetto." Growing up in a ghetto part of San Diego, I know what it was like to live in fear and soon enough to tolerate the world around me, expecting nothing more than the circumstances I had been living in, full of crime, violence, drugs, etc. … Hearing gunshots at 2 A.M., seeing street walls full of graffiti, in multiple colors, and knowing that somewhere in my neighborhood there were people dealing drugs and selling weapons—this was my life. When completing this assignment, I thought about my experiences growing up in the hood, seeing violence so close to home and how it has affected my family, friends, and last but not least me. Fortunately, I made my way to a better life through willpower and determination however, some of my family members did not. The theory that I felt was most appropriate to explain this painting is Social Learning & Modeling Theory. Lanier and Henry best define this theory as, "learning to behave by imitating and modeling the behavior of others, from groups or in media images" (p. 132). All of the behaviors shown through my painting depict the reality of this theory.

CPSIA information can be obtained
at www.ICGtesting.com
Printed in the USA
BVHW081102090421
604507BV00004B/184